Hoover Institution Publications 133

The Soviet Union and the Middle East

THE U.S.S.R.

AND THE

MIDDLE EAST

THE SOVIET UNION AND THE MIDDLE EAST

The Post-World War II Era

Edited by

Ivo J. Lederer

and

Wayne S. Vucinich

Hoover Institution Press
Stanford University
Stanford, California

The Hoover Institution on War, Revolution and Peace, founded at Stanford University in 1919 by the late President Herbert Hoover, is a center for advanced study and research on public and international affairs in the twentieth century. The views expressed in its publications are entirely those of the authors and do not necessarily reflect the views of the staff, officers, or Board of Overseers of the Hoover Institution.

Hoover Institution Publications 133
International Standard Book Number 0-8179-1331-9
Library of Congress Card Number 72-87716
© 1974 by the Board of Trustees of the
    Leland Stanford Junior University
All rights reserved
Printed in the United States of America

Contents

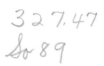

Preface

Constantinople beckoned to the lords and commoners of Russia from the time they first embraced its Orthodox faith a thousand years ago until the Tsarist Empire toppled in 1917. Apart from its wealth, glitter and power, the domed capital of Byzantium stood astride the Bosporus, like Russia itself part European and part Asian, a splendid sentinel guarding the gateway to the Mediterranean and the sunny lands of the Middle East. It was indeed a prize to be sought — and always it lay beyond the grasp of Imperial Russia. When the Bolsheviks came to power the religious lure of Santa Sophia faded, but the new rulers like the old kept their gaze fixed on the Straits and the region beyond. Even during the years of civil strife that began in 1917, years which sometimes saw Soviet forces pitted against Muslims in territories that had been subjugated by the Tsars, the Soviet government was urging Muslims under the rule of Western colonial powers to rise and free themselves.

During the years before the Second World War, the Soviet Union focused its Middle Eastern policy on Turkey and Iran, its neighbors immediately to the south. When the war came, a neutral Turkey stood guard at the Straits to keep away all belligerents. The Soviet Union, in desperate need of military equipment from abroad, joined with Britain to establish a vital supply route across Iran.

At the end of the war the Soviet Union discerned opportunities to extend its objectives in the Middle East. Encouraged by indigenous movements against French and British rule, it now adopted a more active policy, which was manifested in different ways: attempts were made to undermine the national sovereignty and territorial integrity of Turkey and Iran (for example, the Soviets demanded joint control of the Straits and delayed their postwar evacuations in northwestern Iran); there was an increase in communist agitation all over the Middle East; and various local popular movements, in particular national liberation movements, gained the blessings of the Kremlin. Turkey and Iran, vigorously buttressed by United States intervention to implement the Truman doctrine, successfully warded off the more immediate Soviet threats. Nevertheless, the pressures continued, and as early as 1945 the Soviet bid for a trusteeship over Tripolitania, though fruitless, showed that Soviet territorial aspirations were stretching outward to the more remote reaches of the Middle East.

In the Arab world, postwar Soviet activities have varied in intensity from

vii

one country to another and have altered in response to evolving conditions. Whereas in the late forties the Soviet Union supported the establishment of a Jewish state in Palestine, within several years Soviet authorities were publicly endorsing the Arab contention that Israel was an agent of "new Western colonialism." By the mid-fifties the Arab world stood on a par with Iran and Turkey as a target of Soviet attention, and with the collaboration of Egypt and other Arab states the Soviet Union had succeeded in fulfilling one of the long-held dreams of Imperial Russia — it had secured a firm military and political foothold in the Eastern Mediterranean. Moreover although the Soviet position in Egypt has weakened of late, the Soviet presence in the Mediterranean remains an accepted fact. This represents a significant development on the contemporary international scene. No longer can the Western Powers claim exclusive control in that part of the world, and their relations with the Soviet Union are affected accordingly. The destiny of the Mediterranean states is similarly affected, for now they must consider the Soviet Union as well as the Western Powers in the conduct of their international affairs.

Thus the Soviet Union in the Middle East since the end of the Second World War offers a challenging subject for scholarly scrutiny. A group of experts addressed the subject at Stanford University in 1969 in a conference organized by the Center for Russian and East European Studies. This book consists of eight revised papers delivered at that conference, plus a paper surveying the organization of and the major trends in Soviet Middle Eastern Studies.

A collective work of this type usually creates a problem of consistency in transliteration. In this volume, most Arabic names are transliterated according to a system in common use among Arabists; Persian names are written in the forms often used by scholars in the field of Persian studies; Turkish names keep forms now current in the latinized script of Turkey. In specific cases where a contributor has expressed a decided preference for a variant spelling, we have complied with his wishes. For well-known names and terms we have generally used the form that has become familiar to English-speaking readers. Otherwise, for geographic terms, we have followed the spellings given in *Webster's Geographical Dictionary* (rev. ed., 1964).

The editors wish to thank the Center for Research in International Studies at Stanford University for its support, and the Hoover Institution for the publication of the papers. They are indebted to Mrs. Elise M. Johnson for her valuable assistance in the organization of the conference. They are also thankful to a number of their students (especially Ivo Banac, David O. Carson and Nicholas C. Pappas) for their help during the conference, to Mrs. Edna Halperin for her editorial work, and to Dr. George S. Rentz of the Hoover Institution for his active participation in the conference and for his much appreciated counsel during the preparation of the manuscript for the press.

Palo Alto, 1973   *I.J.L., W.S.V.*

Contributors

JOHN C. CAMPBELL is Senior Research Fellow at the Council on Foreign Relations. He has served some twelve years in the Department of State and has written extensively on the Middle East. Among his published works are *Defense of the Middle East: Problems of American Policy*, which first appeared in 1958; *American Policy Toward Communist Eastern Europe: The Choices Ahead* (1965); and *Tito's Separate Road: America and Yugoslavia in World Politics* (1967).

GEORGE S. HARRIS is a Professorial Lecturer at the School of Advanced International Studies. For many years he served in the American Embassy in Ankara. Dr. Harris is the author of *The Origins of Communism in Turkey* (1967) and of *Troubled Alliance* (1972), as well as of many contributions in professional journals.

HARRY N. HOWARD, a retired Foreign Service officer, is Chairman of Near East and North Africa and Country Studies, Foreign Service Institute, Department of State. He has served in various capacities on government and U.N. bodies for some thirty years. His books include *The Partition of Turkey* (1931, 1966); *The Problem of the Turkish Straits* (1947); and *The King-Crane Commission* (1963). He is Associate Editor of the *Middle East Journal*.

FIRUZ KAZEMZADEH is Professor of History at Yale University, where he has served as Director of Graduate Studies in the Russian and East European Program and as Chairman of the Council on Russian and East European Studies. Among his many published works are *The Struggle for Transcaucasia* (1952) and *Russia and Britain in Persia, 1864-1914: A study in Imperialism* (1968).

IVO J. LEDERER is Professor of History at Stanford University. He is currently on a two-year appointment (1972-74) to the Ford Foundation as Program Officer, Office of European and International Affairs. Among his principal works are *Yugoslavia at the Paris Peace Conference* (1963), and *Soviet Foreign Policy* (1962); and he has co-edited (with Peter F. Sugar) *Nationalism in Eastern Europe* (1969).

NADAV SAFRAN is Professor of Government at Harvard University. He is the author of *Egypt in Search of Political Community: An Analysis of the Intellectual and Political Evolution of Egypt, 1804-1952* (1961); *The United States and Israel* (1963); and *From War to War: The Arab Israeli Confrontation, 1948-1967* (1969).

P. J. VATIKIOTIS is Professor of Politics in the School of Oriental and African Studies, University of London. He is the author of *The Egyptian Army in Politics: Pattern for New Nations?* (1961); *Politics and the Military in Jordan: A Study of the Arab Legion, 1921-1957* (1967); *The Modern History of Egypt* (1969); *Conflict in the Middle East* (1971); and editor of *Egypt Since the Revolution* (1968), and *Revolution in the Middle East and Other Case Studies* (1972).

WAYNE S. VUCINICH is Professor of History at Stanford University and Chairman of the Center for Russian and East European Studies. Among his principal works are *Serbia Between East and West* (1954) and *The Ottoman Empire* (1965). In addition he is editor of *The Peasant in Nineteenth-Century Russia* (1968), *Contemporary Yugoslavia: Twenty Years of Socialist Experiment* (1969), and *Russia and Asia* (1972).

JOHN WATERBURY is Associate for the Middle East, American Universities Field Staff, currently resident in Cairo. Professor Waterbury is the author of several books and articles on Morocco, including *The Commander of the Faithful: The Moroccan Political Elite - A Study in Segmented Politics* (1970); and *North for the Trade: The Life and Times of a Berber Merchant* (1972).

— 1 —
Historical Introduction
Ivo J. Lederer

Of all the zones of instability in the world today none is more entangled and unpredictable than the Middle East. The volatile situation in this portion of the globe is of course the product of myriad factors. In the first place the entire area has an unclear distant past — though the picture became somewhat clarified but not simplified during the nineteenth and twentieth centuries. Then there is the irony of a hostile natural environment tempered by the bounty of oil, coupled with the convergence of geostrategy and economic rivalry over petroleum. Add to these the interaction of cultural traditions and values that have never harmonized and perhaps never will. And there is apparently no escape from the tensions inherent in the process of modernization. The list might be expanded almost indefinitely, but I propose to examine in detail only one factor that may well prove decisive today: the role and the position of the Soviet Union in the Middle East.

However the Middle East may be defined geographically, whether it is said to extend from Afghanistan to Libya or to be composed of the triangle between Turkey, the Persian Gulf, and Egypt, for the Soviet Union the area represents a region of multiple opportunities and serious concerns. But in my view the Middle East, despite the amount of attention it has been receiving from the Soviet Union, is not of cardinal importance to the Kremlin. Nor is it a life-and-death matter so far as Soviet national interests are concerned. That place in the Soviet scheme is shared by three other factors and by the interrelation between them: the stabilization of the Soviet-dominated half of Europe; the resolution of the conflict with China; and the maintenance of technological-military balance or parity with the United States. The Soviets regard even partial failure on any of these fronts as a possible prelude to catastrophe. In order to forestall such an eventuality they have been willing to run high risks, including the use of force, and even to run the risks inherent in selective accommodation. The question of an advance or a reverse in the Middle East, as compared with Soviet problems relating to China or to the Eastern European satellites, or with Moscow's urgent need to maintain a strong technological-military posture, is not a matter of paramount importance.

Why, then, the recent Soviet thrust in the Middle East? Why the implacable enmity toward Israel and the tenacious support and subvention of several Arab states? Why a seeming policy of "neither peace nor war" that precludes a settlement and future stability? These and related questions are precisely the concern of this symposium. While this introductory discussion will avoid trespassing on the preserves of the other authors by limiting itself to the period before World War II, several comments on the variety of Soviet motives that are presently at work might nonetheless be ventured.

Considerations of external security forbid Soviet indifference toward the fate of adjacent Afghanistan, Iran, and Turkey. However, given the relatively large and sensitive Turkic, Mongol, and other Asian populations of the Soviet national mosaic, these states also affect questions of internal security. The Arab world, on the other hand, occupies a considerable land mass, sits astride waterways that connect three continents, and, in addition, is blessed with untold deposits of oil. Outright Soviet control of the region, or at least denial of Western control, is a prize not to be lightly dismissed. A Soviet anchor in the Arab Mediterranean offers the added promise of exercising pressure on Turkey, and on Yugoslavia as well. As for Israel, hostility toward the Jewish state is a natural consequence of the Soviet-Arab combination. But it is also a convenience within Russia (and in parts of Eastern Europe), where anti-Semitism has long been a serviceable tool of internal politics.

In the 1960s the Soviet Union established an imposing naval presence in the Mediterranean, especially in the eastern half. By now this Soviet presence has the quality of permanence. It has caused some Western strategists qualms and other anguish, for it has shattered NATO's naval monopoly in the Mediterranean. A Soviet Mediterranean fleet is of course necessary to sustain the Arab combination. Ironically, though, the Arab liaison was probably a precondition of the Soviet naval build-up in the Mediterranean, if only in terms of supply depots and berthing privileges in North African and Near Eastern ports.

The presence of Soviet vessels in Arab ports has doubtless increased Arab-Israeli tensions. But it has at the same time brought new hazards to the Soviets, because Russian ships in Arab ports bespeak a deeper commitment than may be useful, entail more military exposure, decrease diplomatic latitude, and even given rise to some Arab vexation with Soviet action or inaction. Should Middle Eastern events run out of control, or should any of the Arab client governments find themselves unable to steer the Soviet course because of challenges at home, the U.S.S.R. might suddenly discover it has become a captive patron rather than the master in control. The prospect is not too likely, but neither is it inconceivable.

The Soviet push into the Middle East since the mid-1950s must be seen as part of an integral global approach. In this larger field of vision the Middle

East is but one stage-setting in a complex and delicately balanced theater of action. Soviet involvements in Vietnam, in Cuba, and in India, and the experiment with a new German policy are part of an overall dynamic strategy that combines elements of classical imperialism, power politics, and ideological gamesmanship. Such a strategy inevitably generates a momentum that cannot easily be reversed, if only in order that the assumptions on which it rests may not be undermined. A governing Soviet assumption would appear to be that a global power must exercise its power globally. In practice, the system continues to assign higher importance to areas of geographic proximity, though influence must be wielded in distant parts as well. To this must be added the Soviet conception of the U.S.S.R., however challenged it may be, as the guardian and vanguard of the socialist camp. On this front, it is Soviet purpose to maintain, to gain, or to regain paramountcy in the communist parties in power or out. While this desire has produced certain contradictory situations, as in the case of Egypt, doctrinal considerations appear to have been permeated no less than military-diplomatic ones by the rather conventional logic of the eighteenth and nineteenth centuries, to pursue politics "consonant with the status of a great power."

In the overall context, the Middle East and the Mediterranean have become crucial to the assertion of this global role of the U.S.S.R. Relative proximity of the region increases its immediate importance. Of the various other elements involved, one that ought not be overlooked is the burden of history. To gain the upper hand in the Middle East would also signal the fulfillment of a recurring dream.

Russia is too often assumed to have entered the Middle Eastern scene only after World War II. This view ignores centuries of Russian interest and activity in that part of the world. It is not mere chance that over a century ago, around 1848, the poet and ex-diplomat Fedor Tiutchev in the poem "Russian Geography" identified seven rivers as delimiting Russia's natural frontiers: the rivers Neva, Volga, Euphrates, Ganges, Elbe, Danube— and the river Nile.[1] By Tiutchev's day, Russian policy had already established a traditional interest in the regions east of India. It seems not inappropriate, then, to indulge in a brief historical sketch which will, perforce, skim over the centuries, omitting much interesting detail and leaving aside a number of important historical processes.

For ancient Russia the world to the south meant primarily the Byzantine Empire. Commercial connections with Byzantium already flourished in the tenth century. Late in that century Eastern sources mention a variety of Russian contacts with Daghestan and other parts of Transcaucasia. As time went on, these contacts increased in scope.[2]

In the year 1001, according to late Russian chronicles, the Kievan prince

St. Vladimir is said to have sent a scouting mission to Egypt and to Jerusalem, partly out of religious curiosity and partly in the interests of commerce. By the twelfth century Russian merchants were firmly ensconced in Alexandria. The exchange of goods was not massive by the standards of the day, but it was fairly lively. The connection was deepened by the southward travels of Russian pilgrims and by the exportation of Russian slaves to the valley of the Nile. Thus by the twelfth century Egypt had become a visible star on the horizon of outward-looking Russians. In the nineteenth century it was to rise to a star of substantial magnitude.

In the twelfth century, too, the Russians established numerous contacts with various Arabian markets. Some Arab merchants came to Kiev via the great West-East trade route that passed through Prague, Cracow, and Przemysl. Before long, an indeterminate number of Russians are reported to have entered Arabian service. Farther to the east, Russians established connections with most of inner Asia by overland routes, and with Derbent, Baku, and Persia down the Volga and the Caspian Sea.

The Kievan state steadily expanded its vision to the west, the south, and the east. That process was brought to a halt, however, by the Mongol invasion of the thirteenth century and the prolonged occupation of Russian lands. Among other results of the occupation was the transfer to the Mongols of the Russian commerce with the Middle East. By the time the Mongol rule had been broken, however, after some two centuries of struggle, the Russian center of gravity had moved from Kiev to Novgorod and thence to Moscow. Both these principalities had established commercial ties with Europe,[4] but had relatively little experience with Byzantium and the Moslem East. As Byzantium fell in the fifteenth century to Ottoman power, the Russian position was greatly changed. To the south, instead of a kindred Christian state and civilization, the Russians now faced a dynamic, hostile, Moslem foe. Whatever lay beyond Ottoman domains became for a long time inaccessible. From the late fifteenth century to the twentieth, military conflict supplanted the more benign cultural-commercial relations with the Middle East of the Kievan-Byzantine past.

As Mongol hegemony receded, drawing the Russians eastward, so the waning of Ottoman power in the eighteenth century drew them to the south. The conquests of Kazan and Astrakhan by Ivan IV were followed in the eighteenth by Peter's bid for Azov and Catherine's conquest of the Crimea. These were no random exercises; they were calculated preludes to the emergence of Russia as a force to be reckoned with in the Mediterranean.

Peter the Great had consecrated an imperial design involving direct access to and connection with Central and Western Europe in the north and access to the Black Sea in the south. His range of activity swept from Sweden through Poland to all the dominions of the Ottoman Turks. In 1723 he reached even farther south (and, by an invasion of Persia, southeast) in an ineffectual yet portentous gesture of seeking to establish an influence in Madagascar. More to the point, however, was the steady and systematic movement toward the Black Sea and the gateway to the Mediterranean. The policy begun by Peter was continued by his successors, not excepting Catherine.[5] For Catherine, in fact, the notion of controlling Constantinople developed into an ideological fixation that would influence Russian policies for a long time to come.

Throughout the nineteenth and early twentieth centuries the eyes of Russian policy makers were riveted on the Ottoman Empire and the Mediterranean. In a larger sense their interests and their efforts were globally oriented, with two interconnected goals in view. One was the territorial expansion of the Empire, in Northern, Central, and Southeastern Europe, and in Central Asia and the Far East as well. At the same time, the Russians sought — not without success — to establish the parity of St. Petersburg in the councils of great powers.

The process of territorial expansion that began in the eighteenth century with the conquests of Peter and Catherine, was extended in the nineteenth to include Finland, Bessarabia, and vast Asian dominions to the south and east. As a consequence the Russian Empire became veritably multinational, with a significant population of non-Russian stock and of the Muslim faith. Inevitably, too, Russian influence came to be felt widely in world affairs.

Although Russian acquisition of territory was often viewed by contemporaries as part of a master plan, one must guard against discovering design where none was intended. An inner logic evidently connected the sequence of Russian activities, but it would be too easy to impute to it the character of untempered gluttony. For example, while Catherine and her successors sought to dominate Constantinople, and in the nineteenth century to gain outright control over the Turkish Straits, the motives were mixed. They involved as much ensuring Russian access to world waterways as denying to the West any possibility of mounting naval expeditions into the Black Sea.

Attempts to dominate neighboring states, such as Bulgaria in Europe, Persia in Asia, and Turkey straddling both continents, similarly involved the combined desire to establish zones of Russian influence and to deny them to adversary powers. Such efforts, to be sure, were rationalized in the theory of territorial security. Beyond these there were other plans — some quixotic, but not all — to establish the precedent of Russian involvement in diverse parts of the world and thus to assert Russia's global interests and world role. Several such episodes are worthy of mention. A few that might be cited are Emperor Paul's project against India at the turn of the nineteenth century and Nicholas I's insinuations into Egyptian affairs in the era of Mohammed Ali. Nicholas played an important role, too, in the Holy Land imbroglio in the 1850s that triggered the Crimean War. Next, Russia was involved, albeit peripherally, first in the building of the Suez Canal and then in the question of control of the Canal. In the 1880s there was an unofficial attempt to establish a Russian influence in Ethiopia, as well as a scheme in the 1890s to capture Constantinople, and various other activities extending from the Indian Ocean to the westernmost reaches of North Africa.

The military ventures against India and Constantinople remained unfulfilled schemes. So, in effect, did the Ethiopian affair. Nor did tsarist maneuvers in the Holy Land, in matters concerning the Suez Canal, or in Egyptian affairs meet with any success. However, three points emerge from the overall picture. First, during the nineteenth century Egypt, the Holy Land, and the Mediterranean were not primary targets, but rather instrumentalities of Russian efforts to gain control of the Ottoman Empire. These efforts were aimed partly at thwarting British imperial designs, but more importantly at placing Russia in a position where she would become the principal beneficiary of the anticipated collapse of the Ottoman Empire. Second, in spite of the frustrations they suffered, Russian strategists did attune the outside world — and themselves as well — to regarding as legitimate Russian participation in co-determining the destiny of the Middle East. Third, after 1875 Egypt became increasingly pivotal in Russian calculations — no less than those of the British and the French. In the abortive Ethiopian venture — in which the initiative came from the Russian church and not from the government — the monk Porfirii (who once headed the Russian ecclesiastical mission in Jerusalem) saw in the combination of Ethiopia and Egypt the key to a major Russian influence in Africa.[6] That vision was of course ephemeral, but it was also the harbinger of other combinations that came into play after World War II.

As for the eastern Mediterranean, it became increasingly a sphere of Russian naval activity during the nineteenth century. Here, too, we must bear three points in mind. First, this activity was mainly supportive of Russia's Ottoman and Balkan policies. Second, the naval presence really began in 1769, when Catherine sent the squadron under Admiral Spiridov from the Baltic that defeated the Turkish navy at Chesme and Scio. Within three generations Russian movement in the Mediterranean was seen as imperative to the larger designs of St. Petersburg. Third, this was all the more important since tsarist Russia was a land colossus but not a great naval and maritime power. This limitation made it difficult to achieve and then to sustain a dominant naval position in the Mediterranean. Even though the desire to do so may have existed, the resources did not.

The events of 1917 wrought vast changes, both qualitative and quantitative, in the Russian-Middle East equation. To begin with, the Bolsheviks abandoned, though not for very long, the objective of establishing spheres of predominant influence in adjacent lands. This particular game they abjured for a much larger prize: the revolution that was to sweep the world.

Hence, Turks, Persians, and others were now being viewed not as friends or foes but in terms of their revolutionary potentialities. In the Bolshevik world view, considerations of commerce and geostrategy appeared — at least for the moment — to have no place.

Within a month of the Bolshevik seizure of power, Lenin — who had no particular interest in the Arab world — appealed to the Muslims of Russia and the East to join the revolution. Trotsky, as commissar of foreign affairs denounced tsarist arrangements in Persia and elsewhere and offered new relationships all around. But as the chimera of world revolution waned, so the Bolshevik regime assumed more and more the profile of a conventional state. It began to develop new relationships that in effect reflected the patterns of the conventional international system. It reconquered whatever tsarist territories it could, among them the Ukraine and Georgia, and then sought to neutralize politically its new and ancient neighbor states. Turkey and Persia belonged to the latter group. In the Arab world, the Bolshevik call for an anti-British uprising, beyond gaining some measure of sympathy among Arab nationalists, met with little success.[7]

Through the Comintern, at the same time, the Soviets undertook a policy of stirring up mischief throughout the Middle East. This was aimed at fostering instability by undermining the established governments. The apparatus for most of Asia was set up following the Comintern-sponsored Congress of the Peoples of the East, held in Baku in September 1920, and the establishment in Moscow in 1921 of a communist University of the Toilers of the East, which was something of a precursor of Lumumba University of more recent times.

In general, during the twenties and thirties the Soviets made little headway in the Middle East, and for that matter anywhere throughout the Mediterranean. As an isolated and materially insolvent power it was enough of a triumph for them to survive, to Bolshevize Russia, and ultimately to become a serious factor in European politics. As for the Middle East during this period, the Soviets were more concerned with neighboring Turkey and Iran than with the affairs of the Arab world or the problems of Palestine. They were interested in protecting the revolution in Russia from outside interference and with blocking the villain of Bolshevism, "British Imperialism," especially in Iran. In a larger sense, their primary goal was the advancement of the general revolutionary cause; and internal security was, of course, an important aspect of their design.

At the time of the revolution, in addition to over three million Jews, the Russian mosaic contained some fourteen million Turkic peoples and other sizeable Moslem populations in the belt from Northern Caucasia through Central Asia. The great majority were Sunni, with smaller groups of Shiah (Azerbaijanis, Talysh, and Tats). Moslem roots in Russia ran deeper than those of the Jews, but neither religious denomination could be indifferent to the lot of their coreligionists or conationals abroad. For the Bolsheviks this posed delicate problems, especially with regard to the Moslems. Hence, any ideology or political movement within or outside Russia after 1917 became immediately threatening — if it involved or even made an appeal to Soviet citizens.

While it is impossible to deal here with all the relevant movements, a few observations about the Pan-Turanian and Turkist idea and about Zionism are in order. With the exception of the Crimean and Volga Tatars, the Bashkirs, and the Azerbaijanis, most Soviet Moslems live in Central Asia. Ethnically, most are Turkic, though the Tadzhiks are Iranian. The Chuvash, west of Kazan, are Christian, though of Turkic stock. Before and in the years after 1917 there had been various attempts to achieve unity of all or parts of the Moslems of Russia, essentially with a view to autonomy and political leverage. None produced great results. Some of the appeal in these initiatives was based on the idea of coreligiosity, some of it on ethnic communality. Before 1914 some intellectual momentum was gathered behind the Pan-Turanian idea that looked to supranational unity of Turkic-speaking peoples, though some scholars, such as Zeki Velidi Togan for instance, saw it as a search for unity among Turkic, Mongol, and Finno-Ugrian groups, a notion that found several academic supporters in Constantinople and in Budapest.

Pan-Turkism, on the other hand, developed as an expression of concern at the Russification of the Turkic Moslems of Russia, with adherents in Asian Russia as well as in Turkey, especially after the Young Turk coup of 1908. The idea of the unity of Turkish-speaking peoples was promoted further through the Turkish military incursion into the Caucasus in World War I, by official propaganda throughout Caucasia in 1918, and by Enver Pasha's activities in 1921-22 in Turkestan.

The Bolsheviks were understandably nervous about all such impulses, and Stalin had already attacked Pan-Islamism in his famous 1913 treatise on the national question. In the early 1920s Pan-Turkism was attacked as a perversion of bourgeois nationalism and the movement was emasculated. It reappeared in Russia during World War II as an anti-Soviet scheme supported by Istanbul as well as by Berlin. Harsh measures were used to defeat the idea as a political force. But at times the specter has continued to haunt the Soviet scene.

It is no wonder, then, that Soviet policies toward Moslems at home have been ambivalent and inconsistent since 1917. Soviet dealings with Turkey, Iran, and Afghanistan—and to some extent with India and Pakistan—have had to reckon with a possible impact at home. This has not greatly inhibited the pursuit of state or imperial objectives (since methods that cannot necessarily be used abroad can be used at home), but it has called for some delicacy in relations with the Arab states and indeed with the Moslem world. By 1928 Islam within the U.S.S.R., as well as Pan-Islamism and Pan-Turkism, was officially proscribed. From 1944 on Islam, but not supranational ideas or movements, has been tolerated, if only to keep things stable at home.

As for Zionism, the picture has been very different. To begin with, the Bolsheviks inherited a confusing intellectual legacy: one of partly Jewish origins developed in an anti-Semitic environment. For this reason and myriad others Bolshevik attitudes were at first ambivalent. Before 1914 Lenin and Stalin did not consider the Jews to be a *nation*, and in fact in 1917 they had not prejudged the fate of Russian Jews. On the one hand, of course, in line with general Bolshevik policy, Jewish organizations and autonomous communities were suppressed. On the other hand, the Communist Party, whose leadership included a number of Jews, welcomed and even sought Jewish cooperation, both at home and abroad. A Jewish section was organized within the Communist Party. Cultural life was allowed so long as it catered to the party line. Judaism as such shared the fate of Christianity, but in 1934 a Jewish Autonomous Province was created in Birobijan, in the Far East. The experiment was meant to attract Russia's Jews, to make them a formal nationality within the U.S.S.R., and to detract from the actual or potential appeal of Zionism abroad. It failed for many reasons, among them the fact that the inhospitable region of Birobijan had no historic meaning for the Jews.

Zionism as such was not a significant force in the Soviet Union during the interwar years. Yet as early as 1919 it came under attack, not so much as a result of the magnetic attraction of Palestine but because it was seen as a bourgeois aberration and as a bastion of reaction that was separating the Jewish masses from the Russian revolution. Later in the 1920s the tune changed, and Zionism was attacked for its Palestinian orientation, as a tool of the imperialist, anti-proletarian entente.

In the 1930s Stalin's purges began to assume, among other things, the form of official anti-Semitism. Leading Jewish communists perished in the political cannibalism of the day. Jewish cultural life practically ceased to exist, and the party and police made strenuous efforts to sever all contacts between the Jews of Russia with those in Palestine and elsewhere. It became commonplace to charge prominent or nameless Jews with foreign Zionist connections, and thereby with treasonous activities in the service of capitalism. When the Nazi-Soviet Pact was sealed in 1939, so was the lot of Russian Jews. Their situation cannot be said to have improved in the last ten years of Stalin's life.

With the achievement of victory in World War II the Soviets entered directly into the affairs of the entire Middle East. The course of the Soviet involvement in individual countries is analyzed by our various contributors.

But though the postwar era lies beyond the scope of this introduction, reference must be made to it in these concluding remarks.

As was the case before 1917 and before 1939, the Russians were determined to gain the upper hand in the contiguous states, particularly in Turkey and Iran. And as before, their actions in the more distant parts of the region have been directed to the larger end of thwarting the noncommunist world led by the United States and Britain. The principal Soviet objective, as was aptly pointed out in 1969 by Winston S. Churchill, has been "to remove British [and American] political, economic and military influence from the area and replace it with its own."[8] In the pursuit of this design the Soviets have not hesitated to lay aside considerations of internal Soviet convenience or of ideological consistency.

In 1946-47, in the hope of hastening the departure of the British, the Soviets and their satellites encouraged the Jewish exodus from Europe into Palestine. In the United Nations in 1948 the Soviet Union practically sponsored the formation of an independent Israel and was the first state to accord it *de jure* recognition. Within less than a decade the Israeli policy had been reversed and the Soviets had begun to sponsor the Arab cause. The fact that Egyptian and other Arab jails contained numerous local communists was explained away as a regrettable tactical necessity in the service of larger strategic opportunities.

Such opportunities to date have been adroitly used. Soviet influence in the region is pervasive and profound, even if it is not unchallenged. The Soviet position may well require continued instability, for without the fear of Israel the Arabs would hardly be so dependent on the Soviet Union. Hence, "no peace no war" is likely to remain the Soviet formula. But whether such a status can be maintained is a question rather for an astrologer than for a historian.

— 2 —
The Continuing Crisis
John C. Campbell

In the Middle East the word *crisis* has long since become almost meaningless The struggles between the Arab states and Israel and those within the Arab world, interlocked with the competing interests and policies of outside powers, have made high tension and danger of war the normal state of affairs. One is hard put to single out specific instances or episodes that are more critical than others. Thus the problem for all nations concerned, the great and the small, is how to pursue their interests given a climate of danger that leaves them scant room for breaking existing patterns without pushing the situation beyond recall.

In June 1967, moves and countermoves set in train a full-scale local war which the United States and the Soviet Union, though they could congratulate themselves on staying out, proved unable to prevent. It was an experience neither would wish to repeat. Yet even as both powers pledged themselves to the search for a settlement between the Arab states and Israel, all the ingredients of continuing conflict, including their own highly charged competition, remained.

Some observers have seen Russia, since 1967 a Middle East power as it never was before, profiting enormously from these conditions and not seriously constrained by them. Several obvious facts tend to provide confirmation. Soviet influence gained steadily from the mid-1950s until it was firmly implanted in a number of Arab countries and had largely displaced the West in Egypt, in Syria, and in Iraq. Later events extended the Soviet inroads into southern Yemen and Sudan. Soviet warships plied the waters of the Mediterranean, the Indian Ocean, and the Persian Gulf. Soviet officers came to advise the armed forces of Arab countries and to train them in the use of Soviet weapons. Soviet diplomacy played its part, too, in weakening the ties between the United States and its local allies, Turkey and Iran. It seemed as if a grand strategy dating back to the tsars were reaching a new stage of success, with its ultimate aim within grasp: a Russian-dominated Middle East.

Contemporary Soviet policy, however, finds no exclusive explanation in geography, in tradition, or in ideology. Despite facile deductions it is no linear derivative of Peter the Great's will or the dream of the Third Rome, of

11

the manifestoes of the Comintern or Stalin's demands after World War II for footholds in the Mediterranean. It owes something to all of these historical precedents; but for the most part it is a product of initiatives taken and developed since the mid-1950s in the particular conditions, regional and worldwide, of those years. It is a reflection of the Soviet Union's determination to be not a continental but a global power on a par with the United States. The Middle East is the region where that drive has been most successful and where the United States has been most sharply challenged. Yet the Soviet gains were not without corresponding liabilities. It is useful, therefore, to examine the Soviet position in the light both of the local situation and of the conditions in the world and at home under which the Soviet leadership must conduct its policies in the Middle East.

What Khrushchev did was to build up a policy of global involvement— some would say global adventure — with the plunge into South Asia, the Middle East, Africa, and finally Latin America. It was a natural development for Russia to go beyond Stalin's more confined continental horizons at a time when the anti-colonial revolution was sweeping over Asia and Africa. Although accompanied by talk of social revolution the new Soviet policy meant in fact a decided shift in emphasis from communist ideology to cooperation with existing regimes and *Machtpolitik* on a global scale. Khrushchev combined this shift with attempts to exploit a presumed political and psychological advantage in that he thought, or we thought, or he thought that we thought, the Soviet Union was gaining superiority in strategic weapons — the famous missile gap. He accepted the idea of an essentially bipolar world so far as real power was concerned, but did not take that as a bar to action that would unsettle and ultimately shift the balance.[1]

Thus he challenged us in Berlin, in the Congo, and in Cuba. Only when those adventures failed did he turn to actions more consonant with his declared policy of peaceful coexistence with the West. He concluded the nuclear test ban, took other measures of conciliation in 1963 and 1964, and may have been planning to move farther toward cooperation with the West at the same time that he was bringing Soviet relations with China to the point of serious hostility and open struggle.[2] What he would really have done is an interesting "if," which perhaps not even he could have answered.[3] Just at this juncture he was removed from leadership by his friends and colleagues.

Khrushchev's successors inherited the whole mixture: the gains together with the failures and the problems. The record of the collective rule of the new team gives no definite view of the directions of their foreign policies, but some conclusions may be drawn from their reactions to the changing situation. In strategic military terms the world remained for them a bipolar one. They built up Soviet strength in long-range missiles to a position of rough equality with the United States. Learning some of the lessons of the

Congo and Cuba, they tried also to create and expand mobile all-purpose forces for use in every corner of the world. Although they provoked no new crisis similar to that of 1962, the relationship with the United States was still an adversary one. Limited coexistence it might be, but it could hardly be called détente. The accent was on the capacity of the Soviet Union to compete, with greater success and perhaps at greater risk, rather than on the search for areas of cooperation and common interest — except to prevent a nuclear war.

The Arab-Israeli war of 1967 provided an interesting case of crisis management by the two great powers, based on the desire of both to stay out of it. But no sooner was the war over than the Soviet leaders set out to recoup their losses in the Arab world by replenishing the arms supply, thus encouraging the Arabs to scorn peace and to put their hopes in winning back what they had lost without having to make peace with Israel. They were willing at the same time to negotiate with the United States about an Arab-Israel settlement, but with no noticeable change in their own policies that rested on the assumption of continuing conflict. In the panorama of Soviet foreign policy the desire for détente and consolidation was much less evident in the Middle East than elsewhere. There the cold war lingered with a corresponding intensity.

In Europe the Soviet leaders did not change the long-term strategy of their predecessors: to keep their grip on the key countries of Eastern Europe while working for division in Western Europe, the breakup of NATO, and the withdrawal of American power back across the Atlantic. The promotion of "European security," a constant theme of propaganda and diplomatic proposals, was aimed not at a genuine settlement, but rather at confirming the division of Germany and of Europe. Yet these were not policies of aggression, risk, and crisis, but of consolidation. The pendulum swung from the crisis-making to the defensive side. Events in Czechoslovakia in 1968 brought Moscow to a decision for military action. This was essentially, however, a defensive reflex from fear of an upset of the European balance and a threat to the security of the U.S.S.R. and its regime. The invasion of Czechoslovakia did not mean that the Soviets would so easily make a decision to attack Berlin, or Turkey, or even — despite the elaborate working out of the so-called Brezhnev Doctrine—Yugoslavia. The Moscow meeting of communist parties in June 1969 produced the normal quota of anti-imperialist oratory, but left the definite impression that no militant Soviet-led offensive on behalf of communism or in extension of Soviet power was to be expected, either in Europe or in the Far East.

Consolidation of the situation in the east was not so easy, however, because it was the Chinese who set the tone of the polemics and determined the frequency of border clashes. The Soviets took the threat from China very seriously. Hoping to dampen the conflict rather than escalate it, they nevertheless felt the need to show their teeth in the border encounters, and they put enormous pessure on the Chinese in the autumn of 1969 to bring them to the conference table to talk about the disputed frontiers. The polemics were softened while the talks went on — which is what the Soviets desired — but there was probably as little confidence in Moscow as in Peking that those talks marked the beginning of a reconciliation. The Chinese, like the Western nations and the peoples of Eastern Europe, saw the Brezhnev Doctrine as a rationale for Soviet imperialism.[4]

This general picture recalls the old Russian nightmare of encirclement by enemies to the east and to the west. It may partly explain the lack of a sure hand in dealing with either, the shifts and uncertainties, the alternation of hard-line and soft-line moves. It may explain also the extraordinary attention the Soviets have given to the Middle East, South Asia, and the Indian Ocean. In those areas they did not feel hemmed in, despite the presence of America's allies, Turkey and Iran, right up against their own frontiers. They found it a place of opportunity to play imperial power politics. This area, in contrast to Europe and East Asia, is not a main theater of the global struggle for power, but it is one where Soviet leaders may have scented a breakthrough of strategic significance against both the United States and China, or at least a successful sideshow and an opportunity to demonstrate the Soviet Union's ability to act as a global power.

It seems pertinent to consider here the Soviet Union's Mediterranean fleet, the symbol of its enhanced power and prestige and the source of many a scare story during the past few years. Although dating only from the mid-1960s, this force grew rapidly, at times reaching a strength of 60-odd ships including missile cruisers and two helicopter carriers. It thus gave Soviet power a visible presence affecting both the military and the political balance in the region. It was not sent there to do battle with the U.S. Sixth Fleet, for its role in a general war could be only a suicidal one.[5] But it did put an end to the brief era in which the Sixth Fleet, as successor to British naval power, was without challenge in the Mediterranean. Both Soviet and Western observers believe that its mere presence may make impossible any future move similar to the American landings in Lebanon in 1958. The Soviet fleet gives political and potential military support to Moscow's friends and protégés such as Egypt, Syria, and Algeria. It may affect the decisions of Turkey, Greece, Cyprus, Lebanon, Tunisia, Yugoslavia, Albania, and conceivably of Italy. Above all, however, it is a sign of a new strategic naval thinking in Moscow, wishful though it may be in many respects, that carries well beyond the confines of the Mediterranean.[6]

Soviet military leaders, and presumably the civilians as well, chose to pursue a build-up of naval and other power with a long reach, more or less on the model of America's, so that the Soviet Union could deal with situations where its massive striking force was unusable and its continental strategy inadequate. In other words, they proposed to make the Soviet Union capable of acting the part of a global power on the seven seas and all the continents. As their ranking admirals have put it with customary bombast, Soviet forces will be able to deal crushing blows to the imperialists anywhere on the face of the earth.[7]

It may seem ironic that the Soviets were going in for this type of power at a time when America in Vietnam was discovering some of its limitations. The main point is that they saw the Mediterranean not merely as a good place to back up their local diplomacy with naval power but also as a highway to somewhere else, notably the South Atlantic and the Indian Ocean.

How strongly or how ruthlessly the Soviet leaders will use this growing power, either in military encounters or as a back-up for political moves, is an open question. It has been a favored theory in the West that the attainment of parity in strategic weapons enables the Soviet Union to be bolder, at less risk than before, in using its conventional forces to intervene in faraway places. The sending of combat personnel to Egypt in 1970 seemed to support the theory. Yet generalization from that instance is unjustified. External conditions, especially the possibility of loss of control over decisions on war and peace, may be a limiting factor; so also may conditions at home, not least the character of Soviet political leadership and the pressures that bear down upon it.

Western experts have generally rated the men who succeeded Khrushchev as super-bureaucrats, as less imaginative and daring than Nikita Sergeevich. The system of collegial rule with its differing priorities and inevitable compromises almost guaranteed caution and conservatism, or to put it less charitably, factionalism and inertia. The new leadership in the Kremlin was confronted at the outset with almost insurmountable difficulties at home. How could the economy support a greater military burden and still meet the competing demands on limited total resources? What steps could be taken to resolve the need for drastic economic reform — a need whose logic the Politburo could recognize but whose effects on the political system they feared? How could they relieve the mounting pressures from those elements in society that were dissatisfied with their own lack of influence? How should they cope with the stirrings of nationalism among non-Russian peoples, including the Muslims of Central Asia who had some ties with the peoples of the Middle East? Would the restive intelligentsia and the new student generation create additional difficulties for the regime? In brief, they faced all the strains of an evolving industrial society cramped within a system of rigid rule by party chiefs and the party bureaucracy.

Compounding these difficulties was a general decline in faith in the ideology, for which the regime tried to compensate by beating the ideological drums to prove its legitimacy. Some observers believe that the system is outworn, others that it is in deep trouble and may be headed toward internal struggles that will greatly weaken the country's international position. Behind the partial revival of Stalinism at home and the hardening of the line abroad seemed to lie an uncertainty of purpose and a sense of insecurity. Following the shock of the challenge which Czechoslovakia represented in 1968, the leaders called on sentiments of nationalism and chauvinism in a transparent attempt to cultivate loyalty and support and to seek security in the international field when it was under question at home. Add to this what was plainly an increased deference to the military, who were getting a bigger share of the national budget than they had under Khrushchev, and the simultaneous build-up of both strategic and conventional arms. The result might be an overextension of military effort and of commitments that acquire their own momentum and reduce the leadership's caution. Have we been watching what a keen student of the Soviet scene, Richard Löwenthal, has described as the successful outward expansion of an internally declining regime?

That thesis is not now provable one way or the other. It is mentioned only to draw attention to some of the internal factors that bear on foreign policy and particularly affect the relationship with the United States. The dilemmas and the ambiguities appear when the Soviet leaders are forced to face the big issues of the day: to go all out in an arms race, or to try seriously to get some agreed limitations; to find means of cooperation with the United States to curb China, or to carry on a no-compromise struggle with both; to enlarge foreign commitments, or to retrench and build the home economy; to take risks for big stakes in the Middle East, or to establish some kind of limited détente there with the United States. Such decisions had not been made by the end of the 1960s but merely postponed.

Soviet Middle Eastern policy following the crisis of 1967 is open to differing interpretations. At the very least, the decision to rearm Arab states meant there would be no cutting losses and turning back because a defeat had been suffered. More broadly, it seemed to reflect a confidence that support of Arab nationalism against Israel was still the winning ticket, one that had brought substantial gains and should bring more as additional Arab countries joined the radical camp, weakened or broke their ties with the United States, and became more dependent on the Soviet Union. The special position of influence which the Soviets had won in Cairo gave them the opportunity to reap the advantages flowing from Egypt's strategic location and from its leading role in the Arab world, at the same time providing Moscow with some degree of control over Egypt's policies. The degree of Soviet control represented an asset not easily to be given up in exchange for an arrangement with the United States to defuse or settle the Arab-Israeli conflict. The record of negotiations since 1967, though indicating that the Soviets did prefer a political settlement to renewal of the war, showed also that they would not exact a substantial share of the price from their Arab friends but wanted the United States to impose virtually the whole price on Israel. Let the deterioration of American influence in the Middle East continue apace, they appeared to be saying, until a time when stabilization or détente would confirm the Soviet Union in an even more favorable position.

On the other hand, Soviet policy in the Middle East has been far from reckless. The one exceptional instance was its role, still not fully explained, in the events leading to the six-day war. Even here, however, the very strong desire to avoid a military clash with the United States was abundantly clear.[8] We can be fairly certain that the Soviet leaders did not intend to bring on a situation where they had a choice only between risking a major war and accepting a humiliating political defeat. Another crucial point came when they sent Soviet combat personnel into Egypt in 1970 to redress the balance created by Israel's domination of the skies. Provocative as it might have seemed, that move led to a new cease-fire agreement rather than to war.

Many Americans impressed by Soviet successes and by the continuing threat to NATO and to vital oil supplies have seen the remedy in action to counter that threat — by military build-up, more aid to allies, diplomatic activities, warnings by NATO — rather than in negotiations with the Soviet government. Others impressed more by signs of Soviet moderation and by the common interest of both powers in the avoidance of war have favored pressing the endeavor to negotiate at least a common approach to a settlement of the Arab-Israel conflict. Without rejecting the former course, the United States government chose the latter when it went ahead with the series of bilateral talks that took place in Washington throughout most of 1969. The failure of these discussions to produce an agreed piece of paper was not surprising. The significant fact was that they were not propaganda exchanges but serious negotiations dealing with the specifics of boundaries, demilitarized zones, formal peace engagements, and so on, something more than the generalities of the U.N. Resolution of November 22, 1967.

As the Soviet Union and the United States went forward with negotiations, however, they ran up against the formidable obstacle of their own involvement in the local conflict by virtue of their rivalry with each other and their special relations with the contending parties. During the course of Soviet-American talks and the broader exchanges including Britain and France under U.N. auspices, it became clear that the Soviets were not prepared to press upon Abdel Nasser a particular set of proposals he found distasteful, even though they may themselves have thought the proposals not unreasonable.

Soviet-Egyptian relations were never as happy and cooperative, in fact, as the public statements — up to the point when Sadat tore off the curtain by demanding the recall of all the Soviet military "advisers" from Egypt — would have had us believe. The Soviet leaders were not above exercising restraint on Abdel Nasser in order to lessen the danger of war. But because they felt that their position in the area depended on his remaining in power, they had to permit him to be the judge of how far he could go by way of making concessions to Israel. This was the reason for the Soviet decision in 1970 to commit Soviet pilots and missile crews to the defense of Egypt. It did not mean a commitment to back an Egyptian offensive against Israel; on the contrary, the basic idea was to save the Nasser regime. When Cairo accepted the American proposal for a cease-fire and negotiation in the summer of 1970, and again, after Nasser's death, when it stated its willingness to conclude a "peace agreement" with Israel (dependent, of course, on Israel's withdrawal from occupied territory), it did so for its own reasons; we have no evidence to show that either of these decisions was imposed by Moscow.

The United States has been in a different but not entirely dissimilar situation with respect to Israel. Its support to Israel has been limited by the desire to keep some standing with the Arabs and to maintain American interests in the Arab world. Thus U.S. proposals have been aimed at a compromise settlement offering the chance for reduced tension and peace. Nevertheless, the United States has regarded an Arab pledge to respect Israel's sovereign existence within agreed frontiers as an essential part of the settlement, and Israel's survival has been a tenet of U.S. Middle Eastern policy since 1948. The key point, of course, has been whether Israel's stand on frontiers would conform to the American view that the territorial settlement should not reflect the weight of conquest.

Israel was kept apprised of the two-power talks by the United States, as Egypt was by the Soviet Union. Israel had objected to the holding of two-power or four-power negotiations, having no illusions about Soviet or French policy, no confidence in the British, and some fear that her American friends, in their eagerness for compromise, might somehow bargain away some of her vital interests. This was especially true after Secretary Rogers on December 9, 1969, took a public position on the issues that appeared in Israeli eyes to do just that. Even so, the United States continued to be regarded by the Arabs and by the Soviets as the special defender of Israel; and in fact it did agree with the basic Israeli position that in the last analysis the settlement must be founded on binding agreements between Israel and its Arab neighbors. The differences between Washington and Jerusalem have been apparent to the world because they are the subject of public debate in both countries. They make it clear that the United States does not determine Israeli policy, nor does Israel determine American policy. The question whether Washington could "deliver" Israel's agreement to particular terms of settlement might depend on how much pressure the United States could or would exert; but here the strength of pro-Israel forces in this country and the concern of the government to keep the military balance in the area stable have tended to preclude the use of such sanctions as denial of arms or economic help.

It has been suggested that the United States and the Soviet Union should really be negotiating about their own interests and their own competition in the Middle East, rather than on the details of a settlement between smaller states which those states have no desire or intention to make. The idea makes a good deal of sense. Talking on their own behalf, and not as actual or presumed advocates of Israeli or Arab interests, Washington and Moscow might come to a better understanding of what each considers vital and where the points of danger really lie. In both their own interest and that of the entire world, they might explore practical means of keeping the violence of the Arab-Israeli conflict within certain bounds.

Actually there was no yawning gap between American and Soviet views on the terms of an Arab-Israel settlement. Both powers reiterated their support for the Security Council Resolution of November 22, 1967, the essence of which was Israel's withdrawal from the territories occupied in June 1967 in return for Arab recognition of Israel's right to exist as a sovereign state. On the question of withdrawal, a difference was apparent between the Soviet insistence on the return of all occupied territories and the American proposal to leave the door open to minor rectifications to be negotiated by the parties. This was scarcely a divergence that for either power was worth the risk of war. The crucial difference was not a few kilometers of territory in the Middle East, but rather how far each power was committed to its local protégés, and how far each could bring itself to be associated with terms and procedures they rejected. More fundamentally, the similarity in proposed terms masked a divergence of purpose on how a settlement might affect the positions and the interests of each of the two powers. The Soviets saw it as a means of reducing the danger of war while still prolonging a situation of sufficient tension to keep the Arab states looking to Moscow for support and guidance. The United States, on the other hand, looked upon it as a means of ending the state of conflict and tension on which Soviet influence had fed, reopening the path to normal and cooperative relations between the United States and the entire Arab world.

The notion of Soviet-American agreement on the Middle East has inevitably raised the specter of joint domination or agreed spheres of influence. Aside from the pejorative connotation which these terms have taken on in American minds, they are not particularly useful for a sober consideration of what is possible in the Middle East. It is in fact hard to apply any idea of spheres or blocs in an indeterminate region where the neutralist label has been attached to a wide variety of policies on the part of the local states; and it is anything but clear where the lines of alliance or allegiance run. But if there is no stability, it may be possible for the two superpowers to bring about a situation of controlled instability through a practical relationship between themselves. Such a relationship would presumably include a continuing habit of communication that would set certain limits to their competition and would prevent their common interest in peace from being at the mercy of border incidents or of decisions taken in Cairo, in Damascus, or in Jerusalem. Evidence has been accumulating to show how little the great powers control their so-called client states. A degree of practical cooperation might at least limit the more dangerous consequences.

Whether Americans should think seriously about such cooperation depends upon how they judge what the rival power is up to. If the Soviet Union, for instance, is inevitably driven by its ideology or its manifest destiny toward domination of the Middle East or toward a clash with the United States should the United States stand in the way of that drive, then the American choice can only be either to resist or to give way. Yet a less cataclysmic interpretation of Soviet policy and of what the future holds seems more in accord with the available evidence. The Soviet Union, without doubt, is moved by concern for its own security, by a strong consciousness of its role as one of the world's two greatest powers, and by a conviction that this particular region is important to its ability to play that role. But within that general framework for policy the Soviet government has left itself scope for flexibility and for compromise on practical problems as they arise.

In relations with the Arabs, for example, the Soviet leaders have tried to maintain and enlarge their gains but without multiplying their risks and commitments. They have deliberately rebuffed the more intransigent states such as Syria by calling for a political settlement with Israel under the U.N. Resolution of November 1967. They have used ideology as a means of identifying themselves with anti-imperialist and socialist currents, but they have been careful not to let ideological considerations determine policy. They want to make the Soviet Union the preeminent outside power in the Middle East, the arbiter of its destinies; but it is most doubtful that their plans include communizing the entire area or making it a zone of satellite states, or that they really believe they can make it an exclusive sphere of Soviet influence. In the light of their experience elsewhere, it is hard to believe they could be entranced by the idea of taking responsibility for running a flock of Middle Eastern countries whose politics they cannot control and whose economic demands they cannot afford to meet.

The Soviet Union assumed the role of patron of Syria and of Southern Yemen, but did it thereby gain real control or even restraint over their domestic or international policies? Both those countries felt quite free to flirt with Peking. A *Pravda* article in mid-1969 referred with disdain to Arabs who had been influenced by Peking propaganda into calling for a redrawing of the map of the Middle East.[9]

The Soviet Union took on the task of principal provider to Egypt, but that did not mean it was prepared to underwrite the economy of that over-populated and resource-starved country. The Soviet leadership, although talking about a grouping of "progressive" Arab states, refrained from making the cause of Arab unity its own, whatever might be the aspirations of its progressive Arab friends. The Kremlin knew all too well how far from reality was this dream; and it was aware, too, that its own interests could be better served by dealing with many Arab states rather than with one.

The Soviet dilemma over policy toward the Palestinian guerrillas has been especially acute, because this revolutionary movement, itself divided into factions, burst outside of all control, either of the Arab governments or of Moscow. The revolutionaries' aim, the destruction of Israel, is not a Soviet aim; nor are the means they use — subversion and terror that achieve little against Israel but keep the Arab world in turmoil — consonant with Soviet policies. The Soviet Union may seek and may find ways of utilizing the fedayeen for its own purposes, mainly to keep them from becoming an instrument of the Chinese. In general, Moscow has made the choice for a conservative rather than a revolutionary role in its attempt to manage what is a new and not wholly anticipated situation. It would much prefer to have these reckless men firmly under some relatively responsible control.[10] But Arab governments have not found it possible either to control or to ignore them.

The Soviet dilemma extends further, to the role of the patron who cannot gain for his protégés what they want most. Moscow cannot regain the lost territories for the Arabs without force and the risk of war that it is unwilling to assume. Despite the torrents of propaganda from Moscow that the Israeli aggressors must disgorge their gains, the Soviet government pointedly refrained from endorsing the frequent statements of Abdel Nasser and of his successor to the effect that what was taken by force must be regained by force. As time goes on, Arab politicians must ask whether Soviet patronage is worth the dependence that goes with it. Sadat increasingly did so, to the ultimate point of demanding the recall of Soviet military personnel from Egypt in 1972.

The great lesson of the past two decades, which America has learned and Russia is learning, is that local nationalism works against an outside power's pursuit of its own interests unless they coincide with local interests as the local nationalists see them. When a great power, moreover, takes the responsibility of being the great white father to many small nations, it must cope not only with their demands but also with their quarrels among themselves. The Soviets have not been able to avoid shouldering some of the burdens that in the past have weighed upon the British and the Americans.

Some might draw the conclusion from such anticipated troubles for the Soviet Union that the United States would do well to withdraw from the Middle East and watch its chief rival become ensnared in local problems

and repulsed by nationalism. This is an idea that in many ways seemed to fit
the mood of America at the end of the 1960s. But it is one thing to recommend a review or rethinking of American policy, quite another to propose a
withdrawal without regard to existing commitments or to possible future
consequences. As a rule, small nations can maintain their independence and
successfully assert their national will only when there is a great-power
balance to which they can relate. Turkey and Iran, living in the shadow of
Russia, need their Western ties to hold their own. Even while the United
States is suffering a decline in the Arab world, it is important that it find a
combination of policies to keep itself there as an alternative and counterbalance to the Soviet Union. Bad as relations may be, it is a mistake to
assume that we have passed the point of no return with any country beyond
which it is useless to try. For some such counterbalance is important in the
long run to Egypt, to Syria, and to Iraq, presently so violent in their anti-
American pronouncements, just as it is to Lebanon, to Jordan, to Saudi
Arabia, and to Kuwait.

The United States has had a policy of trying to avoid polarization in the
Middle East. It has not desired total alignment with Israel against the Arabs
despite the influence of a segment of the American public advocating
precisely that. It was the closeness of the Soviet ties to Egypt, rather than
domestic or Israeli pressures, that made American policy relatively pro-
Israel in the crisis of 1967 and after. Secretary Rogers's speech of December
9, 1969, which aroused strong objections in Israel, was but one attempt
among many over the years to put this country in a more impartial position, though it must be conceded that "the limits of American flexibility
have always been reached before Arab requirements have been met."[11] Nor
is it in the American interest to see the Arab world polarized between
national and conservative states, with the Soviet Union backing the former
and the United States the latter. Important American economic interests,
notably in oil, have tied us to some of the conservative states in mutually
beneficial relations. But a policy of close involvement on their behalf in an
inter-Arab conflict with the Soviet Union on the other side could not
guarantee peace, or the stability of the conservative regimes, or the
availability of the oil to the West.

Oil, strategic positions, communications, and transit rights are important.
But the only two vital American interests in the Middle East are negative
ones: to prevent any major shift such as might bring a large part of the
region under Soviet domination, and to preserve the world from the danger
of nuclear war. In the absence of an established world order, these interests
require balance and equilibrium, a system capable of absorbing and containing a variety of shifting forces. Although in Europe, where the danger of
a general war was so great, a generally understood line of division has served
the cause of peace since World War II (much as we deplored the denial of

self-determination to peoples to the east of it), no such line, except against a direct Soviet attack on a NATO country, has been or can be drawn in the Middle East. There the need is for a balance, between major outside powers and within the region itself, capable of keeping competition and conflict within bounds, not a rigid stand-off or a brittle structure of commitments and countercommitments almost certain to crack under the strain.

It follows that the United States should continue its presence in the Middle East. This means not just a military presence — though that is a part of it — but an active diplomacy and continuing economic and cultural relations. At the very least the United States should remain in communication with all governments and peoples of the area. It should take account of their interests even if it cannot wholly satisfy them. With Turkey and Iran, it can show generous support for their defense needs and their development programs. With Israel, it can stand firm for that nation's right to live in independence and security, without supporting all of Israel's territorial and other demands as requirements for a settlement with neighboring states. With the Arab states, it can establish a position that shows limits on American support of Israel, pays heed to Arab views and sensibilities (whatever the current pronouncements of contemporary Arab governments may be), and holds the door open for better economic and political relations in the future. Sound policies, even when only declaratory, can themselves create an American "presence" that will be felt in the long run.

Looking at the persisting crisis of "no peace, no war" one finds it difficult to be optimistic for the near or mid-term future. The search for a political settlement has had an occasional boost from a sign of peaceful disposition from one or both sides, but the basic political decisions for the simultaneous concessions necessary to a settlement have not been taken. A new outbreak of full-scale war on the 1967 model is always possible, for Arab fervor may again overcome Arab caution or Israel may find the situation threatening enough to warrant a new strike, aimed at wiping out Arab offensive capabilities. Would the great powers stay out, as in 1967? The chances are that they would, especially as issues of much greater importance to them than anything in the Middle East would be at stake. Yet Soviet involvement with Egypt and other Arab countries has gone deeper since 1967, and there is ground for doubt that the Soviets would stand aside and see their laboriously won positions destroyed by Israeli action without making a military move to save them; and it is most uncertain what the United States would do if they did make such a move.

The melancholy fact is that the parties to the dispute have proved themselves unable to make peace. Israel is not of a mind to make concessions on the "secure boundaries" it needs, whatever the United States may choose to recommend, and has no faith in the capacity or will of the great powers to provide effective guarantees for its security. Arab governments, although knowing in their hearts that they could not win a test of force, have lived under the threat of radical reaction to any steps toward political settlement and may have passed the point when they can make one. The fedayeen organizations, which explicitly reject any settlement with Israel, could succeed in wresting the initiative from governmental hands. In this situation the key question would be not what the parties can be induced to agree upon but whether the United States and the Soviet Union can agree on means of containing the conflict.

While world opinion tends to stress the necessity for American pressure on Israel as the key to a settlement, the decision for greater security and stability in the Middle East lies primarily with Moscow. Soviet policy must be seen not just in relation to the Arab-Israel conflict but as a forward movement into the entire region, and it is here that common interests and agreed limits to rivalry must be found. The United States, for example, has shown its readiness to discuss limitations of arms deliveries to the Middle East without getting any encouraging Soviet reply. It is the general equilibrium between the great powers, not Israel's frontiers, that constitutes the real problem, and both sides will have to recognize it. Washington cannot help matters by making unilateral concessions for the sake of creating a better atmosphere; already on many occasions it has seen the folly of that tactic. Yet knowing that facts and conditions will shape Soviet policies, the United States can by its conduct — conciliatory or tough or indifferent as the situation may require — affect what those conditions are. The United States should not appear as a pleader for cooperation but as a power that offers cooperation in the interest of peace, at the same time following policies of its own which will serve that interest whether Soviet cooperation is forthcoming or not. The United States is obliged to stay the course if it is to provide that equilibrium which, over time, may bring the Soviet Union to reassess the risks of high tension and the benefits of widened cooperation to control conflict in the Middle East.

The two powers may in time arrive at the point where both can accept the proposition that they are better off if neither tries to achieve a status of primacy in the Middle East, that it is enough for each to deny that primacy to the other. Each must recognize the other as legitimately there, so that their competition need not be on an all-or-nothing basis. In a framework reflecting this approach, the "vital" interests of today may come to lose their life-and-death aspect for both sides. The prospects for the long run do not appear hopeless, if only because in the global context the United States and the Soviet Union will have to come to an understanding for the sake of survival. In the Middle East, however, the immediate dangers are such that the long run seems strangely irrelevant.

— 3 —
The Soviet Union and Turkey
George S. Harris

The Second World War marked an important watershed in the relations between Turkey and the Soviet Union. For roughly the first two decades of its existence, the Turkish Republic had been on exceptionally friendly terms with the U.S.S.R. The determination of the Turkish nationalists to gain and maintain political independence from the West provided common ground for cooperation. Not only was Soviet Russia the first major state to recognize the Ankara regime, but Moscow even provided material support to the fledgling Kemalist movement in its struggle against the European powers after the First World War. This cooperation was reinforced by periodic exchanges of state visits and culminated in Soviet economic assistance to the first Turkish Five-Year Plan, which began in 1934.

CAUSES OF FRICTION

With the approach of the Second World War, the factors dictating close relations between Turkey and the U.S.S.R. underwent significant change. The growing threat of Hitler's Germany aroused fears in the Kremlin about the security of the Black Sea. Starting at the time of the Montreux Convention in 1936, the Soviets began pressing the Turks to agree to change the regime of the Straits to prohibit entry into the Black Sea of warships of non-riparian powers. Soon thereafter the Kremlin proposed a pact for the joint defense of the Straits. When Ankara firmly rejected these propositions, Moscow sought other ways to achieve its goals. In secret negotiations with the Nazis in November 1940, Molotov demanded that Hitler agree to permit the U.S.S.R. to establish a base controlling this waterway. The threat of Nazi-Soviet collaboration on this matter, however, was dissipated after the German invasion of the Soviet Union in 1941.[1]

Beyond the Straits there were other areas of discord. For example, Moscow was concerned over Germany's growing economic involvement with the Turks during the 1930s. Turkey's efforts to reinsure its position by concluding the Balkan Pact in 1934, the Saadabad Pact in 1937, and finally the defensive alliance with Britain and France in 1939 all tended to derogate from the Soviet connection. Indeed, by the end of 1939 the Comintern was attacking this last arrangement as a " 'pact with the old enemies of Turkey's independence.' "[2]

The Second World War served only to deepen the mutual suspicions that had already begun to cloud the Turkish-Soviet friendship. Turkish determination to remain outside the war became a major bone of contention, though Stalin was not eager for Turkish troops to play a role in the liberation of the Balkans, an area he hoped to incorporate in the Soviet orbit. The Kremlin was displeased at the active diplomatic and commercial ties that Ankara maintained with the Nazi regime until almost the end of the war. But perhaps more significant for the future was Moscow's suspicion that the Turks had permitted Hitler to use the Straits in ways violating the Montreux Convention. The Kremlin later detailed a series of alleged wartime infractions of this Convention in a stiff note to the Turkish government.[3]

Nonetheless, until the very end of the war Ankara remained interested in propitiating its northern neighbor. In May 1944 the Turks eagerly seized on hints by the Soviet ambassador to probe the possibilities of restoring more cordial relations through security guarantees in the Balkans. Just a year later, in his speech celebrating Germany's capitulation, Prime Minister Saracoglu paid tribute to "Stalin's leadership genius" and, to the applause of the assembled deputies, voiced Turkey's appreciation of the heavy Soviet sacrifices during the conflict.[4] Yet, though the Turkish leaders clearly recognized that such protestations could hardly hope to overcome the points of friction, they were quite unwilling to risk military conflict with Germany or to see Turkey's sovereignty infringed as the price of friendship with Moscow. In this situation, their proposals to restore good relations with the Kremlin were foredoomed.

PLAY FOR THE STRAITS

The U.S.S.R. emerged from the war determined to secure its borders against future invasion. To Stalin and his cohorts this suggested ringing the Soviet Union with buffer states closely allied with Moscow and providing advance bases for Soviet troops.

The question of how Turkey would fit into this design had not been solved during the war. Conversations with Roosevelt and Churchill had left Stalin uncertain whether or not they considered Turkey to lie within the British sphere of influence. Nor were the Western powers willing to clarify their stand at Potsdam. Here the parties agreed merely on the formulation that each state should undertake to work out its desires in the Straits through bilateral conversations with the Turks. The Western powers may have envisaged these talks as the prelude to reconvening the Montreux signatories rather than as carte blanche for Moscow. To the Kremlin, however, it appeared that the Turks might be without any committed patron in the Western camp. And even before the end of the war with Germany, the Soviets undertook to probe Turkish resistance. On March 19, 1945, Molotov presented the Turks a note denouncing the Treaty of Neutrality and Nonaggression in force since 1925. This was followed in June with demands for a base on the Straits and for retrocession of the vilayets of Kars and Ardahan, which Turkey had recovered in the First World War.

While the Soviets coupled these maneuvers with a propaganda campaign and efforts to arouse the Armenians in Turkey, they did not back up their words with force. Nor did they indulge in unambiguous ultimatums. In fact, when in October and November 1945 the Ankara government was so alarmed at reports of Soviet military maneuvers on the Turkish-Bulgarian border that it seriously considered ordering a full mobilization, the Kremlin took care to reassure the Western powers, and through them the Turks, that no invasion was contemplated.[5] For all his bravado, Stalin was not inclined to risk open attack against a determined adversary. Probably at bottom he feared the American monopoly of atomic weapons, and was thus unwilling to risk arousing U.S. retaliation by engaging in overt military invasion.

Indeed, Stalin may have judged Turkey to be a prize attainable even without invasion. Within Turkey political ferment had begun to rise in the last years of the war. By the spring of 1945 burgeoning opposition to the single-party regime was openly mounting in the movement that would spawn the Democratic Party (DP) in 1946 and oust the Republican Peoples Party (RPP) government only four years later. Among the earliest opposition to emerge in 1945 were leftist intellectuals. And at first these elements, who had been involved in anti-fascist activity during the war and were well-disposed toward the Soviet cause, were able to play a role in the political maneuvering disproportionate to their size. They even succeeded in gaining the support of the prominent former foreign minister of the Ataturk era, Tevfik Rustu Aras.[6]

The fortunes of the leftists waxed steadily through most of 1945. In part this reflected the fact that the lines between them and the future DP leaders were not yet clearly drawn. Aras was on intimate terms with Celal Bayar and the other founders of the DP, a connection skillfully exploited by some press organs. In part, too, the initial success of the left in Turkey may have been facilitated by a lingering innocence of the full nature of Soviet designs on Turkish territory.

In December 1945, however, the factors favoring the left in Turkey changed abruptly. Any uncertainty about the U.S.S.R.'s desires was dispelled by the dramatic claims now voiced by two Georgian professors. Arguing on historical grounds, they demanded that Turkey give up vast areas along the Black Sea coast as well as along the eastern frontier.[7] Soviet press and radio gave broad coverage to these extreme demands.

At almost the same time, the efforts of the left to trade on the respectability of Bayar and his colleagues provoked an explosive reaction. A mob — if not set in motion, at least tolerated by the RPP authorities—sacked the offices of leftist publications.[8] This incident, whose anti-Soviet character was bitterly denounced by the U.S.S.R. in an exchange of notes with Ankara, roused the DP leaders to the dangers of further association with the left. Bayar and his fellows repudiated any connection with their erstwhile allies.

The break with the DP was a serious blow to the Turkish left. Efforts throughout 1946 to form socialist parties and to capture the nascent labor union movement, which had come into being with the end of prohibitions on worker organizations, did not prove very successful. In fact, the proliferation of tiny socialist parties split the already small constituency for factions amenable to the Soviet Union. And in the atmosphere of fear and doubt generated by the Kremlin's territorial demands, the left easily became identified with a denial of Turkish sovereignty. Hence, when the Martial Law Command moved in December 1946 to suppress the socialist parties, to close the remaining leftist press organs, and to disband labor organizations affiliated with them, this action was broadly applauded by both DP and RPP circles alike.

Not surprisingly the Soviet press bitterly decried these moves as merely the domestic reflection of a "foreign policy line that seriously compromises Turkey and arouses natural opposition within the country."[9] To make their stand clear, in August 1946, as the date for renewal of the Montreux Convention drew near, the Soviets seized on the occasion to reiterate their request for a base on the Straits. These demands were accompanied by troop movements in the Caucasus and by maneuvers of the Black Sea Fleet.[10] However, the U.S.S.R. did not follow to the letter the procedures specified for altering the Convention, a fact that served to quiet the fears of Ankara, suggesting to the Turkish Foreign Office that Stalin recognized his inability to prevail at a conference of the signatories.[11]

SEARCH FOR SECURITY

Far from isolating Turkey, these demands and pressures merely pushed the Turks to draw closer to the West. The Saracoglu government stepped up its consultations with London and Washington, particularly to compare evaluations of Soviet intentions and military preparations regarding Turkey. The Turks appeared to hope thereby to commit the Western powers either to intervene to forestall Soviet invasion or to come to the rescue should an invasion nevertheless materialize.[12]

Turkey's efforts to reinforce ties met growing response in the West, where suspicion of Soviet designs for aggrandizement mounted steadily after 1945. In this atmosphere, Washington first extended private assurances that the territorial demands of the Georgian professors "related to the UN Charter, which the US government is resolved not to permit to be violated."[13] As public evidence of its support, the Truman administration then dispatched the battleship Missouri to Istanbul in April 1946 to return the remains of the Turkish Ambassador, who had died in Washington during the war. British Foreign Minister Bevin, too, after some initial hesitation, reaffirmed in February 1946 that the Anglo-Turkish Treaty of 1939 was still in effect, declaring that the United Kingdom was unwilling to see Turkey become a satellite of the Soviet Union. The Western powers cooperated closely with the Turkish Foreign Office in constructing their replies to the Soviet demands for a revision of the Montreux Convention.[14] Likewise, in September 1946, British and American ships took part in an ostentatious maneuver in the Aegean designed to demonstrate Western interest in Ankara's defense amid reports of threatening Soviet troop concentrations on the Turkish borders. Yet until 1947 gestures of support remained essentially sporadic and small-scale.

At least in comparison with what was to come, Moscow's reaction, too, was somewhat measured. In the early years after the war, the Kremlin directed its invective especially at Ankara's connection with London, which appeared to be Turkey's chief backer in the West. Soviet press and radio accused the British of setting up a base in the Straits and of seeking to create a "Near Eastern Bloc" including Turkey and the Arab states.[15] But at this stage Moscow obviously still regarded the Western interest in Turkey more as an obstacle to Soviet control of the Straits than as a threat to the security of the U.S.S.R.

THE TRUMAN DOCTRINE

With the enunciation of the Truman Doctrine in March 1947, however, Turkey's strategic position underwent an obvious and basic change. Instead of being a relatively isolated prey, dependent on the faltering British hand, Turkey became overnight part of the rapidly expanding sphere of influence of the United States. The nature of the U.S. commitment was still quite vague; it was by no means clear that the United States and its allies would come to Turkey's immediate defense with military force. But declaration of the Truman Doctrine made unmistakable the general American interest in protecting Turkey against Soviet encroachment. And this interest was further emphasized by the continuing build-up of American naval forces on station in the Mediterranean.

For the Turks, the Truman Doctrine imparted a surge of confidence. By this time, the Turkish Foreign Office had concluded that Stalin was bluffing in his demands on Turkey; the Ankara regime no longer considered a Soviet attack likely in the near term.[16] On one level this new-found assurance was expressed in the bluntness with which, for example, Selim Sarper in October 1947 answered Byshinsky in the United Nations, accusing the U.S.S.R. of inciting belligerency.[17] The Turkish press, too, changed in tone. Editorialists more and more flaunted Turkey's defiance of the Soviet Union. Some even derided the U.S.S.R. for its lack of nuclear weapons, openly boasting that "the vengeful fist of civilization and humanity would soon descend on the Bolsheviks, and the world would be rid of these tyrants and savages."[18] And on another level, the Turkish government — undeterred by Soviet rhetoric — quietly went ahead to secure American military equipment and to refurbish its communications network, with heavy stress on roads, port facilities, and airports.

The Truman Doctrine brought a remarkable and sudden shift in Moscow's attitudes as well. The Straits now ceased to be the focus of Soviet attention, and the Kremlin permitted its territorial claims to lapse. Instead Moscow turned its main attack against Turkey's American connection. To the Soviets, the Truman Doctrine appeared designed to make Turkey an integral part of Washington's worldwide system of alignments to contain the U.S.S.R.[19] The construction of airfields and ports on a scale greater than Turkey had known in the past appeared especially sinister to the Kremlin. Indeed, it seems clear that the Truman Doctrine for the first time raised the specter before Soviet eyes that Turkey might present a military danger to the heartland of the U.S.S.R. This concern that Turkey might serve as a base for U.S. operations against the Soviet Union would be a lasting consideration in Soviet policy.[20]

It was not easy for the Soviet leadership to devise an effective policy to deal with Turkey's new "strategic-military" position. By now Moscow's hopes of seeing a more amenable government installed in Ankara had evidently gone a-glimmering as the left encountered ever more stringent restrictions. At the same time, Soviet foreign policy appeared to be losing its momentum. Moscow had found it necessary to pull back from Iran; and the Truman Doctrine dealt a heavy blow to the prospects for the guerrilla movement in Greece. The outlook for intimidating the Turks, therefore, appeared less and less promising.

In this situation, the Soviets directed their main effort at inflaming latent nationalist feeling within Turkey against close collaboration with the United States. To this end, Kremlin commentators played a number of variations on the theme that American "aid" — which they always categorized as sham — was directed at purposes harmful to Turkey. The rising cost of living at home, the falling value of Turkish currency abroad, and Turkey's rapidly mounting foreign debt were all attributed to the effects of having "sold out" to the "American imperialists." Soviet propaganda gave great prominence also to the influx of American specialists to survey the Turkish economy and military apparatus, contending that they were taking control of the Turkish armed forces and that their presence signaled the revival of the hated capitulatory privileges of the nineteenth century. Moscow further charged that the need to keep a large standing army at the service of the West was imposing an intolerable burden on the Turkish people, a burden not offset by the military assistance furnished by the United States, which was acquiring Turkish soldiers for its own purposes at little cost. All in all the Soviet thesis amounted to the accusation that a tiny reactionary ruling class had sold Turkey to the West in order to assure continuation of its political hegemony and exorbitant profits.[21]

While among the extremes of left and right in Turkey suspicion of the West always ran close to the surface and could be easily aroused, by far the majority of the Turkish elite was unmoved by this propaganda. On the contrary, the leadership of both the DP and the RPP were at one in favoring even closer ties with the West in general and with the United States in particular. Under President Inonu's leadership, Turkish policy was directed at entering an explicit defense arrangement with the United States. When, after the Berlin crisis in 1948, American attention became focused on a collective security pact for Europe, the RPP government became concerned lest Turkey's importance in Washington's eyes decline. Ankara therefore stepped up its exploratory efforts at this time, probing the possibility of forging an alliance with other Mediterranean states that also seemed ineligible for the Atlantic Pact. Yet the underlying aim of the Turkish maneuvers was to secure acceptance by NATO.

THE DEMOCRATIC PARTY REGIME

Under these circumstances, Soviet-Turkish relations could hardly be other than frigid. Nor was there even a hint of a thaw following the victory of the Democratic Party in the 1950 elections. The transfer of political power by the free exercise of the ballot was hailed in Turkey and in the West as the culmination of the long process of developing effective democratic procedures. The Soviets, on the other hand, characterized these elections as no more than "a comedy," the collusion of bourgeois politicians to fool the masses.[22] Soviet commentators greeted the DP's victory pledge to continue the RPP's foreign policy with the immediate judgment that the Menderes government was no improvement on its predecessor.[23]

From Moscow's point of view the new Turkish regime quickly showed itself even worse that the old. Before the DP government had been in office a full three months, it responded to the call to send troops to take part in the Korean War. This was a bold step for Turkey. Prominent elements in both the RPP and the tiny right-wing Nation Party (NP) expressed misgivings about this course, which committed Turkish forces far from home. They argued that, given Turkey's "delicate" geographical position on the border of the Soviet Union, it was unwise to risk provoking the Kremlin this directly.[24]

Predictably the Soviets strongly attacked the commitment of Turkish troops to Korea. Terming this move a course against Turkey's national interest, the Kremlin alleged that the United States had forced Ankara to take this step by threatening to cut off military and economic aid.[25] A miniscule group of Peace Partisans organized by former Ankara University teacher Behice Boran chimed in, appealing to the Turkish parliament to desist from the Korean venture. But these protests had no effect on the DP government, which rounded up the Peace Partisan leaders. The foreign minister seized the opportunity to lump all who objected to sending soldiers to Korea as "communists."[26]

TURKEY IN NATO

More significantly, the Korean episode offered the DP the means it had been seeking to force the doors of NATO ajar. Prime Minister Menderes recognized that dispatch of a significant force to Korea would dramatically demonstrate Turkey's value to the West and reinforce its claims to Western protection from the Soviets. Nor were these calculations far from the mark. First, in September 1950, the Ankara regime was invited to join in strategic military planning associated with NATO. Then, after active lobbying during the ensuing year, the Turks secured the long-sought approval to enter NATO as a full member.

Entry into NATO did little to change Turkey's perception of its position vis-à-vis the Soviet Union. In fact, adherence to the Atlantic Pact was for the Turks not so much an act defining their relations with the U.S.S.R. as one confirming their cherished belief that they were and should be recognized as, an integral part of Europe. The underlying possibility that Moscow might, at some point, seek to advance its claims by force provided a plausible pretext for including Turkey in Western defense arrangements. But although membership in NATO undeniably furnished additional security against Soviet hostility, for Ankara the real advance over the previous Western connection lay in providing assurance that Turkey would receive aid in the quantities that alone could spell the success of the government's development plans.[27]

Even in the Kremlin's eyes, Turkey's entry into NATO did not cause a marked change in relations between the two countries. Naturally Moscow went through the motions of protest over this "provocative" act, declaring that it "could not remain indifferent" to the inclusion of Turkey in this pact. The routine nature of the Soviet stance, however, was clearly evident in the stale repetition of by now well-worn argumentation charging the Turks with aggressive intent.[28] For there could not have been any appreciable expectation in Moscow that its vague and essentially unsubstantial threats would work a change in Turkey's course. Indeed, the Soviet reaction seemed to be a tacit acknowledgment of the U.S.S.R.'s inability to block Turkish association with NATO.

The Kremlin, however, was disturbed by the intensification of efforts to create regional groupings in the Near East and in southeastern Europe that accompanied Turkey's entry into NATO. This was a time when the Western powers were making another effort to piece together a formal defense pact for the Middle East to replace the previous colonial arrangements. Turkey played a key role in the "Middle East Command" that was now projected. Toward the end of 1951, the Turks joined with the United States, Britain, and France in sponsoring a call first to Egypt and then to the other states of the area to participate in the new organization.

Although the Egyptian government lost no time in rebuffing these proposals, the Soviets continued for some time to exaggerate the likelihood that a defense arrangement of these dimensions would in fact come into being. In November 1951, Moscow delivered a sharp protest note against Turkey's attempts "to involve the Near and Middle East in the military maneuvers of NATO aggression."[29] And even after Arab opinion generally had registered unmistakable opposition to formal association with Turkey and the West, the Kremlin persisted in playing on the theme that Ankara might serve as the surrogate of the Anglo-Americans in extending NATO's influence in the Arab world.[30]

By the same token, the Kremlin vastly overrated the Treaty of Friendship and Cooperation concluded in February 1953 by Yugoslavia, Greece, and Turkey. Charging that this agreement represented a branch of NATO in the Balkans, designed to bring Yugoslavia into the Atlantic Pact through the "back door," Moscow made much of the military nature of the compact. And, when in 1954 a formal military alliance was consummated by these same three states, Soviet propaganda took this as confirmation of the earlier diagnosis, despite the fact that the arrangement in reality remained largely on paper.[31]

STALIN'S SUCCESSORS AND TURKEY

Stalin's death in March 1953 brought an immediate change in the Soviet attitude toward the Turks. No one could step into Stalin's shoes; and a struggle for power in Moscow was underway from the first. Yet the new collegial leaders generally shared doubts about the wisdom of continuing the high level of open hostility that had marked Soviet policy toward the West during these years. They were inclined to move toward coexistence between the Soviet camp and the Western powers. To achieve this they were prepared to retreat from some of the more obvious excesses of the Stalinist era.

Turkey was one of the first areas where the new spirit was expressed. On May 30, 1953, the Soviet Union officially renounced its territorial claims on Turkey, stating in a note to Ankara that Moscow had also changed its mind about the need to share in control of the Straits.[32] Thereafter, as was the case generally throughout the world, a new theme crept into Soviet propaganda toward Turkey: regular offers to settle outstanding issues through negotiation. To complement this more temperate approach, the Soviets in March 1954 replaced their ambassador in Ankara. By October 30, only a few short months later, Moscow was able to cause a minor sensation in Turkey through the unaccustomed warmth of tone in its traditional Republic Day commentary.[33] Early the following year Premier Bulganin would even proffer apologies that "Stalin had spoiled Soviet relations . . . with Turkey."[34]

Yet striking as this transformation in Soviet approach appeared, it did not signify a complete about-face. In fact, until after Khrushchev had been installed in power, the essential demands of the collective leadership in the Kremlin remained what they had been for some time: namely, Turkey must leave NATO, must abandon all special ties with the United States, and must drop its efforts to form regional alliances. The cutting edge of Soviet propaganda continued to be turned especially against alleged American colonialist domination of Turkey. Hence, for example, only two days after Ankara's reply to Moscow's renunciation of its territorial demands, the Soviet Foreign Ministry delivered a note of protest, calling scheduled visits of American and British naval units to Istanbul a "military demonstration."[35] Protests on this theme would form a persistent refrain in the Soviet repertory, though Moscow would itself in May 1954 begin to send warships through the Straits for the first time since before the Second World War.

THE TURKISH RESPONSE

Under these circumstances, neither the government nor the press in

Turkey hastened to respond with any enthusiasm to the suggestions of friendship from the collegial leaders in the Kremlin. This may have been partly because withdrawal of the Soviet territorial claims did not seem to represent a notable advance. Since the Soviet Union had not pressed these demands for some years Moscow's announcement seemed merely to confirm the status quo. Furthermore, the language of the Soviet renunciation appeared to imply the sacrifice of a legitimate claim, a position that the Turkish Foreign Office found offensive.[36] More important was the pervasive suspicion in Turkey of Soviet expansionist desires engendered by the experiences of the Stalinist era. It would be some time before Turkish opinion makers would cease to be impressed more by evidences of continuing hostility than by conciliatory gestures.

To suggestions that they undertake bilateral negotiations with the Soviet Union, therefore, the Turkish leaders posed a condition unacceptable to Moscow: they linked improvement in Soviet-Turkish relations to progress toward resolution of all outstanding issues between the Kremlin and the West. Ankara obviously feared that piecemeal attempts at settling problems would merely serve the Kremlin's ends, leaving Turkey exposed and vulnerable to sudden shifts in the Soviet policy.[37] Furthermore, uncertainties over the durability of the collective leadership in the Kremlin and an initial apprehension that Khrushchev might revive Stalinism evidently discouraged Ankara from accepting at face value the new Soviet protestations of friendship.[38] Indeed, in May 1955 *Zafer*, the mouthpiece of the DP, warned that coexistence was a Soviet weapon to dull the fighting spirit of the West. To the question, "to live together?" *Zafer* replied in an article obviously reflecting the government's view, "Never!"[39]

KHRUSHCHEV TAKES CHARGE

It was in this situation that Nikita Khrushchev shouldered Malenkov aside in February 1955 to emerge as the paramount leader of the Soviet state. Even before this formal act, Khrushchev's personality had already begun to shape policies of the government. Under his leadership the Soviet Union undertook actions well beyond the immediate vicinity of Soviet frontiers. His leap over the "northern tier" to establish intimate relations with Nasser's Egypt in 1955 was only the first signal that the U.S.S.R. would insist on its right to play an active role in the Arab world. Indeed, the quest to break out of the bounds imposed by the West's containment policy and to establish a presence in the Middle East — from which the Soviet Union had been all but entirely excluded in the past — became a primary goal of Moscow's policy toward the area. In this scheme of things, efforts to improve relations with Turkey clearly occupied a secondary position.

Whenever a choice seemed necessary, the Kremlin now favored its Arab clients, providing them material as well as verbal backing in their struggle against the West. In this struggle Turkey was invariably identified with the West.

RIVALRY IN THE MIDDLE EAST

Accordingly, the Middle East rapidly became the focus of discord between the Turks and the Russians. Western hopes of assembling some sort of grouping in the Arab world had not died with the failure of the idea of the Middle East Command. In 1954 Turkey took up Washington's suggestion to form a new regional defense organization, this time based on Iraq and the so-called "northern tier" countries of Pakistan and Iran. Disregarding the drumfire of criticism from Moscow, which attacked the venture as an imperialist conspiracy to perpetuate aggressive aims in the Middle East, the Menderes government concluded agreements culminating in the formation of the Baghdad Pact in 1955. Britain joined the regional members from the start, whereas the United States made clear that, though it would not accept full membership, it would provide support for this cooperative arrangement.

Formation of this alliance posed a direct challenge to Khrushchev's ambitions to see the Soviets established as an active participant in the politics of the Middle East. As a result, each step in the pact's genesis evoked sharp protest from Moscow, which accused Turkey of serving as the "gendarme of the United States" in the Middle East. But the Soviet Union took more direct steps as well. When Western reluctance to supply military equipment to Egypt for use against Israel led Nasser to the brink of frustration, Moscow stepped in to sponsor a deal by which Czechoslovakia offered arms to the Egyptians in the fall of 1955.

While the Czechs formally bore the entire onus of supplying arms to Egypt, the Turks never doubted the Kremlin's underlying responsibility for this transaction. Nor was there any hesitation in Ankara to look upon this act as the start of a full-fledged arms race in the Middle East. On this basis, the Turks took the lead in NATO councils in branding the new Soviet policy toward the Middle East as dangerous and provocative.

PEACE OVERTURES TO TURKEY

It was typical of Khrushchev's approach that he try to juggle several more or less contradictory policies at the same time. While boldness in the Middle East was obviously paying dividends for the Kremlin, peaceful coexistence remained the watchword of the era. In his report to the Supreme Soviet at the end of December 1955, Krushchev himself played on both themes. Here, on the one hand, he excoriated Turkey for her role in the Baghdad Pact, and on the other hand held out the prospect of reconciliation.[40]

In furtherance of peaceful coexistence, Khrushchev at the fateful Twentieth Congress of the Communist Party of the Soviet Union in February 1956 put forth a significant new foreign policy line. Here he proclaimed that "even . . . when military alignments exist, the opportunities for improving relations between countries, particularly between neighbors, have by no means been completely exhausted."[41] Accordingly, Marshal Voroshilov, in his message to President Bayar in March 1956 on the twenty-fifth anniversary of the Turkish-Soviet treaty, invited Prime Minister Menderes and a parliamentary delegation to visit the U.S.S.R. To further sweeten its image, the Kremlin offered the Turks a modest amount of economic assistance — proposing to expand trade and to undertake projects such as an oil refinery and a steel mill. But the most important concession from Moscow was voiced only unofficially. Starting in April 1956 articles in *International Affairs* and other Soviet press organs for the first time indicated that the Kremlin was no longer demanding that Turkey abandon its treaty arrangements with the West:

> While advocating normal relations with Turkey, the Soviet Union by no means seeks to impair Turkey's relations with the US, Britain, or any other Western country . . . . What the Soviet Union rejects is that kind of cooperation which makes it possible to subordinate the interests of one country to the interests and aggressive aims of another.[42]

This commentary and others like it did not remove all ambiguity. It was not altogether clear how the Soviets proposed to reconcile their continuing attacks on Turkey's alleged subordination to the United States with their reassurances that a rapprochement with the U.S.S.R. "does not mean that Turkey will be obliged . . . to break with the West, or even to impair her relations with Western countries."[43]

SUEZ AND HUNGARY

Whatever guarded optimism this peace campaign may have aroused in Turkey was soon dispelled by the rapidly mounting tension in the Middle East that was to explode into the Suez war and by the Red Army's forceful suppression of the Hungarian revolt.

Egypt's nationalization of the Suez Canal Company in July 1956 was regarded in Turkey as an act inspired by the Soviet Union. It appeared evident to the Turks that Nasser would not have embarked on such a bold course without Soviet encouragement and without Soviet arms. Yet the Turkish Foreign Office judged it inexpedient to condemn this move as was being urged by some commentators, who advised that "if Egypt will not listen to reason, then it must listen to force."[44] First of all, the Ankara government was reluctant to oppose the right of any state to nationalize property within its borders. Moreover, there was concern in Ankara lest internationalization of the Suez Canal, as requested by the Western powers, could form an undesirable precedent for Turkey in the Straits. In this situation the Turks moved cautiously in support of their Western allies. Even so, they were not spared Soviet condemnation.

The deployment of the Red Army to crush the Hungarian revolt in October 1956 greatly inflamed Ankara's suspicion of the Kremlin. Soviet recourse to force touched off a wave of revulsion in Turkey. Expressing the general indignation, the Turkish newspaper *Cumhuriyet* remarked that "the people who condemned Stalin's tyranny possess the ability to apply the same principles with even greater thoroughness and cruelty."[45] It was widely agreed that this act had stripped away the mask of Soviet peaceful intention, demonstrating the need for vigilance and precautions against being deceived by sweet words from Moscow. Some voices in Turkey even went so far as to call for the expulsion of the U.S.S.R. from the United Nations.[46]

Hardly had the effects of Soviet repression in Hungary had time to sink in before the Israelis launched their military move against Egypt, followed almost simultaneously by British and French occupation of the Suez Canal Zone. This introduced new complications; the war threatened to break apart the newly formed Baghdad Pact. Indeed, the Middle Eastern members felt it necessary to convene without delay to issue a sharp condemnation of the British role in these events. To salve Arab sensibilities, Ankara withdrew its minister to Tel Aviv. But the Baghdad Pact remained unshaken. Even responsible RPP leaders now began to attack it for contributing to the instability of the Arab world.[47]

Soviet conduct throughout the conflict did nothing to reassure the Turks. Khrushchev's vague threats that missiles might fly against the British and French was duly noted in Turkey, though the achievement of a cease-fire was attributed largely to U.S. pressure. The Soviet offer to send volunteers to Egypt — obviously aping Western reaction to the Hungarian invasion — also caused some stir. While a few Turkish observers pointed out the difficulties for the Soviet Union in supporting such a distant operation, especially when the number of volunteers was said to be some 50,000, there was obvious relief after Egypt turned down the Soviet offer.[48]

THE SYRIAN CRISIS

Under these circumstances, the momentum of the Soviet advance in the Middle East became a major preoccupation of the Turkish government and its Baghdad Pact associates. Syria rather than Egypt, however, was the focus of concern in this connection. Not only did Syria border on Turkey and Iraq, but the Baghdad allies judged the leaders of the unstable Syrian regime to be more vulnerable to Soviet pressure than was Nasser. Turkish reports just after the fighting had died down to the effect that Syria was awash with arms and equipment supplied by Moscow and intended for use by Soviet troops evoked a warning from the Foreign Office in Ankara that Turkey would find it necessary to respond should Soviet forces be stationed on Syrian soil.[49] In December 1956 the Turkish foreign minister confirmed his government's belief that Syria had received more Soviet arms "than she could use given her present capabilities."[50] It was clear from his words that the Turkish government affected to believe itself threatened by a Soviet surrogate from the south.

Even enunciation of the Eisenhower Doctrine in January 1957, engaging the United States to defend Middle Eastern countries threatened by "international communism," did little to diminish the concern in Turkey over the intimacy of Soviet ties with Syria. For a period during the spring of 1957 the Turks concentrated troops on their southern frontier. In the summer of 1957 there was renewed talk of plotting by the Baghdad Pact powers to bring down the Ba'athist regime in Syria. Syrian exiles began to collect on Turkish territory amid rumors — promptly denied by Ankara — of the formation of a "free Syrian government."[51] Under these circumstances, U.S. Deputy Undersecretary of State Loy Henderson made a quick visit to the Middle East at the end of August 1957. His trip was accompanied by demands in the Turkish press for international action against Syria. He apparently returned convinced that Ankara's fears about the Damascus regime were well founded. Following his departure from the area, Turkish military maneuvers near the Syrian border were announced, and notice was given of a NATO exercise in the eastern Mediterranean. To add to the tension, Ankara radio, in defending these moves, cryptically declared that "Turkey takes necessary precautions in all fields when necessary."[52] Furthermore, in September 1957 Prime Minister Menderes publicly proclaimed that Syria was in the final stages of transformation "into a bridgehead with subversive purposes and aggressive aims." On these grounds, he cautioned that "one should not be amazed at [Turkey's] reaction to the Syrian-Soviet understanding."[53] This warning was underscored by U.S. reiteration in October 1957 of its commitment to come to Turkey's help without delay in the event of attack resulting from "Soviet infiltration of Syria."[54]

These pressures on Syria struck a sensitive nerve in the Soviet Union. With the Suez experience fresh in mind, Khrushchev obviously wished to avoid the embarrassing position of proving unable to prevent the military defeat of a client state. This apparently suggested to the Kremlin that a public stand in defense of Syria with appropriate warnings to Turkey — though admittedly entailing its own risks — might head off the danger of a repetition of the Suez debacle. To this end, *Pravda* on September 8, 1957, undertook to warn that the Turks were "playing with fire." At the United Nations Gromyko embroidered on this theme, adding that action against Syria would place "Turkey in a situation pregnant with great disasters for her."[55] *Izvestiia* went farther still, noting that "in encroaching against the security of her southern neighbor, Turkey would undoubtedly expose her own security to a direct blow. The Soviet Union, whose frontiers are near the threatened area, cannot adopt the attitude of a spectator to the situation there."[56] These ideas were expressed as well in the letter Bulganin sent to Menderes on September 10, 1957, openly warning that Syria was not alone and that there could be no guarantee that war involving it would remain "localized."[57]

Some have labeled this an "artificial" crisis.[58] For all its long build-up, the dispute petered out with astonishing suddenness after the arrival of Egyptian troops to reinforce the Syrian army in October 1957. Thereafter, the Syrians dropped their request for U.N. action. By the end of November the Soviets had focused their propaganda on other targets. Meanwhile the Turks ceased proclaiming that Syria was on the verge of becoming a Soviet satellite. Their final reply to the U.S.S.R. on this subject in February 1958 appeared quite perfunctory in nature. By this time Foreign Minister Zorlu could officially express his government's expectation that creation of the United Arab Republic had ended the danger of a communist regime's coming to power in Damascus.[59] Never again was Syria to be a serious bone of contention in Turkish-Soviet relations.

Both Ankara and Moscow had ulterior motives for seeing a crisis fomented at this moment. No doubt the heated exchange with Turkey served Khrushchev's domestic imperatives; he was still struggling against the "anti-party" group in the Kremlin, and Marshall Khukov's ouster at this time was apparently linked with the crisis. In addition the contest with Turkey offered a convenient context for asserting the Soviet claim that the Middle East, as "an area situation in direct proximity to the territory of the Soviet Union," intimately "involved Soviet security."[60] Indeed, while Turkish actions clearly dictated some Soviet response, the evidence suggests that Khrushchev inflated the crisis in a deliberate effort to inflame tensions. He had his own penchant for brinkmanship.

Although, to be sure, the Democratic Party leaders in Turkey felt some genuine concern lest Syria install a communist regime and offer its facilities to the U.S.S.R., there can be no question that the Syrian imbroglio suited Adnan Menderes's ends as well. Campaigning for the October 27 elections was proceeding hot and heavy in Turkey. For the first time since taking office, the DP was seriously challenged. Moreover, the restrictions on the press and on the opposition parties added a note of bitterness that boiled over continually during the election period. In this situation, to raise an acute foreign threat impelling the people to close ranks behind the DP held obvious attractions. Besides, Menderes may also have viewed a Syrian crisis as inducement for the United States to increase its support for the Baghdad Pact.

Both the Turks and the Soviets seemed reasonably satisfied with the outcome of the Syrian events. Turkish fears of a communist takeover in Syria were quieted when Egyptian authorities speedily suppressed communist organizations in the United Arab Republic. More important for Ankara over the longer run was the fact that the Kremlin shifted its line toward Turkey on a basic point. Bulganin, in his final message concerning the Syrian affair, officially confirmed that "the Soviet government has no wish whatsoever that the relations between the Soviet Union and Turkey improve at the expense of the worsening of Turkey's relations with the Western powers."[61] This clear statement, the logical culmination of earlier trends, was a prerequisite to any substantial progress toward establishing normal relations between the two countries.

The Kremlin, too, gained. Henceforth, the Turks accepted the U.S.S.R.'s right to participate in the affairs of the Arab world. Even the flow of Soviet weapons to the Arabs no longer elicited significant protest from the Ankara government. Perhaps the Turks reasoned that the Soviets would not themselves man the equipment they supplied to their clients. Certainly there was no doubt that the Turks held little regard for the fighting qualities of their Arab neighbors. In any event, with the end of the Syrian crisis began a noticeable decline in Turkish fears of encirclement by the Soviet Union — whose maneuvers with the Greeks during the Cyprus dispute after 1954 had conjured up for the Turks the specter of their country almost completely surrounded by Soviet states.[62]

LEBANON AND IRAQ

Even the Lebanese insurrection of 1958 and the Iraqi revolution in July of that year gave only momentary fillip to Turkish anxiety. The Menderes government offered some minor items of equipment to the beleaguered Beirut regime and permitted the United States to use the Adana airbase as a staging point for a unit of American troops on their way to Lebanon. Moscow derided the first gesture and protested the second. The newly established clandestine Bizim Radyo, broadcasting in Turkish from East Germany, seized the occasion to appeal for the formation of a "united front" to block Menderes's cooperation with the United States.[63] Rumors in Turkey that the DP was preparing to dispatch forces to upset Qasim in the confused days following the coup in Iraq prompted immediate warnings from Moscow against such a course.[64] Yet there was no suggestion that the Soviets themselves would send troops to the area or would take prominent part in either the Lebanese or the Iraqi events. In this situation, the alarm which these crises generated in Turkey was soon spent and never reached a peak of intensity in any way comparable to that of the Syrian question of the previous year.

It may seem surprising that the Turks were not more concerned lest the Soviets be able to exploit the wave of unrest that swept over the Middle East at this time. But by 1958 Turkish reaction to upheavals in the Arab world had become mixed. To an important degree the consensus on policy toward the Middle East that had obtained until the Suez crisis had now been sundered. Seeing the hand of Nasser rather than that of the Soviet Union as the prime mover in both Lebanon and Iraq, most of the Republican Peoples Party leaders felt the U.S. landing in Lebanon to be counterproductive. They regarded Turkish assistance to this move as a blunder that would facilitate Soviet penetration of the Middle East.[65] Further, in the eyes of RPP policy makers, the withdrawal of Iraq from the Baghdad Pact appeared likely to strengthen, not weaken, that alliance by removing a focus of discord with the rest of the Arab world. These views were expressed forcefully in connection with the extraordinary sessions of parliament summoned at their request in July and August 1958.[66]

In time this line of argument prevailed. The Menderes government overcame its initial hesitancy and recognized Qasim's regime. Moves to establish friendly relations with Iraq came much more slowly, providing Moscow ammunition to accuse Turkey of plotting with CENTO against the Baghdad regime. But the DP government eventually came to appreciate Qasim's attempts to maintain a balance between various competing factions in Iraq, including the native communists. In this frame of mind, Turkish leaders did not become greatly concerned either over the fact that Soviet weapons had begun to displace Western equipment in the inventory of the Iraqi armed forces or that Soviet military missions were installed in Iraq.

THE MISSILE CONTROVERSY

If the Turks could now regard Soviet arms in Arab hands with something approaching equanimity, U.S. weapons in Turkey were a different story for the Kremlin. By 1957 technological advance had made possible the deployment of short-range nuclear missiles (such as the Honest John). To Moscow this prospect threatened a significant degradation of the advantages conferred by Soviet superiority in manpower over the Western armies. By January 1957 TASS was spearheading an attack against the deployment of nuclear weapons and tactical guided missiles by NATO military forces.[67] The following month Foreign Minister Shepilov publicly warned that "it goes without saying that any country . . . which would agree to grants its territory for U.S. atomic task forces would assume full responsibility for the consequences arising therefrom."[68] And in April 1957 *International Affairs* carried an article by I. Chelnokov proclaiming that to put such weapons on Turkish territory ran the risk of embroiling Turkey in atomic war if any conflict should break out between the West and the Soviet Union.

Ankara paid no attention to the Kremlin's rhetoric. The Turks did not see themselves able to avoid entering any conflict between NATO and the U.S.S.R. Hence they saw missiles giving them more, not less, military security. Thus in December 1957 the Menderes government openly announced that it was in the process of obtaining Honest John rockets and Nike antiaircraft missiles.[69] In justifying this position before the parliament, however, Foreign Minister Zorlu was careful to reject the Soviet accusation that these missiles could be fired without Turkish permission. He gave categorical assurances that "the use of [missiles] was subject to the provisions of the Turkish Constitution and to approval by the Assembly."[70]

Honest Johns and Nikes were tactical weapons whose short range precluded use against targets more than a few miles behind the Soviet frontiers. While Soviet propaganda at this time generally blurred the distinction between these missiles and those capable of striking deep in the heartland of the U.S.S.R., the Kremlin's main concern was the prospect that intermediate range missiles (the Thor and Jupiter) might be stationed on the periphery of the Soviet Union. Under these circumstances, as the Atlantic Pact began to consider deploying intermediate range missiles, the level of Soviet opposition markedly increased.

Although this campaign was directed at the Western alliance as a whole, Turkey's proximity to the Soviet Union and her eagerness to receive missiles made her a special focus of attack. Thus Bulganin bore down heavily on Turkey in a round of notes to the NATO states in December 1957, seeking to head off a formal Atlantic Pact commitment to deploy intermediate range missiles. He pressed the Turks not only to refuse to permit missiles and nuclear weapons on their territory, but to intercede with their NATO allies to achieve a two- to three-year moratorium on the testing and use of such arms.[71] Early in January 1958, following a NATO Council meeting, the Kremlin sent another harshly worded communication to Ankara threatening that the U.S.S.R. would destroy such installations without even using ballistic missiles. Exaggerating the likelihood that the Baghdad Pact countries might deploy missiles, TASS now launched the persistent refrain that the Middle East should become a "zone of peace, free of nuclear and rocket weapons."[72] Khrushchev himself repeated this call in Albania in May 1959. As Soviet commentators put it, "if Turkey really wants to improve Soviet-Turkish relations, it should at least refrain from increasing old commitments and assuming any new ones in carrying out the aggressive plans of the U.S.A. and the North Atlantic bloc."[73]

Caught up in the momentum of the Western alliance, the DP government was not swayed by the drumfire of Soviet criticism. On the contrary, the harsh tone of the Kremlin's notes merely increased Menderes's interest in complying with U.S. desires. He undoubtedly hoped that Turkish cooperation in NATO would dispose Washington to be more forthcoming with economic aid. Hence, in 1959 Ankara joined Italy and Great Britain in agreeing to permit the deployment of intermediate range missiles on its territory.[74]

EXCHANGE OF VISITS

Having failed in his campaign to block the Jupiters from being stationed in Turkey, Khrushchev changed his tack somewhat. The more extreme propaganda efforts against the Ankara regime were assigned to the clandestine Bizim Radyo. This organ, which served as the voice of the émigré Turkish Communist Party, took over primary responsibility for the task of seeking to arouse Turkish nationalist sentiment against the United States and especially against the activities of U.S. personnel in Turkey. On the other hand, Moscow radio and the Soviet press generally adopted a more moderate tone, urging Turkey to let down its guard and to join in the détente that was particularly in evidence in the days preceding the Geneva summit conference of May 1960. The Kremlin coupled this propaganda campaign with a diplomatic offensive to press the Turks to agree to a rapprochement. These efforts culminated in the announcement on April 12, 1960, that Prime Minister Menderes had accepted an invitation to visit Moscow in July 1960, to be followed by Khrushchev's return visit to Turkey at some later date.

While for Khrushchev these visits marked another step toward peaceful coexistence, for Menderes they represented a complete reversal of field. So sharp was his turn, in fact, that it led the military leaders who ousted him in May 1960 to justify their move in part on the grounds that he was planning to "sell out Turkey" to the U.S.S.R. Evidence for this charge was never forthcoming, however, and these accusations were soon dropped.[75] Nor does it appear at all likely that Prime Minister Menderes had any intention of making a radical about-face in foreign policy.[76]

Perhaps the main reason for Ankara's sudden change of heart lay in the conviction of the DP leaders that they were being left behind in the process of normalization of East-West relations that was taking place by 1960. The Cold War had entered a stage of cautious contacts, and personal diplomacy at the highest level offered the prospect of easing tensions. At the same time, the Menderes government was beginning to feel the pinch of financial constraints. The $359 million package of economic assistance extended by the Western powers in August 1958 had been largely spent or committed to existing projects. No doubt the U.S.S.R. had led Menderes to expect that he could conclude advantageous economic arrangements during his trip.[77] But most basic of all was the fact that Moscow no longer insisted on radical change in Turkish foreign policy as the price for improved relations. Unhappy as they were over Turkey's alliances and missile bases, the Kremlin leaders were willing to accept them as a fact of life. Under these circumstances it was possible to agree on an exchange of top-level visits.

The Ankara authorities were careful to stress that their trip did not prejudice Western solidarity, but had been arranged in the context of efforts to ensure peaceful and just solution of conflicts.[78] The RPP claimed credit for having long urged a more flexible policy toward the U.S.S.R. Some opposition commentators, however, warned that the timing of this announcement served the Soviets in preparation for the Geneva summit conference.[79] Yet public interest in this surprise announcement did not last long, for by the end of April 1960, domestic troubles had pushed this topic off the front pages of the Turkish press.

Bizim Radyo and the Soviet organs displayed differences in reaction to the visits. The émigré radio was more concerned with urging youth and the military to rise up and join in the "struggle until Menderes is overthrown and the U.S. driven out."[80] Soviet press and broadcasting, however, paid considerably more attention to the visits, which they viewed as a major breakthrough in the Cold War. Nor did this effect wear off entirely even during the U-2 contretemps, with the resulting failure of the summit conference, and the rapidly spreading unrest that would lead to the overthrow of the Menderes regime on May 27, 1960. As late as May 19, Moscow radio was still proclaiming that despite all obstacles it hoped that the visits would promote peace and improve Soviet-Turkish relations.

Indeed, the prospect of this exchange may have tempered the Kremlin's expressions of annoyance with Turkey for its part in the flight of the U-2 reconnaissance plane, which was shot down on May Day 1960 deep within the U.S.S.R. When the Soviets recovered the pilot, they discovered that the craft had been based in Adana, Turkey. Khrushchev exploited this incident mainly to embarrass the United States by sabotaging the 1960 Geneva summit meeting. Of course, the Kremlin did go through the motions of protest to Ankara, and sent a note warning in the usual vague terms that the Soviet

Union would "be forced to take due retaliatory measures" if such acts were repeated.[81] But Khrushchev was careful not to raise this issue to a pitch that would destroy the chances for greater harmony with the Menderes regime.

THE MILITARY REGIME IN TURKEY

The process of détente between Turkey and the U.S.S.R. was interrupted by the military coup of May 27, 1960. To be sure, the ouster of the DP administration did not alter Turkey's basic foreign policy: the military rules had no intention of changing Turkey's role in NATO and CENTO. But preoccupied with internal matters, they were not inclined to rush into any striking gestures to improve relations with the Soviet Union. Moreover, Turkish suspicions of the U.S.S.R. were fueled by the failure of summit diplomacy in 1960 and by Khrushchev's return to a generally truculent posture at the United Nations and elsewhere.

Accordingly, Moscow's early attempts to ingratiate itself with the military rulers in Ankara bore little fruit. The Kremlin initially welcomed the coup as "*a telling blow to the plans of American imperialism,*" and hastened on May 30, 1960, to affirm respect for Turkey's territorial integrity.[82] Soviet proposals for large-scale economic aid followed, allegedly accompanied by suggestions that the military remain indefinitely in power.[83] In the summer of 1960, no doubt to test the firmness of the junta's commitment to the West, Khrushchev sent General Gursel, Turkey's new president, a note suggesting that neutrality would have great economic as well as political advantages for Turkey.[84] Gursel firmly rejected this counsel, making clear that the military regime would be no less determined than its predecessors to preserve ties to the West. The junta refused Soviet offers of aid also, although it did permit some increase in cultural and commercial activity between the two countries. In this context, plans for an exchange of visits were shelved indefinitely. Thereafter, with Khrushchev obviously convinced that his peace campaign toward Turkey stood no chance of success, the Kremlin gradually reverted to a harsher attitude toward its southern neighbor.

Within Turkey the 1960 coup unleashed powerful forces that in time would transform the political scene. Almost from the start, the military regime developed a strong reformist complexion reflecting a concern with social issues — centering on the slogan "social justice" — which both stimulated and itself fed on a rapidly spreading socialist movement. In the freedom of expression engendered by the coup, proponents of left and right emerged (though open advocacy of Pan-Turanism as well as communism was still proscribed). Socialist attitudes affected not the masses, who clung with remarkable tenacity to traditional values, but the educated elite. Indeed, a striking shift to the left took place in the political spectrum. At the same time there was a profound upsurge of nationalist fervor that colored all approaches to Turkey's problems. At first domestic issues formed the chief subject of concern. But gradually foreign policy too began to come under this influence, and Turkey's basic orientation came under fire.

The junta did not remain long in office. Following elections in October 1961 a civilian government took power. But no single party had the required majority of seats in the lower house to form a government unaided. Hence, with the military looking over their shoulders, the civilian politicians patched together a series of unstable coalitions. Until January 1965 Ismet Inonu, whose party had the largest representation in the lower house, served as prime minister and was the dominant figure in the regime. This expedient generally fitted the requirement of inspiring confidence among the armed forces. It did not, however, facilitate effective government. The coalition partners held quite divergent views on priorities and on direction. In this situation it was never easy to achieve consensus to embark on radical departures in either foreign or domestic policy.

THE CUBAN MISSILE CRISIS

The first acute foreign policy issue to face the coalition regimes arose at the end of 1962 in connection with the Soviet attempt to place missiles in Cuba. A direct outgrowth of Khrushchev's frustrations over the West's increasing superiority in strategic weapons after 1960, this bold Soviet move formed the response to NATO's deployment of intermediate range missiles. Khrushchev's conviction that the Soviet Union ought to be able to do what the United States was doing around the world was no doubt largely responsible for Moscow's decision to set up similar missiles in Cuba. But success in this endeavor would also have boosted the military capability of the Soviet Union to a significant degree.

The Kremlin had never forgotten the Jupiters in Turkey. After hope of rapprochement with the military regime had waned, the Soviet government in February 1962 had addressed an aide-mémoire to Ankara demanding clarification of press reports regarding missile-base construction in Turkey.[85] Hewing to established custom, the junta had brushed off this question with the affirmation that Turkey would continue to take "all measures it judges expedient to assure its own security." While this was the last official Soviet démarche to the Turks on this subject made public before the Cuban crisis, press and periodicals in the U.S.S.R. continued the refrain after the civilian regime took office in Ankara. Ironically, in its October 1962 issue, the Soviet periodical *International Affairs* would again characterize the Ankara regime as on "the brink of disaster" because of U.S. plans to turn it into a missile base not only against the U.S.S.R. but also against "the national liberation movement in the Middle East."[86]

In erecting missiles in Cuba, Moscow was clearly conscious of the parallel with the U.S. installations in Turkey. Once Washington discovered the sites in the process of construction and forcefully demanded the removal of missiles from Cuba, Khrushchev produced an obviously well-thought out proposal for withdrawal of American intermediate range missiles from all overseas bases, particularly Turkey, as a necessary quid pro quo.[87] President Kennedy regarded this offer as reasonable, especially because the Jupiters were by then obsolete and no longer essential to a credible deterrent.[88] Feeling it inexpedient to accept a bargain explicitly in the heat of crisis, he passed the word to the U.S.S.R. unofficially that the United States would phase out these missiles from Turkey after the Soviets had withdrawn theirs from Cuba. Forced on the defensive, Khrushchev accepted this compromise and agreed to pull out his missiles in return for a pledge from Kennedy merely not to invade Cuba.

In a real sense, therefore, the Turks were a party to the crisis. From the first they were concerned over the obvious similarity between the Jupiters in Turkey and the Soviet missiles in Cuba. Confirming publicly that Turkey would be loyal to its NATO commitments come what might, Foreign Minister Erkin strongly rejected Moscow radio allegations likening bases in Cuba to those in Turkey. Erkin put forth his government's position that the Turkish installations were for strictly defensive purposes.[89] The emerging left-wing press seized on the occasion to dramatize the threat to Turkish security from the presence of NATO missile bases.[90] Indeed, the Inonu government, which earlier had strongly resisted American suggestions to phase out the Jupiters, now required little prodding to agree to the removal of these weapons.[91] This decision was announced in January 1963.

Withdrawal of the missiles marked a significant shift in Turkey's strategic importance in respect to the Soviet Union. To be sure, the Turks continued to possess an air force equipped with atomic weapons and to have significance for other reasons. But with deployment of intercontinental ballistic missiles in the United States, backed up by Polaris submarines, the imperatives of deterrence no longer assigned a central role to Turkey. Though Moscow maintained its attack on the stationing of Polaris submarines in the eastern Mediterranean as endangering "all the countries of this part of the world," it was clear that these fulminations were addressed primarily to the United States.[92]

Under these circumstances, the dismantling and removal of the Jupiters eliminated a major source of irritation in Turkish-Soviet relations. No doubt this was an important consideration in impelling Khrushchev now to open a new peace offensive seeking to woo the civilian government in Turkey. In 1963 there was a notable decline in the hostility of Soviet press and radio toward the Inonu governments. Articles began to appear on the theme, "Let the Black Sea Unite Us."[93] By the middle of 1963 these blandishments were showing results. A Turkish parliamentary delegation visited the U.S.S.R. in June and was warmly received by Khrushchev. Turkish Foreign Minister Erkin himself agreed to consider an early trip to Moscow. All the pressures within Turkey set in motion by the coup now appeared to suggest cautious exploration of a more individualistic foreign policy.[94]

THE CYPRUS DISPUTE

With the outbreak of the Cyprus crisis in December 1963, the inclination toward a more independent Turkish foreign policy received dramatic impetus. At that time the efforts of the Greek Cypriot majority to eliminate from the constitution the political guarantees for the Turkish community painfully worked out in 1959 led to widespread violence on the island. Ankara's immediate response of overflights to underscore its determination to protect the Turkish community embroiled it with Greece, which also felt committed to take sides. British attempts to end the conflict failed, NATO mediation proved unequal to the task, and the U.N. peace-keeping force had scarcely greater success. In June 1964, when Ankara appeared on the verge of landing an expeditionary force on Cyprus, President Johnson intervened with a harshly worded letter warning the Turks against such a venture.[95] The Turkish government was shocked at the suggestion that the alliance might not operate against the Soviet Union and public resentment against the United States mounted swiftly. Disregarding American pressure, the Turkish air force mounted air strikes in August 1964 to relieve a beleaguered Turkish Cypriot outpost. Though this led to the suspension of major military action in Cyprus, it left Turkey's relations with both the United States and Greece painfully strained.

Khrushchev's policy took little advantage of the opportunities thus offered. Moscow had long opposed Turkey's aspirations on Cyprus. The Kremlin — perhaps out of concern for the fate of the large Communist Party on the island — steadfastly supported independence for Cyprus. Initially Soviet propaganda condemned the outbreak of communal fighting as a NATO plot to provide a pretext for intervention.[96] Ignoring Turkey's sharp conflict with its Western allies, Kremlin commentators labeled the famous Johnson letter "a smokescreen, an attempt to give the United States an alibi just in case Cyprus is attacked."[97] They characterized the Turkish air strikes in August 1964 as "actually the handiwork of NATO at large."[98] Accordingly, Khrushchev's public warning that the Soviet Union "would not stand aloof" in the event of an invasion was not specifically addressed to Ankara. In fact, a *New Times* editorial denied that his statement "was an act unfriendly to Turkey."[99] Not unnaturally it did not seem so in Turkey, where hotheads responded by breaking into the Soviet as well as the American pavilions at the Izmir fair, occasioning an official note of protest from Moscow.[100]

POST-KHRUSHCHEV PATTERNS

A shift of Soviet policy toward Cyprus that would profoundly affect relations with Turkey came early in October 1964 at the time of Khrushchev's sudden ouster. Recognizing that a modest move toward a more even-handed policy on the Cyprus dispute would earn large dividends in Ankara, Kosygin and Brezhnev took advantage of Foreign Minster Erkin's long-projected visit to Moscow to signal a new policy. In the communiqué issued early in November 1964, they proclaimed their recognition of the Turkish community's legal right to coexistence. This position, which Foreign Minister Gromyko reiterated in December 1964, was read by the Turkish Foreign Office as endorsement of the Turkish demands for Cyprus to be an independent federated state.[101]

Turkish response was immediate. A Turkish parliamentary visit to the U.S.S.R. was arranged for January 1965; and a few months later Ankara welcomed a Soviet delegation headed by Podgorny. Foreign Minister Gromyko visited Turkey in May 1965. After Inonu was finally obliged to step down, the new prime minister, Suat Hayri Urguplu, himself journeyed to Moscow in August 1965, a visit which Kosygin repaid in December of the following year. Finally Turkish Prime Minister Suleyman Demirel, who had taken office after the Justice Party (JP) won the elections in October 1965. traveled to the U.S.S.R. in September 1967.

In part, the enthusiasm with which the Turks took up these exchanges represented the depths of their disappointment with U.S. policy toward Cyprus. But to view Turkey's relations with the U.S.S.R. as the mirror image of those with the United States would be, of course, a profound mistake. The desire of all recent regimes in Ankara has been to maintain close ties to the West in general and to the United States in particular, while carrying on not unfriendly relations with the Soviet Union. In this context, one main requisite for the Turks has always been confidence that the Kremlin had abandoned its harsh policy and no longer harbored designs on their country. Given the continuing suspicion in Turkey that the U.S.S.R. might take advantage of weakness, this has always required and still requires that Turkey strike a delicate balance. Thus, for example, while the pace of high-level visits between the two countries rapidly gained momentum in 1965, Ankara insisted as an explicit precondition for this exchange that the Soviet leaders agree to forswear raising the question of Turkey's adherence to NATO and CENTO during these visits.[102]

For the new leaders in the Kremlin to forego any formal assault on Turkey's alliances represented no great sacrifice. Indeed, it was merely a reaffirmation of the official Soviet position of some years' standing. Moreover, CENTO by this time was passing through a stage of acute internal difficulties and no longer appeared to hold any prospect of military or political threat to Soviet interests in the Middle East. This organization, therefore, had become largely a peripheral issue between the U.S.S.R. and Turkey.

As for NATO, Moscow had by no means given up the objective of easing the Turks out of this pact. Clearly the immediate aim of the new bosses in the Kremlin was to discourage Ankara in the first instance from cooperating militarily in NATO and in U.S. bilateral arrangements. A second and related goal for the Soviets continued to be to have the Black Sea closed to Western warships, i.e., to establish the principle of *mare clausum* which Moscow had never renounced.[103] In fact, Moscow sought to extend this principle to airplanes as well as ships to discourage aerial reconnaissance in the Black Sea. A third, but somewhat longer-range, Soviet ambition was no doubt to promote Turkey's complete withdrawal from NATO and to turn Turkey generally from its Western orientation to a nonaligned status. Disruption of Turkey's plans to enter the European Economic Community fell into this category. Regarding any ultimate intention to see Turkey enter the Soviet sphere of influence, however, Moscow obviously did not find it practical to pursue courses of action to this end.

The principal means selected to work toward these goals were propaganda, diplomatic démarches, and economic suasion. For the most part, Soviet open propaganda was directed at emphasizing the legitimacy of friendly relations between Turkey and the Soviet Union. Even when the Kremlin did voice criticisms of the Demirel government, the tone of these attacks was generally restrained and was largely directed against Turkey's cooperation in U.S. activities.

On the other hand, Bizim Radyo and the émigré Turkish Communist Party — whose audience, though never large, nonetheless is probably growing — struck a far harsher note. From the start, the émigré communists called for a "united national-democratic front" to bring down the Demirel regime, which was assailed as the stooge of the Americans and the lackey of imperialism.[104] Not bound by the restrictions imposed on open Soviet media, Bizim Radyo insistently urged that Turkey leave NATO.[105] Indeed, the note of urgency in these unofficial voices was reminiscent of the earlier period of the Cold War, something that could hardly have helped to inspire genuine warmth in the Soviet-Turkish relationship.[106]

Economic relations between Turkey and the U.S.S.R. began a strong upward course in 1967. In March of that year, after long negotiations and many false starts, the Turks finally agreed in principle to a $200 million

Soviet assistance program to undertake a series of major projects, which included a steel mill, an oil refinery, and an aluminum plant. In connection with the program, a Soviet economic aid mission was set up with headquarters in Ankara. A trickle of technicians from the Soviet Union began to flow into the country and a few Turks were sent to the Soviet Union for training. Although progress in carrying out these projects has been slow, it is nonetheless clear that the 1967 agreement marked a significant breakthrough for the Soviets in their campaign to improve relations with Turkey.[107]

THE ARAB-ISRAELI WAR

A measure of the degree of change in Turkey's relationship with Moscow was offered by the 1967 Arab-Israeli war. In many respects this was a repetition of the lightning victory of Israeli forces over the Egyptians just over a decade earlier. But this time the Turks showed little concern over the Soviet role in supplying arms to the Arabs. Whatever nervousness may have been generated by the fighting quickly vanished when it became apparent that despite the expanded scene of battle, now involving Jordan and Syria as well, the Kremlin had no intention of introducing troops on any appreciable scale into the Arab world.

THE SOVIETS IN THE MEDITERRANEAN

The conflict in the Middle East, however, did emphasize the growing Soviet naval presence in the Mediterranean. Since 1964 the Soviet Union had been maintaining ships on permanent station here at least partially in reaction to the deployment of Polaris submarines in this area. Secondarily, the presence of Soviet ships in these waters was probably regarded by the Kremlin also as an adjunct of its developing relations with the Arab world and as a demonstration of its great power status. During the June 1967 war, these naval vessels shadowed the American fleet in the Mediterranean, keeping close tabs on its activity but remaining a careful distance from the actual area of fighting.

By and large this build-up of Soviet warships did not alarm the Turks. The naval capabilities of the U.S.S.R. were still vastly inferior to those of the NATO powers in the Mediterranean. Moreover, the Soviet task force, assembled gradually and without fanfare, did not receive great publicity in Turkey. The voice of retired admiral Sezai Orkunt was almost alone in calling attention to the military implications of this development, which he read as leading eventually to Soviet naval supremacy in the eastern

Mediterranean.[108] On the other hand, elements of the Turkish Labor Party (TLP), embarrassed at these Soviet efforts at power politics, found themselves obliged to demand that all non-Mediterranean states, i.e., both the United States and the U.S.S.R., withdraw their forces from this sea.[109] But most politically articulate Turks dismissed the advent of the Soviet ships as an inevitable response to the presence of the American Sixth Fleet, hence of concern primarily to the United States.

Soviet conduct during the crisis — Kosygin's willingness to talk with President Johnson at Glassboro and Moscow's evident desire to see an end to the war in the Middle East — did much to impart confidence that the Kremlin was not interested in military adventures. In this atmosphere a move to follow the course of France in its independence of NATO gained a foothold among the educated elite in Turkey. This state of mind was reflected to some extent in the ruling JP, which had been conducting negotiations with the United States since 1966 with a view to making adjustments in the series of bilateral agreements that regulated military cooperation between the two countries. But the idea of loosening ties with the West was far stronger within the ranks of the RPP. Indeed, by July 1968, an important segment of this party was apparently recommending the elimination of all remnants of the strategic deterrent — e.g., American strike aircraft and nuclear weapons of all sorts — and removal of the NATO regional headquarters in Izmir.[110] It seems to have taken Inonu's personal intervention to forestall adoption of this position as the RPP's policy in its declaration of July 9, 1968. Most vehement of all in its attacks on association with the West was the TLP. This avowedly Marxist oganization had been in the forefront of an increasingly successful campaign — though one generally disavowed by the larger parties — to arouse animosity against U.S. personnel in Turkey, to conduct strikes against U.S. firms, and to protest such adjuncts of the alliance as routine U.S. fleet visits to Turkish ports.

THE CZECH CRISIS

These developments in Moscow's favor were set back sharply by the display of Soviet military force in Czechoslovakia. While the Turks could and did draw a clear line between those countries they recognized were within the sphere of influence of the U.S.S.R. and those outside, they saw the invasion of Czechoslovakia as a blunt reminder that Moscow had not renounced force where its vital interests were concerned. As a result, therefore, the JP government postponed the visit to Moscow of Senate President Atasagun.[111] Ignoring strong objections from the Kremlin, the Demirel regime now felt it expedient to agree to cooperate in a new multinational force to be created in the Mediterranean under NATO auspices.[112] At the same time, some voices of concern were heard in Turkey over the size of the Soviet Mediterranean fleet. Those in the RPP who had been calling for far-reaching changes in the NATO alliance generally fell silent.

But the effect was most pronounced on the Turkish left. The Turkish Labor Party was simply torn apart. The left in Turkey had always been wracked by differences in personality and in shadings of ideology. Party President Aybar forthrightly condemned the Soviet invasion.[113] In the flush of revulsion at the Soviet act and to disassociate his party's philosophy from anything resembling that preached by the U.S.S.R., Aybar proclaimed that the TLP's socialism was one peculiar to Turkey, reflecting Turkey's own particular conditions.[114] This stand triggered an ideological debate that undoubtedly reflected underlying political rivalries. Party congresses in November and December 1968 proved unable to restore harmony; they merely papered over differences. And in the October 1969 elections, these considerations along with the lingering impact of the Czech events on the people at large led to a decline in TLP voting strength.

The effects of the Kremlin's move into Czechoslovakia, however, soon died out. In general, the climate appeared favorable for a continuing expansion of economic and cultural relations between Turkey and the U.S.S.R. These are the areas in which the Soviet leaders undoubtedly see the greatest prospect for success. In fact, Moscow radio was quick to come forth with a strong endorsement of the JP's victory in the October 1969 balloting, paying special tribute to the party's "concrete steps" toward improving the serious economic situation.[115] While Bizim Radyo called for a left-wing united front opposing the JP, it is clear that the Kremlin is not placing its bets on the Turkish left in the first instance. For the Soviets aim at improving relations with Turkey on a state-to-state level. The results of the 1969 elections merely reinforce the conclusion, obviously long held by the Soviet leadership, that it is extremely unlikely that a left-wing party (let alone the still illegal Turkish Communist Party) would be able to come to power on its own. Nor, indeed, is there any evidence that the leaders in the Kremlin feel they can bank on the Turkish left to follow the dictates of Moscow.[116]

— 4 —
Soviet-Iranian Relations:
A Quarter-Century
Of Freeze and Thaw

Firuz Kazemzadeh

Soviet-Iranian relations since the Second World War have been at once both complex and simple. While specific events may often have seemed random and unrelated; while dozens of personalities have suddenly appeared upon the stage only to vanish just as suddenly; while notes, agreements, and declarations have kept legions of diplomats busy, the basic outlines of policy on either side have seemed quite clear. The Soviet Union has had as its ultimate goal a Persia under a government controlled from Moscow; but in pursuit of this goal it has not been prepared for major political sacrifices, let alone war. Iran, on its part, has been trying to use every available means to stay outside the sphere of Russian domination. Thus the last twenty-five years have continued the pattern established in the nineteenth century: one of Russian pressure and of Iran's attempts to protect herself by exploiting third powers whose Middle Eastern or global interests might bring them into conflict with Russia.

Soviet pressure on Iran has been unremitting, though its intensity has varied with circumstances. In resisting such pressure Iran has had to exercise extreme care lest she commit herself to Russia's antagonists to such an extent that she would lose her freedom of manuever.

The stage for the initial phase of postwar Soviet-Iranian relations was set in 1942-43, when Soviet armies were engaged in a death struggle with Germany and Iran was under joint Anglo-Soviet occupation. Even while the fate of the Soviet Union itself hung in the balance, Moscow did not neglect measures that might assure it control of Iran after the war. In his *Puti sovetskogo imperializma (Paths of Soviet imperialism)*, Lev Vasil'ev tells of the activities of Soviet agents diligently preparing for the struggle they knew would come as soon as Germany was defeated.[1] It was with the aid of Soviet agents, civilian and military, that Iranian communist organizations were formed and armed. When in the summer of 1943 the Soviet embassy in Teheran (Tehran) ordered the newly appointed prime minister, Ali Soheyli, to turn over to the U.S.S.R. 100,000 rifles, 3,000 light machine guns, and

1,000 heavy machine guns, the weapons were not intended for the Red Army. Two years later the Persians found their rifles in hands of the troops raised by the Soviet-sponsored separatist regime of Azerbaijan.[2]

As soon as Soviet victory in the war was assured, Russian activity in Iran was intensified. The Tudeh party, which until the spring of 1944 had taken pains to appear as a united front of all leftists and liberals, began to attack the government of Mohammad Saed. The attacks were the more significant since Saed was a cautious statesman, well intentioned and friendly to the Russians. Simultaneously the Soviet government proposed negotiations concerning the status of an inoperative oil concession (Kavir-Khurian) in. the Semnan area granted to the Soviet Union in 1925.

Sergei Ivanovich Kavtaradze, the newly appointed assistant people's commissar of foreign affairs, came to Teheran in September. It became clear at once that the purpose of his visit went far beyond the settlement of issues left behind by a defunct concession. Kavtaradze demanded that the Persian government grant the Soviet Union concession for the exploitation of oil throughout northern Iran. A veteran Bolshevik only recently returned to favor after years in obscurity, he assumed an exceptionally unpleasant tone designed to intimidate the Persians. Simultaneously the Tudeh party denounced Saed, demanding his resignation and the granting of the oil concession to the U.S.S.R. To justify its demand, which represented probably the only known case of a communist party advocating such an ironic case, the party worked out the thesis of "the security perimeter of the Soviet Union," which proclaimed northern Iran essential to the security of the U.S.S.R. Britain would be excluded from the north. "An oil concession, especially one comparable to that of the British-Iranian Oil Company in the south, would simply consolidate the region as a security perimeter."[3] In Teheran Tudeh demonstrators were transported to the Baharestan Square in front of the Majles (mijles) in Soviet army trucks and "openly escorted by armed Soviet soldiers . . . . In Azerbaijan the Soviet authorities made the population sign petitions and telegrams, demanding that the Government accord the oil concession to the Russians, and force the resignation of Saed."[4] In spite of Tudeh's fury and Russian threats the Persians stood firm. Saed was not intimidated and refused to grant oil concessions either to the Soviet Union or to Western oil interests. In December Dr. Mohammad Mosaddeq introduced in the Majles a bill prohibiting any minister from negotiating oil concessions with foreigners without the prior approval of the Parliament.[5]

Oil, however, was only one of the goals of Soviet policy in Iran, less important in Russian eyes than the establishment of a communist regime in Teheran, though perhaps not less important than the establishment of separatist communist-dominated governments in Azerbaijan and Kurdistan should the acquisition of an oil concession prove impossible of achievement.

In both provinces Soviet agents worked closely with disaffected elements, whether they might be convinced Marxists or pre-feudal tribal chiefs.[6]

In Kurdistan (Kordestan) Moscow was able to exploit not so much anti-Iranian as anti-government sentiments of the tribal aristocracy. After years of oppressive peace imposed by Teheran, the Kurds had had enough of corrupt representatives of a distant central authority, enough gendarmes patrolling their roads, and enough tax collectors, army recruiters, and other such "trespassers." They were ready to revert to their more traditional and happier way of life, to raids, vendettas, and brigandage.

Late in 1941 the Soviets began to work with a number of Kurdish khans. A certain General Salim Atakchiov (Atakchiev) took a group of Kurdish chiefs to Baku, where they were received by Mir Ja'far Baghirov, premier of Soviet Azerbaijan and valued friend of Lavrentii Beria. From this meeting, the chiefs carried away the distinct impression that the Soviet Union was sympathetic to their aims.[7] A second visit to Baku occurred in the fall of 1945. This time Baghirov and his colleagues openly discussed the formation of an autonomous Kurdistan.

The Soviets initially preferred to see this territory as part of a communist-controlled Azerbaijan, but they soon realized that Kurdish khans would not accept such a solution. Since there was no other leadership within Kurdish society than that of the chiefs, the Soviets were compelled to agree to a separate Kurdistan. Baghirov thereupon promised the khans tanks, artillery, machine guns, and rifles, as well as financial support, and invited them to send as many young men as they wished to the Baku Military College.[8] No tanks or cannon were ever delivered, but Soviet trucks soon began to arrive at Mahabad, the center of Kurdish separatism, bringing rifles confiscated from the Iranian army in Azerbaijan, as I have mentioned.[9]

Compared to Azerbaijan, Kurdistan was, of course, only a minor issue. In Azerbaijan the Soviets had assisted at the birth of the so-called Democratic Party, a local version of the Tudeh. The party was to stage a coup d' état, to occupy government buildings, and to proclaim the autonomy of Azerbaijan. However, units of the Iranian army were still stationed in Tabriz and several smaller towns. These had to be disarmed or neutralized before any action could be taken by the separatists. In October fresh Soviet forces arrived in Azerbaijan "to assure by their intimidating presence the success of a 'popular movement.' " With the troops came numbers of armed Soviet Azerbaijanis, identical in appearance and in speech with their southern brothers and therefore able to blend with the local population.[10]

On November 19, 1945, Soviet troops, which had since August kept Iranian forces encircled in the barracks at Tabriz, offered the Persian commander a choice between surrendering and returning to Teheran with his officers, or joining the new Azerbaijani army. The commander chose the first alternative and communicated his decision to the imperial chief of staff in Teheran.[11] Iranian relief forces dispatched from Teheran to test Soviet intentions were stopped by a concentration of Russian armor and infantry east of Qazvin. Assured of total impunity, the local branch of the Tudeh, now renamed the Democratic Party, set up an "autonomous" government of Azerbaijan. Its leader, Ja'far Pishevari, remains to this day a mysterious figure. He had supposedly been a member of the government of the Gilan Soviet Republic in 1920-21, had fled to Russia, and had lived there for the next fifteen years working for the Comintern. In 1936 he returned to Iran, where he was jailed until 1941. After being released he entered politics, published a Tudeh newspaper, and was elected to the Majles. His credentials were challenged, he was refused his seat, and departed for Tabriz. Here he emerged as the leader of the so-called "Democrats," the new name for the reorganized local Tudeh.[12]

Though to outsiders the situation was confusing, the Persian government was aware that a large-scale plan had been put into operation by the Soviets, a plan involving the simultaneous formation of two separatist states and the take-over of the central government itself. The formation of a puppet regime in Teheran was to be accomplished by Tudeh bands from Azerbaijan, Mazanderan, and Semnan, converging on the capital.

> To reinforce the morale of these elements and to weaken that of their adversaries, a Soviet detachment of armoured cars advanced to within 18 miles of Teheran on the Karaj road, whilst to the east Firuzkuh and Garmsar were similarly occupied . . . . The arrival of these Communist elements in the neighbourhood of Teheran was intended to coincide with a popular revolt inside the town by the Tudeh partisans.[13]

The Persian government approached both the British and the Americans with requests for help, but the Western powers were in no mood to quarrel with Stalin. When the Iranian chief of staff, General Arfa', tried to explain the Azerbaijan situation to Wallace Murray, the United States ambassador, "He showed himself without understanding of the situation, telling me," the general reports, "that nobody wanted to take Azerbaijan, that certainly the Russians would evacuate Iran and this province in due course."[14]

In December 1945, Ernest Bevin raised the Azerbaijan question at the Moscow Conference. The British had already suggested to the Persians that an Anglo-Soviet-American team be sent to Azerbaijan as "investigators and advisers on the establishment of Provincial Councils into which the Azerbaijan 'Government' could be assimilated." Provincial councils had been provided for by the Persian Constitution of 1906 but had never come into being. Bevin was proposing to use a constitutional device to lend an air of legality to a fait accompli. At first Stalin seemed mildly interested. However, on December 26 Molotov stated that the Persian question was not on the agenda of the Conference and could not be discussed.[15] Moscow refused to compromise on Azerbaijan because her leaders believed that they would soon achieve all their goals in Iran. The Iranian government took an identical stand because it was afraid of being "sold out." The Majles rejected Bevin's proposal, "refusing to permit the future of Iran to be the subject of a committee decision by the three Allied powers."[16]

The Iranians, though discouraged by both Ernest Bevin and James Byrnes, decided to appeal to the first session of the General Assembly of the United Nations. Accordingly, January 11 they lodged their complaint against Soviet interference in Iran's domestic affairs. The Soviets were furious. They denounced the Persian government and, for good measure, the British, who, it was pointed out, had troops stationed in Greece and Indonesia. The dispute between the Soviet Union and Iran was no concern of the Security Council, the Russians maintained, and they refused to answer any questions on the subject. The Security Council then asked the parties to settle their dispute by direct negotiation and report to the United Nations at a later date. This meant, of course, that Iran could not count on support from the international organization. In the midst of these diplomatic maneuvers the cabinet of Ebrahim Hakimi resigned and Ahmad Qavam (Qavam os-Saltaneh) became prime minister.

Qavam was an experienced, old-style politician. He sensed that Iran had little international support and that his own position in Teheran was insecure. The World War was over; the last British and American troops had left Iran before January 1; Soviet strength in northern Iran and beyond was overwhelming; neither the British nor the Americans seemed willing to risk the breakdown of their alliance with Stalin for Iran's sake; and the Tudeh was rioting in the streets and could, perhaps, overthrow the government. Under the circumstances direct negotiations with the Russians must have appeared to Qavam as the best, or even the only, course of action. Thirty-five years earlier Qavam and his brother, Vosuq od-Dowleh, had been cabinet members when Russian troops invaded Iran in support of Persian counterrevolution. On that occasion, resistance and refusal to bow to Russian ultimatums had led to the disaster of long-term military occupation and the virtual extinction of Persian independence. Would Qavam be justified in running the same kind of risk a second time?[17]

The actions of Qavam following his appointment as prime minister on January 27, 1946, have been the subject of much controversy. The Shah neither liked nor trusted him. General Hasan Arfa', the imperial chief of staff and the officer in immediate control of the army, was suspicious and fearful that Qavam might pay too high a price for a settlement with the Russians.[18] In their memoirs both the Shah and his one-time chief of staff show Qavam in an unfavorable light, as does the Shah's foreign biographer, Ramesh Sanghvi. Others, however, found Qavam's policies astute and his motives highly patriotic.

The Imperial Farman (decree) appointing Qavam was promulgated on January 27. The next day the prime minister sent a telegram to Stalin offering to go to the Soviet Union to discuss Azerbaijan and oil. His offer was accepted and Qavam immediately left for Moscow, where he conducted negotiations with Stalin and Molotov until March 8.[19]

That February and the first week of March may very well have been the grimmest in Qavam's life. In accordance with wartime agreements all foreign troops had been scheduled to evacuate Iranian territory no later than six months after the termination of hostilities, or March 2, 1946. The Americans had left before January 1 and the British had withdrawn most of their forces, the last six hundred men leaving before the deadline. Only the Russians remained firmly in place, using their army as a shield under whose protection the Tudeh in Azerbaijan and the Kurdish khans could consolidate their separatist regimes. On March 2 Stalin summoned Qavam to tell him that Soviet troops would leave Khurasan (Khorasan) and the Semnan area but would remain in occupation of Mazanderan, Gilan, Azerbaijan, and Kurdistan. The next day fresh Soviet forces poured into Iran and moved in three prongs toward Teheran and the Turkish and Iraqui frontiers. Hundreds of tanks and heavy concentrations of artillery and infantry were to be seen all over northwestern Iran as well as on the Soviet side of the Russo-Turkish border.[20]

Stalin's deliberate violation of an agreement with Britain and the United States, the strident propaganda campaign against Turkey, and the troop movements that started on March 3 alarmed the United States. On March 4 President Truman conferred with Secretary of State James F. Byrnes. It was decided to send

> a note to Moscow that would, while still being diplomatically polite, make it very plain that we did not like the way Russia was behaving in Iran, and, specifically, that Russian troops were still there in spite of the solemn promises repeatedly made by the Kremlin that they would be out of Iran not later than March 2.[21]

The American note, delivered in Moscow on March 6 by George F. Kennan, chargé d'affaires, expressed the concern of the United States over the continued presence of Soviet troops in Iran and the hope that the Soviet government would do its part to promote international confidence "by withdrawing immediately all Soviet forces from the territory of Iran . . ."[22]

Face-to-face with Stalin and Molotov and himself the representative of a nation whose population numbered no more than a tenth of that of the

U.S.S.R. and whose military resources were practically nil, Qavam felt compelled to make four significant concessions:

He agreed to recommend to Parliament the establishment of a joint Russian-Iranian oil company (the Soviets to hold 51 per cent of the stock) to exploit the oil resources of northern Iran; to grant three cabinet posts to Tudeh party members; to recognize the rebel Azerbaijan Government; and, finally, to withdraw Iran's complaint against Russia before the United Nations.[23]

We know nothing of Stalin's or Molotov's reaction to Qavam's apparent capitulation, though one can easily guess their satisfaction at having achieved so much at such low cost. However, if there was jubilation in the Kremlin, it was premature. At the United Nations the Iranian delegate, Hoseyn 'Ala, disobeyed the prime minister and, relying on the Shah, of whose sentiments he was aware, refused to withdraw the Iranian complaint. A confusing situation developed with the Soviet delegate claiming that Iran had withdrawn its case while the Iranian delegate was requesting the privilege of presenting it to the world organization.

'Ala addressed the United Nations on March 21. His articulate speech may not have changed history; yet as the first complaint ever brought before the United Nations, it focused attention on events that were sufficiently alarming to make President Truman confer again with Secretary Byrnes and Admiral Leahy. "Then I told Byrnes," Truman writes in his memoirs, "to send a blunt message to Premier Stalin."[24]

Unfortunately the Soviet government has published nothing that would throw light on the process through which Stalin and his associates decided to withdraw from Iran. One can only speculate about their motives and their thinking. The decision to withdraw troops from Iran was probably reached for several reasons. The Soviets seemed already to have achieved all their goals but one. They had Qavam's promise of oil concession; the Tudeh "government" of Azerbaijan had been recognized and the autonomy of Kurdistan seemed assured. Though the Persian government had not been overthrown, it was headed by a man who seemed willing to serve Russia. He had promised to introduce three members of the Tudeh party in his cabinet. The Tudeh was the only political party in Iran worthy of the name. It had no rivals and could be expected to take over the government either through infiltration or through a coup d'état. Of course, withdrawal from Azerbaijan would take pressure off Turkey, but claims on Turkey advanced by a couple of Georgian professors (rather than Armenian ones) and supported by the Moscow press were intended only as a test of Turkish determination to resist.

In late 1945 and early 1946 the Soviet Union was in no position to unleash a war in the Middle East. Furthermore, permanent refusal to withdraw might alert the United States and Britain. Even if these powers became reconciled through time to long-term Soviet occupation of northern Iran, continued violation of the sovereignty of an allied nation on the morrow of Hitler's defeat could not but create greater suspicions. Fears of Soviet expansionism were already being voiced by a few Western statesmen, the most prominent of whom, Winston Churchill, had just made a speech at Westminster College, Fulton, Missouri, sounding a dark warning against the Russian threat. Stalin was not prepared for the sake of achieving all his aims in Persia to jeopardize his European goals. His hold on East Germany, Poland, and the rest of Eastern Europe had not yet been consolidated. Czechoslovakia was still governed by a coalition of "bourgeois" politicians. Eduard Benes was still president and Jan Masaryk was alive. Rumania had not yet been rid of the king and the non-communist politicians, and in Bulgaria the struggle for control had not yet ended with the arrest and execution of Nikola Petkov. Stalin must have weighed opportunities and risks and decided that, having already achieved so much in Iran, he should not needlessly endanger his position. On March 24 Andrei Gromyko announced at the United Nations that, barring unforeseen circumstances, all Soviet troops would evacuate Iran within five to six weeks.

Upon returning to Teheran Qavam proceeded to carry out the promises he had made to Stalin. On April 4 an agreement was signed in which the Soviets promised to withdraw their troops from Iran May 6. Azerbaijan was recognized as an internal Iranian problem, though Teheran agreed to settle its differences with Tabriz through negotiations. Finally, within seven months of the signing of the agreement the Iranian government was to present to the Majles proposals for the establishment of a Russo-Iranian oil company in which for twenty-five years the Soviet Union would hold 51 per cent of shares to Iran's 49 per cent; for the second twenty-five years of the concession the two parties would hold an equal number of shares.

On paper, the granting of the oil concession was contingent upon its ratification by a Majles that had not yet been elected. However, Qavam had no difficulty in assuring the Russians that they had nothing to fear from a new Majles. All the deputies from Azerbaijan and Kurdistan would be hand-picked by the Tudeh. Elsewhere Qavam as minister of the Interior would see to it that the right people got elected. Nothing could have sounded more plausible to the Soviets, especially in the light of Qavam's seeming determination to do everything in his power for the implementation of the promises he had made in Moscow. He took every opportunity to stress his dedication to friendship between Iran and the U.S.S.R., promoted Russo-Persian cultural relations, allowed the Tudeh freedom of the streets, and appointed to the cabinet three of its prominent members, Iraj Eskandari, Dr. Morteza Yazdi, and Dr. Fereydun Keshavarz.

Late that summer an uprising of south Persian tribes occurred. There is still no documented information on the origin of the rebellion or as to its true instigators. In Moscow and in Teheran it was said that the British had armed the Bakhtiaris and the Qashqais. The presence of British warships in the Persian Gulf, the landing of British troops at Basra, and Britain's fear for the future of the Anglo-Iranian Oil Company lent credibility to the theory that the British were using the tribes to split the south from the rest of Iran. However, Qavam's mild treatment of southern rebels suggested to some that he was not unhappy about their demands for the dismissal of communists from the cabinet and the suppression of the Tudeh party. Later this became the official Soviet version enshrined in M. S. Ivanov, *Noveishaia istoriia Irana* (Contemporary history of Iran) and in his portion of the article on Iran in the sixth volume of the *Sovetskaia istoricheskaia entsiklopediia* (Soviet Historical Encyclopedia).

Though Qavam may not have engineered the Qashqai-Bakhtiari uprising, the event nevertheless greatly improved his position vis-à-vis the Tudeh. The critical moment of Majles elections was approaching. The fate of the country hinged on the composition of that body in its next session. Trouble in the south provided the old statesman with leverage against the Tudeh. With seeming reluctance he accepted many of the demands of the southern chiefs, thus forcing the resignation of the Tudeh ministers.

Early in November Qavam proclaimed that elections would at last be held, a move made necessary by the insistence of the Soviets that Qavam live up to his promise to have the Majles ratify the oil agreement. No further procrastination was possible. It was time to act. During the next months, in close collaboration with the Shah and the army, plans were made for the reintegration of Azerbaijan and Kurdistan. At a War Council the Shah himself spoke in favor of an immediate advance into Azerbaijan; "others considered that this would involve the risk of Soviet military intervention."[25] However, Qavam had calculated the odds. He had noticed, no doubt, that Russia had not protested the departure of communists from the cabinet. Moreover, the Soviet embassy, which must certainly have received intelligence reports on the Iranian preparations for a march into Azerbaijan, remained silent. The Shah too felt that "The Russians found themselves in an awkward position; they wanted to support their puppet state, but at the same time they wanted to keep on good terms with Teheran in the hopes of getting oil."[26]

In the opinion of the Iranian government Russia was facing a dilemma. She could send her troops back into Iran to prevent the Iranian army from occupying Azerbaijan. Such an action in a rapidly deteriorating climate of world opinion could lead to dangerous consequences. It would most certainly prevent the election of the fifteenth Majles, since under Iranian law no election could be held while foreign troops were on Iranian soil. Without the Majles the oil concession promised by Qavam would vanish into thin air. Or she could abandon Pishevari's separatist regime in the hope that the subsequently elected Majles would ratify the oil agreement.

On December 3 Qavam announced that the army would march into Azerbaijan so that elections might be held there as in the rest of the country. Earlier he had requested from Washington "strong support should the Soviet Union object to Iranian troops entering Azerbaijan."[27] Reassured by a favorable response from Washington, Qavam felt ready to move. The Soviet ambassador then presented himself to the Shah and, the Shah wrote,

> began to speak in threatening tones, protesting that military moves in Azerbaijan were endangering the peace of the world. In the name of his government he demanded that I, as King and Commander-in-Chief, should withdraw my forces. I told him that on the contrary, the situation until then prevailing in Azerbaijan had been endangering the peace of the world, and that I was refusing his demand.[28]

The Shah ordered the army to march. The separatist regime left without Soviet military protection was paralyzed. Its troops offered practically no resistance. In Tabriz, Azerbaijan's capital, the populace rose against the "government" and took over the city even before the arrival of Iranian army units. The Russians had abandoned the Tudeh. The separatist regime collapsed. Some of its leaders surrendered, others were massacred by vengeful crowds, and still others, including Ja'far Pishevari, fled to the Soviet Union. The Kurdish separatist state at Mahabad was also liquidated by the Iranian army without evoking Soviet action.

The election to the fifteenth Majles returned a heavy majority for Qavam's newest invention: the Democratic Party of Iran. The prime minister now had a firm base in the Parliament and a good working relatonship with the Shah. The army, loyal to the Shah, was also favorably inclined, partly because Qavam was showing increasing interest in it and had purchased for it large quantities of American surplus war matériel. With force on his side, Qavam began to smash the Tudeh in Teheran. Party headquarters were raided and their newspapers suppressed. Tudeh-dominated trade unions were disbanded. In its moment of crisis the Tudeh proved not to have been the strong, monolithic organization it was supposed to be. Hangers-on, opportunists, and fellow travelers of all shades began to abandon the communist sinking ship:

> On 5th January 1947, the Tudeh Central Committee voluntarily divested itself of its powers and confessed its errors. Power had, it seemed, already begun its corrupting process, because in the redelegation of Tudeh Party offices, and especially in the breaking up of the trade union organization, charges of graft and peculation were heard a great deal.[29]

The Soviet government began to lose patience. The original agreement with Qavam had been made in March and signed in April 1946. A year later Azerbaijan and Kurdistan had been lost to the government of the Shah. The fortunes of the Tudeh were ebbing in Teheran and throughout the rest of the country. But the oil concession had not been ratified. Meanwhile American influence in Iran grew rapidly. The deterioration of Russian-American relations was bringing the United States onto the Iranian political scene as a successor to Great Britain in counterbalancing the Soviet presence. The Soviet ambassador in Teheran, I. Sadchikov, protested in rather intemperate language against the interminable delays in the ratification of the oil concession. He threatened dire consequences if the agreement of April 1946 were rejected. Sadchikov's threats were backed up by a show of force. Soviet troops concentrated on Iran's frontiers, Soviet gunboats violated Iran's waters off Bandar-Pahlavi, and Soviet airplanes repeatedly flew over Iranian territory.[30]

Time was still working in Iran's favor. The Truman Doctrine had come into being in the spring of 1947, bringing United States commitment to Greece and Turkey. United States Ambassador George S. Allen, in a Teheran speech, expressed America's concern with Russian threats to Iran. Iran, he said publicly, was free to grant or withhold oil concessions and the Iranians "may, therefore, rest assured that the American people will support fully their freedom to make their own choice."[31] Strange as it may seem, the British assumed an attitude unexpectedly sympathetic to Moscow. The British embassy in Teheran stated to the Persians in September 1947 that Britain "had no objection in principle" to the granting of an oil concession to Russia and advised them "to keep the door open for future discussions with Russia on the subject of oil."[32] The United States government through its ambassador in Teheran, however, publicly dissociated itself from this position.[33]

On October 22, 1947, Qavam presented to Majles the proposal for the granting of an oil concession to Russia. The Majles, feeling that there was no longer a real danger of Russian invasion, adopted by one hundred and two votes to two a resolution that declared Qavam's negotiations with the U.S.S.R. on oil null and void, proclaimed that Iran would exploit its own oil resources, and permitted the sale of Iranian oil products to the U.S.S.R., but would not grant concessions to foreign countries or enter into partnerships with them. The last item of the resolution sounded the opening shot of another campaign: The government was instructed "to enter such negotiations and take such measures as are necessary to regain the national rights" in all cases in which such rights had been impaired and "particularly in regard to southern oil."[34]

The Soviet press denounced Qavam, the Shah, Iranian reactionaries and American imperialists. One can only guess at the thoughts and the feelings of those responsible for Soviet policy in Iran. A year earlier Moscow was certain of achieving most of its goals in Iran. At best, it was felt, Teheran would have a Tudeh government and the entire country would fall within the Soviet orbit. At worst, the Soviet Union would acquire an oil concession that would give it innumerable economic and political advantages in northern Iran. Instead, the U.S.S.R. had suffered a political defeat of the first magnitude. It had evacuated all of Iran. Its Azerbaijani puppets had been thrown out, rebel Kurdish chiefs suppressed or hanged, the oil agreement repudiated, the Tudeh party seriously weakened, and the "feudal-bourgeois" regime in Teheran stabilized. Worst of all, from Moscow's point of view, the events of 1946-47 had aroused the United States and had provoked America into taking an ever greater part in the affairs of the Middle East.

However, the Soviet government did not allow itself to be forced into taking rash action over the reverses in Iran. The Kremlin had other, more important battles to fight. The years 1947 and 1948 were crucial both in Europe and in the Far East. Events of great moment were taking place. Iranian developments had to be viewed in the perspective of Soviet interests in Germany, in Western Europe, and in the Far East. The Marshall Plan had been promulgated during the summer of 1947. In September the U.S.S.R. replied with the Cominform. A "democratic" government under Markos Vifiades was organized in Greece, where the civil war spread and intensified. Communist forces were rapidly winning in China, opening the brightest prospects for the further growth of communist movements in the Far East. In Burma, Malaya, Indochina, Indonesia, and the Philippines a wave of anti-colonialism was rolling forward, ready to be exploited by Moscow. Under the circumstances it would have been imprudent to risk a large-scale conflict involving the United States in the Middle East. Russian leaders knew the political virtues of patience. For the time being, therefore, they accepted the new situation in Iran.

Anti-imperialist movements have frequently provided Russia with opportunities to expand her influence and to promote her political system. The Soviets had never satisfactorily settled the numerous theoretical problems raised by attempts to apply Marxism, a quintessentially Western product of Western conditions, to non-Western societies; but they did not ignore the great movements that were taking shape in Asia and Africa. On the morrow of the Bolshevik revolution Russian communist leaders intervened in Iran, helping to establish the short-lived Gilan Soviet Republic. They gave aid to Mustafa Kemal in his struggle against the Allies. They cooperated with the Kuomintang. In each instance they acted in the hope that Asian anti-Western, anti-colonial movements would bring about the dissolution of European empires and a corresponding weakening of "bourgeois" powers.

The resolution of the Iranian Majles rejecting Russia's demands for an oil concession announced at the same time the intention of the Iranians to get rid of the British in the south. The Anglo-Iranian Oil Company (AIOC), a giant enterprise that wielded tremendous influence in the life of the country, became the focus of all anti-imperialist sentiments. The company, which was immensely profitable for its shareholders, of whom the British government was the largest, was out of touch with the political reality of the times. At first it practically refused to negotiate. Later its offers were too insignificant. When they did become reasonable, it was too late. On March 14, 1951, the British government offered Iran an agreement for an equal division of the company's profits. The next day the Majles adopted in principle the nationalization of the oil industry. On April 28 the Anglo-Iranian Oil Company was nationalized and Dr. Mohammad Mosaddeq assumed the post of prime minister.

The story of the Anglo-Iranian oil dispute is too well known to be retold here. Suffice it to say that the British government showed no more sensitivity to the realities of the situation than had the AIOC. The dispatch of warships to the Persian Gulf only inflamed passions throughout Iran. It was clear to Mosaddeq and to the Shah that a brigade of British paratroopers flown to Cyprus did not constitute much of a military threat, and that in any case in 1951 Britain was no longer in a position to defend her imperial interests by armed force.

The Soviet attitude toward Mosaddeq was ambivalent from the start. His anti-British sentiments that made him willing to wreck the Iranian oil industry rather than permit the British to continue with their concession, made them want to give him support. Yet he was an aristocrat, a landowner, a conservative who distrusted the Russians and was generally friendly to the United States. Being totally devoid of sentimentality in international politics, the Russians were prepared to forget that Dr. Mosaddeq was the author of the bill, passed by the Majles in 1944, prohibiting any Iranian government from negotiating oil concessions with foreign countries without express parliamentary approval. They found it more difficult to forgive him the renewal in April 1952 of the agreement on American aid to the Iranian armed forces. Mosaddeq's government was informed in a formal note on May 21 that the renewal of the agreement had placed the Iranian army under the control of a foreign power. The note further stated:

The Soviet Government deems it necessary to call the attention of the Iranian Government to the fact that, in agreeing to accept American so-called aid and, in this connection, assuming definite commitments of a military nature toward the United States of America, the Iranian Government is in fact setting out on the path of helping the United States Government to carry out its aggressive plans directed against the Soviet Union.

Such actions of the Iranian Government cannot be regarded otherwise than as actions incompatible with the principles of good neighbourly relations, the

The concluding reference to the Treaty of 1921 contained a veiled but obvious threat since it was this treaty, improperly invoked, that the Soviet Union had used to justify its invasion of Iran in 1941.

Through most of Mosaddeq's tenure as prime minister, however, relations between the U.S.S.R. and Iran were eminently correct. The expiration of the Soviet fisheries concession in Gilan produced some minor irritations that were quietly remedied. In Iran's dispute with Britain over oil Moscow maintained a similarly correct posture.

The Soviet press, of course, cheered Mosaddeq and condemned the British. The Tudeh party, freed of recent restraints and revitalized by the course of events, frequently led street demonstrations, strikes, and riots directed against the Anglo-Iranian Oil Company. However, it was noticed that the communists spared no effort to turn the struggle against a British oil company into a general campaign against the Western powers, the United States in particular.

After the death of Stalin relations between the Soviet Union and Iran improved further. In a review of world affairs made by G. M. Malenkov on August 8, 1953, he stated that, "The experience of thirty-five years has shown that the Soviet Union and Persia are interested in mutual friendship and collaboration," and that talks were being held on the initiative of the Soviet Union concerning the settlement of a number of frontier problems and mutual financial claims.[36]

Though Stalin's successors were willing to improve relations with Iran, they, like their predecessor, saw the Persian question in a much broader context than that of the Middle East. An astute writer on foreign affairs has observed that, "The Malenkov-Khrushchev regime, only a few months in office, was making efforts to ease relations with Britain and the United States. An end of the war in the Far East must not be a prelude to a war in the Middle East."[37] Another writer has pointed out that "Caution was the main feature of Russia's attitude." The Soviet ambassador offered to supply Iran with certain goods that could no longer be imported from Britain.[38] However, as the Shah himself did not fail to note, when the International Court of Justice ruled on the Anglo-Iranian oil dispute, declaring it outside the Court's jurisdiction, "The British member of the tribunal voted in support of Iran's case. The Russian member, on the other hand, abstained; in fact he failed to appear during any of the Court's proceedings in the case."[39]

The same ambivalent attitude toward the prime minister was evident in the last months of Mosaddeq's regime. When Mosaddeq broke with the Shah and attempted to gain control of the army, he further complicated an already involved situation. Domestic unity gave way to discord. In his search for allies Mosaddeq had to rely upon extreme reactonaries led by Ayatollah Kashani, a ruthless and powerful cleric, and the extreme left. Yet he did not relish their cooperation. He even tried occasionally to suppress the more violent actions of his supporters. The Soviets were aware of his attitude and made plain their view of him:

> Mosaddeq's government, which struggled against English imperialists for the implementation of the nationalization of the oil industry in the interests of the Iranian national bourgeoisie, attempted at the same time not to permit the deepening of the unceasing democratic workers' and peasants' movement that constituted the main force in the anti-imperialist struggle. The P.P.I. [People's Party of Iran, Tudeh] and the democratic trade unions were compelled to operate semi-legally. Mosaddeq's government did not dare in its struggle against Anglo-American imperialists to rely upon the democratic forces within the country, as well as on the countries of the democratic camp, but attempted to maneuver between them and the imperialist powers. It took no radical actions to stop reactionary provocations and intrigues. All of this created favorable conditions for an offensive by the imperialists and the Iranian reaction.[40]

In the showdown between the Shah and Mosaddeq in August 1953 the Soviet Union remained on the sidelines. The press, of course, hailed the "anti-imperialist struggle of the Iranian people." On August 19 *Pravda* reported that the Persian government had discovered a plot hatched by the Americans and their local hirelings.

> The conspiracy was uncovered and suppressed at the most decisive moment. The Shah has fled Iran . . . . The Iranian people have answered the machinations of the American agency [*agentura*, agents] by a huge demonstration under the slogans: "Death to the plotters!" "The Iranian people demand [the] expulsion of American spies from their country!"[41]

Pravda's writing of the uncovering of the conspiracy at the decisive moment indicates that the Soviet leadership believed in Mosaddeq's victory. (The Tudeh, too, saw him as the Persian Kerenskii.) The American plot had been uncovered; the Shah was gone. The demands of the "Iranian people" for "death to the plotters" was not only reporting but also an expression of wishes and a bit of advice. A revolution had occurred. It must be deepened.

After the Shah left the country, Teheran was virtually in the hands of the Tudeh. The army stayed in its barracks. The police, too, remained out of sight. *Pravda*'s article, however, was already out of date at the moment of reaching its readers. The forces loyal to the Shah struck back. Army units supported by throngs of people surged through the streets of the capital calling for the return of the Shah. Since it was known that the United States was actively involved in these events, the Tudeh could be expected to mobilize all its resources in defense of Mosaddeq, whatever his position may have been from the constitutional point of view. But the party was paralyzed. It knew that it would have to face the army with its own resources, Soviet military aid being out of the question.

> At a meeting of the Tudeh Central Committee in the basement of a house behind the VOKS [Soviet cultural agency] a fight was going on between the extremists and the moderates led by Dr. Kia Nuri; the majority was on the latter's side. Instructions from the Central Committee often contradicted one another. Arms were distributed; then an order came to abstain from the revolt.[42]

Thus Mosaddeq, who only a few days earlier had been hailed by the Tudeh as a national hero, was abandoned by them at the crucial moment.

The Shah returned to Teheran in triumph. For the first time since he ascended the throne in 1941 he stood at the pinnacle of power without rivals. While the Soviet press denounced the victory of reaction in Iran, the Soviet embassy in Teheran continued dealing with the Iranian government as if nothing had changed. Soon "Russian propagandsts declined to offer any further support to the discredited Tudeh party," the Shah later wrote, "and Russia showed every inclination to cooperate with me and with my new Government."[43]

The new government, headed by General Fazlollah Zahedi, suppressed all political parties. The Tudeh received particularly harsh treatment when in August 1954 the secret police discovered a Tudeh organization in the army. Six hundred officers were arrested. Some were executed, while others received prison sentences of varying length or were exculpated. Such measures did not at all disturb relations with the U.S.S.R. On the contrary, the Soviet government seemed impressed with the strength of the regime and willing to improve relations. A mixed Russo-Iranian commission was appointed to work on the old unsettled issue of badly demarcated frontiers.[44] On December 3, 1954, an agreement was signed between the two countries providing for border demarcation and, in Article 4, for the payment of nearly eleven tons of gold and $8,500,000 in the form of goods to Iran in settlement of Russian wartime debts.[45]

The only negative gestures made by the U.S.S.R. for a year after Mosaddeq's overthrow related to the discussions, then in progress, concerning Iran's possible adherence to the Turkish-Pakistani treaty of April 1954. The Soviet government, aware of talks between General Zahedi and Ambassador Henderson, drew the attention of the Persian government to Article 3 of the Treaty of 1927 whereby

> each of the contracting parties undertakes not to participate, either in fact or formally, in political alliances or agreements directed against the security on land or at sea of the other High Contracting Party, or against its integrity, its independence, or its sovereignty.[46]

Soviet apprehension was not baseless. The United States had long relied upon a system of regional alliances. The great gap in the system lay in the Middle East. John Foster Dulles pushed the idea of a Middle Eastern bloc that would include, in addition to Turkey and Pakistan, also Iran, Iraq, and Jordan. On February 24, 1955, at Baghdad, Turkey and Iraq signed a treaty of cooperation "for their security and their defense."[47] To forestall Iran's adherence to the Baghdad Pact the Soviet Union made some friendly gestures that included an invitation to the Shah to visit the U.S.S.R.

In Teheran there was no agreement on the merits or demerits of membership in the Baghdad Pact. Those opposed to joining argued that adherence would needlessly antagonize the Soviets, creating new pressures upon Iran. Since the country bordered on the U.S.S.R., it could not escape this unwelcome contiguity. It was better, therefore, to engage in no acts that could be interpreted by the Soviet Union as hostile. The proponents of the Pact, on the contrary, maintained that Moscow did not respect weakness and that membership in the Pact would enhance Iran's position vis-à-vis her northern neighbor. The strongest argument in favor of adherence to the Pact had little to do with world politics. It was simply that membership was likely to bring about a much larger flow of American economic aid.

On October 11, 1955, the Shah proclaimed Iran's adherence to the Baghdad Pact. The next day the U.S.S.R. protested that this action was "incompatible with the interests of strengthening peace and security in the area of the Near and Middle East and is incompatible with Iran's good-neighbourly relations with the Soviet Union and the known treaty obligations of Iran."[48] The Iranian reply was correct but firm:

> As is known to the authorities of the U.S.S.R. Government and as has been repeatedly stated both in writing and verbally to the Soviet Ambassador in Tehran, the Imperial Government, in accordance with its responsibilities to protect the independence and frontiers of its country and by its sovereign right, will take any action or adopt any policy it may deem necessary.[49]

The Iranian note concluded with the expression of a desire for peace and good relations with the U.S.S.R.

The exchange continued when on November 26 a new Soviet note "explained" why the Baghdad Pact was an aggressive military bloc: "By joining this grouping, Iran, strange as it may seem, has tied up its policy with the interests of forces alien to Iran who are out to maintain or re-establish the colonial dependence of the countries of this area." The note went on to point out that the territory of member nations would, under certain conditions, be open to the troops of other members.

American, Turkish, and British press reports show that the Turkish armed

forces, which under the military plans of the Western powers are given the
assignment of waging an "offensive" in the direction of the Caucasus, will
have to enter Iran and occupy Iranian Azerbaijan and Kurdistan.

The note referred to Iran's obligations under Article 3 of the 1927 Treaty of
Guarantees and Neutrality, stressed Soviet desire for the relaxation of international tension, and sounded an ominous warning:

> The situation which is being created by Iran's accession to the aggressive
> Baghdad bloc is fraught with dangers to the frontiers of the Soviet Union.
> Therefore the Soviet Government cannot remain indifferent to Iran's acces-
> sion to the Baghdad Pact . . . . [The note placed] on the Iranian Government
> the entire responsibility for the probable consequences of the Iranian
> Government's decision to join the Baghdad military bloc.[50]

In its reply on December 6, Iran maintained that the Baghdad Pact was
not aggressive and did not conflict with the Soviet-Persian Treaty of 1927.
Iran had always lived up to that Treaty but not the Soviet Union, which had
repeatedly violated it by its actions, invading Iran, failing to withdraw its
forces after the war, and taking measures to separate parts of northern Iran
from the rest of the country.[51]

This exchange of words and a loud propaganda barrage in the Soviet
press constituted the most important consequences of the latest Russo-
Persian dispute. In addition the U.S.S.R. cancelled the visit to Iran of seven
Soviet musicians and refused to accept delivery of 40,000 tons of Iranian
rice. Within a month or two the political weather had cleared and relations
improved again.[52] By the summer of 1956 they were good enough for the
Shah and Empress Sorayya to make a state visit to the U.S.S.R.

During the visit (June 25-July 13, 1956) the Shah exchanged views with
Khrushchev, Voroshilov, Bulganin, Mikoyan, and Shepilov. The Shah was
asked why, in spite of the peaceful policy of the Soviet Union, he had joined
the Baghdad Pact. His report of the ensuing conversation deserves to be
quoted at length:

> I told them not to forget that in the Second World War they had invaded my
> country in spite of the treaties of friendship which existed between us, and that
> in 1946 they had created a puppet government as a front to take over control
> of Azerbaijan.
>   Khrushchev and his colleagues replied that they were not responsible for
> these aggressions, which had been committed before they assumed leadership.
> Khrushchev admitted that his country had made mistakes, but said that Iran
> should trust the benevolent intentions of him and the other Russians sitting
> there in the room.

Khrushchev went back to the Baghdad Pact, arguing that it was aggressive in nature, but "finally agreed that Iran had no aggressive intentions against the Soviet Union." However, he went on, some big power might compel Iran to make her territory available for staging an attack on Russia.

Certainly, I [the Shah] said, we would never allow either the pact or our territory to be used in furtherance of aggressive designs upon the Soviet Union . . . . Khrushchev and his colleagues generously replied that they believed completely in what I said.[53]

The Shah's visit showed how greatly Iran's position had improved vis-à-vis the U.S.S.R. and how much more flexible was Khrushchev's foreign policy than Stalin's. The Baghdad Pact continued to be regularly denounced in Soviet propaganda, but somehow Iran's membership in the Pact did not seem to figure in the propaganda campaign. New agreements were negotiated with Moscow on questions of transit, frontiers, and the utilization of the waters of the Aras and Atrak rivers for irrigation and for generation of power.

In 1956-58 the Soviet government concentrated its attention on the Arab world. Egypt, Syria, Lebanon, Jordan, and Iraq became international storm centers. The Anglo-French attack on Egypt, the proclamation of the Eisenhower doctrine in the presidential message to Congress on January 5, 1957, the Iraqi revolution of the summer of 1958, and the violent death of the young King Faisal, made a profound impression on Teheran. The Middle East seemed suddenly much less secure than it had been in years. War and rebellion lurked everywhere and small nations survived only when protected by great powers. With a volatile, unpredictable, and angry regime installed in Iraq (and allegedly much influenced by Iranian Tudeh émigrés) the Persian government was undoubtedly nervous and looked for support where support could be found, namely to America.

In the fall of 1958, Iran began discussing a bilateral military agreement with the United States. Soviet reaction was unexpectedly strong. Before Moscow's note of protest had been delivered to the Iranian minister of Foreign Affairs, it was broadcast over radio Moscow. The note itself dispensed with diplomatic propriety and accused Iran of "overstepping the limit beyond which begins direct support for certain foreign circles in carrying out their aggressive plans directed against the U.S.S.R." It grimly pointed out to Iran that there was no security "under the collapsing roof of the Baghdad Pact and under the protection of foreign powers situated thousands of kilometers from Iran." Attempts to seek such protection, "as has been shown by the experience of Iran's recent allies under the Baghdad Pact, can least of all serve that purpose." The note also announced the cancellation of a scheduled visit to Iran of the Soviet head of state, Marshal K. Voroshilov.[54]

The developments that occurred during the ensuing four months are still partly unexplained. In his memoirs the Shah has written that the Russians made overtures to his government in the hope of preventing the conclusion of a bilateral military agreement with the United States. These overtures, initially made "through intermediaries, held out promises of a long-term non-aggression pact and tremendous economic help." On the contrary, the terms offered by the United States turned out to be unsatisfactory. "Feeling militarily ridiculously weak, and without such guarantees as, for example, NATO countries have, we allowed ourselves to enter into negotiations with the Russians on the subject of a non-aggression treaty."[55]

Russian negotiators arrived in Teheran and, as the price of a new treaty, proposed that Iran leave the Baghdad Pact. Confronted with a firm Persian refusal, they dropped the matter but demanded promises that Iran would not sign a bilateral military agreement with the United States. "By then," comments the Shah, "it had become clear to us that in return for a treaty of non-aggression the Russians wanted to separate us from our allies."[56]

The Russian version is different. It is contained in a long note handed to the Persian government by the chief Soviet negotiator, Deputy Minister of Foreign Affairs Vladimir Semenov, after the negotiations had broken down. In reviewing the history of the Soviet-Iranian negotiations Semenov made it appear that the initiative for negotiation had come from the Persians. According to his account, the Soviet side made generous proposals on the principle that it was better to give aid for mutual benefit than to expand the arms race. The Iranian side advanced its own proposals, mainly concerned with the annulment of Articles 5 and 6 of the Treaty of 1921 (articles that had been invoked by Russia as a justification of her invasion of Iran in 1941). The Soviets made certain concessions, but Iran refused to undertake not to enter a bilateral agreement with the United States. How could such behavior of the Persians be explained? Semenov asked.

> The secret of the conduct of the Iranian side is quite plain. The Soviet government has information, confirmed by facts, that already in the first days of the Soviet delegation's stay in Tehran, the Shah entered into a commitment with a foreign state not to conclude an agreement with the Soviet Union and declared that he intended to sign an agreement with the United States.

Throwing all protocol to the winds, Semenov raged on: "What we have said bears out the fact that the Iranian government and the Shah are pursuing a two-faced, insincere policy toward the Soviet Union which cannot but lead to grave consequences, above all for Iran." The note concluded with a threat that "in view of these unfriendly acts of the government of the Shah in relation to the U.S.S.R., the Soviet government . . . cannot be drawing the appropriate conclusions."[57]

On February 14, 1959, Iran's minister of Foreign Affairs, Ali Asghar Hekmat, made a speech before the Iranian Senate. Like Semenov, he reviewed the history of Soviet-Iranian negotiations but with different results. According to Hekmat's version the crux of the matter lay in the Soviet insistence that Iran enter no alliances or military pacts.

> Will the other side [he asked], namely the Soviet Government which has military and defensive pacts with other countries, give us the right to assume that they are directed against us? Do the Soviet authorities have in mind thoughts of war, attack, and aggression as to make them so apprehensive of such defensive pacts?[58]

The departure of the Soviet delegation from Teheran signalized the beginning of a violent war of nerves against the Iranian government and, above all, against the person of the Shah. Speaking in Tula on February 17, 1959, Khrushchev claimed that Iran's military agreement with the United States would convert Iran into an American military base. The Shah, Khrushchev said, "fears his people. He is none too sure, apparently, of his throne and for this reason he keeps his private capital in Britain, and not in Iran."[59] Soviet radio dropped all restraints, filling the air with virulent anti-Shah statements. A station calling itself the National Voice of Iran went even farther in vilifying the Shah and the government. In his memoirs the Shah remarks that the Persian government knew the station to be located in southern Russia, "and the Soviets knew that we knew it was there."[60] It called for the overthrow of the government and daily predicted an early end to the Pahlavi dynasty.

The virulent campaign against the Shah went on for several years. In October 1961 at the Twenty-second Congress of the C.P.S.U., the representative of the Tudeh, Dr. Reza Radmanesh, used language which had by then become familiar:

> The present rulers of Iran, headed by the Shah, who took over the country through a coup d'etat against the legal government of Dr. Mossadeq, have turned our country into open territory for invasion and plunder by imperialists . . . . The defeat of the usurper regime is now near, and the struggle of our masses during the past two years shows that we are now at the beginning of a great national liberation movement.[61]

Shortly thereafter relations between the two countries began to improve, the tone of radio broadcasts began to grow milder, and by mid-1962 the National Voice of Iran faded from the air.

The Baghdad Pact proved no threat to the Soviet Union, whose relations with all its members steadily improved through the 1960s. Iranian statements to the effect that Iran would never become a base for an attack on the U.S.S.R. were accepted "with satisfaction" whereas a year or two earlier they had been scornfully rejected. In 1961 Khrushchev had told Walter Lippmann that the corrupt Iranian ruling class would be overthrown. In 1963 Leonid Brezhnev paid an official visit to Iran. Dozens of agreements, large and small, dealing with economics, irrigation, hydroelectric power, trade, and cultural exchange were signed and implemented.

When in June 1965 the Shah, at the invitation of the Soviet government, visited the Soviet Union for the second time, mutual recriminations were forgotten. A friendly atmosphere prevailed throughout his visit to Leningrad, Volgograd, Sverdlovsk, Irkutsk, the Baikal region, Simferopol, and Yalta. "In Moscow he deposited a wreath in Lenin's tomb," and engaged in negotiations with Brezhnev, Kosygin, Mikoyan, Gromyko, and others. The joint communiqué issued at the end of the visit proclaimed that both sides agreed on issues of universal disarmament and both favored the United Nations.

> *The* [two] parties condemn colonialism in all its manifestations and insistently call for the implementation of the Declaration concerning the granting of independence to colonial nations and peoples adopted by the U.N. General Assembly on December 14, 1960.

The communiqué noted the successful development of Soviet-Iranian cooperation and expressed the desire for further growth in scientific, commercial, and cultural exchange.[62]

In January 1966 agreements were signed for Soviet participation and aid in the construction of a steel mill, a machine-tool factory, a gas pipeline to be paid for by Iranian deliveries of natural gas; water works and hydroelectric power stations on rivers along whose course run sections of the Soviet-Iranian frontier. The U.S.S.R. even began to supply the Shah's army with a certain amount of arms and equipment on a cash basis.

Business ties were further strengthened during the 1967 visit to Moscow of Prime Minister Amir Abbas Hoveida. He brought with him the minister of Water Resources and Electric Power, the Director of the Plan Organization (the Iranian equivalent of the Gosplan), the governor of the Central Bank, the director of the National Gas Company, and several experts. They met and negotiated with Brezhnev and Kosygin as well as with the chairman of the Gosplan, the minister of the Gas Industry, and others among their Soviet counterparts. Again the joint communiqué spoke about peace in the Middle East and expressed disapproval of aggression and concern about the situation in Vietnam. The parties noted, in the unvarying full language of such communiqués, the development of technical and economic cooperation between the two countries and agreed to extend such cooperation into the period of Iran's fourth five-year plan. A real departure from the usual diplomatic practice was the decision to hold a meeting of a mixed commission on the ministerial level every six months.[63]

Clearly Soviet-Iranian relations have become "friendly." Both countries derive considerable advantage from trade. Iran enjoys in the Soviet Union a source of industrial supplies that it needs to promote its own rapid industrialization. The ability to obtain heavy machinery, weapons, or credit from Moscow also lessens Iran's dependence on the West and permits her to pursue a more independent political course. Another important benefit of good relations with the U.S.S.R. is the relative inactivity of the remnants of the Tudeh.

The Soviet Union in its turn derived considerable advantage from good relations with Iran. The growing volume of trade between the two countries speaks for itself. Technical and economic cooperation is profitable. Moreover, Soviet policy makers undoubtedly realize that Iran's internal situation has become extremely stable. Whereas during the 1953-54 period the stability of a "bourgeois" regime may have been something to work against, today it may be desired, especially in such areas as the Middle East and South Asia. Soviet mediation between Indian and Pakistan at Tashkent, leading to the termination of a war between these two states, is a case in point.

To sum up: in the geographic sense the U.S.S.R. and Iran are, of course, inseparable. Relations and contacts between them date back to the era when Russia under Ivan the Terrible succeeded the Khanate of Astrakhan as a Caspian power, and they will continue indefinitely. At the end of World War II the Soviet Union made an attempt to achieve control over Iran, or at least over its northwestern provinces. Stalin's aims were in many ways similar to those of the last tsar, and Soviet policy in Iran in the immediate postwar period was reminiscent of the years 1900-14. Stalin's defeat in Iran was accepted both by himself and by his successors. In spite of occasional conflicts a *modus vivendi* was achieved in the 1950s. Even the clash of 1958-59 did not entirely upset the accommodations worked out in preceding years. Indeed the failure of the last anti-Shah campaign demonstrated the limited capacity of the Soviet Union to influence Iran's domestic affairs in periods of internal stability and strong government.

Though historians should not prophesy, they may express hopes. Our small planet is threatened with destruction by nuclear weapons or suffocation from the population explosion. Air and water pollution may have international or worldwide consequences. Now more than ever one must acknowledge the wisdom of the old Russian proverb: *Khudoi mir luchshe dobroi ssory* (a bad peace is better than a good quarrel). Perhaps the relative calm that has descended on Soviet-Iranian relations may continue and turn into a habit of mind. Both countries, and the world, would benefit thereby.

— 5 —

The Soviet Union and North Africa

John Waterbury

The ostentatious presence of the Russian fleet in the Mediterranean since the spring of 1967 has evoked a spate of Western commentary upon Soviet motives and strategy regarding the Middle East and North Africa. There is no gainsaying the significance of this naval build-up; but as far as North Africa is concerned, it has not led to a quantum jump in Soviet influence or interest in the area. Moreover, there have been no major changes in Soviet policies toward the North African states as a result of her naval presence. The foundations of Soviet strategy and policy concerning North Africa were laid in the late fifties and early sixties. The events of 1967 have simply sharpened Russia's interest in the area, and have made her challenge to Western influence there more credible.

THE FOUR REGIMES:
A TEST FOR STRATEGY AND IDEOLOGY

The four countries of North Africa which this essay will treat—Algeria, Libya, Morocco, and Tunisia—offer to the Soviet strategist and the Marxist analyst a representative sample of the societies, the nations, and the elites with which they must deal throughout the Middle East, and to some extent, of the developing countries in general. Consequently it seems artificial to discuss North Africa in isolation from broader Soviet concerns and objectives. Wherever possible, therefore, I shall try to situate North Africa within the general Soviet approach to the Middle East and Africa. (Table 1, page 81, provides data on the size and other relevant characteristics of the national units with which we are here concerned.)

At the end of the Second World War, all the countries of North Africa were firmly in the imperialist camp. Two, Morocco and Tunisia, were French protectorates with large resident European minorities, and Algeria, a territory four times the size of France, was considered to be an integral part of the French republic. Libya had been colonized by Italy, but the defeat of the Axis nullified Italy's title to that territory.

Of all the North African states, it is in Libya that the Soviet Union has had the least influence; yet it was Libya that first aroused the Soviet interest in North Africa. Perceiving that the undetermined status of the former Italian colony seemed to offer an opportunity to establish some sort of Soviet presence on the southern shores of the Mediterranean, the U.S.S.R. in 1945 requested that Tripolitania be awarded to her as a U.N. trusteeship. The Soviet demand, which I shall discuss more fully below, may have hastened Libyan independence. In 1952 what had amounted to a four-power U.N. trusteeship was terminated, and North Africa's least developed region became its first independent state. Not until 1955 did the U.S.S.R. recognize Libya. Since then relations between the two have been correct but minimal.

From the Soviet point of view, Libya is a feudalist monarchy based on a tribal society with class development confined largely to the European minority. The state has been solidly rooted in the capitalist world through the presence of the American and British military at Wheelus and Idris air bases, and, since 1960, through the proliferation of American oil interests in the country. From this perspective, one whose accuracy can hardly be contested, Libya differed little from Saudi Arabia. The Libyan coup d'état of September 1, 1969, announced the birth of a regime that is as staunchly anti-Soviet as it is anti-Western. Still Qaddafi and the other Libyan officers of the Revolutionary Command have given evidence of a readiness to deal with the devil if need be.

The course of Russian relations with Algeria has been, on most counts, the inverse of the Libyan example. In 1945 there was little question as to Algeria's status within the French republic. Even during the revolution (1954-62), the U.S.S.R. was circumspect in its contacts with Algerian nationalist forces. As a result, Algeria was the last North African country in which the U.S.S.R. tried to make its presence felt; but it has also been the country in which the Soviet Union has been most successful. Soviet analysts see in Algeria perhaps the most viable revolutionary regime among the developing countries. Since 1963 Algeria has been considered, if not actually in the process of "building socialism," at least to be on the "non-capitalist path." The country has a growing urban and industrial proletariat to supplement what some analysts have described as a "revolutionary peasantry." The exodus of the French in 1962 in effect decapitated the capitalist bourgeoisie; and the coup de grâce was delivered in March 1963, when the most productive segments of the agricultural and industrial sectors were placed under self-management and state ownership. Finally, since 1962, Algeria has resolutely asserted her independence from the imperialist camp and has enunciated "progressive" foreign policies. While Algeria's imperfections are not minimized, in Soviet eyes, the country is something of a model for Third World revolutionary states.

As for Morocco, this country is North Africa's surviving monarchical regime. It is fundamentally different from the now-defunct Libyan monarchy and is so regarded by Soviet analysts. The Alawi dynasty presides over a differentiated society with a growing native bourgeoisie and industrial proletariat. The French developed through the years an extensive economic infrastructure and established an important modern agricultural sector. Since its independence in 1956 Morocco has been more or less firmly attached to the capitalist world, especially to France. Nonetheless, Morocco has adopted a neutralist foreign policy, one that has occasionally reflected "progressive" tendencies. It is in regard to nonalignment and stances on given foreign-policy issues that the U.S.S.R. takes an interest in Morocco. In most respects Morocco is seen in the same light as Iran, Afghanistan, and perhaps Jordan. All are regarded as bourgeois monarchies that are gradually abandoning feudal support and accentuating class development within their societies, and as susceptible to being coaxed from the capitalist world in foreign policy matters.

We come now to Tunisia, which represents for Soviet analysts the epitome of the national bourgeois state. Measures undertaken by Habib Bourguiba's regime since Tunisian independence in 1956 have, in many ways, been more revolutionary than those of Algeria. Tunisia's single party, the Socialist Destour (Destur), is far better organized and more firmly anchored in the society, for instance, than Algeria's FLN. In the final analysis, however, it is felt that Bourguiba's domestic progressivism has been designed to control and manipulate the revolutionary forces of Tunisian society in the interests of an emerging bureaucratic bourgeoisie and state capitalist system. Of more immediate concern to the U.S.S.R. is Tunisia's forthright identification with the West in foreign policy questions such as Vietnam. Bourguiba presents the same image to the Soviet Union as Senghor of Senegal and Houphouët-Boigny of the Ivory Coast. These figures are looked upon as leaders who have frozen the revolution at home and who have resisted Soviet influence on foreign policy.

Table 1 represents, in brief, how one might characterize the four states of North Africa from the Soviet perspective. It remains to be seen how the sociopolitical analysis relates to Soviet strategy in the area. While in the remainder of my essay I expand upon the themes of strategy and interpretation, one brief remark on strategy is in order here. As is the case for most nation-states involved in international politics, ideological considerations must keep pace with, but do not often determine, the factors considered relevant for the exercise of Soviet influence in North Africa.

Algeria is the pivotal unit in Soviet strategy in North Africa. With several hundred miles of coastline and ample port facilities, it dominates the southern Mediterranean littoral. Its vast territory extends southward to the states of sub-saharan Africa, westward nearly to the Atlantic Ocean, and eastward in such a fashion as to bracket Libya and Tunisia between itself

Table 1

SOCIOECONOMIC DATA
ON NORTH AFRICAN STATES, 1965-66

Country	Population in 1966 (in thousands)	Total Area (sq. km. in thousands)	Percent of Labor Force in Agriculture	Percent of Labor Force in Industry	Per Capita Gross Domestic Product: 1965 Dollars at Factor Cost
Algeria	12,102	2,382	75	4.4	203
Libya	1,564	1,759	n.a.	n.a.	740
Morocco	13,451	445	71	8.8	180
Tunisia	4,470	164	68	5.7	191

and Egypt. Thus in Algeria, ideological concerns and strategic advantage nicely coincide.

Until recently, Tunisia and Libya could be ignored as far as immediate Soviet strategic objectives were concerned. Tunisia, isolated within the Arab world because of the maverick foreign policy of its president, was easily straddled by the Soviet presence in Algeria and the United Arab Republic. Even with the backing of the United States, Bourguiba has been unable to project his own foreign policy preferences beyond the confines of Tunisia. The Soviet Union has long sought the dismantling of all Western military bases in the Middle East and North Africa, and in recent years has shown a growing interest in Middle Eastern oil supplies.

Thus one could assume that Libya would sooner or later figure prominently in Soviet efforts to diminish the Western presence in the area as a whole. However, there has been no indication of a concerted thrust in this direction, even since the Six Day War. It appears that the U.S.S.R. relied upon Algeria and Egypt to exercise their own influence, propagandistic and otherwise, upon the Libyans to ensure that Libyan foreign policy stances would not be directly hostile to Soviet interests. With the downfall of the monarchy it is inevitable that the Soviet Union will develop more ambitious plans for Libya.

The Moroccan monarchy, to defuse leftist criticism within the country and to buy peace within the rest of the Arab world, has been willing to pursue a neutralist foreign policy in which friendly relations with the U.S.S.R. have been promoted. The Soviet Union has encouraged and will continue to encourage more of the same, even if it means giving support to a "reactionary" regime. The strategic advantages that the U.S.S.R. seeks in Morocco, as I shall explain later, can be obtained without any change in regime.

SOVIET STRATEGIC OBJECTIVES

It may be argued that Soviet strategy in North Africa is predicated upon two fundamental factors. First, for all intents and purposes North Africa is a bonus area for the U.S.S.R., an area of considerable interest but not essential to Soviet security. Considerations of territorial contiguity, such as apply in the case of Turkey, Iran, and Afghanistan, or of a backlog of previous commitments, as in the case of the U.A.R., do not materially affect the Soviet approach to this region. Here the consequences of making and abandoning commitments are not as serious as in the Northern Tier or in the Arab heartland and in Egypt. Second, Soviet strategy is basically preemptive. The aim is not so much to acquire satellites or to integrate new units into the socialist camp as it is to deny the region to the West, to free some countries from imperialist influence, and to leave the recalcitrant isolated.[1]

It might be noted that the same two factors seem to underlie American policy in the area as well. Within these premises, let us look at more specific instances of Soviet strategy in North Africa.

The Russian appetite for warm water ports is assumed, rightly or wrongly, to be axiomatic. There is evidence that such an impulse has prompted Soviet interests in the North African area. As early as 1943, the U.S.S.R. demanded from the Allies and received the right to be represented on the short-lived Mediterranean Committee formed in Algiers.[2] Two years later, at the London Conference, Soviet Foreign Minister Vyacheslav Molotov proposed that the U.S.S.R. be given trusteeship over Tripolitania in Libya for a period of ten years. It was stated outright that such a move would satisfy Russia's desire for an outlet on the Mediterranean. The other Allies apparently did not take kindly to the suggestion.[3] Maurice Pernot, on the basis of Soviet actions at that time, was led to write:

> The time has gone when Russia could not, without the permission of other foreign powers, move her ships from the Black Sea, where they were blocked. Today she claims to enter the Mediterranean when and where she pleases, to possess in that Sea, ports of call and bases, and finally to take part in the control of the three gateways (Gibraltar, the Dardanelles, and the Suez Canal) which separate her from the other seas of the globe or else allow her to communicate with them.[4]

This prescient statement, written twenty-two years too soon, is an accurate summary of the Soviet position after 1967.

It is precisely within the context of sea communications with the major oceans of the globe that the Soviet naval build-up in the Mediterranean should be viewed. The USSR is more interested in acquiring access to port facilities than in establishing naval bases. The predictable use of refueling and refitting facilities in certain ports (Latakia, Port Said, Alexandria, and perhaps Mers-el-Kebir) and the right to call at others (for example, Casablanca, Hodeida, Karachi) give the Soviet fleet and merchant marine a range they have never enjoyed before. It is unlikely, for instance, that the former French naval base at Mers-el-Kebir has been turned over to the U.S.S.R. by the Algerians, because the U.S.S.R. does not really need or want to take over such facilities.[5] In the new order of things, Soviet fleet movements will lend credibility to policy commitments by making possible the delivery of support to beleaguered friends and allies. Probably more important is the fact that the Soviet naval presence may serve as a deterrent to possible American military or naval intervention in other states. Finally, Soviet warships can give protection to the growing merchant fleet.[6]

The sea routes that the Soviet Union is trying to develop run along an east-west axis and are designed to give her ships undisputed access to ports of call and port facilities throughout the southern and eastern Mediterranean coast, in East Africa, in the Red Sea and the Persian Gulf, and finally in the Indian Ocean. At the Atlantic end of the east-west axis, Soviet warships have visited Casablanca (1968). If the Moroccans prove amenable, the Soviet Union may be able to use regularly the excellent facilities of this major Atlantic port. (See Fig. 1).[7]

Figure 1

POTENTIAL SOVIET PORTS OF CALL
AND SEA ROUTES

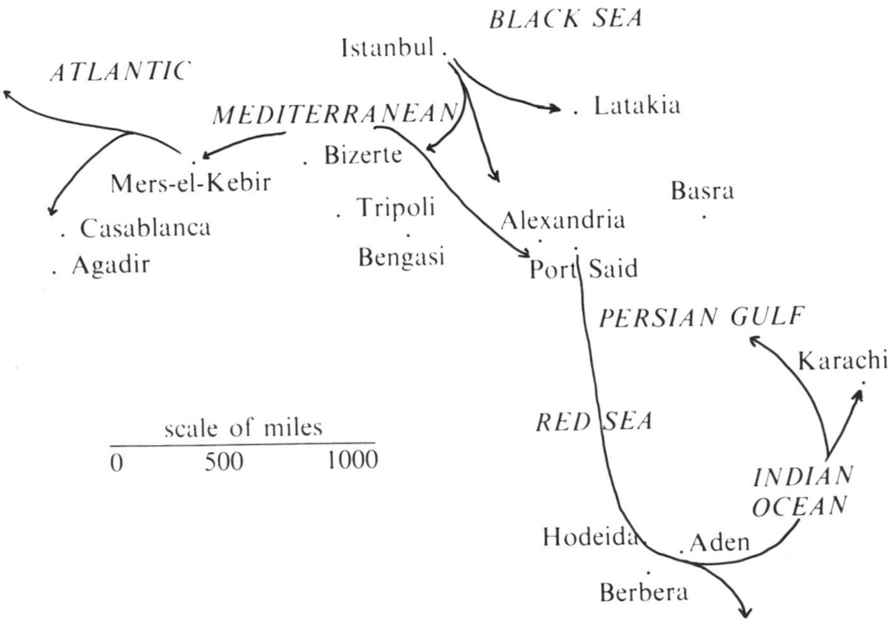

It has been suggested that massive Soviet arms deliveries to Middle Eastern states, especially the U.A.R. and Algeria, may be part of a plan to stock arms at convenient locations in Africa with a view toward intervention elsewhere on the continent. Geoffrey Kemp, for instance, has mentioned the possibility that the amount of Soviet arms received by Algeria is far too great for local needs and may be intended to serve as back-up supplies for the Egyptians in the event of another round with the Israelis.[8] Along these same lines, it may be that both Algeria and Egypt could serve as staging areas for bringing support, if need be, to pro-Soviet regimes in subsaharan Africa, or for direct aid to revolutionary and guerrilla movements. While it is likely that Soviet planners may see their influence in Northern Africa being put to such ends, it does not seem probable that such aims figure prominently in Soviet strategy. Back-up supplies and armaments for Egypt could be stored as easily and as reliably in the Soviet Union as in Algeria. The collapse of friendly regimes in Ghana and Mali with little more than verbal protest on the part of the U.S.S.R. calls into question the staging-area concept. The evaluation of this concept made some years ago by Alexander Dallin is still pertinent:

> It is misleading to think of present Soviet interests in Africa in terms of a geographic penetration from contiguous communist areas. Speculation about Soviet plans to use Egypt, Algeria, or Somalia as "footholds" or "bridges" misses the point of the Khrushchev strategy: to win without fighting.[9]

One of the prime Soviet concerns in the developing areas has been the reduction or elimination of Western military bases. Soviet policy toward individual states may hinge on how host countries treat the presence of foreign bases on their soil. The approach of the U.S.S.R. to North Africa has proved no exception. NATO powers maintained a number of bases throughout North Africa. Some of the major installations were or are the American naval air base at Kenitra on the Atlantic coast of Morocco, the French naval bases at Mers-el-Kebir in Algeria and Bizerte in Tunisia, and American and French air bases scattered across the Maghreb. United States air bases in Morocco were evacuated by 1963, and the agreement providing for the use of Wheelus Air Force base in Libya, capable of giving air cover for most Sixth Fleet movements in the Mediterranean, expired in 1971. France has given up her rights at Bizerte and Mers-el-Kebir, while the United States formally turned over the base at Kénitra to the Moroccans in May 1962. However, the United States still maintains naval personnel at Kénitra (nominally under Moroccan command) and a number of communications stations for the Sixth Fleet.

The lessening of Western military influence in North Africa has been brought about with very little direct Soviet pressure. The antipathy among Middle Eastern states for foreign bases is such that they can exert all the pressure necessary without Soviet prompting. Libya has been frequently criticized by Egypt for allowing Wheelus to continue to operate, and King Idriss was obliged to repeat assurances that U.S. aircraft would never be used in a manner hostile to the Arab cause. Algeria has campaigned against the presence of the remaining U.S. installations on Moroccan soil, particularly in June 1967, when the Algerian radio invited Moroccans to attack or sabotage Kénitra and isolated communications stations.

There is a good deal of convergence between Soviet strategic interests and the Arab desire to rid the area of imperialist and neocolonialist influences.

The Russians can let the radical Arab states take the initiative in furthering their joint interests. If, however, a given state attempts to restrict Western use of a military base, the U.S.S.R. may step in with some sort of reward. After Morocco's 1960 agreement to dismantle the U.S. bases, for example, it received a shipment of Russian arms.

Flowing from the aim of reducing Western military influence is the encouragement of neutrality and foreign policy stances favorable to Soviet policy interests. The major North African target for Russian efforts in this direction has been Morocco. King Hassan II and his father, Mohammed V, both learned that their necessarily conservative domestic policies could be offset by a "progressive" foreign policy. Doing business with the Soviet Union makes it more difficult for radical regimes to attack Morocco as well as more difficult for the Soviet Union to give overt or covert backing to the leftist opposition in the country. The working agreement struck between Morocco and the U.S.S.R. has provided mutual advantages to both parties. Since the monarchy as an institution is vulnerable in a revolutionary environment, the last two monarchs have sought to make themselves as valuable to "revolutionary" great powers as to their Western backers. This has meant that the Soviet Union has been able to win concessions, or the possibility of concessions, from Morocco that Algeria, safe in its radicalism, might refuse. In June 1967, for instance, when Algerian newspapers openly criticized the U.S.S.R. as a fair-weather friend of the Arabs, King Hassan praised the Soviet Union for its judicious behavior and castigated the Arab critics of the Soviets.[10] Since 1966, joint Moroccan-U.S.S.R. communiqués have been issued deploring the war in Vietnam, the last coming in March 1969 at the time of the visit of Podgorny (president of the Praesidium of the Supreme Soviet) to Morocco. The use of Moroccan ports and the continued growth in trade between the two countries reinforce Morocco's commitments to neutralism. Because a revolutionary regime in Morocco might be less accommodating to the U.S.S.R., the Soviet Union will give no encouragement to local revolutionaries nor to whatever plans the Algerians may have for military conflict or for intervention in Moroccan affairs. I might add, by way of fortifying this position, that Moscow appears to me to be developing a relationship of just this kind with Iran.

The influence of the imperialist camp is further diminished by Moscow's policy of promoting trade. There is no denying that many territories in the Middle East, formerly under European control, have been unable to free themselves from complete reliance on trade with their ex-masters. In North Africa, however, the Soviet Union has begun to offer an alternative market to that of France for the export of agricultural and raw produce. This point is treated below in much greater detail. For the moment suffice it to say that U.S.S.R. trade policies represent an instrument with which to chip away at the economic linkages of neo-colonialism. Moreover, the promotion of trade diversification in North Africa has been undertaken as much by the countries of Eastern Europe as by the Soviet Union.

North African oil reserves warrant treatment under a separate heading. It is now generally, although not unanimously, agreed that by 1980 the U.S.S.R. will be obliged to import substantial amounts of crude oil, perhaps fifty million tons a year. Soviet production may not be adequate for internal consumption by that time, and rapidly growing demand for petroleum among Eastern European countries will accentuate the need to increase imports. If this analysis is correct, then Middle Eastern oil supplies may become vital to the continued growth of the Russian and Eastern European economies, and a concerted effort will be made to assure an adequate supply in the future.[11]

In North Africa, Algeria and Libya are major oil producers. Libyan fields were opened up in 1958, and production has soared, particularly since the closing of the Suez Canal, to one hundred million tons per year, a level as high as that of Iran and Kuwait. However, the U.S.S.R. has to date imported no oil from Libya, although with the fall of the monarchy that situation may be rapidly altered. Algerian oil production, too, started in 1958, but has not grown at the same rate as Libya's. In 1968 it had reached about forty-five million tons. The Soviet Union agreed in 1967 to import from Algeria 3,850,000 tons of oil over a seven-year period, a very modest amount by either country's standards. Whether or not the level of imports will be raised in the future is for the moment a moot question. Nonetheless the assumptions that Middle Eastern oil would continue to be marketed primarily in Europe, and that the Soviet Union had ample reserves for internal consumption, have been called into question. In this context the U.S.S.R. may not only be able to weaken the dominant economic links between the Maghreb and European markets but also to gain access to new sources of oil that could meet the domestic needs of the 1980s. The establishment of a revolutionary military regime in Libya may well lead to a policy of trade diversification through oil exports to the U.S.S.R. and Eastern Europe.

Most of the discussion of Soviet strategic objectives so far has dealt with efforts to reduce the influence of the capitalist powers in North Africa. At the same time, a major concern of the U.S.S.R. is to deny the area to Communist China. Efforts in this direction may range from urging revolutionary Algeria to support the legitimacy of Soviet participation in Afro-Asian meetings to pre-empting potential markets for Chinese goods. The voyage of Chou En-lai throughout Africa in 1963 and 1964 raised for the U.S.S.R. the disquieting prospect that some of the promising African states on the noncapitalist path (Algeria, Guinea, Ghana, Mali) might be guided by the Chinese rather than the Soviet example.[12]

Of all North Africa's heads of state, Bourguiba of Tunisia is the most outspoken critic of the Chinese, a stance which, given Bourguiba's position in the Arab world, is of little use to the U.S.S.R. In the case of Libya, although it established diplomatic relations with Peking in 1960, China has for the most part been simply ignored. As for Morocco and Algeria, these countries have tried to maintain cordial relations with both countries. Algeria has always publicly lauded the great revolutionary tradition of China and is grateful for her early support of the Algerian revolution. Good relations with China add luster to Morocco's progressive image in foreign policy and are sustained by the fact that Morocco imports from China the bulk of the green tea consumed in the country. Since the beginning of the cultural revolution, however, Chinese contacts with North Africa have fallen off markedly.

SOVIET IDEOLOGICAL ANALYSIS

As indicated earlier, North Africa reflects the analytic experimentation that has gone on in the Soviet Union during the past quarter-century as Stalin's successors have tried to integrate the developing countries into the Marxist-Leninist framework. The efforts have met with uneven, unspectacular success. Moreover, the policies that would logically flow from Marxist analysis have not often coincided with policies dictated by strategic concerns. In the event of conflict between the two, strategic concerns, at least in North Africa, have always prevailed. One is hard put at times to find any linkage between the abundant ideological debates in the Soviet Union in the 1950s and 1960s and actual policy outcomes in North Africa. Conversely, certain conditions in North African society are obvious grist for the Soviet ideological mill but are, or have been, ignored or downplayed because they conflicted with strategic considerations. The ideological approach of the U.S.S.R. to the Algerian revolution, to be discussed in detail below, is a case in point. For the moment, I shall limit myself to sketching out the evolution of the Soviet ideological framework as it applies to North Africa and to indicating at what points this concept may coincide with strategic objectives.

Zhdanov's Manichean model of the communist and capitalist world was being re-evaluated even before the death of Stalin. The American intervention in Korea, and the testing of the hydrogen bomb, cast doubt on the feasibility of ultimate military confrontation between the two camps, while the example of neutral India seemed to suggest an alternative method to sap the strength of the West. By 1955, Soviet analysts were experimenting with the notion of the "national bourgeoisie" and the "national democratic state" as vehicles for the breakup of the imperialist camp and the promotion of the socialist revolution in their societies. The new orthodoxy was confirmed at the Twentieth Congress of the CPSU in 1956 when Khrushchev declared that the developing countries had joined the "zone of peace."[13]

The Moscow Declaration of 81 Communist Parties in 1960 defined the nature of the national democratic state. In foreign policy such states are 1) nonaligned and anti-imperialistic, and 2) determined to reduce Western economic influence. In domestic policy they are 3) tolerant of local communist parties (which may participate with the national bourgeoisie in broad coalitions and national fronts), and 4) emphasize the development of the state sector of the economy.[14] Points 1 and 2, however, are most likely to coincide with strategic considerations; and if they do, points 3 and 4 can be safely overlooked (as in Morocco and Iran). On the other hand, if a national democratic state fulfills points 3 and 4 but not points 1 and 2, it may well fail to elicit anything but hostility from the U.S.S.R. (as in Tunisia in 1956-63, when the Tunisian Communist Party functioned legally).

In Khrushchev's salad days the new orthodoxy was sustained and elaborated by G. I. Mirski and others at the Institute of World Economy and International Relations. The evolution of certain developing countries seemed to confirm the most optimistic conclusions about the ultimate socialist destiny of the national democratic state. In 1962 Cuba was described as "building socialism," and by 1963 Ghana, Guinea, Mali, Algeria, the U.A.R. and Burma were declared to be on the non-capitalist path. Mirski thrust aside old-guard arguments about inadequate class development in the LDCs, about the absence of a substantial proletariat, and about the impossibility of anything but a communist vanguard leading the society to socialism. He tried to demonstrate that while these judgments were accurate, they did not prove that the national democratic state was incapable of making the transition to socialism but rather that traditional Marxist analysis was inadequate to the task of understanding the revolutionary potential of the new states.[15]

Mirski toyed with ideas that are familiar to Western social scientists, such as telescoping stages of development, the role of modernizing elites, and even the possiblity of forceful, dynamic (read charismatic) leaders allowing a given society to skip stages. In the early sixties it seemed that the leaders of national liberation movements (as in Cuba, Algeria, and the Congo) in conjunction with the national bourgeoisie and communists could quickly lead a society to the noncapitalist path. Ultimately and inevitably the national liberation movement would go beyond the desires of the national bourgeoisie; and the national front, unable to cope with its internal contradictions, would polarize. At this point the communist vanguard would take charge.

Khrushchev was apparently convinced, at least in some instances, by this line of analysis.[16] His policy of cooperation with the national democratic states of the Third World reached its apogee in 1963 and 1964. In the face of opposition from doctrinaire theoreticians, such as Suslov and Ponomarev,

Algeria, in 1964, was declared to have "embarked upon socialism," and thus was the first noncommunist country to receive such an accolade.[17] In May of the same year, during his voyage to the U.A.R., Khrushchev, in a euphoric mood, announced that the U.A.R. was undertaking socialist construction. To the old guard in the Kremlin as well as to various Arab communist leaders (especially Khalid Bakdash) the new approach seemed ill-conceived, improvised, and potentially dangerous. Even before Khrushchev's downfall in October 1964, a reassessment of his policies had begun.[18] The process involved some debunking of Mirski's ideas, but so far no alternative analytic framework has been offered.

Since 1965 much greater caution has been exercised in the Soviet approach to the national bourgeoisie. The sudden collapse of the regimes of Ben Bella, Sukarno, and Nkrumah (and then, in 1968, the downfall of Keita of Mali) left in considerable doubt the possibility that national bourgeois leadership could telescope or skip stages of development, and that national fronts could launch a country on the noncapitalist path. For instance, N. A. Simoniya asserted in 1966 that national liberation revolutions, despite their lofty objectives, were often incapable of breaking the bonds of social reality. "Growing into socialism" is simply not a common result of such movements. Of twenty-eight liberated Asian states, only four have attained socialism and only two—Syria and Burma—are on the non-capitalist path. In Africa, of thirty-eight sovereign states only five (in 1966)—Algeria, Ghana, Guinea, Mali and the U.A.R.—are on the noncapitalist path.[19] Even Algeria, since the downfall of Ben Bella in 1965, has been demoted from "building socialism" to "revolutionary democracy." The new caution in Soviet analysis has influenced the evaluation of national fronts. The example of Algeria and other progressive states has shown that it is virtually impossible for a local communist party to maintain its organizational autonomy within such fronts and that the leaders of national liberation movements are generally intolerant of organized communist activities.

For all these reasons it is apparent that the U.S.S.R. will show restraint in estimating any developing country's chances for transition to socialism; and this restraint will probably be accompanied by greater emphasis on the internal development of the Soviet Union.[20] In terms of the coincidence of strategy and ideology, it would seem probable that with the slackening of ideological interest in the national bourgeoisie, policy will more than ever be determined by purely strategic concerns.[21]

In the final analysis, ideological and strategic objectives meet at the level of long-term systems conversion and the gradual absorption of all national units into the camp of peace. If, in order to weaken the imperialist camp, the U.S.S.R. is obliged to support and perhaps supply aid to "reactionary" regimes, such a policy can be justified on the grounds that Soviet aid may hasten the internal development of the society to an objectively revolutionary situation and, in turn, its transformation to socialism. Such arguments occasionally appear to be *post hoc* rationalizations of hard-nosed strategic choices. For instance, it can be argued that Soviet cooperation with the monarchy in Morocco will lead to Moroccan neutrality and the weakening of the imperialist camp, but also, over the long haul, to trade diversification, economic growth, industrialization, and class development. Morocco's inevitable systems conversion can be accelerated by Soviet aid, trade, and diplomatic support.

SOVIET IDEOLOGY AND STRATEGY IN PRACTICE

The local communist parties

The victims of the lack of confidence of Soviet ideological and strategic objectives in North Africa are the local communist parties. All that can be promised them is that they will be the beneficiaries of the socialist conversion of their societies at some unspecified date in the future. In the meantime they must accept repression by the national bourgeois regimes and must undertake clandestine efforts to infiltrate key sectors of the society with little hope of overt Soviet support.[22]

The communist parties of North Africa were strongest when the entire area was under European control. The leadership and the membership of the local communist parties were drawn largely from among the European colonists in each of the North African territories, and the local organizations were branches of the metropolitan parties. This applied particularly in Tunisia, Algeria, and Morocco, which were directly dependent upon the French Communist Party (PCF) and the General Confederation of Labor (CGT). Because of the internal politics of Italy, communist organizations in Libya were much more loosely aligned with the mother party.

During the thirties and forties attempts were made in the French territories to attract an indigenous clientele and to promote native members to leadership positions. It seemed appropriate also that the local organizations be given at least nominal organizational autonomy from the mother party. Thus in 1934 the Tunisian Communist Party (PCT) was established, in 1936 the Algerian Communist Party (PCA), and in 1943 the Moroccan Communist Party (PCM). Despite their nominal autonomy, party positions faithfully followed the official line of the PCF, and links with the world communist movement were mediated through the French organization.

The native communist leaders trained during and after the Second World War still dominate their organizations today, and their links with the PCF are still quite strong. An exception in this respect is Ali Ya'ta, Secretary-General of the PCM. Well before Moroccan independence in 1956, Ya'ta set about building a nationalist image for his party in order to ensure it a place in the politics of independent Morocco. He has emphasized that his party does not take orders from Paris or Moscow, although it tends to follow the Soviet line in the Sino-Soviet dispute. Beyond this, Ya'ta has been something of a maverick, freely criticizing the PCF for its ambivalent stance vis-à-vis the Algerian revolution, and, more recently, protesting the Soviet invasion of Czechoslovakia. He has taken unusual ideological positions such as praising the progressive nature of Islam, and such unusual political stances as backing Morocco's irridentist claims. With little hope of outside support from the international communist movement, Ya'ta has sought to protect his organization by demonstrating its devotion to nationalist, Arab, and Islamic causes.

The resort to these devices has not been entirely successful. In December 1959 the PCM was officially banned, on the grounds that its statutes and principles were of a subversive nature. The party appealed the ban, and over a three-year period underwent a series of trials that resulted in the Moroccan Supreme Court upholding the ban.[23] Throughout this period of the party's semi-clandestine existence, the Soviet Union pursued a policy of cooperation with the Moroccan government. An arms agreement was concluded in November 1960, with deliveries being made in February 1961 and in the summer of 1962. Soviet policy was aimed at encouraging the Moroccan government to liquidate the American military bases on her soil.

Interestingly enough, in 1959 and 1960 the Chinese also were seeking closer relations with Morocco and, like the Russians, were willing to overlook the suppression of local communist organizations. Such a course is in general less costly for the Chinese than for the Russians. Since the local parties of North Africa and the rest of the Middle East have been fairly staunch supporters of the Soviet line in the Sino-Soviet dispute, their plight quite naturally does not arouse Chinese sympathies. Moreover, the very fact that the U.S.S.R. has failed to defend local parties has contributed to internal splits as well as to the emergence of pro-Chinese factions. To my knowledge, however, such splits have not taken place, at least in a formal sense, in any North African party.

As is the case with the other parties of the Maghreb, the PCM has nothing that could be called a mass following. Its major support has come from students and intellectuals, with a smattering of working-class elements. It has been unable to make inroads into the industrial labor force, which is jealously guarded by the Union Marocaine du Travail (UMT), Morocco's largest trade union confederation. Because the PCM is not a credible force in its own right, Ali Ya'ta has steadfastly backed the idea of a national front of progressive forces that would include the UMT, a leftist political party, the Union Nationale des Forces Populaires (UNFP), and the Istiqlal, a more conservative party now in quasi-opposition to the government. Ya'ta's overtures to these organizations have been consistently rebuffed. As a result, in August 1968 he announced the founding of the Parti de la Libération et du Socialisme (PLS). This was described as a regrouping of the progressive forces of Morocco, but probably involved little more than a change of title for the PCM. Apparently dropping all reference to communism in the new party's name was sufficient to overcome official scruples, and the PLS has been given authorization to carry on its activities openly. One of its gestures, as mentioned earlier, was to condemn the Russian invasion of Czechoslovakia.[24]

In many respects the parties of Tunisia and Algeria have been even less successful than the PCM. Because of their dependence upon the PCF, of their high proportion of European members, and of their ambivalence toward the independence movements, they cut themselves off from the mainstream of political life in independent Tunisia and Algeria. The PCT, which was formally established in 1934, played a minimal part in the attainment of Tunisian independence in 1956. Thereafter it pursued without success a policy of coalition with the Neo-Destour (now the Socialist Destour), the major nationalist party. From 1957 on, it was highly critical of Bourguiba's cooperation with the West, which was dubbed "the policy of collaboration." Perhaps because of such criticism the party was banned in January 1963.[25] Like the PCM, the Tunisian party drew largely on students, and after 1963 proselytizing was carried out from abroad by the PCT's two exiled leaders, Mohammed Harmel and Mohammed Ennafa. After student riots in Tunis at the time of the June war, the government began rounding up "subversive" elements in connection with a conspiracy against the regime. Among those held responsible for the conspiracy were the remnants of the PCT.[26] Through all this the U.S.S.R. maintained correct relations with Tunisia. A commercial accord, first signed in 1962, was renegotiated in 1968. The only Soviet criticism of Tunisia at that time came as a result of official published denunciations of Soviet policy toward Czechoslovakia.

The Algerian Communist Party was founded in 1936. By 1955, one year after the beginning of the Algerian revolution, it was led by native Algerians. In September 1955 the PCA was banned by the French authorities, and its secretary-general, Larbi Bouhali, went into exile. Under the guidance of Sadoq Hadjères, an Algerian Jew, the party attempted to cooperate with the revolutionaries and maintain its European membership. It lost on both counts. On November 29, 1962, just a few months after Algeria became independent, President Ahmad Ben Bella dissolved the PCA. He said at the time: "There will be no anti-communist policy in Algeria; the interdiction of the PCA represents a fundamental position concerning the problem of the plurality of parties."[27] Since then Algerian communist leaders, who have pressed for the formation of a national front, have in no way been accommodated.[28] Following its strategic advantage and the prescriptions of Mirski's analysis of national liberation movements, the Kremlin studiously overlooked the dissolution of the PCA. (Soviet policy decisions regarding revolutionary Algeria and the PCA are considered in greater detail below.)

In Libya, communist activity has been minimal, and largely confined to the period before 1951. In fact there was no Libyan Communist Party *per se* but rather a few Marxist organizations founded by Italians. These included the Italian Association for the Progress of Libya, founded in 1948 and led by Enrico Cibelli, and the Popular Democratic Front led by Albaro Felici.[29] In November 1951, one month before the country became independent, seven leading Marxists and communists were expelled. Since then whatever radical groups may exist in the country have been largely inspired by Nasserism and, more recently, by the Ba'ath party of Syria.

Soviet aid

The economic aid of the Soviet Union and the United States is similar in political intent. In both cases the aim is to convert the political systems of developing countries to what are considered more viable forms. United States aid is designed to encourage economic growth, eventually political stability, and finally democracy. Soviet aid seeks to encourage economic growth and to accelerate development toward socialism.[30] Economic aid is a very tangible means of prodding the national bourgeoisie onto the path toward socialism. Yet in the early sixties a profusion of regimes that were receiving Soviet aid were pressing for the recognition of their status as builders of socialism. While ideological kudos might accrue from such a development, the economic costs appeared prohibitive. As the example of Cuba demonstrated, once a country was conceded the honor of building socialism, the amount of aid and support that such a regime could legitimately petition for was enormous. The prospect of several African, Middle Eastern, and Asian Cubas had no appeal for Soviet planners.[31]

The reappraisal of Soviet aid policies following the upsurge of the late fifties may have triggered the more general reevaluation of the Mirski approach to developing countries. In any event, by 1962 it must have been apparent that the U.S.S.R. had overcommitted itself in its aid program and that the LDCs could not draw fully upon the credits extended. For instance, by the end of 1964 the Soviet Union had made aid commitments of $4.268 billion,[32] of which nearly $3 billion remained unfulfilled.[33] In 1962, the U.S.S.R. tried to slow down the pace of its aid program and made only $53 million in new commitments. However, the Chinese diplomatic and aid offensive in Africa in 1963 and 1964 (including a long-term loan of $50 million to Algeria on October 9, 1963) forced the Soviet Union to make heavy new commitments: $998 million in 1964.[34] The momentum of the aid program has been difficult to slow. By the end of 1967, in fact, total Soviet commitments since 1954 stood around $6 billion.[35] Of that total probably only about $2 billion in credits have actually been drawn by the LDCs. Virtually all of the aid itself is tied to purchases in the Soviet Union. Loans have been repayable over a twelve-year period at 2.5 percent interest, although in recent years shorter term loans at higher interest rates have been used to promote sales of Soviet goods.

The political and economic purposes of Soviet aid are not difficult to discern; several have already been mentioned, including the weakening of Western economic ties with the LDCs and ultimate system conversion. To these should be added the creation of a favorable, non-threatening image for the U.S.S.R. On the other hand, the immediate purposes of substantial Soviet military aid to the LDCs are less apparent. Obviously, furnishing military hardware to various countries (over a billion dollars worth to the UAR alone) entails the risk of the recipient's putting it to use. In the era of peaceful coexistence it is not in Soviet interests to feed the fires of local and regional disuptes that might at some point bring about a great power confrontation. The U.S.S.R. has nonetheless accepted these risks with regard to some nineteen states. The United States, with a similar stake in peaceful coexistence, has accepted similar risks.

Military aid for young states preoccupied with their image and weight in international and regional politics, as well as with their relative strength vis-à-vis some rival state, has a symbolic value that cannot be equaled by economic aid. This is particularly true with regard to the military regimes among the LDCs who see themselves as defenders and saviors of the nation. In a more immediate sense they are faced with the problem of satisfying their constituents in the military establishment, and this can most feasibly be done through the acquisition of sophisticated weapons systems. The U.S.S.R. has, since its first arms deal with Syria in 1954, seized most opportunities to supply radical military regimes, thereby gaining some leverage over the development of such regimes by manipulating the deliveries of new equipment and spare parts.

To some extent the military elite may come to the conclusion that its survival and the defense of the nation are bound up with Soviet good will. This is the sort of attitude that the Soviet Union would like to encourage. The dependency that accompanies military aid is reinforced by the process of paying for the deliveries. Payments may bring about a drastic realignment of trade patterns among recipient states and Western powers. This is likely to be the case when arms are bartered for primary products such as Egyptian cotton, Indonesian rubber, or Algerian iron ore.[36] Despite these advantages, military aid may run counter to the objective of economic development and systems conversion, for the diversion of national resources into the acquisition of arms can only be detrimental to economic growth.

Since this essay was first written, the peculiar dilemma of the Soviet Union's military relationship with Egypt has been bared to public scrutiny. The strategic interest of avoiding confrontation with the United States outweighed the benefits to be drawn from the maintenance in Egypt of a large Soviet military establishment. As this fact became apparent to the Egyptians, the Soviets replied, at least in part, in ideological terms: the liberation of Egypt's territory will not come about through brute military force but only after the process of social revolution has been intensified within Egyptian society. Social liberation must precede national liberation. The threat of Egypt's revolutionary transformation, one may presume, was far more distant in Soviet eyes than that of military confrontation with the United States. The Egyptians reluctantly absorbed the message and invited the Russians out.

Let us now consider the place of North Africa in the total economic and military aid program of the U.S.S.R. Table 2 reveals that of the first eleven aid recipients, nine are Middle Eastern states. However, only one of these, Algeria, is a North African state and it is well beneath the salt relative to the U.A.R., Iraq, and Afghanistan. It is true that Soviet aid to Algeria has been maintained at levels reached in 1964, but with the post-Khrushchevian emphasis on pure strategic concerns, Soviet attention in the Middle East now seems to be directed to territorially contiguous states. For instance, in 1965 alone Turkey, Iran, and Pakistan, absorbed $540 million of $665 million in new economic aid commitments.

What emerges with some clarity from the table is the frequent irrelevance of ideological factors in the determination of who gets aid. Old favorites of the Mirski school, such as Ghana, Guinea, Mali, and Burma, rank behind 'feudal' monarchies such as Ethiopia, Iran, and Afghanistan, and bourgeois states of the imperialist camp such as Pakistan and Turkey. In the case of the U.A.R. there is an ostensible reconciliation of strategic and ideologic factors that governs the flow of Soviet aid to that country. One suspects, nonetheless, that old aid commitments to the U.A.R. have dictated new ones, and that the momentum of past investments explains, more than any other factors, the present ranking of the U.A.R.

The high level of aid to Syria and Iraq, dating from 1954 and 1958, might be explained in similar terms. If so, it seems plausible to argue that the Soviet Union may be alarmed not so much by builders of socialism, such as Cuba, springing up among the LDCs, but rather by new Iraqs and Syrias, who, despite their nebulous ideological underpinnings, can still make heavy demands upon Soviet aid. Soviet aid to Algeria which dates from 1963, has through the years become substantial. Whether or not the Soviet Union will increase the volume of its aid to Algeria may well be determined on the basis of previous experience with the revolutionary states of the Middle East.

To understand the criteria employed by the USSR in directing the flow of aid, we should probably discard the ideological rankings of Soviet analysts.[37] For the purposes of this study, I would suggest the following select group of Soviet aid recipients:

Category 1
a. Strategically vital, ideologically unpromising: Turkey, Iran, Pakistan
b. Strategically vital and neutral: Afghanistan
c. Strategically important, ideologically promising: Algeria, U.A.R., Syria, Iraq, Indonesia (pre-1965), Yemen, Sudan, Somalia, Libya
d. Strategically important and neutral: India
e. Strategically important and potentially neutral: Morocco, Ethiopia, Cyprus

Category 2 — Ideologically most promising: Algeria, Guinea, U.A.R., Burma, Tanzania, Congo (Brazzaville)

Category 3 — Strategically important but ideologically unpromising: Libya (pre-1969), Tunisia, Jordan, Saudi Arabia

Category 1, with its internal breakdown, groups most of the Soviet aid recipients. It is not easy to assess any sub-category in terms of its influence on directing the flow of aid, but generally speaking 1a and 1c are of predominant concern to Soviet strategists. Countries in Category 2 are of only secondary importance in determining aid recipients. While the countries in Category 3 have received little or no Soviet aid, any move on their part away from the imperialist camp would undoubtedly stimulate the flow. If this categorization is at all accurate, it merely re-enforces my initial point that North Africa is a bonus area for the U.S.S.R., a region of considerable strategic interest, but not one, with the possible exception of Algeria, in which heavy commitments should be made.

What aid commitments have been made in North Africa? Some of the specific projects for which Soviet aid has been supplied to Algeria since 1963 range from clearing minefields along the borders to constructing an important steel works at Annaba (formerly Bône).[38] Accords signed in the summer of 1964 have determined subsequent projects and programs. Construction of a number of dams has been undertaken by the Soviet Union, and since 1966 plans have been drawn up for the construction of a distillery (cognac), a plant for treating iron and zinc ore, a power plant, and an agronomy institute. The U.S.S.R. has supplied medical personnel to the public health system and some 200 technicians and equipment to the state oil company, SONATRACH, founded in 1967. In recent years, experts from GOSPLAN

TABLE 2

RECIPIENTS OF SOVIET ECONOMIC AND MILITARY AID, 1954-67*

Country	Military and Non-Military Aid Total: 1954-67 ($ millions)	Rank	Non-Military Aid, 1954-67 ($ millions)	Rank	Military Aid** 1955-67 ($ millions)	Rank
U.A.R.	2,561	1	1,011	2	1,550	1
India	2,203	2	1,593	1	610	4
Indonesia	1,712	3	372	4	1,340	2
Iraq	834	4	184	9	650	3
Afghanistan	820	5	570	3	250	6.5
Syria	693	6	233	6	460	5
Algeria	482	7	232	7	250	6.5
Iran	440	8	330	5	110	8
Pakistan	218	9	178	10	40	10.5
Turkey	210	10	210	8	No military aid	
Yemen	192	11	92	12	100	9
Ethiopia	102	12	102	11	No military aid	
Ghana	99	13	89	13	10	15
Brazil	85	14	85	14	No military aid	
Greece	84	15	84	15	No military aid	
Guinea	83	16	73	16	10	15
Somalia	76	17	66	17	10	15
Morocco	74	18	44	21.5	40	10.5
Mali	60	19	55	18.5	***	18.5
Chile	55	20	55	18.5	No military aid	

Country						
Argentina	45	21	45	20	No military aid	
Kenya	44	22	44	21.5	No military aid	
Cambodia	35	23	25	26	10	15
Tunisia	34	24	34	23	No military aid	
Tanzania	30	25.5	20	28.5	10	15
Ceylon	30	25.5	30	24	No military aid	
Sierra Leone	28	27	28	25	No military aid	
Uganda	26	28	16	30	10	15
Sudan	22	29	22	27	10	15
Nepal	20	30	20	28.5	No military aid	
Burma	14	31	14	31	No military aid	
Congo (Brazzaville)	11	32	9	32	***	18.5
Cameroon	8	33	8	33	No military aid	
Senegal	7	34	7	34	No military aid	
Zambia	6	35	6	35	No military aid	
Mauritania	3	36	3	36	No military aid	

*The figures used in this table are drawn from U.S. Dept. of State (Intelligence and Research) Research Memorandum RSE-120 (Aug. 14, 1968), Table 1, pp. 2-3; and Table 2, p. 6. For a somewhat similar presentation, see Charles B. McLane, "Foreign Aid in Soviet Third World Policies," MIZAN, vol. 10, n. 6 (1968), pp. 210-50, and esp. p.247.

**Military aid figures include all communist countries, not just the U.S.S.R.

***Mali and Congo (Brazzaville) received an estimated $5 million or less in military aid. I arbitrarily assumed $5 million for Mali and $2 million for Congo (B) so that I could have some sort of total for military and non-military aid.

have been advising the Algerians on the implementation of development plans.

In Morocco and Tunisia, Soviet aid has not been extensive, and in Libya, nonexistent. In Morocco the Soviet Union is undertaking the construction of a large dam at Zawia n'Ourbass, a metallurgy complex at Ksar as-Souk, and a power plant at Jerrada. Soviet aid to Tunisia, first extended in 1961, has been devoted to the construction of dams, hospitals, and educational facilities. The first credits were extended at the time of the Franco-Tunisian crisis over the disposition of the naval base at Bizerte (summer 1961).

Through selective but massive military aid to various Middle Eastern states, the U.S.S.R. has demonstrated to local elites that the grip of the West upon their societies can be broken where it seemed to be the strongest—in its near-monopoly of coercive force. Yet the military aid program, as noted above, has not been without pitfalls. The Soviet Union, like the United States, has overlooked the rule of thumb that to arm two or more Middle Eastern States is to arm two or more actual or potential adversaries. The U.S.S.R. has in the past, for instance, delivered arms to Pakistan, India, and Afghanistan; to Iran and Iraq; and to Morocco and Algeria.

During 1961 and 1962 Morocco began receiving Soviet military equipment that included twelve Mig 15s and 17s and fifty-odd tanks. Most of this equipment is today obsolete. In October 1963 Algeria and Morocco fought a brief war to determine the status of territories lying along the ill-defined southern border between the two countries. The war occurred before the U.S.S.R. had made substantial arms deliveries to Algeria. In fact, the poor showing of the Algerian army may have helped soften the Russians when they received Algerian arms requests. The ensuing arms deliveries, probably beginning in late 1964, had by 1966 made available to the Algerians 125 Mig 15s, 17s, and 21s, 35 Il-28 bombers, 150 tanks, and a great deal of other equipment.[39] The deliveries were supplemented with technical and military training missions in Algeria and in the U.S.S.R. Despite the magnitude of Soviet military aid to Algeria it is probably not the intention of the U.S.S.R. to encourage another round with the Moroccans. Other indicators, to be discussed below, would suggest that the U.S.S.R. would like to prevent such a confrontation. It is not, moreover, beyond the realm of possibility that more Soviet arms might be supplied to Morocco. The chief of staff of the Royal Moroccan Army, General Driss Ben Omar, visited the Soviet Union in 1969, perhaps with this in mind.[40]

At the same time King Hassan, clearly underequipped vis-à-vis the Algerians, has called for an end to the arms race in North Africa. It is at least not improbable that Algeria's growing arsenal may encourage her to resume the conflict along the borders, thus embroiling the Russians in a regional dispute that could easily involve the United States. Such are the risks of the Soviet, or any, military aid program. On the other hand, supplying large amounts of matériel to Algeria, and perhaps once again to Morocco, gives Russia a legitimate influence in regional politics and conflict that can inhibit rather than contribute to future military engagements.

Soviet trade

Commercial exchanges provide an accurate measure of the continuing economic grip of the West upon former colonies and territories. Trade diversification is viewed by the U.S.S.R. as a means to break down neo-imperialist linkages. For the most part, however, although Soviet trade with the LDCs has expanded rapidly since the mid-fifties, the nature of the exchange system does not differ greatly from that of the colonial countries. Over 80 percent of Soviet imports from the LDCs consists of raw materials and food stuffs, while the bulk of her exports consists of finished goods and heavy equipment.[41] With only 3 percent of GNP annually taken up by foreign trade with all countries, the Soviet Union is still, among the great powers, a relatively self-contained unit.

The U.S.S.R. has yet to make a substantial dent in the dominant trade patterns of the North African states, although in recent years trade with Algeria and Morocco has expanded rapidly. Nonetheless other newcomers to North African trade, such as West Germany, Belgium, and Italy have expanded their exchanges even more rapidly than the Soviet Union, as have some of the Eastern European countries.

There is, as a result, little prospect that in the near future any North African country will reorient its trade patterns toward the U.S.S.R. to the same extent as has the U.A.R. Taking the year 1964, for example, one finds that total Soviet trade with the U.A.R. reached $279 million compared to $19.5 million with Algeria, the Soviet Union's leading North African trading partner. By the end of 1966 the Algerian figure had risen to about $25 million or roughly 2 percent of total Algerian trade, in that year valued at $1,261 millions. Since 1966 Soviet trade with Algeria has probably trebled. The U.S.S.R. has agreed to import from Algeria 600,000 tons of iron ore (as well as all the production of the Annaba steelworks once it is producing), 3,800,000 tons of crude oil phased over a seven-year period, and 5,000,000 hectolitres of wine over a five-year period. The deal involving wine is particularly satisfying to the Algerians, who regard their vineyards as a poisoned gift from colonialist France. In 1967 French wine-growers forced their government to ignore an agreement signed with the Algerians in 1964 guaranteeing a market for fixed quantities of Algerian wine annually.[42] The U.S.S.R. has stepped into the breach and may tide over the Algerians as they phase out the vineyards.

Under the best of circumstances the Soviet share of total Algerian trade

Table 3

WESTERN AND SOVIET TRADE WITH ALGERIA, 1960-64
(figures in billions of Algerian dinars)

| | Imports from | | | | | Exports to | | | | |
	1960	1961	1962	1963	1964	1960	1961	1962	1963	1964
Total	6,241	5,057	1,938	3,342	3,472	1,946	1,821	949	3,747	3,589
U.S.S.R.	9	3	24	18	49	8	5	4	1	16
France	5,237	4,170	1,474	2,795	2,449	1,573	1,478	806	2,818	2,793
U.S.A.	88	182	107	93	131	3	.5	.5	5	28
U.K.	46	34	10	21	107	79	107	38	101	48

Source: Figures, which have been rounded, are taken from United Nations, Dept. of Economic and Social Affairs, *Yearbook of International Trade Statistics: 1966* (New York, 1968), p. 47. I have not found more recent trade statistics for Algeria that give a breakdown by country. *Total* trade statistics for 1967 may be found in United Nations, *Statistical Yearbook: 1968* (New York, 1969), pp. 394-95.

may rise to 8 to 10 percent by 1970. Nonetheless, the overall contours of Algerian trade will be minimally changed, and may well continue to resemble the distribution shown in Table 3 for the years 1960-64.

France buys about three-quarters of Algeria's petroleum and employs some half a million Algerian workers. There are still seven thousand French teachers and technical assistants in Algeria. Other Western countries, such as Britain, have agreed to increase their imports of Algerian oil and natural gas. With these factors taken into consideration, it would require a major Soviet effort to reorient Algerian trade patterns. The question of Algeria's possible association with the EEC may be of particular concern to the U S S R As an integral part of France until 1962, Algeria was included in the Treaty of Rome and has maintained many of her privileges as a French territory since 1962. Since February 1964 she has periodically entered into contact with the EEC with the possibility of association in mind, but no final arrangement has yet been concluded.[43] The EEC is of course considered by the U.S.S.R., and to some extent by Algeria, to be a Western instrument to perpetuate imperialist dominance over the Mediterranean area. However, the U.S.S.R. may not be in a position to offer sufficiently attractive alternative markets to prevent Algeria from formal association with the EEC.

After King Hassan's state visit to the U.S.S.R. in October 1966, Soviet trade with Morocco grew considerably. In 1968 total trade between the two countries had reached $40 million, not far behind the figure for Soviet trade with Algeria. In December 1966, a joint Soviet-Moroccan trading company, MARIMEX, was established at Casablanca. It is not without interest to note that this company is capitalized on a fifty-fifty basis between the U.S.S.R. and a group of Moroccan private businessmen. Within the terms of a $30 million trade agreement signed in the fall of 1966, MARIMEX will undertake the importation of metals, heavy material, and equipment. This may lead eventually to the construction of warehouses, local assembly shops, and manpower training centers in Casablanca.[44] In addition to the imports handled by MARIMEX, Morocco has begun to import from the U.S.S.R. green tea, chemical products, wood, cotton, and about 15 percent of its petroleum needs. The Soviet Union imports from Morocco citrus fruits (90,000 tons in 1969), canned goods, wine, and vegetable oils. It is perhaps indicative of the growing trade between the two countries that the U.S.S.R. established a consulate at Casablanca in October 1967. Nonetheless Morocco's trade patterns are similar to those of Algeria, and the share of the U.S.S.R. in total Moroccan trade ($941 million in 1967) is not likely in the near future to exceed 3 or 4 percent (see Table 4).

It is a curious but easily explained fact that Morocco, a bourgeois monarchy, has more extensive commercial relations with Cuba and China than has any other North African state, and that its trade with either coun-

Table 4

THE TRADE OF THE U.S.S.R., CHINA, CUBA, AND THE WEST WITH MOROCCO, 1962-66
(figures in billions of Moroccan dirhams)

	Imports from					Exports to				
	1962	*1963*	*1964*	*1965*	*1966*	*1962*	*1963*	*1964*	*1965*	*1966*
Total	2,151	2,243	2,328	2,291	2,418	1,762	1,942	2,186	2,176	2,168
U.S.S.R.	26	36	53	48	81	24	41	27	56	56
China	45	34	60	60	83	21	32	62	47	40
Cuba	113	136	243	186	—	28	48	56	41	—
France	924	952	911	879	944	686	797	931	958	911
U.S.A.	291	223	211	271	287	49	28	27	35	48

Source: Figures, which have been rounded, are from *Yearbook of International Trade Statistics: 1966*, p. 555. The conversion rate is approximately 5 dirhams to the U.S. dollar.

try between 1962 and 1966 exceeds that with the U.S.S.R. for the same period. Cuba has been Morocco's major supplier of unrefined sugar. In 1963 a three-year accord was signed for the importation of one million tons of sugar, and in 1965 alone 650,000 tons were delivered. Morocco annually imports from China about eight million tons of green tea in return for phosphates, canned goods, and Berliet trucks assembled in Morocco. It is probable that in the future, Moroccan trade with Western nations will, as is the case with Algeria, grow more rapidly than with the U.S.S.R. and with other communist states. Significant in this respect is the signature on March 31, 1969, of an accord between Morocco and the EEC, associating Morocco to the Common Market for a period of five years.[45]

Tunisia's total foreign trade in 1966 was about $408 million, of which the Soviet share was $12.5 million or roughly 2.5 percent. Again, while Soviet trade with Tunisia is growing, it has yet to exceed the shares of Czechoslovakia, Poland, and Yugoslavia in total Tunisian trade, nor does it approach the level of exchange between Tunisia and the United States (see Table 5).

The Soviet Union hardly warrants an entry in Libyan trade statistics. In 1966, when total Libyan trade was valued at $1.391 billion, the Soviet Union accounted for only .25 percent of the total. However, given Russia's new interest in Middle Eastern oil, and the fall of the monarchical regime, Libya's predominant trade patterns, shown in Table 6, could be altered in a major way. Indeed, in May 1972 the Libyan Minister of Petroleum signed a contract in Moscow for the exportation to the U.S.S.R. of an undisclosed amount of Libyan crude.

It would be a task of considerable magnitude for the Soviet Union to make appreciable inroads into the dominant trade patterns between the Maghreb and Western Europe. Even if all the North African states ardently wanted to diversify their trade, the U.S.S.R. would probably not be able to buy from nor sell to the countries of the region the kinds and qualities of goods to which they are accustomed. Whether or not we attach the label neo-imperialist to the continued economic dependence of the Maghreb upon Western Europe does not alter the fact that dependence is the prevailing relationship, and it is one that is likely to endure for some time.[46]

Transnational liberation and strategic advance

During the period 1960 to 1965, Soviet strategic and ideological objectives in North Africa coincided more closely than at any time before or since. During this period, when great hopes were placed in the national liberation movements of Africa, it may have seemed to the U.S.S.R. that with proper encouragement and prodding these movements might eventually sweep the continent. Probably by the end of 1963 such sanguine expectations were un-

Table 5

WESTERN AND SOVIET TRADE WITH TUNISIA, 1962-66
(figures in millions of Tunisian dinars)

	Imports from					Exports to				
	1962	1963	1964	1965	1966	1962	1963	1964	1965	1966
Total	905	936	1,103	1,286	1,307	487	529	573	629	737
U.S.S.R.	10	18	17	30	51	10	11	5	6	26
France	473	448	483	502	447	257	264	294	196	255
U.S.A.	145	103	112	209	215	69	36	41	101	100
U.K.	28	36	46	54	39	23	21	22	33	33

Source: Figures, which have been rounded, are from Yearbook of International Trade Statistics, 1966, p. 809.

Table 6

WESTERN AND SOVIET TRADE WITH LIBYA, 1962-66
(in millions of £ Libyan)

	Imports from					Exports to				
	1962	1963	1964	1965	1966	1962	1963	1964	1965	1966
Total	73.5	85.3	104.4	114.4	144.6	49.0	118.6	218.4	282.0	352.3
U.S.S.R.	.5	1.2	1.4	1.1	1.3	.06	.13	.24	.11	.05
Italy	17.6	17.5	20.9	29.0	39.9	9.2	15.7	25.2	27.7	40.2
U.K.	13.5	15.2	18.4	16.9	22.2	17.1	32.3	53.9	58.1	51.3
U.S.A.	14.2	17.0	24.2	19.5	18.2	3.7	4.8	9.0	8.9	19.1

Source: Figures from Yearbook of International Trade Statistics, 1966, p. 481.

dergoing a reevaluation in the Kremlin. However, Chou En-lai's tour through Africa in that year, and his statement that "Africa is ripe for revolution," led the U.S.S.R. to reaffirm its official approval of national liberation movements. Even after Khrushchev was deposed, the threat that the Chinese might take over this issue for their own purposes, and the more immediate need of the U.S.S.R. to maintain its position as a legitimate participant in Afro-Asian politics, evoked continued interest in the notion of national liberation movements. The new realism regarding such movements did not manifest itself until after the Afro-Asian Conference (originally scheduled to be held in Algiers in June 1965) was adjourned *sine die* in the fall of the same year. The downfall of Ben Bella and N'krumah, the evident weaknesses of other African revolutionaries, and the retreat of the Chinese into the cultural revolution, were all factors that permitted a reserved attitude toward national liberation movements. Because Algeria was instrumental first in raising and then in undermining Soviet hopes in the success of revolutions of national liberation, some additional comment on this period is in order.

In October 1960, after Khrushchev had met in New York with representatives of the Algerian revolution, the U.S.S.R. granted de facto recognition to the Provisional Government of the Republic of Algeria (G.P.R.A.). This event was representative of the growing Soviet involvement in movements of national liberation. The Congo crisis of 1960-61 furthered this trend. One of the results of this crisis was the formation of the Casablanca Group, consisting of the U.A.R., Ghana, Guinea, Mali, Morocco, and the G.P.R.A. All of these states, except Morocco and the state-to-be of Algeria, were soon to be proclaimed on the non-capitalist path of development. Their formation of a potentially revolutionary bloc that spanned the Sahara and endorsed the cause of African liberation gave rise to the possibility that national liberation movements could have an impact of transnational or even of continental proportions. From an ideological point of view the movements were promising and, in terms of strategic objectives, provided a vehicle for spreading Soviet influence throughout the continent.

The Casablanca Group, which was formed in January 1961, expired in May 1963. The member states had succeeded in agreeing only upon the decision to condemn the U.N. effort in the Congo and to withdraw their contingents from the U.N. force there. The position adopted by the group suited the immediate foreign policy interests of the individual members. The G.P.R.A., for instance, was interested in improving its international status and in enlarging its role in African politics, while King Mohammed V of Morocco, the sponsor of the group, saw in it a means to isolate his internal opposition from the support of outside radical states. After their initial effort, the participant members could find no common set of interests to bind them together. It therefore proved impossible to bring together the heads of state of the six countries for the scheduled meeting in Morocco in the spring of 1963. In fact by the fall of 1963 two of the erstwhile partners, Morocco and Algeria, were shooting at each other.[47] The demise of the group coincided with the post-independence factional struggle of the Algerian FLN. Neither event was designed to fulfill Soviet expectations regarding the revolutionary impact of national liberation movements.

Almost at the same time that the Casablanca Group was constituted, labor unions in the member states came together, in May 1961, to form the All African Trade Union Federation (AATUF). Once again ideology and strategy seemed to be happily wedded; for here was a movement based upon international labor solidarity, the orthodox path to systems conversion, that could sustain the national bourgeois leaders of a bloc of progressive African states. Enthusiasm for AATUF was tempered, however, by the fact that it had no formal ties with the Soviet-sponsored World Federation of Trade Unions (WFTU).

The provisional secretariat of AATUF was established in November 1959, and the constituent congress met at Casablanca in May 1961. Mahjoub Ben Seddiq, secretary-general of the Moroccan Union of Labor (UMT), was the moving force behind the organization. Like many other African labor leaders, he had first been drawn into unionism under communist auspices. In particular the French CGT had established branches in French territories and colonies. Because the control of local organizations generally rested with Europeans, and because European leaders had mixed feelings about independence movements in the territories, native unionists frequently broke their contacts with the CGT during the nationalist period and founded independent federations of their own. This occurred in Morocco, in Tunisia, and in Algeria. It was encouraged to some extent by Irving Brown of the International Confederation of Free Trade Unions (ICFTU). In fact the labor federations in both Tunisia and Morocco eventually joined ICFTU, the Western counterweight to WFTU.

As a result, the U.S.S.R. could regard as something of a victory the fact that AATUF demanded that its members break all ties with WFTU and ICFTU. Most had already broken ties with WFTU so that the major damage would accrue to ICFTU. The UMT did so only in May 1963. Nonetheless WFTU and the U.S.S.R. greeted the formation of AATUF with enthusiasm.[48] While AATUF has survived a number of crises since 1961, it has been subject to the same strains that proved fatal to the Casablanca Group. Most member unions during that period were involved in the task of defining their positions vis-à-vis the regimes in their countries and had little time left for effective international organization. Tunisia's isolation in Arab affairs, hostilities between Morocco and Algeria, Ghana's growing introversion capped by the downfall of N'krumah, all contributed to the dislocation of AATUF.

By the middle of 1965 it was apparent that the hoped-for process of transnational liberation had failed to develop much momentum. Two of its major manifestations, the Casablanca Group and AATUF, were in disarray. Ahmed Ben Bella, who had been the principal spokesman of armed liberation in Africa and who had wanted to make Algiers the Havana of the African continent, was replaced in June 1965 by Houari Boumedienne, who phased out Algerian assistance to resistance groups in subsaharan Africa. Nasser, tied down in a futile war in the Yemen, was no longer in a position to devote much attention to African liberation. As a result, after 1965 the U.S.S.R. was obliged to devise a new and more cautious approach to Africa.

In North Africa, the new policy took the form of maintaining normal, if not cordial, relations with all the regimes of the region. Systems conversion was simply shelved as an objective with any immediate relevance for policy making. The new emphasis was and is upon obtaining favorable policy stances, trade relations, and ports of call among the North African states. This is an important point, since there has been a tendency for the United States and the U.S.S.R. to view their respective positions in Morocco and Algeria as threatening and incompatible. Some American officials believe that Russia would like to use revolutionary Algeria to overthrow the monarchy in Morocco and create a satellite regime there that would give the U.S.S.R. direct access to the Atlantic. For its part, the Soviet Union has suspected that the United States may try to reverse the revolutionary tide in Africa by using Morocco as a base to overthrow the Algerian regime, in which the U.S.S.R. has made a considerable investment.[49] There is no way of knowing to what extent this mirror image affects policy makers in either Washington or Moscow. But it is clear that both satisfy their immediate strategic needs without fundamental change in any North African Regime. The U.S.S.R., I believe, may actually encourage regional integration within the present political context of North Africa. Cooperation and harmony among the diverse regimes of the Maghreb are not detrimental to short-term Soviet interests, and if they result in economic growth, factors leading to systems conversion may be accentuated. One Soviet analyst of North African economic integration has written that progress toward this goal depends on mutual political trust and on the willingness of the countries involved to make the necessary compromises.[5] Stability, harmony, and economic growth in the Maghreb are as much in the Soviet as in the American interest.

CAN AN INTERNATIONAL IDEOLOGICAL MOVEMENT BE RECONCILED WITH GREAT POWER OBJECTIVES?

The armed phase of the Algerian revolution began on November 1, 1954, and came to an end in the summer of 1962. The domestic revolution has continued, or so its spokesmen assert, right up to the present time. This fifteen-or twenty-year period corresponds to that in which the first steps toward de-Stalinization were taken in the U.S.S.R. and in which a new approach to the national bourgeoisie, the national liberation movements, and the non-capitalist path to socialism was devised. I had initially expected that this entire process would be reflected in Soviet writings on the Algerian revolution, a sociopolitical phenomenon clearly relevant to all phases of the Soviet approach to the LDCs. The Western, particularly French, assumption during the 1950s that the revolution was mounted, *de toute pièce,* by the Kremlin and its minions in Egypt failed to take into account the difficulties faced by the U.S.S.R. in analyzing and formulating policy toward the liberation movement in Algeria. Throughout most of this period Soviet literature on the revolution has been curiously bland and non-analytic, relying largely on stereotypes of the national liberation movement to describe what has gone on in Algeria.

The problems faced by the Soviet Union in dealing with Algeria are old ones, and stem from the fact that the U.S.S.R. is both the center of a worldwide ideological, revolutionary movement and a nation-state that participates in the international state system. These two roles are often incompatible, and the objectives sought in either sphere may be mutually exclusive. Thus stated, the point is one that has often been made by students of Soviet affairs and international communism, but one that does much to explain Russia's uneven and hesitant handling of the Algerian revolution.

If we consider the problems of achieving consensus among the U.S.S.R., the French Communist Party (PCF), and the Algerian Communist Party (PCA) in their interpretation of and strategy toward the revolution, we will have taken a step toward understanding the Soviet dilemma. None of the three actors operated within the same set of constraints nor did they share the same immediate objectives. In one frame of reference the Soviet Union has devised policy toward France and, in another, policy toward the PCF. After 1958, encouraging de Gaulle's hostility toward NATO and the EEC meant noninterference in his handling of Algeria and the French left. Similarly, after 1962, encouraging the noncommunist revolution of Ahmed Ben Bella meant sacrificing the PCA.

The primary focus for the activities of the PCF was the French government and party system. The Frency communists were almost completely preoccupied with defining policy and tactics toward Guy Mollet and the socialists as well as toward General de Gaulle. When the PCF dealt with the Algerian revolution, however, it was the preservation of the PCA rather than the success of the FLN or the independence of Algeria that was uppermost. The objectives sought by the PCF in Algeria and in France often bore little resemblance to those of the U.S.S.R.

In some ways, the PCA was doubly victimized by the other two actors.

First of all, in aligning itself in 1954 with the position of the PCF that the revolution must be won first in France before it could spread to the colonies, the PCA placed itself in direct opposition to the Algerian revolution and the National Liberation Front (FLN). After 1962, the Soviet Union, in befriending the now-triumphant FLN, turned a blind eye to the suppression of the PCA. It has now fallen to the PCF to defend the cause of Algerian communists. In the complicated division of labor that has developed since 1965, the PCF has steadfastly opposed two governments, the Algerian and the French, that the U.S.S.R. has just as steadfastly supported. Only China has chided the U.S.S.R. for its "chauvinistic" policies and its abuse of the world revolutionary movement. But even without the gratuitous Chinese comments from the sidelines, the problems of wearing two hats, one "revolutionary," the other "national interest," have occasionally been insurmountable.

Until 1956 the Soviet Union barely took cognizance of the existence of the Algerian revolution. In July of that year, Khrushchev publicly criticized the policies of Socialist Prime Minister Guy Mollet and called for Algerian independence. After that initial blast, the U.S.S.R. lapsed into silence, especially after de Gaulle came into power in 1958. The silence was not broken until 1960, and then only timidly and in a manner designed to be as inoffensive as possible to the French president. The U.S.S.R. hailed Algerian independence only when it was certain that France had granted that status to Algeria through the Evian agreements in 1962.

Soviet ideological interpretations of the Algerian revolution throughout the period were limited to a handful of analysts who relied upon information published in *Humanité, L'Unità*, and the press of the PCA, and Egyptian news sources. The efforts of R. Landa, who is the most prolific writer on Algerian affairs, have consisted largely of bloodless, non-analytic endorsements of the FLN and the revolution in general.[51] The opportunities of interpretation offered by the Algerian experience were simply not exploited. Indeed, the Marxist analyst who has come closest to studying the revolution in terms of process rather than propaganda has been one of the leaders of the PCA, Bachir Hadj Ali. His dissection of the tactics employed by the FLN in the Battle of Algiers makes a real contribution to our understanding of the revolution. It is significant, however, that this study, published in 1965, was designed to debunk certain notions of the invincibility of revolutionary insurgents and thus to uphold the Soviet end in the debate with China.[52] That the Algerian revolution was not subjected to the same close scrutiny by Soviet observers, at least in print, may be attributable to a desire to avoid reducing the room for strategic maneuver through ideological commitments.

In the years immediately following the Second World War, when Russia still espoused the two-camp theory, the PCF and the PCA shared with the

U.S.S.R. a hostile and deprecating attitude toward nationalist movements. For reasons to be explained below, this consensus among Marxists was lost in the early 1950s and has yet to be regained. Moreover, the PCA and the PCF were not only out of step with the nationalist movement in Algeria but were often pitted directly against it.

Although this antagonism dates back to 1936, the reaction of the communists to the nationalist demonstrations at Sétif in May 1945 provided graphic evidence of communist feelings toward Algerian nationalism. The draconian repression that followed the riots at Sétif was carried out by civilian *colon* militias and the French military. European members of the PCA were prominent in organizing the militias, while in France two communists in the government, Maurice Thorez, vice-president of the Council, and Air Minister Tillon, had at least an indirect role in the military operations.[53] In the case of the PCA the notion that the noncommunist national bourgeoisie could never liberate their societies reinforced the predispositions of the party's European membership to resist the thrust of native nationalists. In 1945, at the Tenth Congress of the PCF, Paul Caballero, the secretary-general of the PCA, stated: "Those who want the independence of Algeria are conscious or unconscious agents of imperialism. We (Algerian communists) do not want to change a one-eyed horse for one that is totally blind."[54]

Within a few years, however, it was clear to the PCA (although not to the PCF) that some sort of accommodation would have to be reached with the increasingly powerful nationalist groups. There was talk of national fronts with a vanguard role for the PCA, of the need to increase contacts with the Muslim masses, and of the need to convince the nationalists to support the revolution in France. Yet accommodation proved impossible to obtain. Despite the growing role of native Algerians in leadership positions in the PCA (Larbi Bouhali, Sadok Hadjerès, Bachir Hadj Ali), the nationalists would cooperate with communists only as individuals, while the bulk of the party's European membership balked at the very idea of cooperation.

The initial reaction of the PCF to the outbreak of rebellion in Algeria in November 1954 was disdainful and condemnatory. *Humanité* of November 9 announced that while the PCF supported the Algerian people in their struggle against repression, it deplored all acts of terrorism.[55] In the following two years it became apparent that this position had served no useful purpose. The French authorities had dissolved the PCA in September 1955, the nationalist tide had swept by the local communists, and the U.S.S.R. in 1956 had made explicit its support of national liberation movements. At its national congress in July 1956, the PCF declared that the Fench government must accept the Algerian national fact and allow the Algerians to decide their own destiny. In Algeria, the PCA had tried to capitalize on the nationalist fervor spreading through the country by organizing its own *maquis*. This only served to antagonize the FLN, which insisted upon the unity of the resistance movement, and to alienate the European backbone of the party. In April 1956 Dr. Hadjerès entered into negotiations with Yussef Ben Khedda of the FLN. The upshot was that the *maquis rouge* was abandoned, and it was agreed that members of the PCA could join the FLN on an individual basis.[56]

The PCA called upon its members to rally to the FLN, proposing that a resistance council be organized in which the PCA could maintain some sort of corporate identity. In 1956 the PCA may have had twelve thousand members.[57] It is thus no surprise that the FLN derided the sincerity of the PCA when only a handful of its members joined the nationalists. Amar Ouzegane, who had quit the PCA in 1948, claims that only thirteen members of the PCA *maquis* rallied to the FLN, and only one, a French girl, signed an oath of allegiance.[58] Moreover, leaders of the PCA, particularly Larbi Bouhali from his exile in East Germany, insisted that in integrating themselves into the FLN they were agreeing only to a unified military command and not to a unified political command.

A congress of the FLN was held in the Soummam Valley on August 20, 1956. In a section entitled "Le communisme absent," the final report of the congress formally condemned the PCA.

> The PCA, despite its passage into illegality and the noisy publicity with which the colonialist press has gratified it in order to intimate an imaginary collusion with the Algerian Resistance, has not succeeded in playing a role worthy of mention.
>
> The bureaucratic leadership of the PCA has no contacts with the people and has not been able to analyze correctly the revolutionary situation. This is why the party condemned the "terrorism" and from the very beginning of the insurrection ordered its militants from the Aures, who had come to Algiers for instructions, NOT TO TAKE UP ARMS. . .
>
> The PCA, as a credible organization, has disappeared because of the preponderance within it of European elements whose superficial nationalist convictions, when faced with armed resistance, were shaken in such a manner as to reveal all their internal contradictions.[59]

Perhaps an even more telling blow was struck against the PCA earlier in 1956 (February 24 to be exact), when the FLN helped found the Union Générale des Travailleurs Algériens (UGTA). This move effectively disrupted the local organization of the CGT and deprived the communists of worker support among native Algerians. To add insult to injury, the UGTA, shepherded by Irving Brown, was admitted to membership in the ICFTU on July 16, 1956.[60] In general, then, it is no exaggeration to say that between 1954 and 1956 the PCA committed suicide as far as Algerian nationalists were concerned,. and with it, the PCF. Because the U.S.S.R. had refrained from taking any defined position regarding the revolution, it did not suffer in nationalist eyes to the same extent as its dependents, the PCF and the PCA. The U.S.S.R. might have been inclined after 1956 to deal directly with the FLN, but for six years the Russians tried to show that they could satisfy several constituencies: that they could be just as militant as the Chinese, that they could support the PCF,[61] that they could encourage de Gaulle along his independent path in Europe, and that they could maintain contacts with the FLN. Trying to move off in several directions at once, all they managed to achieve, at least with regard to Algeria, was immobilism.

Communist China took advantage of the Russian paralysis. On September 18, 1958, the FLN announced in Cairo the formation of the Provisional Government of Algeria (GPRA), which was promptly recognized by Tunisia, Morocco, Libya, Iraq, Yemen, and the U.A.R., and four days later by China, Indonesia, and the Sudan. Later that year a delegation from the GPRA was given a triumphal reception in Peking and met with Mao Tse-tung. In the spring of 1959, China promised to send arms to the Algerians. The Russians tried to counter the Chinese pressure, and during 1959 and 1960 arms carried by Eastern European ships were sent to the FLN via Tunisia and Morocco. Bid to the UGTA was channeled through the International Trade Union Committee of Solidarity with the Workers and People of Algeria, although the UGTA had broken with the CGT and had joined ICFTU. However, the U.S.S.R. went about as far as it could in the direction of recognizing the provisional government when on October 7, 1960, after Khrushchev had met in New York with representatives of the GPRA, it extended *de facto* recognition.

The Soviet Union went on to call for self-determination in Algeria. This was hardly a daring move, since President de Gaulle, in September 1959, had already allowed for that possibility. It is indicative of the problems of coordination encountered by the U.S.S.R., that the PCF attacked de Gaulle's proposals. But on October 31, 1959, when Khrushchev, before the Supreme Soviet, described the proposals as a positive step, the PCF was forced to retract its initial criticism.[62]

With Algerian independence in July 1962, the six-year period of Soviet paralysis came to an end, to be replaced by a three-year period of overcommitment to the new regime of Ahmad Ben Bella. As the Algerian revolution entered its domestic phase, the Soviet Union, through its cooperation with the new regime, seemed to suggest that not only was Algeria proceeding down the capitalist path, but that a vanguard role, or for that matter any role, for the local communists was superfluous.

The PCA followed about the only strategy possible under the circumstances. It sought cooperation with the FLN but not integration; it sought, in short, to realize the old goal of a national front. In the summer of 1962, the PCA approved the Tripoli Charter, to all intents and purposes the manifesto of the FLN for independent Algeria, and refrained from taking sides in the near-civil war between the GPRA and the Oujda group rallied around Ben Bella and Boumedienne. The party began again to publish its two journals *Alger Républicain* and *Al-Houriya*. It announced its support of the Bureau Politique, which had deposed the GPRA by the end of August. Because it could not offer a slate of candidates of its own that would have much hope of victory, the PCA endorsed the FLN list for the fall elections to a constituent assembly. At the same time Bouhali warned that the communist support of the FLN was not unconditional and that the PCA would resist single-party hegemony.[63] On October 12 Ben Bella told Foreign Minister Gromyko that a socialist society was his ultimate objective, and on November 29 he banned the PCA (see p. 93). It was left to the PCF to protest the repression of the communists in independent Algeria.

Since the FLN would not reappraise the PCA, the PCA had to reappraise the FLN and the role of local communists in it. In other words, if the PCA could not play the role of vanguard party, then there was nothing for it but to designate the FLN as a vanguard party itself to which socialists could adhere in good conscience. Bachir Hadj Ali, with a little Marxist legerdemain, professed to discern in the decrees of March 1963, that placed under worker self-management much of Algeria's most valuable land and industry, the opening of the path to the socialist revolution. He went on to note that the FLN had ceased to be an association of all the classes and had become a true vanguard party. In short, the new situation (1964) dictated that all true socialists should unite in the vanguard party and should acknowledge the leadership of Ahmad Ben Bella.[64] The self-effacement of the PCA allowed the PCF to bring about its own reconciliation with the FLN. In a joint communiqué of October 19, 1964, signed by Waldek-Rochet (PCF) and Hocine Zahouane (FLN) the parties threw bouquets at each other without any mention of the PCA.[65] All this came at a time when relations between Algeria and the U.S.S.R. were at their most amicable. Ahmad Ben Bella had made a state visit to the Soviet Union in May 1964. He had occupied the place of honor at the May Day celebrations, and received the Order of Lenin, and had been proclaimed a Hero of the Soviet Union—surely the apotheosis of Mirskiism and the springtime of Khrushchev before the fall.[66]

Soviet observers had also begun to adjust their analysis of the Algerian revolution. R. Landa and Yu. Potemkin both saw in the Tripoli Program the document that launched Algeria on the noncapitalist path.[67] The March decrees for worker self-management furthered this trend. The organization of the self-management units was based on the Yugoslavian model that had in the past been condemned by the U.S.S.R. as anarcho-syndicalist. However, in the Algerian context the establishment of the units was enough, so it was argued, to launch the country into the first stages of socialist construction.[68]

Concomitant with this analysis was a new and somewhat startling reinterpretation of the role of the Algerian peasantry in the revolution. Until 1963, Russian, French, and Algerian communists denied the revolutionary character of the peasantry, thereby striking a blow for orthodox Marxism and against Frantz Fanon and Chairman Mao. Larbi Bouhali, in 1963, reacted to Ben Bella's statement that the peasantry was more revolutionary than the workers by protesting that that was to fly in the face of "historic truth."[69] But Landa and Potemkin, and a little later Bachir Hadj Ali, were already beginning to discern distinctly revolutionary characteristics among the Algerian peasantry. The salaried agricultural workers on the self-managed farms, the migrants to the cities, the peasants displaced during the revolution were all seen as constituting an emerging proletariat with great revolutionary potential.[70]

One of the reasons why Soviet and Algerian communists were eager to reconcile their analysis with the official FLN line was that Ben Bella had surrounded himself with a group of highly intelligent Marxists capable of sophisticated debate but hostile to the PCA and the PCF. These men—Mohammed Harbi, Hocine Zahouane, Mohammed Lebjaoui, Mustafa Lacheraf, Rheda Malik, Amar Ouzegane, and others—had framed the Tripoli Charter in 1962 as well as a successor document, the Charter of Algiers, in 1965. They were as likely to favor the Chinese or Yugoslavian model of revolution as the Russian, and thus could threaten the growing Soviet influence in Ben Bella's Algeria.[71] The question of their opposition became academic after June 1965, when Houari Boumedienne deposed Ben Bella and rounded up most communists and Marxists.

The downfall of Ben Bella forced everyone back to the drawing boards. Boumedienne combines a certain Islamic militancy with devotion to socialist principles in a way that is common among Middle Eastern politicians. His style and outlook are closer to Ouzegane than to Harbi, and one of his first tasks was to purge the Algerian revolution of scientific socialists. Inadvertantly, perhaps, Boumedienne forged some unity in the Marxist left by arresting Hocine Zahouane, Bachir Hadj Ali, and Mohammed Harbi and by driving Mohammed Lebjaoui into exile. The short-lived *modus vivendi* between the PCF and the FLN was shattered, and the PCF (along with the Italian Communist Party) has been consistently hostile toward the Boumedienne regime. A number of opposition groups, organized by Algerians, have sprung up in France since 1965. One group, the Parti de l'Avant-Garde Socialiste (PAGS), associated with Hadj Ali, Zahouane, and Harbi, has been officially endorsed (October 29, 1968) by the PCF.[72] Beyond this, the PCF was clearly sympathetic to the effort of Tahar Zbiri and the Abd al-Aziz Zerdani to reorient, if not overthrow, Boumedienne's government.

By 1967 Boumedienne appeared intent upon destroying the little remaining autonomy of the UGTA and student groups, as well as easing out of important posts the last guerilla commanders. He had thus evoked in the fall of 1967 a counter-coalition of the Marxist left, labor, students, and army officers, such as Tahar Zbiri, Said Abid, Salah Boubnider (Sawt al-Arab), and others. A confrontation developed when two men close to the labor movement, Zerdani and Abdennour Ali Yahya, were dismissed from their posts as minister of labor and minister of agriculture. On December 15, disgruntled army elements concerted with the labor leaders to organize an attempted putsch. A tank column, commanded by Zbiri's brother, advanced on Algiers, but was easily if brutally stopped by an air attack ordered by Boumedienne. Tahar Zbiri escaped and joined the opposition in Exile. Boumedienne has since then consolidated his control, and on November 13, 1968, was confident enough of his position to release from jail Hadj Ali, Zahouane, and Harbi. These men were forbidden, however, to take up residence in Algiers. It may be that this new-found tolerance toward the Marxist left will permit a rapprochement between the PCF and Boumedienne.

The Soviet Union had its hands tied in its reaction, or lack of reaction, to the overthrow of Ben Bella. A leader of great promise had suddenly and easily been removed from power, and yet there was no way that the U.S.S.R. could rebuke Boumedienne. This was so, at least in part, because the new regime announced its intentions to reschedule the Afro-Asian Conference for the fall of 1965. The U.S.S.R. wanted to ensure that it would be represented at the conference and knew full well that the Chinese would try to deny them representation. In fact, China immediately recognized the new regime, and on June 22 Chen Yi arrived in Algiers to consult with Boumedienne. On July 14 Kosygin sent fraternal greetings to Boumedienne, and by the end of the month the Kremlin had indicated that it would do business with him. It must have come as something of a relief to the Soviet Union that because of the opposition of several participant states, the Afro-Asian Conference was not held in the fall of 1965.

The U.S.S.R., as indicated above, oscillated between immobilism toward the FLN in the years 1956-62 and overcommitment to the Ben Bella regime in 1962-65. In the case of Boumedienne the Soviet Union has sought the happy medium of support without euphoria. This has meant a reversion to the earlier stage of non-coordination between the U.S.S.R. and the PCF (one hesitates to add the PCA, for there is no discernible organization that can be identified as such).

The repression of the left, and the hostile criticism of the PCF, have for the most part been overlooked in the Soviet approach to Algeria. Even Soviet analysts have sought a new balanced perspective on the revolution. In some ways Boumedienne left them no choice. After he had emphasized (and

attributed to Ben Bella) the disorganization of the self-managed sector of
the economy and the slipshod methods used in building the FLN for peace-
time purposes, it was a bit difficult for Soviet observers to talk with much
confidence about the construction of socialism and the vanguard party.
A.M. Goldobin reflects the new realism, although R. Landa is still stub-
bornly optimistic.[73]

All in all then, Soviet policy toward Algeria operates today within the
context of the following goals: to keep the revolution alive at minimal cost
with maximal pay-offs in terms of trade and facilities; keep Chinese influence at a minimum; acquiesce in the death of the PCA; allow the PCF to
carry the cudgels of the Algerian left; and, finally, encourage Pompidou to
continue the policies of his predecessor towards the EEC and NATO.

CONCLUSION:
AN ASSESSMENT OF NORTH AFRICA
AS A SOVIET BONUS AREA

In recent years, the rhetoric of the bipolar world of the 1950s has, for both
the United States and the Soviet Union, fallen gradually into disuse. Adding
units to the Free World or the Socialist Camp is no longer a basic and immediate objective for either power. Many of the advantages of empire can
be obtained without maintaining one, and many of its costs thereby avoid-
ed. In the more flexible approach to the LDCs of this decade the great
powers are willing to tolerate a great deal of "deviance" on what are defined
at any moment as nonessential matters as long as there is conformity on
what is seen to count. Both countries are prepared to treat with any regime
that resists the military and trade influence of the other major power and
that adopts favorable stances on crucial international issues. One important
result of this trend is that the whole notion of camps and what unit belongs
in which, becomes very fuzzy. If it is difficult to determine the alignment of a
given state, it will also be difficult to establish whether or not either great
power has lost or gained influence as a result of some internal regime change
or policy reorientation in that state.[74]

If we conceive of a continuum ranging from total alignment at one pole to
effective neutrality at the other, most of us would agree that the four North
African states lie closer to the middle than to either pole. This has not
always been so. Before the *coup d'état* in Libya, that country was virtually a
client of the United States. It is for this reason that any change in regime
there, and certainly the one that actually occurred, could only have been interpreted as a blow to the American position in the Mediterranean. The
United States may wish to avoid in the future (if it is even given the chance)
By 1967 Boumedienne appeared intent upon destroying the little remain-
the kind of overcommitment represented by military bases and massive

private investments. The Soviet Union has been more subtle in expanding its military and economic influence in North Africa, but Algeria under Ben Bella had moved toward the polar position of alignment with the U.S.S.R., and his downfall was, whatever else it might have been, a major setback for the Soviet Union.

Both powers are now in a position to be fairly flexible in their policies toward all four countries. The collapse of any given regime can be viewed with *relative* equanimity for none of the regimes is claimed by the United States or by the Soviet Union as its own. The gradual replacement of the zero-sum perceptions of the bipolar world by the variable-sum game of today means that both powers (as well as others such as France and China) can simultaneously extend their influence into any one or all of the North African states.

Initially, it may always appear that the Soviet Union is gaining influence at the expense of the West, but this is because the Soviet Union had so little influence in the region to begin with. Conversely, the U.S.S.R. can take greater policy risks for it has less to lose. However, except in foreign trade, where the Soviet Union plays a minor role, a rough parity of influence in North Africa seems to be developing between the Soviet Union and the West, a situation that will tend to sustain the already cautious Soviet approach to the region. No matter how great Soviet influence may become in North Africa, policymakers will continue to treat the area as a bonus region. The area contains no states that impinge upon Soviet borders (such as Afghanistan) nor any communist regimes that do not (such as Cuba). As a result, the U.S.S.R. will undertake no binding commitments to any regime in the area.

The Soviet Union wishes to offer the North African states an alternative to the West; and to the extent that individual regimes opt for the alternative, Western influence will be weakened. This is the primary objective, and it has been well served through the phasing out of Western military bases and installations. Less successful has been the effort to offer new markets to North African states with the aim of impeding their progress toward association with the EEC. Beyond the policies of pre-emption, however, the U.S.S.R. has sought immediate payoffs in the form of port facilities, markets for its own goods, and congenial foreign policy stances. On these matters the Soviet Union has enjoyed a reasonable measure of success.

The ultimate objective, or ultimate rationalization, of Soviet foreign policy is to hasten and shape the process of systems conversion. It is believed that economic development will stimulate the revolution in the states already on the non-capitalist path and will bring about a revolutionary situation in states functioning within the capitalist mode of production. And, in the Soviet view, a coincidence of short-term strategic interests and long-term ideological goals is likely to be found somewhere within these terms. Many Western analysts, on the other hand, seem to believe that time and development will tell in favor of capitalism and liberal democracy. While such beliefs may be unjustified on both sides, they do help minimize the tendency to view each conflict situation as bearing the seeds of an apocalyptic showdown between the two systems. They also promote flexible, accommodationist policies that satisfy immediate strategic objectives and that may thereby spare areas such as North Africa from becoming the setting for confrontation between the great powers.

— 6 —
The Soviet Union and Egypt:
The Nasser Years

P. J. Vatikiotis

Even under the best of circumstances there are difficulties in dealing with Soviet policy in the Middle East.* But in my discussion of the Soviet Union and Egypt, rather than embarking on a tedious account of Arab-Soviet and, particularly, Egyptian-Soviet relations, I propose to limit my discussion of the subject to the examination of several controversial views on the Soviet Union and Egypt.

Perhaps the first question calling for some sort of answer is, What circumstances, or what combination of circumstances, brought the Soviet Union to its present position in the Arab Middle East generally, and in Egypt particularly? Equally relevant is the question how and why some of the Arab states, primarily Egypt, find themselves in a close relationship—at least on the surface—with the Soviet Union.

In considering these questions, we may argue about whether there is such a thing as a Soviet "Arab" or a Soviet "Egyptian policy"; about whether there can be one: and if not, why not?

I suspect most of us have been talking more these days about Egypt and the Soviet Union mainly because of the Arab-Israeli conflict, particularly the Six Day War in June 1967. For some of us the fact of the presence of a sizable, if not formidable, Soviet Mediterranean fleet has been pushed home with greater force. Still for others the recent apparent entrenchment of the Soviet Union economically, diplomatically, technically—and militarily—in Egypt came at a time when Great Britain was about to retreat from and relinquish its last military foothold in the Arab Middle East—as announced by its plan to withdraw from the Gulf by 1971. Many argue that the timing was too close for comfort, when the Soviet Union was also making marked

*This essay was written expressly for the Conference on Russia and the Middle East held at Stanford University on November 6-9, 1969. As I feel that my assessment and depiction of the Egyptian-Soviet relationship are realistic for that period, I have not tried to update it in the light of events and developments since that time.

inroads in the "buffer states" of the Middle Eastern periphery, namely, Afghanistan, Pakistan, Iran, and Turkey—the last three still members of the CENTO sub-system of the Western global defense system devised in the mid-fifties, not to speak of Iraq. It began to look, they went on to argue, as if the Russians were reviving the North-South strategy of the Mongols. Yet none of these countries is as crucial to Soviet strategic calculations for a growing Mediterranean, southern European, North African, and Central and East African role as Egypt.

It seems apparent, however, that the June 1967 Arab-Israeli war emphasized the difficulties a great power faces with its involvement in an area that generates as much conflict as the Middle East. There are those who have followed the Soviet-Egyptian relationship with fascination and anxious anticipation, because they hope and expect that the senior partner will eventually suffer the same feeling of dénouement over the precocity or naughtiness of its client as experienced by other powers before it. Finally, there is that brand of lachrymose breast-beaters, the "Glubbites," who see every conflict in the Middle East in which Egypt is involved as part of a huge Soviet conspiracy. Thus General Glubb's five-shilling tract, published two weeks after the June 1967 war, went into two or three printings immediately.

One closely related aspect of the subject that I hardly feel qualified to discuss is the relationship between Soviet ideology and foreign policy. But I understand from writers on the Soviet Union that after Tito's challenge in 1948 of the Stalinist view of a sharply dichotomized, polarized world, the Soviets in 1953-54 no longer considered war between the two major power blocs as imminent. I understand from them also that the bipolar view of the political world was officially abandoned after the Twentieth Party Congress.

The new, post-1953 Soviet view meant, first, that the Soviets themselves were no longer adamant about a Russian-dominated authority structure directing international communism—if there ever was one: second, that they accepted the existence another world interposed, so to speak, between the two major blocs—a "Third World." They assumed also that much of the rivalry between the two blocs, led by the two superpowers, would be over that Third World.

In the practical terms of policy, this shift in ideology meant first, an attempt to render the Third World friendly—preferably allied or tied—to the U.S.S.R.; and second, the decision to dismantle, to remove or to neutralize any anti-Soviet arrangements in it. In short, the strategy of global conflict was partially shifted from an East-West one in Europe to a North-South one in Asia and Africa.

All anti-colonialist, anti-imperialist movements in these two continents presented immense possibilities for Soviet diplomacy. The fact that these movements in the mid-fifties were led by local (and, in Soviet terminology, bourgeois) nationalists who were more often than not violently opposed to local and international communism was to be overlooked by Soviet diplomacy. Orthodox ideological considerations were dispensable in the face of the potential advantages to Soviet state-national interest which this assessment and projection offered.

In the Middle East at that time Western powers, such as Britain in Iraq, South Arabia, and the Gulf; France in North Africa; and the United States with its oil investments and operations in the Peninsula, were all respectable targets for Soviet policy to undermine. A local power, such as Egypt, most vehemently opposed to these positions of Western power and interest, was emerging at the time. The easiest and most sensible policy for the U.S.S.R. was therefore the undogmatic support of this new radical nationalist regime, as well as others like it in the area. After all, CENTO and the bilateral relations of its respective members with the Soviet Union in 1954-55 were not very good. What better way, then, to render the buffer zone between Russia and the core Middle East ineffective, meaningless? In fact, it could be argued that the entry of the Soviet Union in September 1955 into the Arab Middle East was partly responsible for the revised policies of CENTO member countries toward it, and the gradual establishment of closer bilateral relations with it.

The sovietization of the Middle East, or the installation of a communist regime in Cairo, can for the moment be discounted as an objective of Russian policy. That the Soviet Union achieved a near economic and diplomatic hegemony over Egypt, however, is a credible proposition. While it did not completely neutralize Egypt in the sense of having rendered the country inaccessible to Western diplomacy and trade, the U.S.S.R. nevertheless did succeed in getting a near monopoly of economic and military aid. It managed also to re-orient the Egyptian trade pattern toward the Eastern bloc (about 65 percent). The West, in other words, was effectively kept at bay in Egypt. Last but most relevant to Soviet interests and wider strategy, all of these advantages converged on the acceptance by Nasser in the summer of 1968 of a Soviet naval-military presence (in whatever guise) in his country.

Before I make any remarks about Egypt's relationship with the Soviet Union, I should like to refer briefly to certain indigenous, deep-seated characteristics of the Arab Middle East that generate a great deal of conflict. It is fair to say that domestically there is hardly an Arab state, including Egypt, that is not weak, or at least that does not face serious—almost insoluble—social, economic, and political problems.

In the Fertile Crescent, for instance, one could hardly gloss over the terribly low level of national integration, which acts as an obstacle to any meaningful societal cohesiveness or solidarity, and vice versa. Abstract ideological attempts at cohesiveness remain superficial. Iraq and Syria in particular continue to be plagued in the final analysis by sectarian, ethnic, and communal divisions. In a different degree and at another level, Jordan and Lebanon face parallel problems. An added difficulty—indeed, danger —there is that of the Palestine Liberation Movement. Egypt, however, faces different yet equally enormous problems, such as overpopulation and economic and political uncertainty. Moreover, all of these countries are directly affected by the ongoing Arab-Israeli conflict.

In the case of Egypt, its so-called neutralist policy of earlier years (1955-58) was predicated upon the ability to steer a balanced course between the two superpowers in the Cold War. That is, Egypt could benefit from this interposition only so long as both superpowers were directly involved in supplying it with aid. The retreat or disengagement of one or the other endangered Egypt's "independent" course.

* * * * * * *

The antecedents of Egypt's present relations with the Soviet Union are meager. In 1943, during the Second World War the U.S.S.R. and Egypt established diplomatic relations on the legation level. One might say that this development was within the stream of the wartime alliance against the Axis powers. By 1945-46, local communist party factions appeared more active than ever before; but they faced two serious disabilities. One was the fact that their leadership and much of their membership consisted of foreign residents. The other was the determination of the Ismail Sidqi government to suppress them, a policy continued by the Nuqrashi government in 1947-48, that of Ibrahim Abdul Hadi in 1949 and, to some extent, the last Wafd government in 1950-51.

Meantime, the relations of Egypt with Britain were deteriorating so rapidly during the period 1946-51 in the face of the intractable problem of the 1936 Anglo-Egyptian Treaty that both the Nuqrashi government in 1947 and the Wafd government in 1951 considered a neutralist course in the United Nations. In fact, this elementary neutralism included the possible strengthening of Egyptian relations with the Soviet Union as a makeweight to the relationship with Britain. To this extent Nasser's neutralist policy of the years 1955-58 is not altogether original or surprising. No ideological considerations were involved in either instance.

Why, then, did Egypt appear to need a closer, firmer relationship with the Soviet Union after 1954? There were, it seems, domestic and external reasons for this. The external factors came to bear on the situation long before any domestic policy considerations.

After the Anglo-Egyptian agreement in October 1954, Western efforts to produce alternative regional defense arrangements culminated in the Baghdad Pact. It was not so much Egyptian apprehension of a Hashemite Iraqi domination in the Fertile Crescent and thus the isolation of Egypt from the Arab East that annoyed Nasser and caused him to embark upon an extreme anti-Western policy so soon after the resolution of the long-standing Anglo-Egyptian problem. Rather, it was the unfortunate timing of the new defense pact. This came at a time in the winter of 1954-55 when the Egyptian Free Officer regime was emerging from an abrasive, dangerous internal power struggle; when the virtual severance of the relationship with Britain created a climate of uncertainty and insecurity; when the Israelis were applying a policy of massive retaliation against Jordan and Egypt in response to Palestinian irregular guerrilla infiltrations on the border. The original though eventually indirect involvement of the United States in the negotiations for the Baghdad Pact further compounded Egypt's feeling of uncertainty over security matters, specifically with regard to arms supplies. After all, in a period of precarious domestic conditions, the regime's major constituency and power base—the army—had to be given a feeling of well-being and protection.

The matter of Western arrangements for Middle Eastern defense and greater Egyptian exposure to the vagaries of the Arab-Israeli conflict, that is, converged at a time when Egyptian rulers assumed that they had finally attained the desired measure of national independence. It was not really, as many assume, Arab nationalism or Egypt's new deliberate Arab leadership policy that was crucial in the shift to an Eastern orientation. That came later. To put it differently, Egypt, to be sure, badly needed arms after the punitive Israeli raid on Gaza in February 1955; but it needed them even more to strengthen the domestic power base of the regime. Thus, all three dimensions of the relationship of any Arab state, and particularly Egypt, with a foreign power were involved in the eventual Arms Agreement with the Soviet bloc in September 1955: the domestic, the inter-Arab, and the Arab-Israeli.

Yet this first serious penetration of the U.S.S.R. into Egypt in September 1955 was confined to the supply of arms. True, it did bring Egypt on a limited scale into the Soviet pattern of barter trade, but the offer of extensive economic, technical, and other aid to Egypt did not occur until two to three years later. Nor did the Arms Agreement imply or indicate that the Nasser regime had irrevocably committed itself to a pro-Soviet orientation equal in intensity and determination to its anti-Western one. Sincerely, though ignorantly and perhaps stupidly, Nasser continued to justify his new relationship with the Soviet Union (the diplomatic representation between the two countries had been raised to embassy level in March 1954) on the basis of the overriding national goal of independence, i.e., a release from total dependence on the West for the supply of arms.

Between the spring of 1955 and the autumn of 1956, or between Bandung and Suez, two new factors or variables entered the Egyptian political experience; on the one hand, neutralism and the country's promising—so it seemed—possibilities in Asia and Africa (as well as its advantages in

further combating the Western position in the Middle East); and on the
other, the attractive features of a radical Ba'ath-led Arab nationalist movement in the Fertile Crescent, mainly in Syria and Jordan. These ushered in
—perhaps facilely motivated—a new activist Egyptian policy in the Arab
region and Africa. Needless to say both policies ended in failure, in Africa
by 1963 and in the Arab region in 1965-67. But they conveniently facilitated
further Soviet penetration into Egypt to the extent that there is now no comparison between the nature of Egyptian-Soviet relations in the period 1955-
57 and 1964-67 or 1967-69.

It was really the Suez War in 1956 that created both the conditions of
urgent economic need and a popular efficacious myth for the promotion of
closer relations between Egypt and the Soviet Union. The nationalization
of the Suez Canal Company in July 1956 came upon the heels of the Western
rejection of Egypt's request for massive financial assistance to construct the
High Dam at Aswan. It was not so much the alternative Soviet offer to
finance the dam's construction that prompted Egypt's greater orientation
toward the East, for the agreement to do so was not negotiated until
January-October 1958. Rather Egypt's immediate economic difficulties in
1956-57 played a more crucial role in the matter.

Egyptian assets in Britain, France, and the United States had been
blocked in 1956. Hard foreign currency was almost impossible to obtain.
The Soviet Union provided Egypt with badly needed wheat and, together
with Rumania, supplied it with petroleum and fertilizers. Besides the
economic effect, the psychological-political impact of such immediate
assistance was great. For it also came at a time when the myth that Russia
had saved Egypt from the worse effects of the so-called tripartite agression
in 1956 was already widespread among Egyptians and Arabs in general.
Eventually, it became a potent enough myth to inspire complacency and folly in Egyptians, and was to cost them dearly ten years later.

This assistance (for many Egyptians, indeed deliverance) also came at a
time when Arab and, generally Afro-Asian, sympathy for Egypt's plight in
1956 was vociferous and apparently unanimous. Nasser accelerated his so-
called Arab policy in Syria and Jordan, and inaugurated a very active
African policy. His bid for a form of leadership of the so-called Third World
was manifested in the inauguration of the Afro-Asian People's Solidarity
conferences in December 1957, and the launching of "Voice of Free Africa"
broadcasts from Cairo, as well as an active Islamic propaganda campaign.

All of this must have presented attractive opportunities for Soviet policy
in the Middle East. At the end of 1956, the West appeared really at bay in
the area. The Suez campaign not only had failed, but it had also left the major Western allies divided. Attractive new forces were, moreover, emerging
in Syria and Jordan (e.g., the Ba'ath), the British were leaving Jordan in
mid-1957, and a serious crisis was building up in the Lebanon.

Meantime, the Nasser regime had launched its first major, sweeping nationalization program. Economic planning had just become a major state activity, and widespread discussion and consideration of so-called socialist measures were taking place.

In these circumstances, it looked as if Egypt had no choice but to look more and more to the Soviet Union for the promotion and implementation of both its domestic and its external policies. Thus, the question of arms was being faced again so soon after 1954-55. The 1956 Sinai war had wiped out most of the Soviet military assistance received a year earlier.

So far though (i.e., the period 1955-58), Nasser's greater dependence on the Soviet Union did not rob him of his much-vaunted flexibility in steering a relatively independent course in foreign affairs. His closer relationship to Moscow, that is, at this time, was still very much a function or a reflection of what appeared on the surface a temporary break with the West. The public was comforted with the facile argument that, unlike Western aid, Soviet economic and military assistance was *li-wajh illah*—manna from heaven — without strings. Massive, long-term credits at 2.5 percent interest sounded to the uninitiated so attractive as to be tantamount to charity. Except for the rulers, few Egyptians were aware of the more intricate—tricky—aspects of these loans, or of the ways in which these overtaxed Egypt's meager economic resources and limited capacity. Thus by 1958 the Soviet Union was extending to Egypt massive economic aid directly related to the regime's most important (and prestigious) single project—the Aswan Dam. This had a glamour all to itself, related as it was to the "revolution's" modernization goal via industrialization. Soviet military aid had also by that time been extended to the construction of fortifications and to the training of Egyptian officers and other personnel both in Egypt and the Soviet Union.

Yet Nasser could counter any charges of growing political dependence on the Soviet Union with his apparent success in the arena of Arab nationalist policy (e.g., the union with Syria, the overthrow of the Hashemites in Iraq and, temporarily, the civil war in the Lebanon—all in 1958). He could point to the fact that communist and other extreme leftist elements in the country were in no way serious contending forces; that the new cultural propaganda of the Soviet Union was neither encouraged by, nor was it eliciting any enthusiastic response from, Egyptians. In short, Nasser could take the position that he had successfully countered Western encroachments, had pursued radical Arab nationalist policies, and had secured economic and military aid from the Soviet bloc without compromising Egypt's independence or its nationalist revolutionary goals.

An occasion to prove his position presented itself in the deteriorating relations with Qasim's Iraq in the winter and spring of 1959. The Egyptian-supported, abortive Shawwaf uprising in Mosul in March led to a cooling of relations with the Soviet Union. Nasser argued that Qasim was being supported by local communists and, by implication, by the Soviet Union. At the same time, he clamped down on his communists in Egypt and Syria.

Significantly though, the developments of that year also enabled Nasser to restore a certain balance in his relations with East and West. During the period 1959-64 Egypt achieved a veritable bonanza in the area of economic aid from both East and West. While in the years 1961-64 the United States provided the country with surplus food (mainly wheat) amounting to $700 million payable in local currency, and other loans amounting to $500 million, the Soviet Union poured in another million dollars, mainly in military and technical assistance.

By 1962, however (when Nasser's radical Arab nationalist policy was in retreat), other developments had intervened that marked a distinction between Western and Eastern aid. Far-reaching "socialist" measures had been taken in 1961-62, and further ones in 1963-64. Greater emphasis was being placed on accelerated industrialization, on agrarian and rural cooperative reconstruction, and on nationwide political mobilization programs. The first stages in the construction of the Aswan Dam were complete in mid-1964. A more relaxed, benevolent state policy toward local communist and leftist elements occasioned by Khrushchev's visit to Egypt that year was balanced by the methodical repression of the extreme right, specifically the Ikhwan, the Muslim Brethren (in 1964-65).

Meantime the war in the Yemen from September 1962 onward was costing Egypt about 50 million pounds a year. In less than four years the country had accumulated a military debt with the U.S.S.R. of over 150 million pounds exclusively over the Yemen operation. Deferred payments and greater arms costs further compounded this indebtedness, until food assistance from the West became essential to feed the masses. Then, despite improved relations with West Germany that produced more economic, industrial, technical, and military aid, by 1966 Egypt had come to play an important role in Soviet trade. Moreover, in terms of economic and military aid, by the late 1960s it ranked first among countries receiving Soviet aid.

On the whole, it looked as if the regime had concluded during the period 1960-65 that the country's new national, socialist programs for development depended for their success largely on an ever closer relationship with the Soviet Union. Given the Yemen war (including American pressure on Egypt to end it), the country's relations with other Arab states, and the revived Palestine Question in 1964-65, it looked as if Egyptians had concluded also that the U.S.S.R. constituted a genuine friend in time of need. After all, in that year, the presumed new friend in the West, that is, West Germany, recognized Israel and thus forced Egypt to break relations with her. Also in those five or six years, relations with Britain, following the first financial agreements after Suez in 1959, steadily improved. Similarly, relations with France improved steadily after the end of the Algerian war in 1962. Nasser and his lieutenants may very easily have felt a certain euphoria over their renewed ability to play successfully the game of the third party in the Cold War. Unfortunately, both the nature of the Cold War and the pattern of inter-Arab and regional politics were entering a slightly different phase.

Events in South Arabia (the upheaval in Aden and the stalemated Yemen war), the rise to power of a radical Ba'ath regime in Syria in February 1966, and the growing activities of the Palestine guerrillas from Jordan and Syria against Israel all combine to produce critical conditions in the Arab East. For a start, these developments elicited a renewed and more vigorous Israeli policy of military retaliation. Although active Egyptian military commitment in the Yemen and political involvement in Aden offered the Soviets perhaps an alternative though indirect potential in these areas once Britain had withdrawn, the returns for Egypt were nearly disastrous. In effect, it lost both the Yemen war and the political game in South Arabia. In the process, it lost also the foreign policy lever it had recaptured in the period 1961-65, namely, American aid.

More significantly, these developments reflected clearly Egypt's tarnished image and reduced role as the leader of the radical Arab nationalist movement. The post-February 1966 Syrian regime was bitterly anti-Egyptian. The Iraqis were cultivating a partial return to a semblance of civilian rule and grappling with their own civil war. Hussein's Jordan was, for a change, experiencing some economic prosperity and, perhaps superficially, political stability. The so-called conservative monarchies of Saudi Arabia and Kuwait were in a position to gloat over the humiliation of the overextended Egyptians. In general, the Nasser-led Arab radical movement was not simply in retreat, but its very chief was abjectly mending his fences with his erstwhile enemies, the arch-reactionary Arab rulers. The common enemy of all Arabs, Israel, was punishing the Palestinians (the so-called conscience of the Arabs) with impunity, with its retaliatory strikes on the West Bank region of Jordan in the bargain. Egypt was faced with a situation in which both its prestige and its credibility among the Arabs had reached an all-time low, especially in connection with the Arab-Israeli conflict. It had just burnt its bridges where the United States was concerned. Inevitably it had to lean even more heavily on the Soviet Union. Locally, it was forced to accept a realignment of forces with the extremist Syrian regime—with disastrous consequences.

The Middle East crisis of 1966-67 coincided with a concerted effort in Egypt to improve the economic condition of the country, and even to rationalize the administration of expanded state services. The Yemen war was being phased out, thus permitting even greater possibilities of development at home. A certain revulsion on the part of Egyptians against adventurous schemes was visible. But the Six-Day War in June 1967 that may have put paid to any aggressive Egyptian policies at home and abroad created not only a heavier dependence on the Soviet Union but changed fundamentally the very nature of the relationship between the two countries.

Whether it was 3,000 or 10,000 Soviet military advisers who were stationed in Egypt; whether the U.S.S.R. had replaced Egyptian arms and equipment lost in the June 1967 war without charge, the fact remains that, in the absence of that balancing alternative—some relationship with the United States — Egypt was more of a Soviet client state and less of an independent, neutralist sampler of aid. The question raised by many students, Was the Egyptian-Soviet relationship tantamount to an alliance? is an academic one. There was no formal alliance, of course. On the other hand, as early as 1964, but clearly after July 1968, without saying as much, Nasser had no alternative but to permit a peculiar type of Soviet military presence in his country, but nonetheless a military presence. Storage and maintenance facilities for the Soviet navy, the use of air bases generally and even for operational missions in the Mediterranean, and some say in the further training, equipment, and administration of the Egyptian armed forces, do not amount to what the Italians would describe as a slap in the Soviet eye! Basically this fundamental change in the Soviet-Egyptian relationship came about because Egypt simply could not pay for Soviet military and economic aid after June 1967.

The consequences of this nearly total military and economic dependence on the U.S.S.R. for the domestic development program in Egypt are too serious and, in the long run, too dangerous to be lightly glossed over. Nasser apparently had to assign top priority to two concerns: the training, arming, and equipping of his armed forces; and the feeding of his population that was increasing at 3 percent per annum. All other schemes and projects of development had to take second place.

Despite the fact that Egyptians had been disappointed in the Soviet Union as the vaunted "shield of progressive Arabs," the fact remains that Nasser came to rule alone and almost absolutely. His credibility had been eroded after June 1967, while the public was feeling ever more insecure and yet resigned to the uncertainties of its situation. Tension and resentment of the Russians were only a function of the country's dependence on them. The reality of a regime, a ruler who to some extent retained power on the basis of his total reliance on a superpower was not hidden from most Egyptians. To this extent Nasser had become more transitional than ever. Then, because of its economic, financial, and military needs, Egypt had once again become truly a client state. The question was or is, Can Egypt ever be any other kind of state?

But what of the Russians? In their growing close relationship with Egypt they invested over a billion dollars. They sustained the Egyptians with alacrity and apparent magnanimity, even after Cairo stumbled into gross blunders. Within Egypt itself their ideas, their economic and political style, even their social ethos were hardly accepted or emulated; in fact, educated Egyptians of the Left or Right showed a consistent, tenacious preference for what I might arrogantly call Western ideas, style of life, even an emulated social ethos. In short, what did the U.S.S.R. achieve or gain by this relationship?

That the Russians considered Nasser, during the 1955-68 period, as the most successful energizer of an anti-Western "radical" Arab movement is clear. While also supporting such regimes as those in Syria since 1957, and Iraq intermittently since 1959, they clearly preferred the relatively more stable, forceful, and charismatic Nasser, whose country had the further advantage of straddling Africa and the Arab Middle East. Furthermore, Egypt presented the best or optimum conditions and communications facilities required by Soviet naval-military, political, and diplomatic strategy in the Middle East after 1956.

It would be foolish to argue that after 1967 the Soviets still considered Nasser or the Egyptians as essential for a so-called radical Arab nationalist movement. After all, with the exception of the Peninsula and the Gulf, the West has clearly disengaged. Then, the kind of conflict that may arise in the Peninsula and the Gulf in the seventies will probably involve non-Arab states (Iran definitely; Turkey probably) toward which the Soviets have been evolving a definite policy. In fact, except for its nuisance, conflict-generating value, the Russians do not particularly care about the radical Arab nationalist movement. They may even be more interested at this stage in the kind of regional stability that facilitates the further strengthening of their newly acquired diplomatic, economic, and strategic position.

It could easily be argued, therefore, that the Soviets throughout the sixties considered Egypt, whether under Nasser or his successor, the essential center of their hoped-for power position in the Mediterranean. This, in turn, is linked to their emerging global naval strategy that encompasses the Indian Ocean. It gives them not only a deterrent against the U.S. Sixth Fleet, but affords them also several potential political advantages, apart from the Middle East, in southern and western Europe and Africa.

The Egyptians presently, especially since 1967, have argued that if only the Americans would behave better (i.e., abandon the Israelis), Egyptian foreign policy would automatically return to its normal, or even middle course, between the two superpowers. One wonders though how easy it would be for any Egyptian government to effect a drastic disengagement from this unequal, dependent relationship with the Soviet Union.

To assert that from 1955 until 1967 the Soviet Union comfortably pursued a negative political and diplomatic policy in Egypt is to state the obvious. This consisted simply of exploiting Egyptian apprehension over Western-sponsored regional defense pacts, Nasser's ill-considered radical

Arab policy directed against both the West and Israel, and his domestic development schemes. What is not clear yet is what positive policy, if any, the Russians have or contemplate in Egypt and the Arab Middle East, apart from what I have already suggested. They may find such a task just as difficult as did other states that preceded them in the position of patron powers of Egypt. The Russians, of course, may have learnt that this relationship does not, cannot perhaps, necessarily produce an Egypt modeled after the Soviet Union. This condition is unimportant, however, and absolutely not of the essence when one considers the type of regimes Egypt has had in the past. It is also surely a lesser consideration in the policy calculations of the Russians. They have also learnt that certain regimes and states in the Middle East (in fact, most of them) are not viable without a relationship—a client relationship at that—to a Big Power. If that is imperialism which is accompanied by conflict and yet a measure of development, some Middle Easterners may prefer it to no imperialism, possible peace, and certain stagnation.

Most, if not all, of the Arab states as presently constituted will continue to require arms and economic, financial, and technical assistance not only for so-called rapid development, but also, perhaps more importantly, in order to change occasionally the status quo both within their own boundaries and in those of their neighbors. Domestically, they need arms absolutely (perhaps not in great quantities) for the coercion so essential in their retention of power. Thus, some Arab states, chief among them Egypt, for purposes of their own, quite unrelated to those of the Soviet Union (except for a fortuitous convergence of the common interest to undermine and remove Western influence in the area) accepted first massive military then economic aid from the U.S.S.R. Such assistance has been eminently useful—perhaps profitable—to Egypt so long as it was used to buttress its policy within an inter-Arab, inter-African context (Syria, Yemen, South Arabia, Solidarity Conferences, etc.). But how useful or profitable has it been since June 1967?

It would be inaccurate to explain or justify Egypt's relationship to the U.S.S.R. during the past decade by its relevance to the 1952 revolution or its ideology. The two are not related. Rightly or wrongly, this relationship evolved from a policy based on the national-state interest of Egypt as viewed by Nasser and his regime. It was deemed essential in three areas of state endeavor: internal or domestic development, Arab policy, and in order to meet the problems engendered by any relationship (confrontation of otherwise) with the West, not to mention Israel.

It would indeed be ironic if during the seventies or eighties the United States or some Western power combination were to emerge in the eyes of Egyptians as the liberator of some Arabs—especially the Egyptians—from a new imperialism, a new "Cromerism." Within the context of this hypothetical projection, the Soviet presence in Egypt and/or the Middle

East seemed as stable or as guaranteed as that of Britain was earlier in this century. It would have been foolish of anyone, however, to assess with any measure of accuracy the kinds of risks the Soviets might have been prepared to take in order to retain, to strengthen, and to defend their new position and role in the area which, to a great extent, derived from their relationship with Egypt. It would have been equally foolish of anyone to assert that Egyptians were particularly happy with or about this relationship.

— 7 —
The Soviet Union In Lebanon Syria, and Jordan

The year 1955 marks a watershed in the development of Soviet policy in the Arab world, if not a new departure in Soviet interest and policy in the Middle East. As Louis Fischer pointed out some forty years ago, the Bolshevik Revolution did not alter the geography of southern Russia. Whatever the new dynamism, there are continuities in Imperial Russian and Soviet policy and interest in the Middle East, or in the changes in direction and ideology.[1] While the antecedents in Russian and Soviet policy reach far back through the centuries, it may be well to recall briefly the more immediate past of World War II, when the Soviet government sketched out some basic considerations and guidelines for policy in the Middle East. The policy set forth in the Hitler-Ribbentrop-Molotov discussions during November 12-13, 1940, clearly encompassed much of the Arab world.[2] During the course of these negotiations the Soviet government, as a price for possible entry into the Axis, demanded a new regime of the Turkish Straits, with land, naval, and air bases in that area, and declared that the center of gravity of Soviet interest lay south of Baku and Batum, in the general direction of the Persian Gulf. The Soviet position did not change with the end of World War II. On the contrary, Soviet ambitions were pressed at all points along the Northern Tier of the Middle East; and during 1945-46 demands for a trusteeship over Libya and for a commercial (naval) base in the Dodecanese Islands were added. Indeed, it was the development of the Soviet position at the time, along with the Palestine problem, that brought the United States, in an enduring politico-strategic sense, into the Middle East and inaugurated the Soviet-American rivalry in that troubled area.

The Soviet Union had entered into diplomatic relations with Lebanon and Syria in 1944, at substantially the same time that the United States took such action, with the designation of a diplomatic agent in Beirut. By the end of 1944 the United States became the first of the great powers to grant unconditional recognition to Lebanon and Syria.[3] But neither at that time nor when World War II came to a victorious conclusion did the Soviet Union have an overriding interest either in Lebanon or in Syria. Not until late in

1963 did Moscow enter into relations with the Hashemite Kingdom of Jordan. During the immediate postwar era of 1945-46, after all, Soviet attention was riveted more firmly in other directions, particularly on Greece, Turkey, and Iran, with an eye to possible action farther south and west, as the Truman administration suspected.[4] There was, to be sure, an acute awareness of the Arab character of the area in general, and some interest in the Palestine problem. It is refreshing to read, however, in the light of all that has happened since, that in the winter and spring of 1945-46 the Syrian government appealed to the United States, not to the U.S.S.R., for assistance in training its gendarmerie and armed services. The Syrian request was acutely embarrassing to the French government, which, only very reluctantly, was giving up its tutelage over Lebanon and Syria.[5]

When in February 1946 the Lebanese and Syrian governments brought the problem of the continued presence of Anglo-French troops in Lebanon and Syria to the attention of the U.N. Security Council, in one of the very first cases to come before that body, the U.S.S.R. vetoed a draft resolution on the ground that it did not go far enough in indicting Great Britain and France.[6] Although the forces were, in fact, withdrawn in 1946, the Soviet Union, whatever the ambiguities of its position, was evidently seeking to establish its *bona fides* in support of Middle Eastern national movements, and of the independence of Lebanon and Syria in particular. When the United States, on January 31, 1949, extended *de jure* recognition to the Hashemite Kingdom of Jordan, the Soviet Union did not bother to follow suit. Nor did it support the Jordanian application for membership in the United Nations until the log jam on membership was broken in 1955.

THE DEVELOPMENT OF SOVIET POLICY AND INTEREST

With its concentration along the Northern Tier in the immediate postwar period, the Palestine issue aside, the U.S.S.R. showed little apparent interest in the Arab East as such. It was very skeptical of the establishment of the League of Arab States on March 22, 1945, and of its early development. While Moscow seemed to have little choice among the various Arab states, it appeared to show a preference for Syria, partly because of its strategic location for outflanking Turkey and Iraq and for penetration southward, and partly because the Syrian Communist Party and its apparatus of front organizations in the cultural and trade union fields had established some strength. There was, of course, no preference for Syrian governments down to 1954, all of which were accused of persecuting "communist" and other "democratic" or "progressive" groups in the country. Husni al-Za'im, for example, was accused of being both an American and a French puppet, while Sami al-Hinnawi, who overthrew him in 1949, was characterized as a

British tool. Adib al-Shishakli, who followed, was cast in an unfavorable light after he was overthrown in 1954, when a parliamentary structure was reestablished in Damascus.

Within three years the Syrian Communist Party, under the leadership of Khalid Bakdash, a Kurd, who was elected to parliament in 1954, emerged as probably the strongest of the Arab communist parties. The professed primary aim of the Communist Party was to establish a national popular front, which came into being for a brief period in 1956. Bakdash proclaimed that the party was "Arab Nationalist" and would remain that in ideology and purpose above all else. Before 1958, too, the Syrian Communist Party publicly refrained from anti-religious activity and even tried to win over to its various front organizations unsuspecting religious dignitaries.

Soviet sympathies, naturally, were with the Syrian Communist Party, although Soviet influence was not confined to the communist element. Other political groups were regarded as rivals of the communists, although Moscow considered the so-called National Party of Sabri al-Asali with some favor, while distrusting the Arab Ba'ath Socialist Party, which was condemned as "fascist." Both these parties were regarded as representing essentially the national bourgeois elements and landowners, while favoring independence and opposing Western imperialism. On the other hand, the People's Party, the largest down to 1955, was considered to represent "monopoly capitalism" and as deficient in patriotism and, therefore, undesirable from the Soviet viewpoint.[7]

In view of Lebanon's strong commercial and cultural ties with the West and its basic commercial economy, Soviet policy had much less success in Lebanon during the early postwar era. The small and weak Communist Party had to compete in a more sophisticated society, fragmented in a confessional political structure. During the period of the Cold War in the 1950s Lebanon experienced little trouble in pursuing a policy of nonalignment, with a very obvious Western orientation. The country was not very active in purchasing arms; and its basic danger, sometimes exaggerated, lay in the fact that it had formed part of Greater Syria, as viewed at least from the vantage point of Damascus. While Beirut had been a kind of political and organizational center for Arab communism, that subversive doctrine made no great headway in Lebanon, and the Communist Party, as such, attracted few adherents. After 1953 communist demonstrations in cities like Beirut, Sidon, and Tripoli ceased essentially, although there was a brief revival in 1955. The fact that family, clan, and tribal politics tended to dominate in a confessional society militated against the development of a strong communist movement. The basic achievements lay in the field of "popular front" activities, such as the "Partisans for Peace," and similar movements. While communists participated with other dissidents in the anti-Chamoun movement during May-October 1958, they were never a dominating influence, whatever the appearances at the time.[8]

The Soviet Union had neither diplomatic relations with Jordan, nor economic or cultural exchanges of any consequence. Soviet policies were influential and attractive among some Jordanian circles, especially in connection with the Arab-Israel conflict. A statement of Andrei Vyshinsky in the U.N. Security Council in April 1954 evoked a vote of thanks from the Amman Parliament. The Jordanian government was denounced as feudal, reactionary, and a colonial dependency of the United Kingdom. The October 1954 elections were characterized as having taken place under police terror. The tone changed by 1956, when Soviet propaganda stressed the strength of the U.S.S.R., both in the military and industrial sense, and urged that it was the better part of Arab discretion and wisdom to strengthen ties with Moscow, to which all Arabs could look for national liberation.[9]

The Communist Party in Jordan, which in 1954 acted through a National Front, achieved its zenith in 1956, when several National deputies were elected to Parliament. It exercised considerable influence through alliance with the Ba'ath and Suleiman Nabulsi's National Socialists. Moreover, it played an active role in the demonstrations against General Sir Gerald Templar, Chief of the Imperial General Staff, when he visited Amman in December 1955 in the interest of Jordanian adherence to the Baghdad Pact. After a number of cabinet shifts, King Hussein called upon Nabulsi to form a new government, which Nabulsi did on October 29, 1956, the very day on which Israel, in collusion with France and the United Kingdom, sent its forces against Egypt.

During the winter of 1956, the Nabulsi government, which desired diplomatic relations with both the Soviet Union and Communist China, proposed that Jordan seek arms and economic and technical assistance from the Soviet bloc. Nabulsi also noted the offer of Syria, Egypt, and Saudi Arabia to replace the annual British subsidy to Jordan, which was ready to end the British alliance. An agreement was reached on January 19, 1957, and the Anglo-Jordanian alliance was formally terminated in March.[10] The Nabulsi government now appeared ready to enter into closer relations with Syria and to allow Russian and foreign communists to come into Jordan. On February 2, however, King Hussein warned the country against communist infiltration and urged Nabulsi to take steps to destroy "destructive propaganda" in the country. All communist publications, along with Soviet newspapers and movies, were banned. But there were no violent demonstrations. Nabulsi expressed his determination to enter into relations with Moscow and Peiping, and declared his intention to pursue a course of "positive neutrality" in Jordan's relations with the United States and the Soviet Union. On April 10 King Hussein ordered the resignation of the Nabulsi government, and soon formed a new government. The troubles in Jordan persisted, however.[11] In October 1957 the King convened Parliament and denounced the sympathizers with the Soviet Union, and both the Ba'ath and the communist parties were duly outlawed.

SOVIET ASSISTANCE IN THE MIDDLE EAST

Soviet cultural policy in the Middle East met with varying degrees of success. After 1954 Soviet cultural efforts shifted from Beirut to Damascus, where the first Arab Writers Congress was held in September 1954, and the effort concentrated on Syria with movie technicians, performances in Damascus and Beirut, and festivals here and there. While no similar activities took place in Jordan, books edited in Damascus and Cairo made their impact. A new Soviet-Syrian cultural agreement was signed in 1956. In the summer of 1957, large delegations from Egypt, Syria, Lebanon, and Jordan attended the Sixth Moscow Youth Festival, the Syrian delegation consisting of no less than 450 people.

A highly selective Soviet program of economic, technical, and military assistance began on a substantial scale only in 1955. The effort was concentrated for the most part on Egypt, Syria, and Iraq, not on Lebanon and Jordan. During 1954-56, for example, credits to the Middle East totaled some $4,298,000,000, out of a world total from the Soviet bloc of some $8,729,000,000, with about two-thirds from the U.S.S.R., and with Syria receiving some $363,000,000.[12] Substantial trade with the Soviet bloc was also initiated during 1954-55. Bloc share in Syrian imports, for example, was only 2.5 percent, or $4,800,000 in 1954 and rose to only 3.9 percent in 1956, or $12,700,000. The Soviet bloc took only 0.5 percent of Syrian exports in 1954, or $700,000. This rose to 7.8 percent by 1956, or $11,200,000, although trade shifted sharply to the U.S.S.R. in 1957. The International Trade Fair in Damascus in September 1956 provided a significant opportunity to promote trade connections, and only India entered into more trade agreements with the Soviet bloc during this period.

The U.S.S.R. sought in its various programs to impress the Arab world with its own progress toward industrialization under a communist regime and communist ideology. Moscow appeared especially eager to establish good will among politically significant groups with pro-Soviet orientation that might come to power. Soviet economic arrangements were also fitted within the framework of broader political activities. They looked toward the expansion of Soviet influence, if not outright domination, and sought to encourage neutralism of the more "positive" variety and the lessening, if not elimination, of Western influence, the development of an anti-Western orientation, and the undermining of Western alignments and alliances. While the spread of communist influence remained a constant objective, the U.S.S.R., perhaps for rather obvious reasons, did not appear to be driving toward a crude "satellization" of Syria, Lebanon, and Jordan.[13]

During 1954-58 virtually all Soviet and satellite assistance took the form of interest-bearing credits to finance specific projects. Up to February 1, 1958, Soviet bloc credits to the Middle East, for economic and military assistance, reached $808,000,000, of which $455,000,000 was for economic and $353,000,000 for military assistance. Of this amount, Syria received some $294,000,000 with $194,000,000 in economic and $100,000,000 in military assistance, as compared with a total of $485,000,000 for Egypt. The bulk of the grand total for military assistance, of course, went to Egypt and Syria, and about 80 percent of all Soviet bloc technicians went to Egypt, Syria, India, Indonesia, and Afghanistan, with some 360 in Egypt and 110 in Syria (1957).

Syrian economic ties with the Soviet bloc, in contrast with those of Lebanon and Jordan, became progressively closer after 1955. This would appear to be a reflection more of politics than of economics. Syria was especially receptive to Soviet assistance and to a pro-Soviet orientation, partly as a result of Soviet policy in the Arab-Israel conflict. Before the formation of the United Arab Republic in 1958, Syria rejected any American assistance, on the stated ground that such assistance would prejudice its independence. Its anti-Western orientation became much more pronounced following the Israel-Anglo-French invasion of Egypt during October-November 1956, when both Soviet aid and Soviet trade increased sharply. The government of Sabri al-Asali, which had come into being in June 1956, was in serious trouble during the summer and fall, and the political climate was one of constant plot and counterplot. The regime needed arms not only for the prevention of a possible coup, but also to strengthen its position relative to both Israel and Iraq, and for its own purposes relative to Jordan. The Syrian army as well was increasingly active on the political stage, and very anxious for large supplies of modern arms. A military aid agreement was signed in May 1956, followed by a second in November. On November 3, during a visit to Moscow of President Quwwatli, the U.S.S.R. promised assistance in strengthening Syrian independence. Early in December Syrian military sources indicated that arms had been secured from the Soviet bloc because Syria could not accept the restrictive conditions imposed by the Western Powers in return for military aid.

Supplies now began to flow from the U.S.S.R. About $60,000,000 in tanks, MIG-17 jet fighters, and other military equipment poured in during 1956. Defense Minister Khalid al-'Azm visited Moscow and Prague during August 1957. Once more, at a critical period in American-Syrian relations that ended in the withdrawal of the respective emissaries, the Soviet government promised extensive military assistance.[14] On his return home Khalid al-'Azm announced a loan of $150,000,000. In addition projects were revealed in the amount of some $570,000,000, to be financed by Soviet bloc credits, along with an economic and technical agreement with the U.S.S.R. Western statesmen, and sympathizers within Syria, became somewhat alarmed at the extent of Soviet activities in Syria. They were troubled lest Syria mortgage itself to the Soviet bloc, and feared that a possible communist takeover might well be imminent. To many it seemed that Syria was slipping ineluctably behind the Iron Curtain and into the Soviet bloc.

Large-scale Syrian-Soviet economic collaboration really began with the agreement of October 28, 1957, which extended credits of some $168,000,000 to finance equipment and technicians for nineteen major projects. By the end of 1957, as already observed, the Soviet bloc had extended some $294,000,000 in credits. Czechoslovakia extended $50,000,000 in military and $20,000,000 in economic assistance. Bulgaria and East Germany too furnished substantial credits. The agreement of October 28, in reality a formalization of the Soviet offer of August 6, 1957, essentially marked the major entry of the U.S.S.R. into the field of economic assistance, and constituted an innovation in economic relations with Middle Eastern states. It provided for construction of hydroelectric plants on the Euphrates, the Orontes, and the Yarmuk rivers, and in the region of Lake Homs; irrigation projects on the Euphrates, the al-Kabir, and the Barada rivers; construction of the Aleppo-Latakia-al-Qamishli railways; construction of bridges on the Euphrates and the Kabir rivers; exploration for petroleum, asbestos, iron, manganese, and chromium; geological surveys; construction of thermoelectric power stations in Damascus and Aleppo; construction of a nitrate fertilizer plant; and development of an agricultural laboratory for scientific research.[15] The fact that Syria was desperately short of adequately trained and qualified technicians opened the door to Soviet bloc technicians. As a result, it was estimated that by May 1956 there were some 200 military and 100 other technicians in Syria, more than half of whom were from the U.S.S.R. and the remainder from Czechoslovakia and Poland. The greatest number of nonmilitary technicians were drawn from Bulgaria, East Germany, and Czechoslovakia. While the Soviet military experts were involved primarily in training Syrians in the use and maintenance of the equipment, some served as advisers in the field. In addition, several hundred Syrians went to Soviet bloc countries for special military training, some to the Moscow Military Staff College and about a hundred to other bloc countries for further study.[16]

The Soviet indifference to Lebanon had undergone some change by 1954. On April 30, for example, an economic agreement was signed by which the two governments undertook to exchange goods in the amount of some $3,500,000. A trade and payments agreement was signed with East Germany on November 12, 1955, under which Lebanon was to export agricultural products and import manufactured goods. A Soviet survey team arrived in Lebanon on February 2, 1956, to investigate economic and industrial possibilities; and on May 5 the U.S.S.R. offered the free services of engineers to reconstruct villages destroyed by earthquakes in March. Communist China signed a commercial agreement with Lebanon on August 20. But this kind of activity was hardly comparable with that in Syria, even though Lebanon looked out over the Mediterranean, where much of its trade went, and its cultural heritage pointed in the same direction. In aid, in trade, and in ideology, therefore, the country remained oriented essentially toward the West.

INTERNATIONAL POLITICS IN THE MIDDLE EAST

Soviet policy, with its heavy stress on Syria, had its underpinnings in support for Arab positions in the Arab-Israeli conflict, along with other problems. When the United States joined with France, Turkey, and the United Kingdom during October-November 1951 in the proposal for a Middle East Command or Middle East Defense Organization (1952), a proposal on which the Arab States had strong reservations, the U.S.S.R. bitterly opposed this regional defense project.[17] Later, when Secretary of State John Foster Dulles outlined his project for the Northern Tier, the U.S.S.R. not only denounced the new pact as a revival of colonialism designed to keep the Arab States in tow, but hurdled over it to take a dominant position in Syria and Egypt. Lebanon remained "neutral" and Jordan was torn in strife over the issue. The U.S.S.R., although it had supported the partition resolution of November 29, 1947, and had temporarily blocked American attempts during March-April 1948 to retreat into trusteeship, had already established itself as a firm supporter of the Arab cause in Palestine.[18] Soviet arms shipments both to Egypt and to Syria, however, began essentially after 1955, following the Israeli attack on the Gaza Strip on February 28, 1955, and were signaled by the Egyptian-Czechoslovak arms arrangement of September 27, 1955. With the onset of the Suez conflict in October 1956, developments took a decided turn in the direction of the Soviet Union, especially in the instance of Egypt and Syria.[19]

For a very brief moment after the Suez affair it appeared that the United States had achieved a very high and very solid moral position in the Arab world—in Egypt and Syria, as well as in Lebanon and Jordan.[20] Nevertheless, a number of developments served to complicate the situation in the Middle East at the time. In the first instance, the ill-starred Eisenhower (American) Doctrine was announced. This was approved by Congress on March 9, 1957. Under the new Doctrine, reminiscent of the Truman Doctrine of March 12, 1947, President Eisenhower was authorized to render assistance to any group of states that desired it "in the development of economic strength dedicated to the maintenance of national independence."[21] Military assistance was offered also. It was stated in addition that the United States regarded "as vital to the national interest and world peace the preservation of the independence and integrity of the nations of the Middle East." The President was authorized to use the armed forces to assist any nation or group of nations "requesting assistance against armed aggression from any country controlled by international communism." In the spring of 1957, Ambassador James P. Richards was sent to the Middle East as special representative of the President to inaugurate the new Doctrine. But among the Arab States only Lebanon and Iraq endorsed it. Syria refused to receive the President's emissary, and the situation in Jordan was so serious that he was asked not to visit that country either.[22] Whatever the good intentions of the Eisenhower Doctrine as originally conceived, states in the area generally were not prepared to accept its implications. Some were offended by the assertion that a serious power vacuum existed in the area.[23]

The Soviet Union was now heavily involved in the Middle East. On February 11, 1957, it set forth a series of proposals for a Four-Power Declaration (France, the United Kingdom, the United States, and the U.S.S.R.) to guide Great Power policy in the area.[24] The U.S.S.R. called for 1) the maintenance of Middle Eastern peace by the settling of outstanding issues exclusively by peaceful means; 2) noninterference in internal affairs and respect for sovereignty and independence; 3) renunciation of all attempts to involve Middle Eastern states in military blocs with Great Power participation (as in the Baghdad Pact, 1955); 4) liquidation of foreign bases and withdrawal of foreign troops from the territory of the Middle Eastern countries; 5) reciprocal refusal to deliver arms to Middle Eastern states; and 6) promotion of Middle Eastern economic development "without any political, military, or other terms incompatible with the dignity and sovereignty of these countries."

These comprehensive principles, which were already somewhat shopworn, were to be used time and again. They were hardly acceptable to the United States, which on March 11 advised the U.S.S.R. that it would deal with the Middle East in accordance with the U.N. Charter. The United States took the position that along with other principles it fully supported peaceful settlement, noninterference in internal affairs, and respect for sovereignty and independence. It was prepared to cooperate with any country in the implementation of these principles. On the other hand, the United States did not wish to be a party "to any attempt by the great powers, as suggested by the U.S.S.R., to arrogate to themselves decisions on matters of vital importance to the nations of the Middle East." Nor would it prevent states which considered themselves threatened "from assocation of their own free will with other nations in legitimate collective security arrangements, in accordance with the provisions of the United Nations

Charter." As to foreign bases and the withdrawal of foreign troops, the United States considered the states of the Middle East "fully capable of deciding whatever cooperative efforts" were "required to enable them to play their part in the defense of the area." While it favored limitation of arms shipments, the United States regretted that the U.S.S.R. had seen fit "to effect massive shipments of arms into the area at a time when regional disputes there had become sharply exacerbated."

In contrast to the Soviet position, the United States observed that the Eisenhower Doctrine had been designed to promote the peace, security, stability, and economic development of the area. On April 19, the U.S.S.R. substantially reiterated its position, to which the United States replied on June 11 that what was now needed was implementation of the principles of the U.N. Charter. "If the Soviet Union sincerely" desired "to contribute toward the establishment of peace and security in the Middle East, it could do so by working constructively within the area," in connection with the Arab-Israel conflict. But the U.S.S.R. restated its proposals once again on September 3, 1957, and still called for a Four-Power Declaration as a first step "in the direction of restoring to health and normalizing the situation in this area."

Far from developing normally, however, the situation in the Middle East, especially in Jordan, had by this time grown even more critical; and that in Syria soon deteriorated badly, too.[25] As already observed, under the government of Suleiman Nabulsi there was a sharp turn to the left. Jordan adhered to the Declaration of Arab Solidarity with Egypt, Syria, and Saudi Arabia on January 19, 1957, and on February 13 terminated its alliance with the United Kingdom. The United States was much concerned with a possible threat to the independence of Jordan, whether from without or within, and on April 24 President Eisenhower found that "the preservation of the independence and integrity of the nations of the Middle East" was "vital to the national interest of the United States and to world peace." The reminder seemed appropriate in view of King Hussein's statement concerning the threat of "international communism."[26] Not only Saudi Arabia but the United States came to the assistance of the Hashemite Kingdom with military and economic assistance (June 29, 1957).

By August the Syrian situation seemed out of hand, when the Syrian government charged the United States with an attempt to overthrow it, and the respective ambassadors were declared *personae non gratae*.[27] American "imperialism" was evidently unhappy "to see Syria free, enjoying the successful steps it achieved in its independent life." In turn there were American fears that Syria might fall under the control of "international communism." President Eisenhower did not want to speculate as to whether it would be "tolerable to have in the heart of the Middle East a regime subject to Communist control which at any time could deny the Free World a vital part of its oil supply." Nevertheless, he thought the Syrian situation would have to be closely watched, and that "we must not get into a position that would be intolerable for us."

Ambassador Loy W. Henderson, deputy undersecretary of state was sent to the Middle East during August 22-September 4, 1957, to confer with officials in Turkey, Lebanon, Jordan, and Iraq concerning the complicated Syrian situation. While it was difficult to get people to speak frankly and explicitly, Mr. Henderson "found concern lest Syria should become a victim of international communism and, as such become a base for further threatening the independence and integrity of the region." He reported to President Eisenhower and Secretary Dulles that he had found in the Near East deep concern at the apparently growing Soviet Communist domination of Syria and the large build-up there of Soviet bloc arms, a build-up which could not be justified by purely defensive needs. There was particular concern over border incidents and intensive propaganda and subversive activities directed toward the overthrow of the duly constituted governments of Syria's Arab neighbors.[28] The President appraised the situation in the light of the U.N. Charter, which denied members the right "to use force except in self-defense." He recalled his message of January 5 to the Congress. He noted that after describing "Russia's long-time ambition to dominate the Near East and the current activities there of international communism," he had sought authority "to help the nations of the area to defend their independence." The President affirmed his intention to implement the Eisenhower Doctrine, and authorized acceleration of arms deliveries and economic assistance that had been programmed for their use. He hoped "that the international Communists would not push Syria into any acts of aggression against her neighbors and that the people of Syria would act to allay the anxiety caused by recent events."

On the other hand, on September 10, 1957, the Soviet Union presented an entirely different picture of the problem and charged the Western press and governments with pressures, propaganda, and plots against an innocent Syrian government.[29] The Turkish government, in particular, was charged with preparing an attack upon Syria, especially in the Aleppo area. While denying any Syrian threat to any of its neighbors, the U.S.S.R. noted that such charges should be brought to the U.N. Security Council. The Soviet government warned the Turkish government on September 11[30] that it could not "conceal its concern over the situation that is taking shape in that area at present—first and foremost around Syria." Ambassador Henderson was charged with a desire "to organize military intervention. . . in Syria's internal affairs." He had sought, it was alleged, to organize a plot against Syria, to overthrow the Syrian government, and to change the situation in the country to satisfy "the big American monopolies" in "the interests of the major colonial powers." A role was being assigned to Turkey in "the plans to unleash military action against Syria." "Profoundly alarmed" that Turkish statesmen had been inclined in that direction, the U.S.S.R. was concerned about "Turkish troop concentrations on Syria's borders, as well as about the shipment of American arms to Turkey to effect an attack against Syria." These were developments to which the Soviet government could not remain indifferent:

> Taking into account the proximity of the Middle East to Soviet frontiers and the interests of its state security, the Soviet Union naturally cannot ignore such a course of events that could lead to armed conflict in that area, more so since the danger of violation of the peace would not be limited to that area alone. That is why it should wish to approach the Turkish government in the most friendly manner with an appeal, in the name of the Middle East as well as the world peace, not to take part in such an act as armed intervention against Syria which is fraught with great danger, and help to avert an undesirable turn of events in the Middle East and unleashing of an armed conflict there.

President Eisenhower announced on October 10 that both the Eisenhower Doctrine and NATO would be used to protect Turkey from Syrian aggression and promised to help any Middle Eastern country against Syria, while the Soviet Union continued to denounce the United States for meddling in Syrian affairs. In turn the United States denied the Soviet charges, and on October 16, Mr. Dulles considered the Soviet furor over Turkey reminiscent of "similar furors" in the past. The secretary cited specifically the Soviet actions in 1945-46, in connection with demands relative to the Turkish Straits, and later, the uproar in 1952, when Turkey became a member of NATO.[31] Secretary Dulles did not feel that there was any danger at the time that the smaller Middle Eastern states might commit the power and prestige of the United States and the U.S.S.R. But if there were a Soviet attack on Turkey, "it would not mean a purely defensive operation by the United States, with the Soviet Union a privileged sanctuary from which to attack Turkey." As to the oft-repeated project for a Four-Power Declaration, Mr. Dulles did not know why the United States and the Soviet Union "should set themselves up as a kind of protectorate over the Arab countries," which wanted independence and were entitled to have it. Mr. Dulles thought the United States must be on guard against the possibility of a Soviet-Syrian attack against Turkey. In accordance with usual practice, the Syrian complaint against Turkey was inscribed on the agenda of the U.N. General Assembly with U.S. support. In the end, the draft resolution on the subject was not pressed to a vote, although the complaint was fully aired, with the Soviet Union in complete support of the Syrian contention that Turkey was preparing an aggression against Syria.[32]

The year 1958 produced another crop of continuing problems. For one thing, on February 1, the establishment of the United Arab Republic, composed of Egypt and Syria (the Northern and Syrian regions), was announced. Despite immediate impressions at the time, the proposal for a United Arab Republic came largely on Syrian initiative, more especially on the part of Michel 'Aflaq and Akram Hourani, as an anti-communist move, not on that of President Nasser. The Soviet Union was quite reserved in its attitude toward this step. Secondly, on February 14, the Arab Federation between the two Hashemite kingdoms of Jordan and Iraq came into being. This was a much less viable arrangement, although both, as events soon well demonstrated, were fragile in character.[33]

Civil strife broke out in Lebanon in May 1958, largely occasioned by the evident determination of President Chamoun to maintain himself in his high office in violation of the Lebanese constitution. There were some indications of intervention on the Lebanese domestic stage by the United Arab Republic, especially from across the Syrian-Lebanese frontier, but also directly from Egypt. The press and radio attacks from both Damascus and Cairo were venomous, and the Lebanese government countered, of course, with charges against the United Arab Republic.[34] While the United States did not initially consider the troubled Lebanese situation as one calling for implementation of the Eisenhower Doctrine, the problem nevertheless seemed serious. Mr. Dulles indicated on May 20 that it was unlikely that there would be "an attack, an armed attack, from a country which we consider under the control of international communism, although that did not signify that nothing could be done."

Lebanon charged the United Arab Republic and brought a complaint before the U.N. Security Council on May 22,[35] which was fully supported by the United States, although the United States advised the Lebanese government that its evidence should match its case. The United States supported establishment of a United Nations Observation Group in Lebanon (UNOGIL).[36] Ultimately, following the Iraqi coup on July 14, the United States landed some 15,000 troops in Lebanon beginning July 15. The troops, who remained until October, were sent not only in response to the situation in Iraq and as an indication that Lebanon was entitled to an opportunity to choose its president in accordance with its own constitutional procedures, but as an earnest display that the United States had both the power and the resolve to take action. TASS immediately denounced the American "aggression" in Lebanon. On October 16, Arkady Sobolev, the Soviet representative in the U.N. Security Council, declared that American troops had "absolutely no right to be in Lebanon, whatever excuses" might be "invoked to justify their arrival there," and accused the United States of "dirty work against Arab nationalism." The Kremlin demanded withdrawal and declared that the U.S.S.R. could not remain indifferent "to the events creating serious danger in this region adjacent to her border" and reserved "the right to take necessary measures to preserve peace and security."

The case was duly brought before the Security Council on July 15, and immediately the Soviet representative called for the withdrawal of American forces.[37] In a radio-television address on July 15, 1959, President Eisenhower explained the problem to the Congress and to the people.[38] On July 17, at the very time that two batallions of British troops were landed in Jordan for the protection of King Hussein's government—a move which the United States fully supported[39]—the government of Jordan filed a complaint concerning alleged intervention by the United Arab Republic. The U.S.S.R. now demanded immediate withdrawal of both American and British forces.[40] The United States responded that its forces would be withdrawn when the Lebanese government so requested. In turn, on July 18 the Soviet representative proposed the calling of a special session of the U.N. General Assembly to consider the "intervention of the United States of America and the United Kingdom in Lebanon and Jordan."[41]

While the General Assembly was in session from July 19 to August 7, 1958, many proposals were advanced for the solution of the problems in Lebanon and of the Middle East as a whole. On July 19 Chairman Khrushchev wrote to President Eisenhower proposing the immediate convocation of a summit conference of the U.S.S.R., the United Kingdom, France, the United States, and India, with the participation of U.N. Secretary-General Dag Hammarskjöld. Mr. Khrushchev believed that a solution could and must be found "conforming to the vital interests of the Middle Eastern peoples, insuring their sovereign rights, and with due regard for the interests of all states associated with the countries of this area." A conference could consider the question of discontinuing arms shipments to the Middle East, as the Soviet Union had already proposed. Furthermore, Mr. Khrushchev deemed it necessary to work out concrete proposals for ending the conflict in the Middle East for submission to the Security Council.[42]

President Eisenhower's reply of July 22 rejected the Soviet thesis that the United States had acted in Lebanon in a manner calculated to disturb the peace. Nor was he aware of any factual basis for the extravagant Khrushchev fear of the danger of a general war.[43] He noted the July 14 plot against the government of Jordan and the Lebanese appeal for immediate assistance. The United States government "knew that the plea was based upon solid facts that showed that Lebanon was gravely menaced." It was not "aggression" to respond to the appeal, and the President knew of no armed conflicts outside the events in Iraq, Lebanon, and Jordan. While the United States was not dedicated to the maintenance of the status quo, it did not want "a progressive destruction of the small nations which occurred during the 1930's and which led to the Second World War." The Soviet proposal was calculated to derogate from the authority and prestige of the United Nations. If it thought world peace threatened, the President suggested, the Soviet Union should take the problem not to the five great powers, but to the U.N. Security Council, which was already dealing with certain aspects of the matter.

Mr. Khrushchev apparently had no desire to enter into fruitless discussion as to the origin of the problem. On July 23, therefore, he agreed to a discussion of the Middle East in the U.N. Security Council, with the participation of India, at the summit, and proposed a special session on July 28.[44] On July 25 President Eisenhower suggested an exchange of views among permanent members of the Security Council to ascertain the acceptability of the Soviet proposal. But "to put peace and security on a more stable basis in the Middle East" required "far more than merely a consideration of Lebanon and Jordan," which were "but isolated manifestations of far broader problems." In the Eisenhower view, "the instability of peace and security" was "in large measure due to the jeopardy in which small nations are placed."[45] Khrushchev was disappointed with the American suggestion, accused the United States of dilatory tactics, and charged that in the Middle East "an unceasing accumulation of armed forces" was "taking place," and more and more the area was "becoming a powder-magazine" which could "explode from the smallest spark and evoke a world catastrophe." He adverted to his five-power proposal as a quick way to reach possible solutions, and reiterated the peaceful intentions of the Soviet Union, which evidently still feared that the situation might detonate a world conflict.[46] The calling of an immediate conference was "imperative." Secretary of State Dulles felt that under appropriate auspices a meeting would dispel "the false allegations" that the United Kingdom and the United States were involved in aggression. Such a meeting might also tend to stabilize the political situation and contribute to economic development.[47] Accordingly President Eisenhower advised Khrushchev on August 1 of his intention to seek a special meeting of the U.N. Security Council. But on August 5 he acquiesced in the Soviet preference for a special session of the General Assembly to discuss the Middle East.[48]

When the General Assembly met, the secretary-general reported on the situation in Lebanon and Jordan, and Foreign Minister Gromyko called for the immediate withdrawal of British and French forces (August 12). A propaganda battle now ensued.[49] On August 13 President Eisenhower presented a broad program for the Middle East centering on the dangers to Lebanon and Jordan, calling for respect for their independence and integrity, defending the dispatch of troops, and urging the establishment of a regional Arab development institution, with both Arab and broad international participation. He particularly urged a regional approach to the solution of Middle Eastern economic problems and set forth a six-point program calling for the following: (1) An expression of United Nations concern for Lebanon, (2) United Nations measures to preserve peace in Jordan,

(3) a United Nations Peace Force, (4) a regional economic development plan to assit and accelerate improvement in the living standards of the people in these Arab Nations, and (5) steps to avoid a new arms race spiral in the area.[50] The President thought that "within the Near East and within this Assembly" were "the forces of good sense, restraint, and of wisdom to make, with time and patience, a framework of order and peace in that region." On August 18, the United Kingdom and the United States notified the General Assembly of their intention to withdraw their forces from Jordan and Lebanon on the request of the duly constituted authorities.[51]

The 1958 crisis now appeared to be passing into history. On August 18 seven states introduced a resolution substantially in line with President Eisenhower's proposals, and on August 21 the General Assembly adopted a resolution dealing with the problems of peace, security, and economic development in the Middle East. On October 8 the United States and Lebanon reached agreement on the completion of American withdrawal. American forces were out by October 25 and British forces by November 2, while the work of UNOGIL in Lebanon was basically completed by October 30. For the moment, at least, the crisis had passed, although no basic problems were really solved. Secretary of State Dulles felt that the Anglo-American action in Lebanon and Jordan had served to stabilize the situation, and that it had had a "very great effect in giving reassurance to small countries in the world that if they felt imperiled they could get help."[52]

THE AFTERMATH, 1959-67

The well-established pattern of Soviet interest and policy continued to the *blitzkrieg* of June 1967, with concentration on Syria, although there was a period of relative quiet up to 1966. The United States continued to express its interest in the political independence and the territorial integrity of all Middle Eastern States, as President Kennedy had written to the heads of Arab States on May 11, 1961.[53] While Lebanon maintained its "neutral" position, and Jordan was oriented toward the West, Syria split off from the United Arab Republic on September 29, 1961, and moved more steadily, whether in foreign or domestic policy, in the direction of the U.S.S.R.[54] A coup on March 8, 1963, brought the Ba'ath firmly into power in Damascus. Despite certain Soviet misgivings the party approved a policy of "nonalignment," and made abundantly clear that "nonalignment should not prevent strengthening of ties of friendship with the socialist countries of the world." Moreover, solidarity was proclaimed with countries of the "third world," which pursued a course of "positive neutrality" that would "strengthen the anti-imperialist front." Federal political union with Iraq, at least in principle, seemed to be in the offing.[55] After 1963 especially, the

Syrian military regime proclaimed socialism as its basic doctrine, stressed modernization of the economy, and in pursuit of dynamic foreign policies emphasized expansion and equipment of the Syrian armed forces, especially in connection with Israel and the unyielding problem of Palestine. With the coup of February 1966, the ousting and exile of Michel 'Aflaq and Salah al-Bitar, and the advent of Alawi officers (Maj. Gen.Salah Jadid), dependence on the Soviet Union in international politics increased.[56] The U.S.S.R. in turn appeared to find the Syrian government a very useful tool for exerting influence in the heart of the Middle East. On the other hand, Soviet writers were evidently as confused as others in their attempts to unravel and interpret Syrian politics in the years following 1963. As one wrote:

> The political merry-go-round continues. This is the picture of Syria today: Ministers and high officials, appointed solely on the strength of their loyalty to the Ba'ath and with little or no knowledge of the country's problems, are interested only in political intrigue; every officer seems to assume that his hour is nigh—if he can master a batallion, plus a dozen armoured cars, he can be ruler; journalists spend their time speculating who will engineer the next coup; plots, rumors of plots, counter-measures, suspicious troop movements make up the day's news. No one is trusted, everyone is out to cheat someone else; superiors suspect their subordinates and vice versa; political alliances and coalitions are formed only to fall apart the next day.[57]

As already noted, King Hussein resisted entering into diplomatic relations with the U.S.S.R. Following the events of 1956, with the dismissal of Lt. Gen. Sir John Bagot Glubb and the renunciation of the British alliance, under the Arab Solidarity Agreement assistance was to have come from Egypt, Syria, and Saudi Arabia. But the promises were not kept; and even Saudi Arabia met only the first quarterly payment of its promised $14,000,000. The United States then proceeded to assist Jordan under the Eisenhower Doctrine, which King Hussein accepted. Thereafter the United States paid an annual subsidy to the Jordanian budget, which jumped from $40,000,000 in the first year to $51,000,000 in 1960, and by 1965 was reduced to $44,000,000.[58] But it was announced on August 22, 1963 that Jordan had agreed to the exchange of diplomatic representatives with the Soviet Union; and on October 6 King Hussein, although expressing preference for the United States, indicated that Jordan might in the future purchase arms from the Soviet bloc. He declared on October 31 that Jordan was not necessarily moving closer to the U.S.S.R., and added on November 7 that establishment of diplomatic relations did not signify any basic change in Jordan's foreign policy.[59] When King Hussein visited the United States in April 1964, President Johnson expressed his desire for friendship with all the Arab states and for the maintenance of peace and stability in the Middle East.[60]

The United States continued to express interest in the "peace, security and welfare of the Middle Eastern states and peoples, but without taking sides in regional disputes."⁶¹ In a statement on February 3, 1964, before the Senate Committee on Appropriations and the Committee on the Armed Services, Secretary of Defense Robert McNamara observed that both Syria and Iraq were rent by internal power struggles, and that the only ostensible objective which all the Arab states appeared mutually to share was the destruction of Israel, and that Israel's plan to divert Jordan waters presented a "current problem."⁶² The primary American objective was to prevent "the Arab-Israeli feud" from escalating into overt hostilities, although realization of that objective had been made more difficult by the injection of substantial Soviet economic and military assistance, especially to the United Arab Republic, Syria, Iraq, and Yemen. Because of that aid, Mr. McNamara said, the United States, on a very selective basis, had been providing military matériel to Israel, Saudi Arabia, and Jordan. On the other hand, Chairman Khrushchev continued to stress Soviet assistance and support to Egypt and Syria. When the Syrian-Israeli demarcation line flared into open conflict in November-December 1964, the United States registered its disappointment and called upon the parties to cooperate fully with the U.N. Truce Supervision Organization (UNTSO), while the Soviet Union, once more, gave its full support to Syria.⁶³

THE JUNE 1967 CONFLICT AND ITS AFTERMATH

As in the instance of the United Arab Republic, relations between the United States and Syria continued to deteriorate, particularly after the coup of February 23, 1966, which brought the extreme left of the Ba'ath to power in Damascus and intensified the troublesome situation along the Syrian-Israeli demarcation lines. Syria gave full support to the newly established Palestine Liberation Organization (1964). While the U.S.S.R. continued its full support of Syria, the United States held both Syria and Israel responsible for the increasingly difficult situation, and called upon Syria to insure that its territory not be used as a base for guerrilla (Al Fatah) activity against Israel. On April 2, 1966, the United States announced that it had been providing Jordan with limited defense armaments to promote a degree of stability in the Middle East. At the same time it regretted "the massive Soviet sales of arms to certain countries in the Middle East," which had "intensified the arms race in that area," and observed that the United States would "continue to strive for agreed limitations on arms buildup there." Troubled over the unvarying and increasing pattern of violence that appeared to be developing in Israel, the United States joined in condemning that country for its attack against Jordan at Es-Samu in November 1966.⁶⁴

The Arab-Israel conflict of June 1967 brought some change in Soviet relations with Syria and Jordan, if not basically in those with Lebanon. There were some interesting implications in connection with Lebanon as a result of the severe crisis through which Lebanon passed during the fall of 1969. These developments are so recent and the documentation so elusive that it would be pointless to deal with them in detail.[65] Suffice it to say that the U.S.S.R. appeared to work very closely with both the United Arab Republic and Syria, whatever the motivation therefore. In the period immediately following the June conflict the Soviet Union appeared to identify itself almost completely with the Arab position generally and with that of Syria in particular. Nevertheless the Soviets formally supported the Security Council Resolution of November 22, 1967, and the dispatch of Ambassador Gunnar V. Jarring's mission to the Middle East in the interest of a peaceful settlement of the Arab-Israeli conflict.[66] Moreover, by mid-1968 it was reported that the Arab states—largely the United Republic and Syria—had received some $1,000,000,000 in economic aid and $1,700,000,000 in military assistance since June 1967. While the U.S.S.R. set forth its views as to peace in the Middle East, notably on December 22, 1968, there was little if any indication that the Syrian government was prepared to follow suit.[67]

Meanwhile, Soviet relations with Jordan underwent some changes in the wake of the June 1967 conflict. King Hussein assumed direct command of his army in October 1967, dismissing some forty officers. But he resisted nationalist pressure to become a military client of the U.S.S.R., as the United Arab Republic and Syria had done. Early in 1968, after a six-month interval, the United States resumed military assistance to Jordan. Nevertheless, King Hussein visited Moscow for the first time during October 2-5, 1967. It was believed that at this time the Soviet Union offered Jordan both economic and military assistance. The chairman of the Presidium, who had visited Damascus somewhat earlier, considered the royal visit an important step in the improvement of Soviet-Jordanian relations. He noted the importance of socialist assistance to the Arab countries in contrast to that of the Western powers, which sought to divide the Arab countries. King Hussein thanked the U.S.S.R. for denouncing Israeli aggression, looked forward to strong and permanent relations with the Soviet Union, and expressed a special desire to strengthen cultural and scientific ties.[68] Some months later, however, on August 13, 1968, King Hussein still resisted pressure that he turn to the U.S.S.R. for arms, indicating that he preferred to rely on the United States.

The year 1969 brought further complications to the picture in Jordan, Lebanon, and Syria that produced problems for the Soviet Union, particularly in connection with the national liberation movement, which operated in all three countries. For a while the very existence of Lebanon, the political and constitutional foundations of which rested on a delicate confessional basis, seemed threatened. Encouraged and openly supported in

Syria, guerrilla activities also threatened to undermine the Hashemite Kingdom of Jordan, and certainly to complicate the prospects, if any really existed, of a peaceful settlement of the Arab-Israeli conflict. There were many indications that the U.S.S.R. itself, perhaps for obvious reasons, did not want the guerrilla problem to get out of hand, lest the confusion and conflict in the Middle East escalate into a much larger conflict on the world stage.[69]

Much of the confusion and conflict centered around Lebanon, hitherto cautious and reserved, in the very nature of things, as to the Arab-Israeli conflict. Now, however, there were guerilla operations from southern Lebanon against Israel, and incursions of Israeli forces into Lebanon. There was grave danger that serious attacks would follow, and that the character of the state would be seriously menaced, leaving aside the fears that others might be drawn in. With reports of Syrian troop movements and the probability that Israel would not stand idly by, American officials were deeply concerned with developments in Lebanon. On October 10, Assistant Secretary of State Joseph Sisco already had indicated that the United States continued "to attach great importance to Lebanon's independence and integrity" and "would view with great concern any threat to that integrity from any source."[70] Nevertheless, it was agreed that any substantive statement or open American moves would only aggravate the Lebanese situation, and that any public support for the Lebanese authorities would only inflame the anger of the Palestinian liberation movement. Although there were some fears of a "major catastrophe" and of long-standing contingency plans for the dispatch of American troops, it was pointed out that the United States had no military commitments, by treaty or otherwise, to Lebanon, that it was maintaining a "moderate posture," and that it was counseling others to act in a similar manner. It was indicated also that the situation was much different from that in 1958, when some 15,000 American troops had been landed in Lebanon. There was now a considerable Soviet naval force in the Mediterranean, leaving aside the very volatile situation involved in continued Arab-Israeli hostility. It was doubtful that the United States would ship arms to Lebanon in view of the possibility that such action would increase Middle Eastern tensions. A major move by the United States carried the possibility of a wider conflict.[71]

Although there had been every indication of caution and moderation on the part of the United States and of other Western powers, as well as public advice to Israel to keep out of the situation in Lebanon, on October 25 the U.S.S.R. expressed concern relative to Lebanon and called upon the great powers to avoid involvement. TASS, the Soviet news agency, coupled its call for nonintervention with an accusation that the United States was meddling in Lebanon, and charged that American support for the independence and integrity of Lebanon might be a pretext for intervention. As TASS remarked:

> The aims pursued by the United States are evident from the statement itself. . . . It is reminiscent of the old colonial practice when big powers referred to violations of their interests in some part of the world to interfere in the national affairs of states and peoples and deprive them of their inalienable right to settle their own affairs themselves.[72]

Although the U.S.S.R., under the so-called Brezhnev Doctrine, had acted otherwise in Czechoslovakia during August 1968, it now asserted that no outside intervention in Lebanon by a Great Power could be justified. It called upon the Arab states themselves to settle the crisis, brought on, in the Soviet view, by conflicts between the Lebanese army and the Palestinian commando forces. Moveover, TASS added:

> The Lebanese Republic is an Arab country closely connected with the other Arab states and nobody but the Arab states themselves can decide better the questions arising over Lebanon.
> They know best their interests and their aims. It is understandable why the public of Arab countries, including the Lebanese public, met with indignation the United States statement, rightly assessing it as an attempt to impose on the Lebanese a sort of American patronage.

It is also possible, of course, that the U.S.S.R. was seeking to assert its own patronage, for different purposes, not merely in Lebanon, but in Syria and over the Palestinian liberation movement as well.

The problem in Lebanon continued to develop in serious vein, and there were numerous efforts to settle the crisis with the Palestinian commandos. In view of an urgent appeal from President Helou of Lebanon, President Nasser strove for restraint and compromise, while President al-Atassi of Syria pledged full support to the commandos. At the same time, Sarvar A. Azimov, the Soviet ambassador in Beirut, conferred with President Helou, evidently in the interest of a settlement. American officials acknowledged that Soviet mediation reflected the possibility of increased influence in Lebanon. Admittedly on the defensive, they judged that an open American initiative would only provoke all sides and further inflame the Lebanese situation. On October 27 the Department of State chided the U.S.S.R. for "making propaganda from the difficulties confrontng the people of Lebanon," and called for "quiet diplomacy." There was some fear that any compromise would strengthen the guerrillas, which, it was said, would be a blow to American policy and interest in support of Lebanese restraint. On the other hand, the Soviet Union had no inhibitions, although it had on occasion criticized more radical action on the part of the Palestinians. Nevertheless, without access to any of the parties in the contest American diplomats were unable to play a direct mediatory role. Some officials considered that it would be a bitter outcome of the conflict if the Soviet Union were able to assist in a settlement and establish a political influence with the Lebanese government, with which the United States had had the closest and most cordial relations.[73]

While there were still difficulties ahead, developments now moved toward a compromise, although the Syrian government publicized and supported the guerrillas in Lebanon in conformity with Ba'ath ideology. The government seemed to particularly favor As-Saiqa. Syria continued to supply the guerrillas with everything from boots to bazookas and allowed the use of Syrian territory as a sanctuary. On October 31 the U.S.S.R. announced its approval of the guerrilla movement and reiterated its opposition to any foreign intervention in Lebanon. It also expressed cautious optimism that American-Soviet and four-power discussions would lead to some kind of political settlement in the Middle East. The Soviet statement repeated the charges against the United States government, which found the statement "disappointing" and the allegations "totally false." Indeed, the United States wondered whether the U.S.S.R. really wanted a peaceful settlement. Nevertheless, agreement between the Lebanese government and Al Fatah was reached in Cairo on November 3, under which commandos were to maintain their lines of communications from the Arkoub region to Syria and to cross the demarcation line into Israel without interference from the Lebanese army. The Palestine Liberation Organization now appeared to have tenure agreements in all Arab countries around Israel.[74]

Soviet policy continued to center on Syria, with which new trade, technical (oil industry), and economic agreements were signed in 1970, as they were with Lebanon. But despite Lebanese authorization of Communist Party activity (August 15, 1970), Lebanese-Soviet relations hardly developed into intimacy, as in the instance of Syria. There was some Jordanian-Soviet flirtation during 1970, with Soviet friendship visits and a cultural agreement, but this did not appear serious. The Palestine problem complicated all Soviet relations in the area. Serious questions arose after June 19, 1970,[75] when the United States proposed a cease-fire, which ultimately went into effect on August 7. This proposal, in which the Soviet Union acquiesced, was accepted by the United Arab Republic, Jordan, and Israel, but opposed by Syria and extremist elements in the guerrilla movement.[76] Very serious clashes took place in Jordan during September-October 1970. In the official American view, indeed, the conflict in Jordan and "the intervention of armored forces from Syria created the gravest threat to world peace" since the advent of the Nixon administration. With the deep involvement of the Soviet Union in United Arab Republic military operations and the firm American support of Israel's existence, the risk of a great-power confrontation seemed very real. At one point, evidently the

United States and Israel were preparing to take coordinated military action to sustain King Hussein's government. The United States acted, it was said, to stabilize the situation, not to threaten—to "discourage irresponsibility without accelerating the momentum of crisis." The forces from across the Syrian border withdrew, the government of Jordan reestablished a degree of order, and a tenuous and "fragile agreement" was achieved as to the future role of the Palestinians.[77]

Few could speak precisely of the role of the Soviet Union in these developments and fewer, perhaps, would care to predict as to the future. If the Middle East had become "the most important area of the world for Soviet economic, political, and military penetration,"[78] there seemed little doubt that Syria was one of the major keys to that penetration, and that the U.S.S.R. was seeking to play a significant, if lesser, role both in Lebanon and Jordan, as it was in the Arab-Israeli conflict. Whether the Soviet Union would succeed in its policies and in the achievement of its possible objectives, however, was another matter. Problems in Lebanon remained very complicated. Although the image and the prestige of the United States remained at a very low point in the Middle East after June 1967, there were serious problems and choices for the Soviet Union. There was room for doubt that it had gained commensurately with the American loss. The government of Jordan, which was very disappointed with the part played by the United States, still distrusts the Soviet Union. It is also clear that the U.S.S.R. is confronted with complicated problems in Syria—where the somewhat more moderate Major-General Hafez al-Assad seized power in November 1970—and that there is resentment in that country against the Soviet Union partly because of its position on the Palestine problem. One result of the *fedayeen* movement has been an increased suspicion of the U.S.S.R., now associated with the Arab defeat in June 1967 and with an unwillingness on its part to support another conflict with Israel. The future remains uncertain, and speculation concerning it, beyond the assumption of continuing problems and turmoil in the Middle East, appears fruitless. Nevertheless, the Egyptian ouster of Soviet technicians in the summer of 1972 suggests that the path of the Soviet Union in the Middle East will be anything but smooth.

— 8 —
The Soviet Union and Israel:
1947 - 1969

Nadav Safran

Soviet policies toward Israel, from the birth of that state to this day, present an interesting parallel with the more familiar American policies toward the Jewish state. Like the policies of the United States, Soviet policies toward Israel have been determined by an interplay between an internal "Jewish factor" and the perceived requirements of the country's interest in the Middle East region as a whole in the context of the big power struggle. However, while the internal "Jewish factor" predisposed the United States to take a *favorable* attitude toward the Jewish state that was checked or modified only when this attitude seemed to endanger broader interests in the region, that same factor predisposed the Soviet Union to take an *unfavorable* attitude toward Israel that was checked or modified only when broader Soviet interests in the region could be served by such restraint or modification.

The roots of the Soviet Union's generally hostile attitude toward Israel go back to the late nineteenth century, when the nascent Zionist and communist movements competed for the support and loyalty of the several million Jews in the domain of the tsars, who were caught at the time in a major transition crisis.

The traditional communal structures and belief system of the Jews in Russia were rapidly breaking down in the second half of the nineteenth century under the impact of incipient industrialization and the spread of "enlightenment"—secularism and rational thought. Among the Jews of Western and Central Europe who had undergone a similar process in the preceding generations, the simultaneous process of "emancipation" (the abolition of legal discrimination and disabilities against Jews and their enfranchisement) had opened for them the opportunity to reconstitute their lives as equal members of the national communities in which they lived—a course known in the vocabulary of the time as assimilation.

In tsarist Russia, however, the option of assimilation, opened up slowly in the liberal period of Alexander II's reign, was shut tighter than ever before from the eighties onward by new discriminatory laws, underscored by frequent large-scale pogroms often supported or instigated by the authorities themselves. In face of the crisis, many Jews reacted in the traditional way of their ancestors by fleeing to safer havens (this is how one and a half million East European Jews came to the United States in the decades preceding World War I). Those who did not flee westward, however, were presented by their leadership with two alternative solutions. On the one hand they were told that since Jews were not permitted to form part of the surrounding national society, they must constitute their own national society, in their ancestral homeland. The second choice suggested that since Jews could not become part of the existing national society, they must work for the transformation of that society through social revolution and internationalism.

Not only were the two alternatives antithetical in theory, but they sprouted rival movements, founded in the same year, that fought each other bitterly for the loyalty of the Jewish masses. The Bund, the revolutionary Jewish workers' organization, denounced the Zionist movement as a force that deflected the efforts of the Jewish working masses from the class struggle into a reactionary nationalist utopia, while the Zionist movement attacked the Bund for diverting the activities of Jews from national emancipation into hopeless internationalist utopianism. The communist as well as other revolutionary movements naturally upheld the Bund against Zionism; but these movements also quarreled with the Bund for its effort to retain its identity and its autonomy as a revolutionary movement of *Jewish* workers.

As the political and social ferment in Russia exploded in revolution, Britain's endorsement of the idea of a Jewish National Home in Palestine through the Balfour Declaration provided added impetus to communist hostility toward Zionism. For not only did the Declaration threaten to deflect or subvert the support of Jews for the revolution at a critical moment, but it also seemed to reveal Zionism as a vehicle of British imperialism and as a means of keeping suppressed the presumably revolutionary toiling Arab masses.

This last consideration, though it was not of much practical significance, figured prominently in communist propaganda during the interwar years.[1] The Soviet Union was compelled by war and the course of events to take an interest in its immediate neighbors to the south, but it was far too weak and too distant to play an important role in the Arab Middle East. Consequently its hostility to Zionism affected the situation in Palestine only indirectly. As Zionist activity in Russia was gradually outlawed and as Jewish emigration was first restricted and then barred altogether, one of the main springs of Jewish settlers in Palestine dried off.

The outcome of World War II drastically changed this situation. The Soviet Union, now one of the three world powers besides the United States and Britain, proceeded to surround itself with a ring of satellite countries for reasons of national security and also to propagate communist ideas and institutions. The Middle East, as the southern belt, was an area of obvious interest. However, it was necessary to be more cautious there than in Eastern Europe; for Eastern European countries had been "liberated" from the German foe whose defeat left a power vacuum, whereas the countries of the Middle Eastern belt were under the protection of Russia's allies, who could be presumed to offer effective resistance.

The Soviets made their first probe in Iran, where they delayed the withdrawal of their occupation forces, set up a puppet state in Azerbaijan, and pulled out only under American pressure and after having extracted a favorable treaty from the Iranian government. In Turkey their pressure to "share" in the defense of the Straits and then to revise the Montreux Convention and to gain the border provinces of Kars and Ardahan eventually brought them face to face with the United States. Under the Truman Doctrine Washington committed itself explicitly to the defense of Greece and Turkey, and implicitly to resisting communist expansion anywhere.

From this moment on the stage was set for the big power struggle in the Middle East. It is in the context of this struggle that the Soviet Union developed its policies toward Israel. We propose to examine these policies in their changing context in terms of six phases. Some of these phases are more clearly demarcated from their neighbors than others, and a periodization different from what we suggest may be equally plausible. On the whole, however, we find the sixfold scheme most convenient for clarity of presentation.

PHASE ONE: 1947 TO 1949
SOVIET RECOGNITION AND SUPPORT OF THE NEW STATE

At the conclusion of World War II, Great Britain seemed for the first time in history to emerge as the sole dominant power in the Middle East. It had 60,000 troops in Greece, a newly concluded treaty of alliance with Turkey, and a considerable force in Iran. It had ejected the Italians from Libya and had replaced them there; it had helped ease the French out of Syria and Lebanon and had established a position of influence with the new independent governments. It had longstanding treaties of alliance with Egypt, Iraq, and Jordan and held a mandate over Palestine. British bases dotted the entire area. Even after the 1947 Truman Doctrine transferred to the United States responsibility for the defense of the Greek-Turkish fringes of the Middle East and committed the country to a policy of containing communist expansion everywhere, the United States was quite content to leave primary responsibility in the Middle East heartland in British hands.

The strength of Britain's position, however, was more apparent than real. Already before the end of the war, nationalists in Egypt and Iraq had begun to agitate violently for the termination of the unequal treaties of their countries with Britain. In Palestine the Jews had launched a campaign of terror and other illegal activities aiming at the repeal of the 1939 White Paper that restricted Jewish immigration and settlement in Palestine. Back at home, Britain faced what John Maynard Keynes called the threat of a "financial Dunkirk" unless it took drastic measures to cut down its overseas commitments and bring them into line with the exhausted state of its resources. In the face of the economic squeeze at home and nationalist pressure abroad, the British government was compelled to revise its entire imperial position, including its position in the Middle East.

In going about this task, Foreign Secretary Bevin had one primary object in mind: to secure a few viable bases in the region from which the Suez and overland routes to the east and the Iraqi and Persian oil could be protected. Just where and how these bases should be sought was a relatively open question that might be resolved either under some collective arrangement (e.g., through the British-sponsored Arab League) or by separate negotiations with the individual Arab governments. But two things were quite clear to the Labor government's foreign secretary: first, that any bases which could serve this purpose, if they were to be viable and held cheaply, had to be held with the consent of the Arab governments concerned; and second, that the consent of these governments would depend largely on the kind of policy he adopted in Palestine.

In an effort to use the Palestine issue as a bargaining chip in his negotiations with the Arab governments, Secretary Bevin decided on a continued rigorous application of the 1939 White Paper provisions against Jewish immigration and colonization. In so doing he not only had to cope with the increasingly violent resistance of the Jews in Palestine, but he also ran more and more afoul of the American government and public opinion who were pressing hard for the resumption of large-scale immigration.

Finally, early in 1947, as it became clear that negotiations with the Arab governments for treaty revisions were leading nowhere, and in the face of mounting pressure from the Palestine Jews and the American government, the British government decided to turn the entire Palestine problem over to the United Nations. By this action, Whitehall hoped to escape the crossfire in which it was caught, either through a renewed mandate to apply an explicit policy, or through divesting itself of formal responsibility and thus being free to choose sides. In the meantime, the British move gave the opportunity to third parties, including the Soviet Union, to have a say on the future of Palestine.

Given the traditional Soviet hostility toward Zionism, it came as a great surprise when in the fall of 1947 Soviet spokesmen in the United Nations declared their support for the idea of partition and the creation of independent Jewish and Arab states in Palestine. In May 1948, when the Palestine Jews proclaimed the establishment of their state, the Soviet Union was the third nation, following the United States and Guatemala, to extend diplomatic recognition to Israel. Moreover, its recognition was *de jure*, not just *de facto* as in the case of the United States. The Soviet note of recognition, signed by Foreign Minister Molotov, read in part: "The Soviet Government hopes that the creation by the Jewish people of its sovereign state will serve the cause of strengthening peace and security in Palestine and the Near East, and expresses its confidence in the successful development of friendly relations between the U.S.S.R. and the State of Israel." The Arab invasion that followed the proclamation of Israel was condemned with indignation by the Soviet Union, which exerted itself vigorously in the United Nations on behalf of the new state. Even more significant, arms shipments from the Soviet bloc to Israel were of great and perhaps even crucial importance in helping the improvised Israeli forces to stem and eventually to reverse the tide of the Arab invasion.

This more than benevolent attitude toward Israel seems surprising not only in the light of the previous Soviet hostility to Zionism but also in the perspective of subsequent Soviet policies to the present day. However, the explanation is rather simple. As the Palestine issue came up for decision, the United Nations had before it three alternatives. The first, recommended by the majority of its own Special Committee on Palestine, urged partition; the second, advanced by the minority of the Committee, advocated a federal Jewish-Arab state; the third, pressed by the Arab delegations, insisted on independence for Palestine under rule of its Arab majority. All these proposals envisaged the termination of the British Mandate, which was what the Soviets were interested in most. However, a tally of the votes after the discussion had gone on for some time showed clearly that partition was the only proposal that had a chance of commanding the necessary two-thirds majority, and was therefore the only proposal that promised to bring about the ending of British rule in Palestine. Consequently, even though the Soviets would have intrinsically favored the federal proposal, as Gromyko indicated in one of his speeches, they cast their vote and their weight in favor of partition for the "practical reasons" that otherwise the United Nations would have reached a deadlock that would have worked in favor of continued British presence.

What about the other side of the question: did not the Soviets fear alienating the Arab countries and driving them farther into the arms of the West? The answer is that, in the first place, the West itself was divided, with the United States lining itself on the same side as the Soviet Union and against Britain, and thus in no position to take advantage of Arab resentments on this issue. In the second place, Moscow suspected that Britain was so strongly established in the Arab countries that the Soviets would not be able to cash in on any pro-Arab position they might take, and would end up sacrificing the real prospect of getting rid of British rule in Palestine for the sake of a gain in popularity of dubious real value. In the third place, the Soviets expected that insofar as nationalist agitation against Britain in various Arab countries expressed a strong force, such agitation would not be appeased by the British pro-Arab gestures over Palestine and would therefore give Moscow opportunities for gaining favor in the area in the future.

It is sometimes suggested that the Soviets had some additional reasons for supporting Israel and disregarding Arab feelings. It has been argued, for example, that the Soviet leaders may have shared in the general opinion that, after the terrible fate that had befallen the Jews of Europe, something had to be done for them; or that the Soviets were still resentful of the fact that Arab nationalist movements had taken a pro-Axis orientation in the thirties and early forties. The tendency of states to polish the pursuit of real interest with the veneer of moral virtue, when they can do so, suggests that there may be something to these arguments. On the other hand, inter-pretations such as the one suggested by Walter Laqueur to the effect that Stalin approved of the recognition of Israel in a fit of absent-mindedness seem irresponsible and gratuitous.[2]

As to Israel, which might never have been born as an independent state had it not been for the concurrence of the world's two biggest powers, its in-itial foreign policy was one of "non-identification," that is, of neutrality between the emerging blocs. At that time many Israelis, mindful of the fact that the two largest Jewish communities outside Israel were in the United States and in the Soviet Union,[3] hoped and believed that their newly born "innocent" state would manage to steer a middle course between the two superpowers and their allies. In particular, they hoped that continued good relations with Russia would lead to a resumption of Jewish emigration from that country at a time when Israel badly needed such a demographic shot in the arm, while close ties with the United States would help economically.

PHASE TWO: 1951 TO 1953
THE END OF THE HONEYMOON

This second phase in Soviet policy was marked by a progressive deteriora-tion in the relations between the two countries, a process that culminated in the break of diplomatic ties on February 11, 1953. There seem to be two reasons for this deterioration: one related to the domestic situation in the Soviet Union, the other to the international situation, in particular to the onset of the Cold War and its extension to the Middle East.

Regarding the domestic situation in the Soviet Union, it seems that one side-effect of the establishment of Israel as an independent Jewish state was to force upon the Soviet leadership the realization that, in spite of thirty years of communist rule, Zionism still had a most powerful appeal for Russian Jews. This was clearly brought to the fore by Golda Meir's visit to the Moscow Synagogue after she had been appointed Israel's first minister to the Soviet Union in 1948. On that occasion tens of thousands of Jews packed the streets of Moscow to extend a spontaneous and extremely warm welcome to the representative of the first Jewish state in almost two thousand years. Needless to say, such spontaneous mass demonstrations were not exactly a daily occurrence in the Soviet Union of the late 1940's.

The significance of incidents like this was to revive in the minds of Soviet leaders the memory of the old struggles between communism and Zionism for the loyalty of Russia's Jews, a struggle they had considered practically settled after the suppression of all traces of Zionist activity and after Russia's Jews had been subjected to over thirty years of Soviet "socialization." An indication of that concern was given in an article by Ilya Ehrenburg, the prominent Soviet Jewish writer, published in *Pravda* on September 21, 1948.[4]

It is not difficult to imagine what impact incidents like this must have had on the mind of the Stalin of those years, who had just ordered the forceful resettlement of a number of ethnic groups and who, according to Khrushchev, had refrained from deporting the Ukrainians only because there were too many of them. Starting with the arrest of the Moscow Yiddish writers in 1948, a wave of anti-Semitism of the crassest and most rabid sort engulfed not only the Soviet Union but nearly the entire Soviet bloc. It culminated in the so-called Moscow doctors' plot and the notorious Slansky trials in 1953. Naturally, this wave of anti-Semitism affected the Soviet Union's relations with Israel, which was viewed as the source of the alleged disloyal attitudes of Russian Jews.

We come now to the second reason for the deterioration of Soviet-Israeli relations, stemming from what the Soviet Union considered to be Israel's sellout to the West. Even as Israel was fighting to establish itself and defend its existence, tension between the United States and the Western powers on the one hand and the Soviet Union and its satellites on the other reached a high point with the Prague coup, the Berlin blockade, the fall of China to the communists, and Tito's defection from the Eastern bloc. In the Cold War that ensued, the United States formally espoused a policy that sought to organize a "containment" belt around the Soviet Union in order to resist any effort at communist expansion. As a first order of business the United States sought to stabilize and strengthen Western Europe. It succeeded in great measure in this aim through the launching of the Marshall Plan and the North Atlantic Treaty Organization. Thereupon the United States turned its attention to the Middle East, which was seething with the consequences of the Arab-Israeli war and the agitation of nationalists against continued British domination.

On May 25, 1950, the United States, Britain, and France, following a meeting of their foreign ministers, issued a declaration regarding security and armaments in the Middle East. After proclaiming the determination of the signatory powers to resist any effort to alter existing boundaries by force, the Tripartite Declaration went on to announce a program of arms rationing designed to prevent an arms race while allowing the countries of the region to take care of their internal security and permitting them to "play their part in the defense of the area as a whole." This last statement was understood by everyone concerned to forecast the intention of the Western powers to set up a regional defense alliance in the Middle East. The pursuit of that intention was delayed by the outbreak of the Korean War the following month, but it was resumed after that conflict had reached a stalemate and took the form of a proposal submitted to Egypt in October 1951 to join in establishing a "Middle East Defense Command."

From the point of view of the Soviet Union, "containment" was just another word for the old-fashioned "capitalist encirclement," and the formation of a Middle Eastern military bloc meant the consolidation of a Western military position in a region that bordered on the heartland of Soviet power. At a time when Soviet military thinking was still entirely dominated by conventional notions and by the recent experience of World War II, this threat appeared to be of enormous magnitude, even without the added factor of American nuclear superiority. The worse aspect of the situation was that the Soviets could do very little about it except sit back and hope that the Middle Eastern countries would turn it down—for to attempt to press them not to join and to threaten them if they did might only convince them of the reality of the Soviet danger and push them into Western arms. This is why Israel's apparent eagerness to join the Western project was particularly infuriating to them.

From the point of view of Israel, its own primary interest in the Western plans derived from its relations with its Arab neighbors. On the one hand, it thought it could not afford to stay out of an arrangement that bid fair to strengthen its enemies militarily, economically, and diplomatically. On the other hand, joining in a regional defense organization with its neighbors might just prove to be the way to circumvent their opposition to reaching a peace settlement with it. In addition, a number of reasons contributed to inclining Israeli policy toward the West. First, the Korean War aroused the concern of the Israeli government lest, in case of a general war, which looked like a real possibility at that time, Israel should be isolated not only militarily but also economically. Secondly, the Korean conflict led the United States to press members of the United Nations to "stand up and be counted." Israel, who saw in the American intervention against the invasion of South Korea by North Korea a precedent from which it might benefit at some future date, responded by voting with the West on all questions in this critical East-West issue. Finally, the beginning of the Soviet anti-Jewish campaign and the bitter attacks against Israel which, starting with a Pravda article on November 24, 1949, went on at a steady crescendo, had a feedback effect on the Israeli government.

This combination of internal and external reasons made a vicious circle that drove Israeli-Soviet relations to their lowest point. On February 9, 1953, the Soviet legation in Tel Aviv was bombed and several members of its staff were wounded. The Israeli government promptly denounced the action and extended profuse apologies, but two days later the Soviet Union broke off diplomatic relations with Israel while denouncing its government in some of the harshest terms in the Soviet vocabulary.

It is important to note that the Soviet quarrel with Israel at this juncture was not motivated by an effort to gain the favor of the Arabs. The deterioration of relations between the two countries did not lead the Soviet Union to side automatically with the Arab states in the Arab-Israeli dispute, as it was to do later. Thus, on April 17, 1950, the Soviet Union, which had voted for the General Assembly's resolution of December 9, 1949, calling for the internationalization of Jerusalem, informed the secretary general that "in view of the opposition of the people of Jerusalem" it was withdrawing its support of internationalization—a switch that could only please Israel, even though it was surely not so meant. On September 1, 1951, the Soviet Union cast its vote in favor of a Security Council resolution calling upon Egypt to open the Suez Canal to Israeli shipping. In this case it is possible that the Soviet Union may have joined the other members of the Security Council in condemning Egypt's interference with Israeli shipping as a violation of the Constantinople Convention governing navigation in the Suez Canal because it feared that this violation, if condoned silently, might encourage Turkey to start tampering with the Montreux Convention governing navigation through the Straits. On the other hand, in 1952 the Soviet Union abstained on a resolution calling on Israel and the Arab countries to enter into direct negotiations when it was considered by the United Nations *ad hoc* Political Committee. When the resolution was submitted to the General Assembly, the U.S.S.R. joined the Arab states in voting against it.

PHASE THREE: 1953 TO 1955
DETENTE AND LOST OPPORTUNITIES

With the death of Stalin (March 5, 1953), relations between the Soviet Union and Israel changed rapidly. Following informal talks, diplomatic ties were resumed on July 21, 1953. As part of the agreement to renew these ties, Israel committed itself not to join any anti-Soviet pact, treaty, or arrangement, an indication of the substantive issue at the center of Soviet concern once the internal Jewish question was laid aside.

In December 1953 an oil-for-citrus barter trade agreement provided for the import by Israel of Soviet fuel oil in sizable quantities. This was an important deal because, as a result of the blockade of the Suez Canal and the Tiran Straits, Israel was entirely cut off from the oil fields in the Persian Gulf and had to import oil from as far away as the United States. Thus, in effect, the Soviet Union was instrumental in helping Israel circumvent the Arab economic boycott in the sphere where it hurt most.

In June 1954 the Soviet legation in Tel Aviv and the Israeli legation in Moscow were raised to embassy level and the Soviet ambassador presented his credentials in Jerusalem, the capital, rather than in Tel Aviv. The Soviet Union was, after the Netherlands and Chile, the third country and the first power of some consequence to do so. For the Israelis, given the unwillingness shown by most other powers to recognize Jerusalem as the country's capital in view of the United Nations internationalization resolution, this was a crucial issue.

While the Soviet Union thus gave important tokens of its willingness to restore good relations with Israel, it did not side systematically with Israel in the Arab-Israeli dispute. Thus, on a number of occasions—such as the Nahalin incident, the Lake Huleh conflict, the follow-up on the 1952 resolution on free passage in the Suez Canal—the Soviet Union espoused the Arab point of view in the United Nations. This ambivalence pointed to a desire on the part of the new Soviet leaders to leave all their options open while an issue that they considered crucial hung in the balance.

The change in the Soviet attitude toward Israel was related not only to the general domestic relaxation that followed the death of Stalin but was connected also with changes that had intervened in the general international situation and, in particular, with an altered political-strategic relationship between the superpowers and its implications for the Middle East. Beginning with the first Eisenhower administration, the United States replaced the old global containment policy, of which Korea represented the most dramatic application, with the so-called New Look or massive retaliation policy generally associated with the name of Secretary of State John Foster Dulles.

Strategically, the key feature of the New Look policy was that it no longer bound the United States to meet communist aggression at the point of its occurrence or to use only conventional weapons. Rather it declared that the United States would meet such aggression with massive retaliation by means and at places of its own choosing.[5] In practice, this policy had become possible because, after Korea, the United States Congress had loosened the purse strings, thus permitting the launching of a vast nuclear and thermonuclear armament program which by 1953 had given the United States a distinct superiority over the Soviet Union. The core of the New Look policy was an American second-strike capacity that rested on a ring of air bases around the Soviet perimeter from which American bombers could attack any part of the Soviet Union. This put a premium on obtaining through alliances access to bases in the Middle East among other places. In order to explore the possibilities of such alliances, Secretary Dulles had toured the area in early 1953 and, upon his return, had reported that at least the "Northern Tier" countries (Turkey, Iraq, Iran) seemed to be responsive. The explorations led to action that eventually produced an alliance that came to be known as the Baghdad Pact, officially signed in 1955.

The Western attempt to establish a Middle East alliance in the context of the New Look strategy was even more worrisome to the Soviets than the previous effort to fit the Middle East into the containment strategy. For where the containment strategy at least pretended to be defensive, that of the New Look frankly fused defense and offense. As the Soviets took stock of the ways and means that could be used to frustrate the Western efforts, Israel appeared to them to be an obvious asset. For not only had Israel just committed itself not to join in any anti-Soviet alliance, but its own real interest seemed to dictate a policy of vigorous opposition to the proposed pact.

Back in 1950, Israel had been directly asked about its willingness to participate in a regional defense scheme. The following year, it had not been excluded from the Allied Middle Command scheme, though it was left under no illusion that participation by the Arab states and in particular Egypt took priority. In the elaboration of the project that was to produce the Baghdad Pact, however, it was clear from the outset that Israel would be kept out of it. This could not but fill the Israelis with apprehension. They had visions of their Arab opponents being supplied with large quantities of military hardware through their participation in the Western-sponsored defense pact while they were left out in the cold to fend for themselves. Thus in 1953 and 1954 there was a real convergence of interests between a Soviet Union bent on opposing Western efforts to draw the Arab countries into the anti-Soviet alliance and an Israel spurned by the Western powers in favor of its Arab opponents and desperately seeking some source of support for its security.[6]

It is tempting to speculate on the subsequent course of events had this convergence of interest led to some kind of Israeli-Soviet entente. Although from the perspective of the present such an entente may seem far-fetched, it is hardly more inconceivable than the association of the Soviet Union with the regime of the Egyptian colonels, whom the Soviets had initially denounced as a reactionary fascist clique. In Israel, at least, there has always been a strong socialist minority ready to go to almost any length to strengthen Israeli ties with the Soviet Union (principally the Mapam party and the Leachdut Haavoda party). But be that as it may, the fact was that the Israelis were still too shocked by their recent experience with the Soviets to contemplate any entente with them.

When their strenuous exertions against the Baghdad Pact proved of no avail, the Israelis sought to obtain a security guarantee from NATO, if possible, or from the United States alone. As we know, nothing came of these efforts, since the Western powers wanted to avoid antagonizing the Arab countries whose participation or acquiescence in the regional defense pact they deemed essential. However, the very exertions of Israel to obtain a Western guarantee did not fail to sour the Soviet Union, who saw in them a violation of the commitment Israel had made at the time diplomatic ties were resumed in 1953. The Israelis thought of a Western guarantee as a means to underpin their security in their conflict with the Arabs, but the Soviets could conceive of such a move only as being directed against them.

While the Israelis were exerting themselves in the vain effort to obtain a security guarantee from the United States, the Soviet Union found another candidate in the region to carry the burden of "local" opposition to the Baghdad Pact. For reasons that we cannot consider here, from the middle of 1954 Egypt, which had earlier been responsible for scuttling the Middle East Defense Command proposal, revealed itself as an opponent of the Western alliance project at once more determined and more promising than Israel. This led the Soviets to revise their judgment of the new Egyptian regime, specifically with respect to its willingness and its ability to stand up to the West. The resultant change in Soviet policies toward the Middle East ushered in a new phase in the relations between the Soviet Union and Israel.

PHASE FOUR: 1955 TO 1958
THE COLD WAR IN THE MIDDLE EAST
AND RENEWED SOVIET-ISRAELI ESTRANGEMENT

In 1955 the Soviet Union, seeing an opportunity to fight the Baghdad Pact while getting around the Northern Tier countries, concluded the epoch-making arms deal with Egypt.

At the time the deal with Egypt was concluded, Soviet diplomats were almost apologetic about its implications for Israel. Again and again they assured one and all that the deal had nothing to do with the Arab-Israeli conflict. Although this assurance did not reduce a bit the military advantage gained by Egypt over Israel, it did reflect genuinely the Soviet position toward the Arab-Israeli conflict at that time. The position, quite unlike later Soviet attitudes, was one of relative detachment.

Indeed, at the time of the first arms deal with Egypt, there were widespread reports and speculations that the Soviet Union might be willing to supply arms to Israel, too.[7] Moreover, on April 17, 1956, the Soviet Union issued a statement saying that the Palestine question should be resolved on a "mutually acceptable basis," which was, of course, anathema to the Arabs. It was only after the 1956 Suez war that the Soviets began to explain their arms shipments to the Arab states more and more in terms of contributing to the defense of the Arab States against Israeli aggressiveness and thus to depict themselves as champions of the Arabs in their conflict with Israel.

The Soviet Union could not have failed to be impressed by the tremendous excitement caused in the Arab world by its arms deal with Egypt. This excitement was, of course, due to the fact that the Arab public saw in the deal only a promise of a victorious contest with Israel and of Soviet support for the Arabs in such a contest. While gratified by the tremendous, unexpected propaganda dividends thus gained, the Soviets were at first wary lest the Western powers should read the deal in the same light and react accordingly. They did nothing, therefore, to encourage the Arabs in their belief. In their diplomatic notes to the Western powers at that time they were careful to stress that they were not espousing wholly the Arab cause against Israel.

However, as the arms deal eventually impelled Israel to enter into collusion with France and Britain to attack Egypt, and as the United States condemned its own allies and worked actively to frustrate their aim, the Soviet Union felt it safe to reach out for all the credit that Arab opinion was wishfully eager to attribute to it. Thus, during the crisis itself, but only after it had passed its dangerous phase, Premier Bulganin sent two notes to Israel in which Israel's very existence was put in question. Thereafter, the barter trade agreement was cancelled by the Soviet Union and the Soviet ambassador was summoned back to Moscow, where he remained for five months. Finally, the Soviet Union began right away to replace with more and better weapons the arms Egypt had lost in the war. All this was done with maximum fanfare and amidst resounding declarations portraying the Soviet Union as the Arabs' savior and faithful ally. At the same time, however, the Soviets were careful to remind the West every now and then in little-publicized formal diplomatic notes that they still recognized Israel's right to exist, and had by no means espoused the Arab position that denied it that very right and sought to destroy it.

In the two years following the Suez war, relations between the Soviet Union and Israel settled down to a pattern of "qualified hostility." The hostility aspect of the pattern was nurtured, on the Soviet side, by the continued supply of arms to the Arab countries and by periodical propaganda attacks on Israel designed to keep alive in Arab minds the image of Soviet support of the Arab cause. On the Israeli side, it was nurtured by Israel's qualified endorsement of the Eisenhower Doctrine in May 1957, by the development of a tacit Franco-Israeli alliance, and by Israeli military cooperation with West Germany which, in Soviet eyes, put Israel unequivocally in the Western camp. The hostility was somewhat tempered by occasional indications of Soviet interest in settling the problems of the region on the basis of respect for the sovereignty and integrity of the countries in the area, on the one hand, and on the other by Israel's refraining from playing any active role in the American anti-Soviet anti-Nasser offensive launched under the aegis of the Eisenhower Doctrine.

Thus, for example, during the Syrian crisis of 1957, at a time when Turkey, Iraq, and Jordan massed troops on Syria's frontiers while the Sixth Fleet cruised in the vicinity of Syria's coast, Israel sat completely still, to the surprise and unacknowledged pleasure of the Soviets. Much the same was true during the 1958 crisis in Lebanon and Iraq, when Israel's contribution was restricted to allowing the overflight of British and American planes on their way to Jordan.

PHASE FIVE: 1959 TO 1967
REORIENTATION OF SOVIET POLICIES
AND SHARPENED ANTAGONISM

Soviet relations with Israel during the 1959-67 period and until the crisis of May-June 1967 appeared to be no different outwardly from the pattern of qualified hostility that had characterized the previous phase. To be sure, there were moments during this nine-year period when relations seemed to incline toward improvement (as when cultural exchanges were taking place or when the Soviet Union allowed the dribble of Jewish emigration to increase to a trickle of a few hundred a year). And there were other moments when relations seemed to be headed toward deterioration (as when the Soviet Union supported the Arab claims in the Jordan waters dispute or when it vetoed resolutions in the Security Council that aimed at condemning renewed Arab sabotage actions against Israel while it consistently advocated the sternest condemnation of Israel for its retaliatory actions). But at no specific moment did these fluctuations seem to forecast any *qualitative* change in what had apparently become a well-established and predictable pattern.

In reality, however, the Soviet attitude toward Israel underwent a basic alteration during this period that was nonetheless crucial for being subtle and for passing largely undetected even by the parties themselves until its consequences were upon them. The reason for this elusiveness is that the change came about not as a result of any deliberate decisions by the Soviets vis-à-vis Israel but as a consequence of a modification in the conception of their interests in the Middle East as a whole, which always provided the context for their relations with Israel. To explain this we must make a slight digression.

Generally speaking, we may say that until 1959 the interest of the Soviets in the Middle East heartland was essentially a function of their interest in the Northern Tier. We have already seen how the Soviet Union tried after World War II to extend its "security belt" to Turkey and Iran (as well as Greece), and we have indicated how this effort boomeranged and ended up by driving these countries into the powerful embrace of the United States. Lacking any promising wedge to alter the situation in these countries, which had long been accustomed to suspect and to fear Russian expansionism, the Soviets leaped at the opportunity by Nasser to establish for themselves a position in the Middle East heartland in the hope that they could afterward trade it for the neutralization of the Northern Tier. Indeed, the record shows that each time the Soviets scored or appeared to score an advantage in the area's heartland—after the arms deal of 1955, after the 1956 Suez war, after the failure of the 1957 American effort to topple the pro-Soviet Syrian regime, and after the Iraqi revolution of 1958—they made formal proposals inviting the Western powers to discuss the neutralization of the *entire* Middle East.

At the beginning of 1959 the thinking in Moscow changed. On the one hand, the Soviet position in the heartland seemed by them to be too strong and too well entrenched to be traded away for advantages in the Northern Tier. The U.S.S.R. was now established in Iraq and in Syria as well as in Egypt, and the wave of Arab nationalism on which the Soviets were riding appeared sufficiently powerful to engulf the rest of the Arab East. Moreover, in Iraq itself the communists had quickly captured a powerful position in the regime established by General Kassem and bid fair to establish the first communist stronghold in the Arab world. On the other hand, the importance of the Northern Tier countries from a strategic point of view had begun to decline as the United States, as well as the Soviet Union, proceeded to rest its strategic deterrent on intercontinental missiles and missile-carrying submarines. Moreover, the governments of Turkey and Iran were beginning to show greater responsiveness to Soviet offers of friendship, aid, and trade, an attitude that gave the Soviet government hope of improving its position there without sacrificing its hold on the heartland.

Consequently four or five years after their 1955 breakthrough, the Soviets came to consider their position in the Middle East heartland as an end in itself, for which specific rationalizations could easily be found. A reflection of this change is seen in the fact that Khrushchev withdrew the offer he had made after the 1958 Iraqi revolution to discuss the Middle East with the big Western powers, although the West had for the first time signified its willingness to accept the Soviet offer.

As the Soviet Union became established as a Middle Eastern power with several Arab clients, it began to find itself caught up in the vagaries of inter-Arab and intra-Arab politics that had caused the United States and Britain so much trouble in previous years. Thus Soviet support of Kassem on the grounds that he gave the communists a free hand brought Moscow into an open clash with Nasser; nor did the Russian communists' support of Kassem prevent his turning around afterward and pulling the rug from under them. Kassem's war against the Kurds, with tacit communist acquiescence, cost the Soviets the confidence of these allies of long standing. By the same token, the Iraqi chief's savage repression of opposition at home, in which the Soviets were implicitly compromised, meant that when the Ba'athists overthrew Kassem in 1963 they all but broke off relations with the Soviet Union after wreaking terrible vengeance on the Iraqi communists. Similar troubles confronted the Soviets with regard to Syria as they first supported its merger with Egypt, then opposed it, then recognized and helped the secessionist regime before it was overthrown by Ba'athists and Arab nationalists, and so on. Meanwhile the United States, which had been forced by events and by its reduced need for strategic positions in the Middle East into a more detached role, found itself in the position of sitting back and gathering up the fruits of Soviet troubles in much the same way as the Soviets had previously profited from U.S. difficulties. Washington was thus able to establish good working relations with Egypt and to consolidate at minimum cost and trouble its remaining positions in the region so recently threatened with collapse.

As the Soviets attempted to solidify and to make permanent their hold on this area embroiled in strife and factionalism, they began almost imperceptibly to regard Israel and to use it as a convenient rod to absorb some of the inter-Arab strife that was working to their own disadvantage. Then, as Israel reacted and the Arab-Israeli borders flared up again, the Soviets began to look upon Israel and to treat it as an immediate and dangerous threat to the regimes on which their position in the region rested. This approach was to contribute to the precipitation of the 1967 explosion. Briefly, the process unfolded in the following way:

For several years after 1959, while the Soviets struggled with the problems raised by the "Arab cold war," they continued to treat Israel according to the already established pattern of qualified hostility. Then, early in 1964, the opportunity of gaining some relief from inter-Arab turmoil presented itself in the form of Nasser's call for an all-Arab summit to consider the question of Israel's diversion of part of the Jordan River's waters for irrigation projects. The Soviets seized the opportunity and backed the Arabs' water claims, even though these had as their basic premise the denial of the legitimacy of Israel's existence. In addition the U.S.S.R. expressed its support for the resolutions of the several summits even though these had war as their logical conclusion. Perhaps the need for a respite blinded the Soviets to the dangers implicit in their stance, or perhaps they thought the danger of war would not materialize if the Arabs remained united instead of egging one another on to extreme courses. In any case, the fact was that before long the Arabs fell back to quarrelling and fighting among themselves. The net outcome of the "summitry" was that Syria, in its desire to make its contribution in the Arab counter-diversion project and to prove to the other Arab countries that the strategy of guerrilla it had proposed at the summit meetings was workable, became engaged in a small war with Israel.

In February 1965 a coup d'état brought to power in Syria a "left Ba'athist" government that proclaimed an even more militant stance against Israel than its predecessor. The Ba'athists proceeded forthwith to organize in earnest and to launch guerrilla operations against the enemy. The Soviets, who were particularly pleased with the new government because it included at least one communist minister, belatedly advised caution. When their counsel went unheeded, they tried to spare their wayward client the consequences of its actions by securing for it additional protection against Israeli retaliation. No less a personality than Premier Kosygin himself undertook in the course of a visit to Cairo in May 1966 to reconcile the Egyptian and Syrian regimes. Kosygin succeeded in having the two states conclude in November a mutual defense treaty with provision for a unified command under Egyptian leadership. But the treaty failed to deter Israel from responding to Syria's actions in various ways including air strikes, one of which resulted in an air engagement over Syria's territory in April 1967 in which seven Syrian planes were shot down and Israeli planes buzzed Damascus.

This last operation apparently shook the Syrian regime, which, however, vowed to continue the fight. Israel at the same time threatened worse. With typical insight the Soviets recognized that the Syrian regime was in danger. But with typical logic they attributed the roots of the danger not to the obvious chain of immediate cause and effect, but to "broader historical forces" according to the following syllogism: The Syrian regime is "progressive" by definition since it has a communist minister. The United States hates progressive regimes, by definition. Israel is a tool of the United States, by definition. Therefore, by definition, the Israeli attacks and threats against Syria are part of a United States design to bring down the Syrian government, just as it had brought down the progressive government of Indonesia, Ghana, and Greece, to mention only the most recent examples.

To ward off the threat, the Soviets turned to Nasser, the leader of the "alliance of progressive Arab states" that they had promoted the previous year, and informed him on May 13, 1967, that the Israelis were about to invade Syria. Their idea was probably to induce him to make some sort of military demonstration in order to deter Israel from undertaking even a limited action. Nasser was quick to oblige, but, alas, went much farther than they had intended him to go. The result, the unfolding of which is analyzed elsewhere,[8] was war and crushing defeat, not only for Egypt and Syria, but for Jordan as well.

A NEW PHASE? 1967 TO 1969

It is too early as yet to generalize about Soviet relations with Israel in the two and one-half years that have elapsed since the war. The repercussions of that war are still with us, and even if we knew the Soviet intentions for certain, they could still change under the pressure of the course of events. The following remarks are therefore presented as hopefully informed speculations which, even if they should be now on target, may yet be invalidated by a subsequent abrupt turn of events.

A chronicler of "the facts that made the news" would be most likely to draw the conclusion that Soviet relations with Israel have reached their nadir in the two and one-half years that have elapsed since the 1967 crisis. The Soviet Union has not only broken off diplomatic relations with Israel, as it did in the previous low point of 1953, but it has also frequently voiced veiled military threats against Israel. In addition Moscow has done its utmost to mobilize diplomatic opposition to the young state, and has exerted itself to rearm and retrain the armed forces of the Arab countries. In short, the U.S.S.R. has lined itself up completely with Israel's enemies.

These facts are, of course, incontestable. Yet the conclusion I would draw from the crisis and its aftermath is that they provide at least the basis for a very "positive" relationship between the two countries. The apparent paradox of this view would disappear if we were to switch the emphasis from the surface facts, which may have only tactical relevance, to the more important underlying attitudes. We have seen in this analysis that the Soviet policies toward Israel and the Arab-Israeli conflict have undergone several mutations since 1948. Yet throughout these mutations, up to 1967, the Soviet Union had consistently viewed Israel as an object rather than as a subject, or, more precisely, as a country that could at most protect itself against Soviet moves but could not, by itself, initiate moves that could hurt the Soviet Union.

The Soviet Union could therefore afford to treat Israel in cavalier fashion and to play the Arab-Israeli conflict to its own advantage, secure in the knowledge that Israel could not seriously hit back at Soviet interests. To be sure, Israel had shown in 1956 that it could be a catspaw for bigger powers; but precisely the outcome of the 1956 venture made it clear that theoretically only the United States could make use of Israel, and the United States was practically inhibited by its interests in the Arab countries from doing so. During the year or two preceding the 1967 war, the Soviets seemed to begin to develop a greater respect for Israel (i.e., a greater sense that it might be capable of hurting them); but this feeling was evidently not strong enough to overcome the tradition of contempt for the Jewish state and its capabilities. Rather than attributing Israel's toughness to its confidence in its strength and in its cause, and rather than chalking up its demonstrated military achievements in the limited encounters with the Arabs to intrinsic capacity, the Soviets chose to attribute the achievements to contingent reasons and to attribute the toughness to the implausible explanation of American egging on. The crisis of 1967 compelled the Soviets to change their views fundamentally and to look upon Israel as a power capable of affecting very seriously, if not decisively, their interests in the Middle East. Accordingly Moscow seemed impelled to think of handling its relations with Israel on the basis of calculations that sought to accommodate the basic interests of both countries rather than on the basis of unilateral, peremptory initiatives.

The change in attitude, as I have just implied, resulted from the Soviet acceptance of two realities, an acceptance forced by the events themselves: first, the demonstrated strength of Israel, and second, their own vulnerability in the region. The acceptance of these two realities is related to and conditioned by several other pertinent perceptions. First, the Soviets had to acknowledge, at least to themselves, that the United States had not wanted the war and had done its best to prevent it; and that the war was consequently the result of the interplay of local and regional forces to which they themselves may have contributed more than the United States. There is a tacit outward admission of this fact in the eagerness of the Soviets to negotiate a settlement with the United States.

Secondly, the Soviets had to recognize that within the framework of local regional politics, it was the Arab states themselves, led by Nasser, who took the initiatives that made war inevitable, and consequently that it was the Arabs who chose the time and the terms of the trial of strength. However much the Soviets attempted to disguise the fact that the war was a "fair test of force" by labeling Israel's action as aggression, their real conviction visibly lurks beneath the disguise.

Thirdly, the Soviets had to admit not only that Israel was much stronger than they had thought, but that the Arabs were much weaker than they had estimated.

Fourthly, the reflection of their double mistake in the short duration and devastating outcome of the war brought the Soviets face to face with a realization that had hardly entered the strategy of their overall planning: the possibility that their *entire* position in the Arab Middle East might collapse within days as a result of a sudden military collapse of the regimes on which that position rested.

Fifthly, the Soviets had to recognize that they had much less control over the situation than they had thought, and that their own clients could take actions which not only endangered their position in the Middle East, but also exposed their interests beyond the region and risked embroiling them in a disastrous confrontation with the United States.

The result of all this learning process has been to impel the Soviets to seek to terminate the Arab-Israeli conflict through some form of peaceful settlement. Many people contest the sincerity of Soviet expressions to this effect on the grounds that the continuation of the conflict, perhaps at a mitigated level to avoid an explosion, best serves the interests of the Soviets since it makes greater the Arabs' dependence on them and places the United States on the spot because of its traditional support of Israel. However, these people fail to take into account the following crucial factors: 1) that greater dependence on the Soviet Union means also a very high price tag in roubles and kopecks. To take only one form of dependence, what with the arms lost in the war by Syria and Egypt and the replacements that were provided gratis after the war, the Soviet Union must have lost one and one-half to two billion roubles; 2) that, if the conflict is to continue, there is no assurance at all that it can be kept at a "mitigated" level short of explosion and that, explosion or no explosion, if continuation of the conflict hurts the American position in the Arab world, it exposes the Soviet position in that world to total collapse as a result of the danger of collapse of client regimes under the pressure; 3) that the Soviet Union may very well be looking now to interests that are broader than the Middle East and that could best be served by a settlement in the Middle East rather than by continued conflict. The growth of the Soviet merchant marine and navy and the creation of a Mediterranean fleet, which made its debut a few months before the 1967 war, are strong pointers in that direction and certainly suggest that the Soviets could profit greatly from a reopening of the Suez canal.

What then, it might be asked, has prevented a settlment for two and one-half years? This is a fitting subject for at least a separate paper;[9] but I would point out here than one crucial factor is the weakness of the leverage the Soviets could use to induce Nasser to agree to peace. This, if my point in the last few pages has been made clear, is another reason for the Soviets to desire some sort of settlement in the Middle East.

— 9 —
Soviet Studies on the Middle East
Wayne S. Vucinich

For the purpose of this study the Middle East is defined as including the Arabic-speaking countries of North Africa and Southwest Asia, Israel, Turkey, Iran, and Afghanistan. I have not included Mauritania, though Arabic is one of its two official languages; nor have I included Pakistan, despite its strong ties of culture with Afghanistan and the rest of the Middle East.

Middle Eastern studies in the Soviet Union fall within the broad field of Orientalism, which embraces the whole of Asia and Africa. Certain Orientalists and sections of academies of science and universities concentrate on Arabic, Turkish, or Persian studies, or on archaeological or ethnographical studies that have a bearing on the Middle East. Sporadic work on this area is carried on also by various centers of learning whose research tends not to be circumscribed by geographical limits. In reviewing Soviet studies on the Middle East, therefore, we must examine the whole range of Soviet Orientalism in an effort to isolate those segments that relate specifically to the Middle East.

Since the beginning of the eighteenth century Russians have produced important works on the Middle East. They have collected published and unpublished materials and have trained experts to follow in their footsteps. The October Revolution caused a momentary disruption in this scholarly activity. During the First World War and immediately afterward, a number of Russian Orientalists died. Some left Russia as political refugees to continue their work abroad. Many of those who remained were thwarted by the unsettled conditions, by their inability to conform to communist ideological requirements and to secure institutional sponsorship, and by limited opportunities for publication. The few who were able to adjust to the new circumstances became the founders and pillars of contemporary Soviet Oriental studies.

The importance of the Muslim world looms large in Soviet eyes. Millions of Muslims are Soviet citizens and many millions more live abroad along the Soviet borders. Soviet leaders after the first World War took advantage of the revolutionary movements in many parts of the Middle East to appeal to the peoples of that region to rise against their colonial oppressors. At the

177

same time they took steps to reorganize the old centers of Oriental research and to found new ones equipped to train experts and agitators who could promote the cause of communism among the peoples of the Middle East and Asia. While some of the centers were attached to academic institutions, others were affiliated with the government, the Communist Party, or the army. With the purpose of coordinating Oriental studies, the Vsesoiuznaia nauchnaia assotsiatsiia vostokovedeniia (All-Union Scientific Association of Oriental Studies [VNAV]) was founded in 1921. The VNAV, which was attached to the government, was organized into two departments and a number of sections and commissions. The section on the Middle East was responsible for research and publications concerning the countries of this region. Besides the journal *Novyi Vostok* (New East), VNAV published a number of monographs.[1]

Several scholarly and semi-scholarly journals published in the interwar period carried articles on the Middle East. During these years a number of classics were translated, some good monographs were written, and collections of documents were published. A few textbooks and anthologies appeared, as well as the proceedings of professional meetings. The main efforts of the Soviet Orientalists of this period were directed toward discrediting Islam, encouraging national liberation movements, exposing colonialism and imperialism, and rewriting the history of the Middle Eastern peoples in accordance with Marxist-Leninist ideas.

THE INSTITUTE OF ORIENTAL STUDIES

By the end of the twenties it was decided that the study of the Orient no longer required separate academic, governmental, and party institutions. After much discussion, the Asiatic Museum, the College of Orientalists, the Institute of Buddhist Culture, and the Turcological Cabinet were merged in 1930 into a single Institute of Oriental Studies of the Academy of Sciences, with headquarters in Leningrad. While the army and the party, each in its own way, continued to investigate developments in the Orient and to train bureaucrats and agents, most of the basic research was done in the Institute of Oriental Studies, in certain other institutes of the Soviet Academy of Sciences, and in the academies of other republics.

In both quality and quantity, Soviet interwar research on the Middle East was low. The Institute of Oriental Studies passed through a series of crises and was purged and reorganized. Official interference with scholarship, shifts in government and party tactics, the Stalin personality cult and the purges in the thirties, controversies over historical interpretations—all these and other difficulties seriously impeded Middle Eastern studies and resulted in frequent reorganizations of research centers.

With the advent of the Second World War, Soviet Oriental studies were disrupted and priorities were affected as military and political interests dictated that primary attention be focused on Japan, China, and the Pacific Basin. However, research on the Middle East did not come to a complete halt. When the Institute of Oriental Studies was moved from Leningrad to Tashkent at the beginning of the war, only some of its staff members went along. Others went to Moscow, and still others were drawn into government, military, or party service. Those who went to Moscow, including I. Iu. Krachkovskii, the leading Soviet Arabist, continued to do research under difficult conditions. In the midst of the war, Krachkovskii organized the Moscow Group of the Institute of Oriental Studies of the Academy of Sciences.

After the war the Institute returned to Leningrad, but again not all the Orientalists made the move. Indeed, those who remained in Moscow were joined in sufficient numbers by colleagues who had spent the war in Tashkent so that there were now more Orientalists in Moscow than in Leningrad. Nevertheless, the Institute of Oriental Studies in Leningrad remained principally responsible for research and publications on the Middle East. Under its sponsorship Soviet Orientalists met on several occasions to discuss research problems, to take stock of Oriental studies in the Soviet Union, and to resolve some of the controversial questions regarding the interpretation of historical events. Government leaders in the late forties often criticized the Institute for failure to provide leadership and for allowing mistaken and dangerous views to appear in published works.

In 1950, in order to establish firmer control over scientific inquiry in the Soviet Union, the Central Committee of the Soviet Communist Party took steps to cleanse research centers of persons considered untrustworthy. The Institute was transferred from Leningrad to Moscow and its research program was reassessed and focused. Thereafter, reorganized and enlarged through the absorption of other research institutions, it became the coordinating body for Oriental studies in the Soviet Union. The well-known historian S. P. Tolstov was named director.

The recast Institute of Oriental Studies consisted of several sectors (smaller than sections), three of which were engaged in the study of the Middle East and adjacent territories. These were the sectors on Iran, on Turkey and the Arab countries, and on India and Afghanistan. Research on Turkey and the Arab countries was assigned to a single sector because of a shortage of Middle East experts, especially economists.

Among the major questions debated in Soviet historical and political circles during the immediate postwar years were colonialism and the national liberation movement.[2] In 1947 F. Zhukov wrote that the Soviet Union was the implacable enemy of all forms of colonialism, and added that Marxism-Leninism called on all oppressed peoples to fight for their complete liberation. In so doing, he pointed out, they would unite the national liberation movements of the oppressed peoples with the revolutionary struggle of the proletariat.[3] Soviet spokesmen argued that national liberation was not possible without communist leadership. After the founding of the Cominform in September 1947 and Andrei Zhdanov's proclamation of the "two camp" theory, the communists in different Asian countries were urged to seize power.

Between 1949 and 1951 a new Soviet line was adopted according to which the workers, in their struggle for national independence, were asked to join the "national bourgeoisie" (composed of liberal landowners and intelligentsia).[4] From this time on the Soviet Union gave more attention to the colonial and dependent peoples. It also began to participate in international trade and economic conferences (Singapore, 1951; Moscow, 1952) and in the United Nations technical assistance program.

The new Soviet policy, which was implemented in 1953 after Stalin's death, imposed added responsibilities on the Institute of Oriental Studies, and in that year the Institute was given a new organization. This time it was divided into three regional sections, one of which was responsible for research on the Near East and the Middle East, and three independent sectors, including that on the Ancient East, which sponsored research on the Near East and the Middle East, and a sector for Oriental manuscripts located in Leningrad. The Institute was directed to draw up a plan for research and publications on the Middle East and the rest of the Asian world and to train more experts proficient in the languages, history, and contemporary affairs of the countries in the region. The plan called for monographs on specific problems, as well as for guidebooks and brief historical surveys on the Middle Eastern countries. The result was a series of hastily compiled works cloaked in Marxist-Leninist garb, which had as their purpose the promotion of Soviet state interests. In these writings Soviet authors concentrated heavily on condemning European colonialism and imperialism and lauding the national liberation movements. Historians were told that they had made mistakes in denying a progressive role to the national bourgeoisie, in exaggerating the role of the working class in the anti-imperialist movements,[5] and in failing to appreciate the extent of capitalist development in some of the Middle Eastern countries. The national bourgeoisie was looked upon as an ally of the workers because its struggle against imperialism coincided with popular aspirations. The focus thus was shifted from the internal class struggle in the Middle Eastern countries to the united "anti-imperialist struggle." Soviet historians were prodded to do more meticulous investigation of the national liberation movements. The experts were expected to discredit Western historiography on the Middle East, to hold the Western powers primarily responsible for the backwardness of the Middle Eastern countries, and to show that the Soviet Union, unlike the Western powers, was the genuine friend of the Middle Eastern peoples, always ready to aid them in their struggle for national independence.

But despite the pressure on historians, the study of the Middle East continued to lag. In 1955, in fact, only sixty-six of the two hundred and twenty persons in the Institute of Oriental Studies engaged in research specialized on the Middle East. During the fifties, however, a number of developments—among them the Iranian oil crisis of 1951-54, the signing of the Baghdad Pact in 1955, and the Suez War of 1956—prompted the Soviet Union to adopt a more flexible foreign policy attitude toward the Middle Eastern countries. Moscow sought the friendship of the Middle Eastern peoples and tried to bolster their resistance to Western hegemony over the region. Until 1955 the Kremlin was still vacillating in its policy toward the liberation movements. Some movements, such as Pan-Islamism and Pan-Arabism, were almost consistently rejected.[6] But since 1955 Soviet policy had tended to throw its support behind the national liberation movements in the Middle East because the goal of these movements has been to free their countries from Western domination. The Kremlin expanded trade and diplomatic ties with the Middle Eastern countries, concluded cultural and scientific agreements with them, and sent Soviet scholars to these countries for study and research. In addition the Soviet Union extended scientific and educational assistance to several Middle Eastern countries.[7]

On August 12, 1955, the Institute of Oriental Studies was reorganized once more, this time into twelve cabinets. One cabinet took charge of research on the Middle East and another of research on the languages of the Near East and the Middle East.[8] A separate cabinet was set up for research on Ancient Asia. Special groups were established from time to time as the need arose.

In an address to the Twentieth Congress of the Communist Party on February 14, 1956, Nikita Khrushchev spoke at some length on the disintegration of the imperialist colonial system. After noting that Egypt, Syria, Lebanon, and the Sudan had gained their independence, he explained that the winning of political freedom by the peoples of the former colonies and semi-colonies was the first and most important prerequisite to their economic independence. He denounced SEATO and the Baghdad Pact and criticized the imperialist powers for using the Baghdad Pact as a wedge to divide the Arab countries.[9]

The Soviet leader went on to say that "the Leninist principle of peaceful coexistence of states with different social systems" had always been and would remain the general line of Soviet foreign policy.[10] He was sure that peaceful competition between socialist and capitalist states would end in socialist victory. In fact he was convinced that all nations would arrive at socialism, even though not all would follow identical paths. Whatever the form of transition, the working class, headed by its vanguard, would lead the way.[11]

Among other points re-emphasized by Khrushchev was the progressive role of the national bourgeoisie.[12] He argued that the support of the national bourgeoisie was necessary only during the struggle for national independence. Once independence had been achieved, the national bourgeoisie would tend to compromise with imperialist forces and would lose its progressive character. In this second period the workers would oppose the national bourgeoisie and fight for socialism; but this process would not apply to underdeveloped countries such as those of the Middle East, for they lacked strong communist parties. Yet these countries should be supported because they were anti-capitalist and anti-Western.[13] Soviet theorists continued to argue, therefore, that the national bourgeoisie still played a progressive role; and after much discussion they supplied a theoretical formulation to justify Moscow's policy toward the Middle Eastern countries. The new line of reasoning stipulated that once the united national democratic front had won national independence, a national-democratic state, that is, a non-proletarian transitional state, would be organized whose purpose would be to strive toward socialism.[14]

Criticism by Anastas Mikoian led the Congress to adopt resolutions calling for the expansion of the facilities and the research efforts of the Institute of Oriental Studies.[15] The Congress took occasion to criticize the Institute for publishing inferior materials, for lacking originality, and for simply ignoring basic problems of history. Many works published under the Institute's auspices were said to contain mistaken interpretations of the national liberation movements and of the role of the bourgeoisie. The Institute was charged further with not doing enough toward exposing the fallacies of bourgeois historiography and was asked to improve its staff and to publish more and faster.

To meet official criticism, the Institute drafted a five-year plan (1956-60) for studies based on the Middle Eastern policy of the government initiated in the mid-fifties. The plan stressed contemporary social, economic, and political problems, called for the publication of a long list of historical, literary, linguistic, economic, and other studies, as well as of the writings of prominent Soviet Orientalists. Facilities were provided for the publication of manuscripts and documents on the Oriental world, and a popular journal, *Sovremennyi vostok* (Contemporary East), was to be launched. The Institute planned in addition to stimulate study on the impact of the October Revolution on Asian countries and to assess the effect on these countries of Soviet economic aid.

On September 7, 1956, the Institute of Oriental Studies was reorganized into six departments, each subdivided into sectors.[16] The department of the Near East and the Middle East was made up of three sectors—Iran, Turkey, and Pakistan—and the department for the Arab East of two sectors—the Arab countries of the Near East and the Arab countries of North Africa. The Leningrad Branch of the Institute was organized into three sectors: history, philology, and Oriental manuscripts. The Middle East research done there dealt predominantly with ancient and medieval history, whereas that done in Moscow concentrated on contemporary times. But despite all the changes and the greatly expanded research and publications, official criticism of the Institute continued. The complaints remained the same: insufficient publications, mistaken interpretations, and inadequate criticism of bourgeois historiography. The Institute was requested to do better and to coordinate its work with other research centers.

By 1958 the Soviet Union had established a strong diplomatic position in the Middle East, as reflected by the increased output of published material on the area. However, Moscow suffered occasional setbacks in its Middle Eastern policy. At the Twenty-First Congress of the Communist Party of the Soviet Union, Khrushchev, on January 27, 1959, addressed himself specifically to the Arab countries. He welcomed the national liberation movements of the Arab peoples who had succeeded in freeing themselves from colonial oppression, and cautioned them that the colonial powers would try to regain hegemony over the Middle East. He warned that the Western powers, especially the United States and Great Britain, aimed to play them against one another.

Khrushchev explained that the Soviet Union had given strong support to leaders of the national liberation movements—for example, to President Gamel Abdel Nasser ('Abd al-Nasir) of the United Arab Republic and to Abdal al-Karim Kassem of Iraq—and that it would continue to back these movements while refraining from interference in the internal affairs of Middle Eastern countries. Now that the national tasks (expulsion of the various colonial powers) were completed, Khrushchev added, the Arab countries must find answers to such social problems as the agrarian-peasant question and the struggle between labor and capital.

Yet the Soviet leader was pained by the fact that Egypt and some other countries were waging an anti-communist campaign. He could not see how the communists could be accused of weakening the struggle against imperialism and fighting against national Arab interests when in reality they were the most steadfast fighters against imperialism. The anti-communist campaign, in Khrushchev's opinion, was evidence of a reactionary trend that would split the national forces. Although the communists and others in the liberation movement differed ideologically, their objectives in fighting against colonialism and imperialism and for freedom and independence were the same. According to Khrushchev, the Arab countries needed the support of the socialist countries, who stood ready to provide it. Moreover, he promised that the Soviet Union, unlike the capitalists, would give them aid with no strings attached.[17]

Not only did the Soviet Union object to the anti-communist campaign being waged in Egypt and in certain other Arab countries, but it also had misgivings about Nasser's goal of achieving Arab unity under his leadership. Khrushchev warned that the struggle for Arab unity was premature and would create dissension among the Arabs. For a time relations between the Soviet Union and Egypt thus became somewhat strained, but Egypt, in view of its dependence on the Soviet Union for arms, had to avoid a break at all costs.[18]

Meanwhile, in order to cope with changing conditions and to conform to state interests, Moscow continued to maintain close supervision over Soviet research and publication on the Asian world. On July 22, 1960, the name of the Institute of Oriental Studies was changed, to Institut narodov Azii (Institute of the Peoples of Asia), a name it retained until 1970, when its earlier name, Institut vostokovedeniia (Institute of Oriental Studies), was restored. The Institut Afriki (Institute of Africa), which directs research on Africa, had been founded the previous year.

On February 10, 1961, the Institute of the Peoples of Asia was reorganized into regional and country departments (otdel) subdivided into sectors.[19] There was a department for the Near East and the Middle East with two sectors: (1) economy and contemporary problems and (2) history; and a department for the Arab countries of Asia and Africa. The Leningrad Branch of the Institute was organized into three sectors, one of which was in charge of research on the Near East and the Middle East.[20] This reorganization of the Institute introduced research groups involved with specific problems, the first group being formed to investigate workers' movements.

The latest five-year-plan (1966-70) of the Institute called for an extensive research program covering every aspect of Middle Eastern history and culture. The emphasis was once again on such subjects as national liberation movements, imperialism and colonialism, contemporary developments in the Middle East, and Soviet relations with the Middle Eastern countries. The plan provided also for continued investigation of such matters as the workers' movements and the role of the Soviet Union in the social and economic development of Asia.

ADDITIONAL FACILITIES FOR STUDY
OF THE MIDDLE EAST

The Middle East is investigated not only under the auspices of the Institute of Oriental Studies, but in a number of other institutes of the Academy of Sciences of the Soviet Union,[21] in special government and party institutes and agencies,[22] and the academies of sciences of Armenia, Azerbaijan, Georgia, Uzbekistan, Tadzhikistan (Tajikistan),[23] and of some other republics. Besides these, several Soviet institutions of higher learning offer courses on the Middle Eastern peoples, sponsor conferences, and publish the research efforts of their staffs. The best programs on the Middle East are to be found in the universities of Baku, Erevan, Leningrad, Moscow, Tashkent, and Tbilisi. The largest and the most prestigious of these centers are the Institut vostochnykh iazykov (Institute of Oriental Languages) of Moscow State University and the Vostochny fakul'tet (Oriental faculty) of Leningrad State University.

In furtherance of the policy of stimulating interest in the Middle East, the Soviet Union has organized a number of societies for the promotion of cultural relations with the Middle Eastern countries. These various societies, concerned with relations of Soviet-Arab, Soviet-Turkish, Soviet-Iranian, Soviet-Afghan, and other similar groups, are represented in the Soiuz obshchestv druzhby s narodami zarubezhnykh stran (Union of the Societies of Friendship with the Peoples of Foreign Countries).

The most important collections of manuscript and other documentary materials on the Middle East are located in Leningrad, Moscow, Erevan, Baku, Tashkent, and Dushanbe.[24] The largest and most valuable Oriental collections—Arabic,[25] Iranian,[26] Turkish,[27] and other[28]—are held by the Institute of Oriental Studies.[29] In addition, the libraries of Baku, Erevan, Tashkent, Tbilisi, and especially those of the Institute of Oriental Studies in Moscow and Leningrad, the Lenin Library in Moscow, and the Saltykov-Shchedrin Library in Leningrad, contain substantial collections of published materials.[30]

During the sixties the Institute of the Peoples of Asia published bibliographies on Afghanistan,[31] on Iran,[32] and on Turkey.[33] Occasionally various Soviet research centers publish reviews of Soviet historiography on the Middle East,[34] as well as reviews of Arabic,[35] Islamic,[36] and Iranian studies in the Soviet Union.

The Nauka publishing house of the Soviet Academy of Sciences has been publishing several series of books on the history, culture, and contemporary affairs of Middle Eastern and other Oriental peoples.[37] It has also been translating Western works, Muslim classics, and Russian travelers' accounts, such as the one by merchant Fedot Kotov, who visited Persia in 1623-24.

Until 1959 the principal journal for Oriental studies was *Sovetskoe vostokovedenie* (Soviet Oriental Studies), published by the Institute of Oriental Studies. The first issue appeared in 1940 and the second in 1941. The journal was suspended after the German invasion, the third volume not appearing until 1945.

In 1959 *Sovetskoe vostokovedenie* was succeeded by *Problemy vostokovedeniia* (Problems of Oriental Studies), which was itself succeeded in

1961 by *Narody Azii i Afriki* (Peoples of Asia and Africa). *Narody Azii i Afriki* is a very useful journal, containing important articles, book reviews, professional news, and reports on teaching and research. Consequently it mirrors the trends and the quality of Soviet Middle Eastern and other Oriental studies. In 1960 the popular journal *Sovremennyi Vostok* (Contemporary Orient) was succeeded by *Aziia i Afrika segodnia* (Asia and Africa Today).

At irregular intervals the Institute of the Peoples of Asia, like its predecessor, published *Uchenye zapiski* (Scientific Notes) and *Kratkie soobshcheniia* (Brief Reports). Individual issues of these publications are usually dedicated to a single country or a single discipline.

The Institute of Oriental Studies and other centers of Oriental research in the Soviet Union participate in or sponsor periodic meetings, conferences, and consultations. At these professional gatherings the results of Soviet Oriental studies are assessed, plans for future research and publications discussed, coordination of research and publications considered, and particular historical and ideological problems debated. Meetings are held to honor dead or living Orientalists, to celebrate anniversaries of institutions and major historical events, and to investigate major historical developments, the roles of prominent men in history, and the historiography on specific problems, countries, or regions.

At conferences held during the past several years subjects such as the following have been discussed: the status of Turkish, Iranian, and Semitic studies in the Soviet Union; Oriental toponymy and textual investigation; medieval Asian art; the periodization of medieval Oriental literature; the problem of the transition of underdeveloped peoples to socialism; imperialism and colonialism; bourgeois historiography; non-socialist development; the genesis of capitalism; the national liberation movements; the impact of the October Revolution on Oriental peoples; and the influence of Lenin on Asia. The proceedings of professional meetings are reported in appropriate journals and are frequently published in book form.

THE PRINCIPAL SUBJECTS OF INQUIRY

Soviet historians have published works on almost every aspect of the ancient history of the Middle East.[38] They also have kept abreast of western historiography and of the most recent archaeological discoveries. Improved relations between the Soviet Union and the Middle Eastern countries have made it possible for some Soviet archaeologists and other specialists to engage in excavation work in Egypt, in Afghanistan, and in certain other areas of the Middle East. New finds have enabled Soviet scholars to advance novel hypotheses about ancient Media, Achaemenid Persia, Parthia,

Sogdiana, Bactria, and Khwarizm. Many works, including textbooks and sourcebooks, have appeared on every aspect of the ancient and medieval cultures in the entire area. Important work has been done in Egyptology,[39] in Semitic civilizations and languages (Assyrian, Aramaic, Hebrew, Phoenician, Arabic, Syriac, Sabaean, and Ethiopian),[40] and in Urartology and Hittitology.[41]

The section on ancient history, founded in Leningrad in 1959 as an integral part of the Institute of Oriental Studies, sponsors research and publications on the ancient Middle East. Among the leading historians affiliated with this section are I. M. D'iakonov, V. A. Livshits, A. G. Perikhanian, and M. D. Dandamaev. A three-volume history of the ancient Orient is currently in preparation for publication, and several good works on ancient Iran have emanated from this section. The late V. V. Struve, the founder of the Soviet school of ancient history and a scholar who was at home in the ancient history of several Middle Eastern countries, published many works on the social and economic structure of ancient Egypt. A number of scholars from the Caucasus, especially B. B. Piotrovskii (author of *Urartu*, Erevan, 1944), have done excellent work on Caucasian ancient history. S. P. Tolstov and one or two others have made substantial contributions in their investigations of Central Asia, Khwarizm, Bactria, and Sogdiana; and theoretical questions concerning various developments in ancient and medieval history, including Marx's and Lenin's views on these questions, have been discussed in several works.[42]

Much of the Soviet research on the ancient Middle East appears in the *Vestnik drevnei istorii* (Bulletin of Ancient History), published by the Institute of History of the Soviet Academy of Sciences, in the various publications of the Institute of the History of Material Culture of the Soviet Academy of Sciences, and in *Sovetskaia arkheologiia* (Soviet Archaeology) and a number of other archaeological publications. As for the medieval Middle East, extensive research has been done on the genesis and character of feudalism at different stages, on anti-feudal movements, on the medieval state and society, on classes and class conflict, on economy (trade, taxation, agriculture), on towns, and on crafts and guilds. Peasant disturbances and various social movements have been investigated thoroughly. The Turks, the Mongols, the Hulagids, and the Mamelukes have been the subjects of published works. There are also important studies of medieval art, literature, learning, science,[43] and social thought. Many Muslim classics have been translated and early documents analyzed and published. There are studies on medicine, mathematics, navigation, and arithmetic, as well as on epigraphy and numismatics. Such prominent personages as Avicenna, al-Biruni, Ulug Bek, Firdausi, and many others have been studied and their works translated.

In the field of Byzantine studies many sources have been translated and a large number of monographs and articles published.[44] At the Ninth All-Union Session on Byzantine Studies in the Soviet Union, held in Erevan on May 11-13, 1971, Soviet Byzantinists discussed the problems of transition from a slave-owning order to feudalism and the genesis of feudalism in the Byzantine Empire and adjacent territories, and Z. V. Udal'tsova read a paper on "The Typology of the Genesis of Feudalism in Byzantium."[45] Much of the material on Byzantine studies is published in the *Vizantiiskii vremennik* (Byzantine Annals), the principal organ of Soviet Byzantine studies. Frequent essays appear also in journals and collective works,[46] and some half-dozen surveys have been published on the medieval history of the Middle Eastern peoples.[47] The most important centers for research on Byzantine history and civilization are located in several institutions in Leningrad, at the University of the Urals in Sverdlovsk, at the Georgian Academy of Sciences in Tbilisi, and at the Armenian Academy of Sciences in Erevan.

It is not surprising that Soviet scholars should display a keen interest in the origin and history of Islam and in such attendant developments as the Muslim conquest of Central Asia and the Caucasus. Although Marx and Engels wrote very little on Islam specifically, they did consider Muhammad's "religious revolution" just as reactionary as any other religious movement.[48] This view in itself furnished a sufficient guideline for Soviet historians. During the interwar period the negative Soviet attitude toward Islam hampered Soviet policy in the Middle East. Not only did the Muslims resent Soviet criticism of Islam and of the Muslim way of life and Pan-Islamism, but the Arabs were alienated also by Soviet support of Zionist aims in Palestine.[49]

Since 1956 Soviet authorities have toned down their criticism of Islam and have abandoned their pro-Zionist policy. To placate the Muslims abroad as well as at home, they now acknowledge that Muslim teachers speaking in the name of Islam have sometimes played a prominent role in the struggle against imperialism and that in the past not *all* Muslim teachers have been agents of colonial powers. The Muslim teachers, they say, must be judged in terms of their attitude to imperialism.

The origins of Islam were debated at great length in the early thirties when the Pokrovskii school and the idea of "commercial capitalism" held sway in Soviet historiography. Many views were expressed, some highly speculative, others varying slightly from what was to become the official explanation. Such prominent Islamicists as M. A. Reisner, B. N. Zakhoder, N. A. Morozov, S. P. Tolstov, F. A. Beliaev, L. I. Klimovich, V. T. Ditiakin, and N. Bolotnikov participated in the debate.[50] These scholars were confident that by means of scientific-materialistic analysis of socioeconomic conditions they had succeeded in explaining the origin of Islam[51] and the founding of the Islamic state.[52]

According to Beliaev and A. Iu. Iakubovskii, Islam emerged from a social and economic crisis that occurred in seventh-century Hejaz. This crisis was precipitated by the breaking down of the communal system and the development of private land ownership, and by conflicts between the tribal leaders and ordinary members of the tribes and between the slave-owning element and the slaves. To meet this crisis Arab leaders embarked upon a war of conquest that promised their followers more lands, slaves, and booty. The emergence of new social relations was accompanied with a new ideology, Islam, which combined elements of the pre-Arab religious cults, Judaism, and Christianity.[53] To Soviet Islamicists Muhammad is a historical figure, a prominent Arab, a member of the house of Hashim in the tribe of Quraish. They say, however, that Muhammad, whom the Muslims accept as their prophet, became an object of legend.[54]

For many years Soviet writers differed concerning the character of early Islamic society. Now, however, there is general agreement that in the beginning Islamic society corresponded to the early stages of feudalism, and that Islam was an ideology of feudalism. In historical circles much lively discussion has taken place over the interpretation of the Arab conquests of Central Asia and the Caucasus. A large amount of material on this subject has been published since the Second World War. The conquest, which was once considered a complete disaster, is today viewed somewhat differently: the Arabs facilitated the development of feudal relations, and Arab culture became a source of cultural enrichment for the conquered peoples.[55]

The work published by Soviet Islamicists in recent years covers Islam in general,[56] slavery under Islam,[57] Shamil and Muridism,[58] the ideology of contemporary Islam,[59] Islam and the contemporary world,[60] Muslim sectarianism,[61] the class essence of Islam,[62] and Muslim survivals in the Soviet Union.[63] Many short essays on Islam and the Muslims are scattered through various journals and collective works, and Krachkovskii has published a new translation of the Koran with a lengthy introduction.[64]

Several articles have appeared on Sufism[65] and on Islamic sects,[66] including a number on Ismailism[67] and Wahhabism.[68] V. V. Bartol'd,[69] A. A. Semenov, V. Viatkin, A. E. Bertel's, and more recently, Petrushevskii have written on Ismailism and Sufism. Bartol'd thinks, for instance, that Ismailism emerged from the struggle between the landed aristocracy and the peasantry on the one hand, and the towns on the other,[70] while Petrushevskii contends that the Ismailis were originally drawn from the ranks of artisans and peasants.[71] Bertel's has done a valuable study on the Ismailis of Pamir, who owe their origin to the activities of Nasir-i Khusrau.[72]

Soviet writers consider Islam an ideology of the ruling classes. They see Islam as an idealistic and metaphysical ideology and criticize earlier Russian Islamicists (V. R. Rozen, I. N. Berezin, G. S. Sablukov, N. A. Mednikov, A. F. Schmidt, A. F. Krymskii, and V. V. Bartol'd) for viewing Islam as a set of beliefs detached from the material life of society.[73] They say that Islam contains many negative and undemocratic ideas and practices, and that it impedes progress and perpetuates antiquated institutions. Beliaev observes that Islam justifies man's exploitation of man, sanctions property ownership and social inequality, discriminates against women, and accepts the notions of predestination and fatalism.[74] L. I. Klimovich contends that the Koran justifies class society and considers labor a divine punishment.[75] I. A. Genin and B. M. Dantsig[76] write that Islam today is still a tool of the exploiting classes and an ideology that recognizes class differences and stands in the way of the national liberation struggle.

Several authors criticize the United Arab Republic (U.A.R.) and other Arab states for allowing Islam to flourish while persecuting communists. Klimovich explains that in modern times the Western imperialist powers have used Islam and Pan-Islamism for their own purposes. For this and other reasons Soviet writers consider Pan-Islamism a reactionary movement manipulated by the imperialist powers. Soviet writers observe that Germany threw its support behind the Islamic cause in both world wars.

Soviet writers disagree with Western interpretations of Islam and Islamic institutions[77] and charge bourgeois writers with subjectivism.[78] They criticize those who see Islam as something more than a religion, those who consider it as a social and ethical system and as a "third force" to be used in the struggle against socialism and communism. At the same time Soviet scholars are critical also of Islamic modernism on the grounds that Islam cannot be modernized and reconciled with science. They ridicule those who are attempting "to paint Islam red." They warn that Islam impedes the development of socialist culture, and that it is antagonistic to a socialist-realist world view. According to Soviet critics, the foreign Islamicists and the talibs (young graduates of Islamic schools known as madrasahs) in the Soviet Union are trying in vain to discover in the Koran and in the works of prominent Muslims, such as al-Farabi, Ibn Sina, and Ibn Rushd, passages that could prove that Islam and science are compatible. Soviet writers insist that the Islamic dogma and the provisions of the Shari'a cannot be revised to answer modern needs.[79] They hope that the deeds of the Soviet cosmonauts have convincingly discredited many of the Islamic beliefs.[80]

But the Muslim modernists in the Soviet Union are persistent in their Islamic beliefs and in their faith in the reconcilability of Islam with science.[81] They are using "patriotic" phrases in an attempt to harmonize Islam with communism, and argue that the Soviet system and socialist democracy represent the fulfillment of the prophetic ideas contained in the Koran.[82] Soviet critics, for their part, thinking that it is easier to combat Muslim modernists than Muslim traditionalists, urge relentless struggle against Islamic feudal-patriarchal survivals.[83] However, they think that many Muslims are not genuinely religious but profess Islam just in case (na *vsiaki sluchai*) there is a supernatural power.

Of all the subjects pertaining to the Middle East investigated by Soviet historians, none receives more attention than the national liberation movements.[84] The external and internal conditions that culminated in these movements and the role played in the struggle by workers, peasants, tribes, and other social groups are investigated in great detail. Lenin's views on the subject are discussed in a number of works.[85]

Other questions that have received high priority in Soviet historiography are imperialism and colonialism.[86] A number of collective works and monographs on these subjects treat the policies of the United States,[87] of Great Britain,[88] of France,[89] and of Germany[90] as they concern the Middle East or sometimes Asia as a whole. A series of books entitled *Politika imperialisticheskikh derzhav v stranakh Azii i Afriki* (The policy of the imperialist states in the countries of Asia and Africa) is being published by Nauka. Soviet writers express confidence that the world socialist system, in its struggle against imperialism, will determine the historical process and the direction of human social development.

The Soviet Union seeks to undermine the Western powers in the Middle East by encouraging the colonial peoples to fight for their independence even if the struggle must be led by the middle classes. Taking their cue from Lenin, the Soviet leaders theorize that the subject states and colonies can arrive at communism without going through capitalism.[91]

Soviet writers divide the Arab states into those that are independent and those still under the yoke of colonialism. In a number of works they endeavor to explain the development of colonialism, to describe its legal, economic, and political features, to note the differences between the colonial policies of the different powers, to define the anti-colonial movements, and to refute Western interpretations of colonialism. American aid to Middle Eastern countries is equated with neocolonialism.[92] Soviet authors charge that such aid is intended to stifle the democratic forces in the Middle East and to undermine the friendly relations between the Middle Eastern and the socialist countries. Soviet writers regard Western oil exploitation in the Middle East as the foundation of imperialism and look upon American oil companies and American imperialism as the greatest enemies of Arab independence.[93]

The struggle of the Arab working masses for political independence and social liberation is discussed in several Soviet works, which argue that the two kinds of struggle cannot be separated, since the capitalistic system, which is responsible for colonialism and neocolonialism, is the enemy of both.

It is understandable that the subject of Russian and Soviet relations with the Middle Eastern countries should be one of the most popular areas of inquiry in Soviet historical circles. Many Soviet writers have set out to demonstrate that cordial relations have long existed between the Russian and the Middle Eastern peoples, that the Soviet Union today is the only true friend of the Arabs, and that Russia has exerted a powerful political and cultural influence on the peoples of those countries. The impact of the First Russian Revolution (1905-1907),[94] of the October Revolution, and of the Russian Civil War on the peoples of the Middle East and on their national liberation movements has been given a great deal of attention.[95] Various examples of Soviet benevolence and positive influence on the Middle Eastern peoples have been played up in historical works. There are studies on Soviet diplomacy in Asia (1921-27),[96] on Comintern policy toward and activities in Asia,[97] on the relations between Soivet and Asia communist and workers' groups, on Soviet economic aid to the developing nations, and on economic relations with them.[98]

Other major areas of investigation are the nationality question and nationalism,[99] the growth of bourgeois nationalism, the formation and the activities of bourgeois political parties, the genesis of capitalism,[100] noncapitalist development,[101] state capitalism,[102] classes and the class struggle,[103] the working class and the workers' movement,[104] the Communist Party in the Middle East, and communist competition with other political groups for popular support in the anti-imperialist front.

Among other areas to which Soviet historians devote a good deal of attention are agrarian reforms,[105] agriculture, land tenure, and peasant movements.[106] Many aspects of the economy are investigated as well, including the financial and credit system of socialist and non-socialist countries,[107] economic development and planning,[108] and foreign trade. Nor have Soviet Orientalists neglected international relations of the Near Eastern and Middle Eastern countries,[109] and the influence that Lenin and his ideas exerted on the peoples of Asia[110] and on Asian culture, learning, and science. In recent years they have published on the history of science and technology,[111] on sociology,[112] and on philosophy.[113] They have translated works by many Middle Eastern writers such as al-Kawakibi,[114] ar-Rihani,[115] and al-Jabarti.[116] In addition they have turned out many short studies and a few larger ones on ethnography and ethnic problems.[117]

LITERATURE AND LANGUAGE

Soviet scholars have produced many creditable works on the literatures of the Middle East. They have undertaken the translation of Arabic, Persian, and Turkish classics,[118] have published Arabic sources on Eastern Europe, on the Caucasus, and on Africa, and have written surveys of Oriental literatures from ancient to modern times.[119] After lengthy debates Soviet literary historians have worked out a Marxist periodization of the history of the literatures of Oriental peoples,[120] and have produced studies on different literary genres.[121] They have examined the impact of the October Revolution and the influence of individual Russian authors, such as Pushkin, Gogol, Turgenev, Tolstoy, Gor'kii, and Bunin,[122] on Middle Eastern literatures. Soviet writers have prepared studies on such widely diverse subjects as the treatment of the Soviet Union in the literature of various Asian peoples,[123] the interaction between between Eastern and Western literatures,[124] realism in Oriental literature.[125] literary theory and esthetics,[126] and epic poetry. Many novels and poems by Middle Eastern authors have been translated. Anthologies of Middle Eastern literary works have been published, as well as textbooks that survey the history of one or all of the Middle Eastern literatures.[127] A number of special series on Oriental literatures were initiated in 1957. These include both translations and studies of contemporary literary problems.[128]

Soviet Orientalists have investigated nearly every aspect of the classical and modern literature of the Arabic peoples. In recent years surveys of classical[129] and modern[130] Arab literature have appeared, as well as a list of monographs devoted to individual Arab writers;[131] and many Arabic works have been translated. There are studies also on typical themes and motifs in Arab literature.

Soviet specialists have compiled anthologies of Turkish literary masterpieces and have made studies of Turkish authors, such as Nazim Hikmet and Mihri Hatun. Tatarly has studied Pushkin's impact on Eastern authors,[132] and Aizenshtein has dealt with realism in Turkish prose.[133] Kiamilov has written a short survey of nineteenth-century Ottoman Turkish literature in which he gives special attention to the social and literary environment of the Ottoman Empire and to the lives and works of Ibrahim Shinasi, Namik Kemal, Abdülhak Hamid, Ahmed Midhat, and Sami Pashazade. These figures are seen as the ideological precursors of contemporary Turkish writers. Aizenshtein points out that despite limitations in the political, philosophical, and esthetic views of the nineteenth-century Tanzimatists, these men provided the real inspiration for the Young Turk revolution of 1908, and their traditions were alive during the national struggle in 1919-22. Mustafa Kemal's work in transforming Turkey, he says, followed largely the ideological principles espoused by nineteenth-century authors.[134]

In the field of Turcology, a broad area that includes many Turkic languages and dialects, Russian and Soviet scholars have made valuable contributions. Extensive work has been done on Turkic languages, and a number of grammars, readers, and textbooks have been printed. Many ancient Turkic writings have been published, and there are works on the so-called Altaic theory, on the history of Turcology in the Soviet Union, on Turkic manuscripts in Soviet repositories, and on bibliographies of Turkic philology.[135] At the Third Turcological Conference, held in Leningrad on

June 2-4, 1969, more than a hundred papers were read on various aspects of Turkic languages and literature.

As for Soviet study on Iranian literature and language, a voluminous amount of material has been published on medieval and more recent writers (Sadeq Hedāyat, Malik al-Shvari'ah Bah, Iraj Mirzā, Hoseyn Makki, 'Abbās Eqbāl) and on various Persian literary genres.[136] Soviet Iranists have studied a number of Iranian-Tadzhik epics, poems, proverbs, and sayings. They have written on classical and recent history of Persian and Tadzhik literature and have assessed the works of Kamal al-Din, of Ismail Isfahani (a thirteenth-century poet), of Rudaki, of Iskandar Bek Turkmana (a sixteenth-century historian), and of several others.[137] A number of important medieval classics and tracts have been translated.

In a short paper N. A. Kuznetsova discusses the October Revolution and Iran in Soviet literature.[138] Half a dozen other Soviet writers—M. V. Ivanov, A. M. Gurevich, A. N. Kheifets, B. G. Gafurov, G. F. Kim, and A. Kh. Babakhodzhaev—have written on the same subject;[139] and one or two Soviet Iranists assess the influence of M. Gor'kii on Iranian literature.[140]

The study of Iranian languages, initiated by V. A. Zhukovskii, also has a long tradition in Russia.[141] Because many Iranian peoples inhabit the Soviet Union and because of the Soviet Union's geographic proximity to Iranian peoples abroad, it is natural that the study of ancient and modern Iranian languages should receive a great deal of attention.[142] Although Leningrad is the principal center of Iranian studies in the Soviet Union, there are several other important centers at which Iranian languages are taught and investigated.[143]

Of the two schools specializing in Iranian studies, the one headed by A. A. Freimann concentrates on historical-comparative grammar and the compilation of an etymological dictionary of Iranian languages.[144] The other, associated with the name of I. I. Zarubin, is devoted to the study of living Iranian languages and dialects. This school was the first "to apply the phonological method in the study of the phonetics of the Iranian languages and dialects."[145]

Soviet work on ancient Iranian languages is particularly impressive. It involves the study of the Avestan language and the Old and Middle Persian, Parthian, Sogdian, Khwarizmian, Sacae-Khotanese, and Bactrian languages and writings, as well as the Scythian-Alan dialects. Soviet Iranists have produced works on the New Persian literary language, on Iranian grammar, and on the language employed by Nizami, Sa'adi, Rudaki, and other classical writers. Every aspect of Iranian languages has been investigated,[146] even the Iranian influence on Slavic and other languages.[147] Various aspects of Tadzhik, a language akin to Persian, the study of which for practical purposes has been made an independent discipline in the Soviet Union, are being investigated.

With the aim of coordinating all research on Iranian studies, the All-Union Coordination Conference on Iranian Linguistics was held in Moscow on December 7-10, 1962. The subsequent publication of the proceedings of the four All-Union Conferences on Iranian Philology, held in Leningrad, Baku, Tashkent, and Dushanbe between 1962 and 1966, attest to the high quality and the diversity of Soviet work in this field.

Soviet scholars have investigated numerous questions concerning the Semitic tongues[148] and have published extensively on every aspect of Semitic linguistics. They have compiled dictionaries, grammars, and textbooks of the Semitic languages.

Arabic Studies

After the Second World War the Soviet Union was in no hurry to renew diplomatic relations with Saudi Arabia and Yemen,[149] and was the first country to extend *de jure* recognition to Israel. Although the U.S.S.R. criticized Colonel Nasser when he first came to power, Middle Eastern developments in the fifties prompted Moscow to re-examine its policy. The Soviet Union sympathized with Arab protests against attempts by the United States and Great Britain to control the flow of arms to the Middle East and to draw the Arab states into a Western military defense system. Arab nationalists interpreted the Western-sponsored Middle East Security (Baghdad) Pact, which included Iraq, Turkey, Iran, and Pakistan, as an attempt to split the Arabs by separating Iraq from the rest and as a factor that would weaken the Arab anti-Israeli front.[150] The Kremlin for its part saw the Baghdad Pact as a Western military instrument directed against the Soviet Union. The new situation in the Middle East, therefore, favored Soviet-Arab rapprochement.

At the Twentieth Congress of the Communist Party of the Soviet Union, official approval was given to a new Arab policy. Moscow thenceforth encouraged the Arabs to resist Western pressure and offered its help. With the change in Soviet policy opening the doors for cooperation, the Soviet Union expanded trade with the Arab countries, reached arms agreements, proclaimed respect for the national independence of the Arabs, and demanded peace in the Middle East. The Soviet government even displayed benevolence toward such conservative regimes as Saudi Arabia and Yemen.[151] Most importantly, it threw its support behind the Arabs in their conflict with Israel.

The improvement in relations between the Soviet Union and the Arab countries was manifested in still other ways. Moscow supported Iran's claim to Bahrain, Yemen's anti-British stand, and the emir of Kuwait's quarrel with the British. In February 1954 the Kremlin lauded Saudi Arabia's rejection of American military aid. One direct result of improved relations with the Arabs was that it became possible for many Soviet Arabists to travel and study in the Arab world. The Soviet Union and various Arab countries entered into scientific and cultural exchange programs, and many young Arabs went to the Soviet Union for university study and specialization. Small contingents of Soviet Muslims were allowed to go on pilgrimage to Mecca.

The change in policy provided a tremendous boost for Arabic studies in the Soviet Union. New programs were inaugurated, old ones were expanded, and the training of Arabic experts received higher priority. Numerous professional conferences and meetings were held at which Arab history, culture, and contemporary problems were discussed and plans for future research and publication were adopted.[152] Among the distinguished specialists who participated in the planning were N. V. Pigulevskaia, A. I. Pershits, and S. R. Smirnov.

However, official spokesmen complained about research lags, mistakes in the interpretation of historical events, and various other shortcomings in Soviet Arabic studies. They prodded the Arabists to give more attention to the training of experts, to the collection of documentary material, to improving the quality of published work, and to investigating neglected fields such as Arabic political and social philosophy.[153] Published proceedings, monographic studies, and numerous collective works that soon began to appear attested to progress in various branches of Arabic studies.

The diversity of interest of Soviet Arabists and Semitologists was demonstrated by the many conference papers presented at various meetings held in the Soviet Union between 1953 and 1969. At the Third All-Union Conference of Arabists in Erevan on June 23-27, 1969, for instance, 112 papers were read. This conference, in which several Arabs participated, was sponsored by the Institute of Oriental Studies of the Academy of Sciences of the U.S.S.R. and the Armenian Academy of Sciences.[154] On this occasion E. A. Lebedev reported on the progress of Arabic studies in the Soviet Union and G. Sh. Sharbatov on Soviet investigations of the Arabic language and literature. Since the fifties many books and shorter works on the Arab world have been published.[155] About sixty books, most of them of inferior quality, have appeared in the series called *Arabskie strany* (Arabic countries), published under the auspices of the Soviet Academy of Sciences.

In addition to the basic topics for inquiry, such as the national liberation movements and Western, especially American, imperialism,[156] which have been given top priority in the research plans of the Institute of Oriental Studies and other research centers, many specific questions concerning the Arab world are investigated. Among the more important of these questions are Ottoman rule over the Arabs,[157] the building of modern Arab states, the current political and economic situation in the Arab world, the problem of oil, the Israeli-Arab conflict, the Suez Canal, and relations between the Soviet Union and the Arab states.

Arabic studies have received less attention than Turkish and Iranian, largely because the Soviet Union has been more closely involved with the countries bordering on its frontiers and because an ethnic affinity exists between the populations of Iran and Turkey and many of the Soviet peoples. It is interesting to note that the annual issues of the bibliography *Literatura o stranakh Azii i Afriki* (Literature on the countries of Asia and Africa) often list more titles on Turkey and Iran than on the Arab countries. Occasionally more items are listed on Afghanistan than on Egypt, the most populous and most important of the Arab states. Even the quality of the published material on Turkey, Iran, and Afghanistan appears to be better on the whole than that on the Arab countries. The Soviet Union has had more success also in training experts on Turkey and Iran than on the Arabs. Furthermore, Soviet Arabic studies suffered a heavy blow with Krachkovskii's death in 1951. No other Soviet Arabist of comparable stature and distinction has appeared to fill the void.

Egypt

Of the material published on the Arab world the largest amount deals with Egypt, which from 1958 to 1961 was linked with Syria in the United Arab Republic.[158] Much attention is given to ancient and medieval[159] Egypt, and there are studies on the Egyptian crisis of 1833,[160] on Ottoman and British rule over Egypt, on the rise of Egyptian nationalism, and on the development of Egyptian capitalism.[161] The history of Egypt in the twentieth century is given full coverage as well.

According to one Soviet source, bourgeois historians ignored the spread of socialistic ideas in the Arab countries in the early twentieth century because they saw socialism as an ideology alien to the Arab national character and to Arab individualism. In 1913 a brochure on communism was published in Cairo, and two years later a book on the subject appeared. The origin and growth of socialist thought among the Arabs now form an important area of research for Soviet historians. They contend that Muhammad Farid, a prominent figure in the Egyptian national movement from 1908 to 1917, was under the influence of socialism. After the First World War, a growing number of Arabs were attracted to socialism and communism, even though Western-oriented rulers castigated them as "Moscow agents."[162]

Soviet-Arab relations and the influence of Soviet revolutionary thought and culture on the peoples of the Middle East have been the subjects of many Soviet works.[163] The Russian Revolution of 1905, according to Soviet historians, aroused the Egyptians from medieval lethargy and inspired them to fight for basic human rights and for democracy. The result was a special kind of national liberation movement in Egypt directed against the English. In 1907, Mustafa Kamil, publicist and enlightener, organized a national party that expressed the aspirations of the young Egyptian bourgeoisie.

Soviet historians such as Voblikov, Seiranian, and Petrov argue that the October Revolution exerted a powerful influence on the growth of the Egyptian national liberation movement. This was demonstrated by the 1919 revolt in Egypt, which marked a new stage in Egypt's resistance to imperialism. While revolutionary Russia was making this impact on Egypt, the Western powers sought to isolate the Arab world from the Soviet Union, rendering direct contacts between the Soviet Union and the Arabs difficult. Thus, according to Soviet sources, the imperialist powers guided trade between the Soviet Union and the Arabs through Western commercial channels and introduced measures aimed at stopping the spread of communism in the Middle East. These sources point out that the Western powers were unable to seal off the Arabs in many different ways. The Arabs allegedly sympathized with the Bolshevik cause and were inspired by Bolshevik ideology and revolutionary action.

Soviet authors maintain that the Bolshevik Revolution accelerated the Arab struggle for national independence and induced the leaders of the Arab liberation movements to seek closer ties with the Soviet Union. In addition, they link many of the popular interwar disturbances in the Arab world to Bolshevik inspiration; and they say that although the Arab national movements did not at first succeed in driving the imperialist powers out of their countries, they laid the foundation for further successful struggle and obliged the imperialist powers to modify their colonial rule by making concessions to the countries they controlled.[164]

In addition to the study of revolutionary thought, one of the most thoroughly investigated topics concerning Egypt has been British imperialist rule. According to Soviet writers, the Egyptians never reconciled themselves to this rule. At the very start, under 'Arabi Pasha, the Egyptians rose against British intervention. After this first unsuccessful uprising they remained essentially passive until 1919. The revolt in that year marked a new stage in the country's resistance to imperialism. Although the superior British forces were once again able to suppress the Egyptian revolt, the British government was obliged to make concessions. In February 1922, Britain renounced its protectorate over Egypt, and Egyptian independence was formally proclaimed. Great Britain continued, however, to occupy and to rule Egypt. In 1936 the British imposed a treaty of alliance on Egypt that formally terminated the British military occupation but allowed British troops to remain in the Suez Canal Zone. According to Soviet writers, the treaty was repeatedly violated and Egypt failed to win genuine independence.

The period of Egyptian history since the Second World War receives a great deal of attention from Soviet specialists. Following the general ideological pattern, Soviet historians are most interested in workers' and communist movements,[165] in the peasantry and agriculture,[166] in Egypt's struggle for full independence (1945-52), in the Palestinian War (1948-49), in the Anglo-Egyptian conflict (1950-51), in the Egyptian Revolution of July 23, 1952,[167] in the Suez Canal crisis, in British and American imperialism, in Soviet-Egyptian relations, and especially in the Egyptian national liberation movement. Soviet historians portray their country as a benevolent and positive influence on the course of contemporary events in Egypt. They say that the Soviet Union throughout the interwar period waged a relentless struggle against imperialism and consistently backed those Arabs who fought for their country's independence.[168] They cite diplomatic and other actions initiated by the Soviet Union in favor of the Arabs—e.g., Soviet protests against British oppression of the Egyptians, against Spanish persecution of the Moroccans, and against British attempts to isolate the Arabs from the Soviet Union.[169] Readers are told that the Soviet Union consistently espoused the principle of self-determination of the Arab peoples. One author observed that when the Second World War broke out, the Western powers issued no definition of their aims. It was only after Stalin's statement of July 3, 1941, and the Soviet Declaration of September 24, 1941, on the independence of colonial peoples that this was done.[170]

Moreover, Soviet heroism during the Second World War is said to have inspired the Egyptians and to have aroused sympathy for the Soviet Union. As a result, in 1941 a number of Marxist and other progressive groups emerged in Cairo and Alexandria. These groups, according to Soviet observers, although unable to establish a united front, were as one in their dedication to the cause of Egypt's liberation. Compared to the Western powers, who seek to hold Arabs down and exploit them, the Soviet Union, according to Voblikov, has been the only true friend of the Arabs. This theme is repeated in nearly all Soviet publications. In the United Nations, the Soviet Union has "always" supported the Arabs.[171] Voblikov says that Soviet aid to the Arab countries has been offered on the basis of the principle of equality, and is calculated to promote the economic independence of the Arab states with no strings attached. He further notes that the Soviet Union has often protested against American, British, French, and Turkish military activities in the Middle East inimical to the Arab peoples.[172]

Soviet writers attribute Egypt's success in winning full independence largely to the strong backing that country received from the Soviet Union. They represent the Middle Eastern crisis as a struggle between the imperialistic powers and the peoples fighting to maintain national independence. One author says that when the Arabs, and especially Egypt, rose against the Baghdad Pact and Western imperialism, they turned to the Soviet Union for support.[173] The Soviet Union claims credit for the fiasco of the Anglo-French-Israeli aggression against Egypt. Had it not been for the Soviet Union, they say, Israeli aggression would have developed into a major armed conflict.

As the friend and protector of the Arabs, the Soviet Union, according to Voblikov, opposed the Eisenhower Doctrine, the American intervention in Lebanon, and the British intervention in Jordan, as well as alleged Western attempts to suppress the Iraqi revolution in 1958. Voblikov says that the Soviet Union stood ready to sign a four-power declaration of noninterference in the Middle East and in favor of the withdrawal of foreign troops from the area,[174] but that the Western powers failed to respond. He adds that during the internal upheaval in Yemen (1962-67), the Soviet Union backed the forces of the newly established republic and opposed foreign intervention in that country.

The Soviet Union is described in Soviet publications as a peace-loving country that seeks to stop the Western powers from interfering in the internal affairs of the Middle Eastern states. Moreover, the Soviet Union, which is portrayed as a staunch supporter of peace, progress, and international security, helped prevent the Israelis and their Western backers from detaching the Arab world from the socialist countries.

The Egyptian national liberation movement has been exhaustively studied by Soviet historians. According to Russian experts, the Egyptian national liberation struggle entered a new stage in 1945 and accelerated during two periods—the period from February 1945 to March 1946 and the period from October 1951 to January 1952, the climax of which was armed struggle against the British in the Suez Canal Zone. The Canal Zone affair demonstrated that there was no political party in Egypt capable of assuming leadership of the anti-imperialist movement.[175]

According to Seiranian, the national bourgeoisie was not capable of heading the popular anti-imperialist movement, although the Wafd—the party of the national bourgeoisie—had the largest following among the legal political groups. Seiranian says that as a "class of exploiters," the national bourgeoisie feared the "deepening" of social antagonism and the "democratization" of the national liberation movement. For this reason, he believes, the national bourgeoisie, which was allegedly preoccupied with the promotion of its own class interests, was inclined to negotiate with the British imperialists.

One Soviet version holds that after the Wafd assumed power in 1950, a split over policy occurred in its leadership between the upper bourgeoisie and the lower, which needed an organization to speak for it. This need was filled by the Free Officers, a secret group that engineered the revolution of July 23, 1952.[176] It was therefore the lower bourgeoisie, whose most revolutionary segment came from the left wing of the Wafd,[177] that marched in the front rank of the liberation movement in Egypt.

The most significant role in the Egyptian national liberation movement, according to Seiranian, was played by the "national intelligentsia," which was composed largely of petty bourgeoisie. When Soviet authors speak of petty bourgeoisie as revolutionaries, they have in mind not artisans and merchants but the intelligentsia made up of army officers, students, teachers, and public servants. Seiranian divides the intelligentsia into three uneven categories. In the first he puts those who defended the interests of the large property owners, the monopolistic bourgeoisie, and the monarchy. Next comes the anti-British element and those opposed to the social groups on which imperialism was based. This group, which was nationalistic and patriotic but not consistently revolutionary, was numerically the largest. In the third category, which was somewhat larger than the first but much smaller than the second, he puts the "democratic intelligentsia," made up of the most patriotic and the most revolutionary elements, whose radicalism and revolutionary character are attributed to the constant threat of pauperization that hung over them.[178] Soviet sources contend that this group exerted a powerful influence over the masses and played an important role in the national liberation movement.

One Soviet author writes that at first the Free Officers had no well-defined program or common ideology. They harped on the miserable conditions in their country, for which they blamed British imperialism, the decadent monarchy, the large native feudatories, and the rich bourgeoisie. As far as their ideology was concerned, the officers were influenced to varying degrees either by the Wafd or the Muslim Brotherhood,[179] or by the ideas of Marxism and Leninism. Their main objective, according to the same source, was to win independence for their country through an unconditional evacuation of the British troops, and then to introduce a number of basic reforms, to liquidate their political enemies, and to free political prisoners.

Soviet writers calculate that the number of Egyptian workers increased during the Second World War. As they became more class-conscious they became a factor in the political life of the country,[180] and by the end of the war they had established themselves as an important anti-imperialist force. Although conditions for the formation of a united front for the struggle for national liberation did exist, the working class was not yet strong enough to assume the leadership. Soviet experts attribute the weakness of the Egyptian working class to the fact that it was under the spell of bourgeois ideology. The workers were simply unable to create a unified avant-garde of the working people. And because the working class was weak, it was obliged to share the leadership of the national liberation struggle with the middle and lower sectors of the middle class and with the lower village bourgeoisie.[181] A large part of the working class was still under bourgeois influence and backed such middle class organizations as Wafd, the Muslim Brotherhood, Vatan, and the Socialist Party. Soviet writers consider that the lack of leadership and organization[182] explained the failure of the Egyptian masses to participate fully in the momentous events of 1952.

Soviet specialists point out that the Egyptian peasantry, compared with its counterpart in Algeria, played a lesser role in the struggle for national independence than did the working class and the petty bourgeoisie. The peasants in Egypt participated in demonstrations that took place in major cities. The auxiliary police (*Buluk an-nizam*), made up of peasants, joined the "partisans" who were fighting the British during the period from October 1951 to January 1952.[183] In the final stages of the armed struggle, as more and more peasants joined in, partisan units and committees for defense were created in the rural committees of the Suez Canal Zone. Seiranian says that after the "reactionary coup" of January 27, 1952, the partisan war in the Zone began to wane, and the struggle again shifted to the major cities.[184] The partisan units were made up mostly of the lower bourgeoisie, including the small rural bourgeoisie, and workers. The lower bourgeoisie is said to have been the main moving force in the liberation movement during and after the armed conflict in the Suez Canal Zone in 1951-52. Soviet authors endorse Nasser's statement to the effect that the Egyptian revolution took place not only as a result of the Palestinian war but had its roots in far deeper and more fundamental social and national grievances.

Soviet historians initially characterized the 1952 Egyptian revolution as a bourgeois undertaking by reactionary officers who could not be expected to achieve national independence. Muhammad Nagib, the head of the revolutionary government for a short time, was looked upon as a representative of the reactionary middle class. Since the mid-fifties, however, Soviet writers have given a new interpretation to the Egyptian national liberation movement. They now say that the movement, including the revolution, was anti-imperialist and anti-feudal, and that it was directed against British rule as well as against the native feudatories, the upper bourgeoisie, and the monarchy. In the final struggle with the British, according to Soviet sources, an "absolute majority" of Egyptians—workers, peasants, the middle sector, and the national bourgeoisie—took part. Earlier studies of the movement written by K. A. Troianovskii, V. Abuziam, E. Veit, and others, were criticized from 1956 on for underestimating the Egyptian struggle against British imperialism and for ignoring the progressive role played by the national bourgeoisie.[185]

Since 1956 Soviet writers have become less critical of the middle class and have tended to draw a distinction between the upper bourgeoisie, which is said to have worked against the national welfare, and the "national bourgeoisie," or the middle and petty bourgeoisie, which is said to have played a progressive role in the struggle for independence. Initially Soviet theorists held to the view that the Arab bourgeoisie was not capable of heading a movement for national independence and that only the working class as a consistent fighter for freedom could do this. The progressive role of the Arab bourgeoisie in the successful struggle for national independence has since 1956 been acknowledged by Soviet historians.[186] Thus, as we have seen, Soviet sources now contend that the lower middle class in particular supplied the fighters for the struggle while the upper middle class was collaborating with the foreign imperialist powers.

Soviet writers observe that after the dismissal of Muhammed Najib in February 1954, the Egyptian regime evolved more rapidly in an anti-imperialist direction. Viewing Egyptian political developments in retrospect, they concluded that the seizure of power in 1952 and Nasser's part in this event constituted revolutionary action that secured full national independence for Egypt and transformed the country into "a bourgeois-democratic state." Several events are said to have attested to the anti-imperialist direction of the Egyptian government after 1954: the Anglo-Egyptian agreement (1954), the nationalization of the Suez Canal Company (1956), the anti-capitalist reforms (1959-64), and the proclamation of the United Arab Republic (Egypt) in March 1964 as a democratic and socialist state.[187]

Soviet published materials on Egypt insist that Nasser's decision of July 1956 to nationalize the Suez Canal Company had popular endorsement in the Arab world, and they condemn the tripartite Sinai campaign and the attacks on the Suez Canal Zone. After explaining the reasons for the Suez crisis and the "imperialistic aggression" against Egypt, A. S. Protopopov re-emphasizes the benevolent Soviet role toward Egypt and the Arabs. Both he and Seiranian argue that the Soviets were primarily responsible for stopping imperialist aggression against Egypt. The Soviet Union warned Britain and France that it could not remain indifferent to their activities in the Middle East and that it would use force if necessary to maintain peace in that region.[188] Furthermore, Moscow extended moral and economic aid to the Egyptians[189] and prevented the Anglo-French-Israeli invaders from isolating Egypt. Soviet aid along with that of other socialist states, we are told, has enabled Egypt to overcome the consequences of Israeli aggression.

Soviet sources make much of the alleged worldwide popular sympathy for Egypt during the Suez crisis as well as of arms deliveries to that country by the socialist states. They see the crisis as a serious setback for British and French imperialism. According to Protopopov, the crisis proved that United States policy was no different from that of the other two Western powers, even though the United States publicly feigned displeasure over the tripartite aggression. While warning Britain and France against the use of force to resolve the crisis, he says, the United States at the same time was supplying them with oil.[190] In fact, Protopopov charges, the United States supported the suspension of hostilities against Egypt in order to extend its own influence over the Arab world.

The Suez crisis profoundly affected subsequent relations between the Soviet Union and Egypt. Before the Second World War the U.S.S.R. occasionally backed a movement for Arab unity simply because it was anti-British and anti-French. For a time after the war, especially during the 1948-53 period, Moscow condemned the Arab League, founded in 1945, because it saw the League as a tool of British imperialism directed toward the destruction of "the progressive forces" in the Arab world.[191] Until 1956 such Soviet writers as Vatolina and Lutskii treated Pan-Arabism and the Arab League as tools of reaction.[192] They saw no justification for Arab unity and simply assumed it could not be achieved. The proposals for the establishment of an Arab federation and the Greater Syria scheme were condemned as evil-intentioned devices of the capitalist states.

After 1956 the Arab League was accepted as a positive force that sought to coordinate the Arab struggle for independence and served as a necessary step toward Arab national and economic unity. Soviet writers now stressed the importance of Arab unity, which they felt was favored by economic conditions and was justified on the grounds that the Arabs shared a common language and culture. It was pointed out that because of the powerful influence of foreign "monopoly capitalism," some Arab countries that had achieved "political independence" had not yet won "economic independence." This they could do through Arab unity, and Egypt was recognized as the political and cultural leader of the Arab world.

The Western powers and the United States were singled out as the enemies of Arab unity and independence. A systematic campaign was undertaken to refute and discredit Western interpretations of men and events in the Middle East. For example, certain Western authors were criticized for allegedly saying that the defeat of Britain, France, and Israel in the Suez campaign was an accident and not the result of "objective factors."[193] The Soviets could not comprehend how Western authors could blame the 1956 crisis on the Egyptians.[194] Western works, they contended, were seeking to whitewash the Western powers and Israel in regard to the Suez affair and moreover to minimize the positive steps taken by the Soviet Union to stop the hostilities. They say that subsequent events have shown that Egyptian policy in 1956 was correct, and that the Egyptian victory has proved to all who are fighting for their own country's independence that the colonial powers no longer possess their former strength.

The formation of the United Arab Republic in February 1958, which was enthusiastically received in many Arab circles, was viewed in the Middle East as a first step toward full Arab unity. The immediate Soviet response to the move was not sympathetic, however, Soviet spokesmen reasoning that it might be exploited by Arab reactionaries. Actually, it appeared that the United Arab Republic would pose a threat to the Soviet aim of building a strong base in Syria. Relations between Gamal Abdel Nasser and Nikita Khrushchev therefore became strained, and they deteriorated further when the Soviet Union threw its support behind the new nationalist government that came to power in Iraq in July 1958. At that time the Iraqi government appeared more pro-Moscow than pro-Cairo. Nasser expressed displeasure at Soviet interference in internal Arab affairs, and accused Moscow of seeking to further its own selfish interests in the Middle East.[195] These momentary strains in Soviet-Egyptian relations are hardly mentioned in Soviet works.

The Israeli attack on Egypt of June 5, 1967, has been given a great deal of attention in Soviet publications. Protopopov, who has reviewed Western literature on the subject and has examined many aspects of it, including the United Nations Security Council discussions, maintains that the Israeli attack was not accidental but was part of a Western scheme to gain mastery over the Middle East. The 1967 aggression, he says, has once again shown the Arabs that the Soviet Union is their friend.

Soviet publications describe the United States as a foreign power consistently unfriendly toward the Arabs.[196] This, they say, was amply demonstrated during the Suez crisis, which showed that the United States was the main source of reaction and a principal exponent of colonialism. To further its objectives in the Middle East, says Protopopov, the United States backed Muslim religious circles and tried to strengthen Saudi Arabia vis-à-vis Egypt. [197] But the Arabs, he argues, refused to be misled by United States policy, although they did express willingness to accept the proffered American economic aid if no strings were attached.

In the eyes of Soviet historians American imperialism is the main enemy of the economic and national independence of the Arab states. Thus the United States allegedly seeks to control the key military bases in the Middle East and in North Africa. They charge that the Eisenhower Doctrine showed clearly that the United States was the principal imperialist power in the Middle East. It is argued that Israel has been assigned an important role in American and British imperialist schemes, and that in addition the United States has backed Israel in an armed conflict with the Arab states in order to divert world attention from Vietnam. According to Soviet sources, Britain, the junior partner of the United States, still hopes with American support to preserve whatever influence it retains in the Middle East.[198]

The Sudan

Although some material on the Sudan was published before the Second

World War, much more has appeared since 1945. The Sudan fascinates Soviet scholars because of its unique history and its ethnographic diversity, and since the Second World War the Soviet Union has attached to it great strategic and political importance. A short survey of Sudanese history from 1821 to 1956, published in 1968, is based almost exclusively on Western sources.

Probably the best Soviet work on the Sudan has been done in the field of ethnography. A number of prominent ethnographers, including D. A. Ol'derogge,[199] S. R. Smirnov,[200] and I. I. Potekhin, have investigated the area. Ol'derogge challenges some Western interpretations of African culture. Smirnov contends that the Sudanese people are a product of the fusion of different ethnic elements, but he considers them a nation by virtue of their national consciousness and their common territory, language, culture, and economic interests. Potekhin says that the Sudanese national consciousness developed faster than the country's economy, and that although the Sudan has won political independence, it has not yet achieved economic independence.[201] He recognizes the existence of a Southern problem in the Sudan, but he feels that Western scholars exaggerate its magnitude.

Until 1955 Soviet writers looked upon the Sudan as a part of Egypt,[202] but since that year they have adopted a policy favoring its independence. Before 1955 Moscow supported the Ashiqqa (Brothers) and the National Unionists, seeing them as a petty bourgeoisie movement, and opposed the Ummah (Nation) Party on the grounds that it spoke for the upper bourgeoisie, which betrayed the nation by siding with colonial interests. Since 1955, Soviet writers have backed what they call the national bourgeoisie, which embraces all progressive groups, including the workers and peasants, and which is said to be striving toward the country's economic and political independence.

The Mahdi movement, one of the more investigated topics, is described by Soviet writers as a national liberation movement directed against British rule. According to Smirnov,[203] this movement had its roots in the social and economic conditions resulting from the transition from the primeval-communal to the slave-holding social order. Not all Soviet historians share this interpretation. Lutskii and Pershits, for example, hold that the Sudanese had already gone through the slave-holding stage of development before the Mahdi movement appeared. Smirnov maintains that Mahdism failed both as a national and as a social movement, but he concedes that it did facilitate the development of the Sudanese nation. He believes that the failure resulted from the inherent class conflict between the ordinary tribesmen and the tribal aristocracy. This conflict undermined tribal unity and weakened Mahdi resistance to the British. Smirnov has been criticized for not distinguishing clearly between the political and the religious objectives of Mahdism, for assuming erroneously that the Mahdis fought to secure equality under Islam, and for exaggerating the non-feudal character of Islam and underestimating its "reactionary essence."

Soviet scholars describe the period of Egyptian and British rule over the Sudan as a time of extreme oppression and backwardness. Between 1821 and 1881 the Egyptians not only allowed the slave trade to continue but actually fostered it. The extension of British rule over Egypt produced native opposition in the Sudan and did nothing to improve the situation there.[204] Smirnov says that British rule in the Sudan had disastrous consequences. The British stifled Sudanese culture and reduced the area to nothing more than a colony that supplied raw materials for British industries and markets for British goods. As a result, he says, the British reaped heavy profits overtaxing and exploiting the Sudan while the toilers grew steadily more impoverished. The same writer accuses the British of pursuing a policy of divide-and-rule and of playing one Sudanese tribe against another. The British, to facilitate their colonial rule, resorted to money bribes for the "tribal aristocracy." Their rule preserved the archaic tribal organization, impeded the country's social and economic growth, and retarded the development of the Sudanese nation-state.

Soviet writers have published a number of works on the Sudan's economy, on its geography, and on its natural resources. They have written on the agrarian problem, on the peasantry, and on the nationalization of the Gazira (El-Jezira) Scheme (1955). There are short studies on finances[205] and on the credit system.[206] Studies have been made also on Sudanese relations with other Arab states and with the Soviet Union. The Sudanese are praised for their neutralist policy and for their support of the cause of Arab unity and of Afro-Asian solidarity. According to Soviet writers, Soviet influence on and assistance to the Sudan stimulated the Sudanese movement for independence, a movement accelerated by the Second World War. After fifty years of struggle the Sudanese, with some backing from Moscow, finally did win independence from Great Britain.[207] Several short items have appeared concerning Soviet aid to the Sudan, but relations between Moscow and the Sudan broke down in 1971 after an abortive coup led by Sudanese communists failed to overthrow the regime of President Ja'far al-Numairi.

North Africa

Soviet publications on the North African Arab countries tend to be of recent origin,[208] most of them journalistic in character and attesting to the strategic importance of the area for the Soviet Union. Literature on Libya includes two short surveys of the country's contemporary history[209] and a few articles on Libyan oil, on Soviet-Libyan relations, and on the country's government and economy. The growing importance of Libya on the international scene since the revolution of 1969, however, is now attracting much greater Soviet attention.

The published materials on Tunisia and Algeria consist for the most part of short articles on the French penetration of Tunisia beginning in the seventeenth century and on the later French occupation and administration of the country. Several brief works discuss the national liberation movement in Tunisia, the Dustur (Constitution) Party, and Tunisia's economy,[210] its government,[211] and its relations with the Soviet Union and France.[212] A brief survey of the history of contemporary Tunisia has appeared recently.[213]

As for Algeria, this country's national liberation movement and its struggle for independence have received the most attention from Soviet specialists.[214] One book discusses the French conquest of Algeria in the nineteenth century and the activities of Abdal Kader (1832-47). Additional topics covered either in short studies or at greater length include the Algerian Commune (1870-71), the Algerian workers' movement and the communist party, Algerian relations with the Soviet Union and France, and Algeria's conflict with Morocco, as well as Algeria's government, its economy, its culture, and its literature. A few articles have appeared on the oil of the Sahara, on European neocolonialism, and on contemporary political developments in Algeria.

Morocco has for the most part been neglected by Soviet scholars. The limited amount of material published since the Second World War concerns the Moroccan national liberation movement, the Republic of Rif,[215] European imperialism in Morocco, the winning of independence from France and Spain, the Moroccan government and political opposition, the workers' movement,[216] United States activities in and policies toward Morocco, the threat to Morocco of neocolonialism, the Moroccan economy, and socioeconomic developments. At least one survey of the modern history of Morocco has been published.[217]

Syria, Lebanon, Jordan

Soviet historians have been long interested in Syria, Lebanon, Jordan, and Palestine, in their history in the Biblical period, in the Muslim conquest of these lands, and in Ottoman and Turkish[218] and French and British rule over them. Special studies have been published covering the French expedition to Syria (including Lebanon) of 1860-61[219] and the establishment of the French mandatory system in Syria and Lebanon at the end of the First World War. One of the best Russian histories of the region is K. M. Bazili, *Siriia i Palestina pod turetskim pravitel'stvom* (Syria and Palestine under Turkish rule).[220]

Soviet authors stress the influence of the Russian Revolution of 1905 on the intelligentsia and the middle class in Syria and Lebanon, and show that the impact of the October Revolution on these countries, especially on the workers and peasants, was far greater than is usually believed. As for French mandatory rule, Soviet writers say that the French took advantage of the confessional differences of the population to play one group against the other. As a result, opposition to the French mounted and led to national uprisings. Soviet authors attribute the economic backwardness of the two countries to French colonial policy, and give the Soviet Union the major share of credit for Syria's and Lebanon's having achieved their independence in 1946.[221]

The subject of the Soviet Union's economic and cultural relations with Syria and Lebanon, which were greatly expanded from the mid-fifties on, has received considerable attention from Soviet historians. One or two short surveys of modern Syrian history have been published. On the political front, Soviet writers tended before 1956 to criticize the Syrian and Lebanese bourgeoisie for collaborating with the French. Since then, however, they have been drawing a distinction between the "national bourgeoisie" and an upper bourgeoisie. For a time, Moscow, because it considered Lebanon pro-Western and doubted its friendship, tended to favor Syria over Lebanon.

One short article discusses the development of contemporary Lebanon and notes that the Lebanese Communist Party is fighting against the outmoded confessional system of government representation.[222] Other studies cover the national liberation movements,[223] workers' movements, the economy,[224] the peasantry,[225] and contemporary political affairs and government in Syria and Lebanon. A short handbook on Lebanon was published in 1963.[226] Some attention has been given also to Lebanese literature, to Soviet-Lebanese literary ties, to Lenin in Arab poetry,[227] and to Arabic dialects spoken in Lebanon. The most productive experts on Syria and Lebanon are V. M. Fiodorenko and I. M. Smilianskaia.

The few Soviet writers who have written about Jordan are critical of Jordan and of its close relations with Great Britain and the United States: and they are unsparing in their criticism of the monarchy. They are outspoken in expressing sympathy for the anti-monarchist movement and for the Arab guerrilla forces. They have turned out one or two short histories of contemporary Jordan.[228]

Iraq

Good work has been done by Soviet scholars on Iraq's ancient precursors, Babylonia, Assyria, and Sumeria; on the buffer states along Iraq's frontiers with the expanding early Islamic state; on the Baghdad caliphate and its institutions; and on the forms and practices of Iraqi feudalism.[229] Much of the published material covers the country's struggle for independence from Ottoman and British rule. Soviet writers contend that Ottoman rule had devastating effects on Iraq, because it delayed the country's social, cultural, and literary revival.

According to Soviet experts, since the end of the nineteenth century Iraqi peasants, tribesmen, and workers have participated in the liberation movement directed against their Ottoman rulers. The impact of the Bolshevik Revolution inspired the Iraqi liberation struggle. The Iraqi uprisings of 1920, 1935, and 1953 and the general social ferment in the country have been closely studied by Soviet historians.[230] Of particular interest is a book by G. I. Mirskii, entitled *Irak v smutnoe vremia, 1930-1941* (Iraq in the time of troubles, 1930-1941).[231] There are also short studies on Soviet-Iraqi diplomatic relations during the Second World War and on Iraq's position in the war. Interestingly enough, Rashid 'Ali al-Gailani's coup d'état of April 1941 has been treated lightly; the Soviet Union was at the time on friendly terms with Nazi Germany and had in fact recognized Rashid's government (May 1941).

The social and economic development of Iraq, according to Soviet writers, was impeded by the British mandatory system and by misapplied postwar American technical aid and interference in Iraq's internal affairs. Under what these writers call the unpopular government of Nuri al-Sa'id, backed by Britain and the United States, Iraq's oil revenues were spent on the military establishment rather than on improvement of the position of the workers. In view of the stringent repressive measures of the Nuri government, the political opposition was unable to force it to carry out badly needed reforms.

Another topic frequently discussed in connection with Iraq is the Baghdad Pact. Soviet authors view the pact as an American maneuver to achieve hegemony over the Middle East and to help encircle the Soviet Union with military bases. The pact is said to have strained relations between the Soviet Union and Iraq and to have caused Nuri al-Sa'id, under British pressure, to sever diplomatic relations with the Soviet Union, thereby wrecking the movement for Arab solidarity.

A great deal has been written on Iraq as a British mandate, on British economic interests in Iraq, and on the Anglo-Iraqi treaty of alliance. King Faisal II and Iraqi ruling and feudal circles are condemned for their alleged support of Great Britain. The so-called Anglo-American neocolonialism and alleged attempts to fasten an economic stranglehold on Iraq and recurring themes in Soviet writings.

Until the assassination of King Faisal II and Premier Nuri al-Sa'id in 1958, the Soviet attitude toward Iraq was one of ambivalence. Iraq did not receive the attention given to Egypt; for instance, only a few lines in the two-volume *Novaia istoriia stran zarubezhnogo Vostoka* (Modern history of the countries of the non-Soviet East), published in 1952,[232] were allotted to Iraq.

After the 1958 assassinations the Soviet attitude toward Iraq became more sympathetic. Lengthy papers were published on the exploitation of Iraqi oil[233] and on Anglo-American rivalry to control it, on the question of Mosul, and on Iraq as a strategic base in the Western military encirclement of the Soviet Union. More recently the Soviet Union has become extensively involved in the oil industry of Iraq and has signed a fifteen-year treaty of alliance with that country.

Other aspects of Iraqi history that have been investigated are internal political affairs, the national front (1946-58),[234] Iraq's relations with the Arabic states and Turkey, Kurdish unrest, and the development of agricultural cooperatives.[235] Frequent articles criticizing the Ba'ath Party have appeared, as well as two or three short surveys of Iraq's history that have very little scholarly value.[236] In several studies published on Iraqi literature and language, Soviet writers have drawn attention to a number of "progressive" Iraqi authors who have come forth as a result of the mounting anti-British movement.

Soviet historians write on Iraqi minorities, such as the Kurds and the Assyrians.[237] They are interested especially in the Kurds, who pose a special problem for the Soviet Union. The October Revolution, according to Soviet writers, greatly affected the Kurdish national movement directed against the alien bourgeoisie, the Kurdish feudal leaders, and Anglo-American imperialism. Soviet writers note with interest the growth of the Kurdish proletariat and Kurdish progressive literature. Kurdish ethnography and society are studied, as well as Kurdish anti-British activity. At one time the British were accused of promoting a united Kurdistan with the purpose of using it against the Soviet Union. After the Second World War, however, the Soviet Union itself expressed sympathy for the Kurdish national movement and for the Kurdish Democratic Party that represented it.

The Arabian Peninsula

The national liberation movement in Saudi Arabia, Saudi relations with the West and other Arab states, and Western imperialism and oil exploitation receive a great deal of attention in the Soviet Union. Writers repeatedly stress the fact that the U.S.S.R. was the first country to establish diplomatic relations with King Husain of Hejaz (al-Hijaz) (1924) and to recognize Saudi Arabia (1926). So long as Ibn Sa'ud was anti-British, Soviet writers treated him as an "objectively revolutionary" leader, a unifier of the Arab people; and they spoke favorably of his *Ikhwan* (Brothers) movement.

In the late thirties, even though the U.S.S.R. extended credit to Ibn Sa'ud in 1931 and Amir Faisal visited Moscow in 1934, relations between the Soviet Union and Hejaz were allowed to stagnate. The Soviet Union during this period changed its foreign policy to advocacy of collective security and resistance to fascism, and Moscow became convinced that Ibn Saʻud could not rally the Arabs behind an anti-British movement.

During the Second World War and until 1955 the Soviet Union manifested no sympathy for Saudi Arabia and Yemen, even though Yemen remained anti-British. Soviet writers criticized both countries for being feudal and socially backward. Wahhabism, which Soviet writers had at one time praised for its progressive character in seeking the unification of the Arab tribes, was rejected after the Second World War as the reactionary ideology of a feudal regime opposed to the Arab national liberation movements.[238] King Ibn Saʻud was dubbed a tool of British and American imperialism.

Since 1955 Saudi Arabia has received a somewhat more sympathetic treatment; yet little of importance has been published on this country in the Soviet Union. Apart from one or two brief items on social conditions in pre-Islamic Arabia, no scholarly work on the early period of Arabia's history has appeared. One article of some merit discusses the teaching of Muhammad ibn ʻAbd al-Wahhab, the conditions in Arabia on the eve of the Wahhabite takeover, the domain of al-Darʻiyah (the original Wahhabite capital), the founding of the Saudi state, and the Egyptian campaign against the Wahhabites.[239] Another study supplies a Marxist-Leninist interpretation of Wahhabite religious principles.[240] After 1955, when Soviet writers reverted to a more lenient treatment of Wahhabism, they tended to concentrate more on its political than on its religious aspects. The doctrine was again praised for its "progressive" character in striving to unite Arabian tribes as well as for its opposition to British imperialism.

Since 1958 Saudi Arabia has been criticized for having abandoned the original Wahhabite aim of restoring Islam to its pristine purity, and for becoming a tool of the feudatories and trading bourgeoisie. Wahhabism has been criticized also for seeking to redirect the working classes from their real social and economic interests to religion.[241]

The history of Saudi Arabia is treated in a few general works on the Arab world and the Middle East. A score of articles have appeared on the Saudi monarchy and society, on the slave trade, on ethnic problems, on Western imperialism and oil concessions, and on King Faisal. Soviet writers cover in detail the meandering political course of King Saʻud and King Faisal and the Saudi-Syrian-Egyptian defense pact of October 1955, and show sympathy for the Saudi Arabian claims in the Buraimi dispute with Britain over boundaries in eastern Arabia. Saudi Arabia is cited as an example of a country which, though not yet liberated from the economic oppression of imperialism, has pursued a sovereign foreign policy.[242] However, the Saudi regime, growing alarmed over the activities of Egyptian officers in its country and over Soviet objectives, expelled the Egyptian officers on August 1, 1956.

Several works have been produced on British and American imperialism in Saudi Arabia,[243] as well as on the relations between Saudi Arabia and other Arab states. These relations have been followed closely in the Soviet press. At least one general work treating the history and economy of Saudi Arabia has been published.[244]

Even when approving some of the Saudi Arabian actions in foreign affairs, Soviet authors have not ceased to be critical of the social backwardness of the country. This state of affairs they attribute less to the undemocratic Saudi government than to Western imperialism. They note the growing popular opposition to imperialism, the oil workers' strikes, and the alleged activity of the illegal parties. In 1957 the friendly Soviet attitude toward the country suffered a setback because of the weak Saudi stand on the Eisenhower doctrine and because of the Saudi agreement with the United States for use of the Dhahran airfield.[245]

When Crown Prince Faisal, a supporter of Arab unity and an opponent of Western military blocs, assumed control of foreign and domestic affairs in 1958, the Soviet Union seemed pleased. Moscow resented the country's friendly relations with the United States, however, and criticized the regime for not being closer to the socialist countries.[246] The U.S.S.R. became somewhat more outspoken at this juncture about Saudi domestic and foreign policies. The Soviet press played up the strikes and the reported founding of a Front for National Liberation in March 1958, which was regarded as indicative of growing internal opposition to the Saudi regime. One Soviet author charged that the government demanded and obtained a larger share of oil profits from the Arabian American Oil Company under the pressure of growing popular opposition. Yet Soviet writers welcomed Saudi criticism of the British and American landings in Jordan and Lebanon (July 1958), King Sa'ud's visit to Cairo in September 1959, the improved relations between Saudi Arabia and Egypt, and the Saudi support of Khrushchev's démarche in the United Nations (September 1960) for the "liquidation of colonialism."

Perhaps the best Soviet work on Saudi Arabia has been in the field of ethnography. Soviet writers have long been interested in the life and social organization of the desert nomads, and A. I. Pershits at one time described contemporary Arab nomad society as feudal with certain capitalistic features.[247] In his book, *Khoziaistvo i obshchestvenno-politicheskii stroi Severnoi Aravii v XIX-pervoi treti XX vv.* (The economy and the social and political order in northern Arabia in the nineteenth and the first third of the twentieth century),[248] Pershits provides a Marxist interpretation of the economic, social, and political order in northern Arabia during the period of the formation of the Saudi kingdom. He discusses the sedentary, nomadic, and semi-nomadic populations, the cities, the patriarchal-clan system, slavery, feudalism, tribes and tribal alliances, and the emirates of Jabal-Shammar and Najd. Under Arab conditions, according to Pershits, the emergence of the Saudi monarchy from among the major feudatories was a progressive historical development.[249]

The Soviet Union became interested in Yemen during that country's border dispute with Great Britain, and in 1928 concluded with it a treaty of friendship and trade. The U.S.S.R. sent doctors there and helped build the country's first electric power plant.[250] Soviet historians have argued that the establishment of diplomatic relations with the Soviet Union enabled Saudi Arabia and Yemen to break out of the isolation to which the imperialist powers had subjected them. Moscow praised Imam Yahya of Yemen, whom they looked upon as the "objectively revolutionary leader" of the anti-British movement, and placed the blame for Yemen's backwardness on the landlords, the merchants, and the British.[251] Soviet-Yemeni relations stagnated during the late thirties despite a ten-year treaty concluded in 1939.

Since the war, Soviet spokesmen have often criticized Yemen's antiquated social and political organization. After 1955, however, and especially after 1957, their attitude became more tolerant, and Soviet historians lauded Yemenese and South Arabian resistance to British imperialism. The Soviet press endorsed Yemen's anti-British policy aimed at expelling the British from Aden and the Protectorates, and like the Yemenese they saw the British-proposed federation of the south Arabian emirates as an instrument of British imperialism. The federation, Soviet authors pointed out, was contrived to preserve British control by producing a pro-British state on Yemen's borders. The Soviet-Yemenese treaties of friendship and trade, concluded in October 1955 and March 1956, respectively, were hailed in Moscow as a renewal of the 1928 arrangement; and hopes were expressed that the treaties, because of their equalitarian character, might serve as a model for Soviet treaties with other Arab states. Soviet writers noted a growing anti-imperialist sentiment in Yemen and in other Arab countries.[252]

Soviet works took note also of Yemen's endorsement of the United Arab Republic, especially by the younger generation,[253] and of its apparent adherence to Arab unity through the device of the United Arab States. Through 1960 the Soviet press still praised the Imam's anti-British stand and played down his acceptance of American aid and his grant of an oil concession to an American firm. But Soviet writers continued to call attention to the social backwardness of Yemen and to the miserable lot of the Yemenese peasantry, women, and children. Once again, as they had on earlier occasions, they placed the major blame for these conditions on Western imperialism rather than on the royal family. In fact, the Imam was commended for his variuos attempts to improve the health, education, and economic conditions of his people.

The visits of heir apparent Ahmad al-Badr to Moscow and the

agreements he concluded are set forth in Soviet writings, as is Imam Ahmad's falling out with Nasser of Egypt. There is almost complete silence on the expulsion of the Egyptians from Yemen. But much is said about Soviet aid in the construction of the Hodeida port, about Soviet economic, technical, and medical assistance, and about expanding Soviet trade relations with Yemen. The Soviet press took note also of Yemenese anti-communist activities and of the indignities to which Russian and Chinese representatives were at times subjected.[254] Relations between Yemen and the other Arab states, especially Egypt, as well as the progress of the abortive Yemenese revolt that broke out in 1957, have been well covered, as have the relations between the Soviet Union and Yemen and the Yemenese-British dispute.[255] A brief history of modern Yemen was published in 1965.[256]

Until the early 1950s little appeared in Soviet publications about the British protectorates in South Arabia and the Persian Gulf. After the adoption of the new Middle East policy, the Soviet Union began to recognize the strategic importance of countries ruled by Arab nationalist and traditionalist governments. Many popular articles have since been published in which the Arab movement for national independence is praised, the liquidation of foreign bases urged, and the "unequal" treaties that placed many small Arab states under British control condemned. Although attention is called in these articles to the backwardness of such small Arab states, it is the foreign rather than the native rulers who are held responsible.[257]

Soviet writers trace the beginning of British imperialism in South Arabia to the British acquisition of Aden in 1839, dividing the history of British imperialism in the nineteenth century into two periods: the period from 1839 to 1869, in which British imperialism took root, and the period from 1870 to 1905, when British rule expanded.

The formation in 1958 of the United Arab Republic and the United Arab States aroused Arab nationalism everywhere, and facilitated Yemenese subversive activities in Aden. Some of the rulers of the Protectorates resented Yemenese interference and backed the British Federation plan, a project equally disapproved of by the Yemenese and the Russians.[258]

The Soviet press, which has closely followed the tribal, social, and political frictions in various parts of South Arabia, hailed the 1958 war of the Imam of Oman and his tribal forces against the Sultan of Muscat as a "national liberation struggle."[259] The press discerned an increase in anti-colonial sentiment in Kuwait, in Qatar, in Bahrain, and in other Arabian principalities, and repeatedly condemned the British presence and British activities in the South Arabian sheikhdoms.[260] In addition to the press coverage on this area, a short history of modern Kuwait was published in 1964.[261]

Israel

The works published in the Soviet Union on Israel, except for two or three studies on Judaism, deal mostly with the Israeli-Arab conflict. They are essentially propagandistic accounts, highly critical of Israel. For years Soviet spokesmen made no distinction between the Jews and Zionism. The Soviet Union was a leading supporter of the 1947 resolution of the General Assembly of the United Nations, which provided for Jewish and Arab states in Palestine; and the Soviet Union was also the first country, as we have mentioned, to give the new state of Israel *de jure* recognition in 1948. Since then, the Soviet Union has altered its policy. The 1952 edition of the *Bol'shaia Sovetskaia Entsiklopediia* (Great Soviet Encyclopedia) expresses sympathy for the Jews who suffered from Hitlerian persecution but finds fault with Zionism as an ideology.[262]

Soviet writers criticize Israel's foreign and domestic policies. Although they laud what they recognize as "progressive" forces in Israel, especially the Israeli Communist Party, which is said to support peace, social progress, and a united Jewish-Arab anti-imperialist front, they depict the "rulers" of Israel as tools of imperialism who subscribe to bourgeois-nationalist Zionist doctrine and pursue policies whose objective is to resist the national liberation movements and socialism. Israel is accused of grabbing Arab territories, of violating the borders established by the United Nations, and of causing suffering to masses of Arab refugees.

Soviet experts contend that since the twenties the Zionists have been planning in one way or another to rid Palestine of Arabs and to seize Arab lands. With British backing, the Zionists are said to have resorted to various tactics, including economic discrimination against the Arabs, in order to achieve their objective. According to Soviet critics, Israeli leaders exaggerate the achievements of their state. To speak of the kibbutz as "an island of socialism," they say, is nonsense, because socialism cannot exist in a capitalist society. Soviet writers charge that the kibbutzim exploit workers in a capitalist manner, that they are sinking into ever deeper debt, and that the number of Israelis who live in the kibbutzim has been steadily declining. These Soviet scholars say further that as a result of colossal military expenditures, of a mounting national debt, of a declining standard of living, and of rising unemployment, Israel's economy is on the verge of bankruptcy. They argue that this economy could collapse without a steady inflow of foreign capital, American loans and credits, and until recently, German reparations and compensations.[263] Israeli leaders are accused of plotting war against the Arabs in order to divert the attention of the workers from their plight. The only hope for Israel, according to one Soviet writer, is the Communist Party of Israel, because this party opposes discrimination against the Arabs and the seizure of Arab lands.

Soviet authors reject the argument that the persecution of the Jews in Germany and anti-Semitism made it necessary to found a Jewish state. The founding of Israel, they say, cannot prevent anti-Semitism, which can be destroyed only through the victory of socialism. They charge further that the Arab minority in Israel has been subjected to various kinds of discrimination, and that it has been denied equal political rights and an equal opportunity to acquire citizenship. Israel is accused of instilling chauvinism in its youth and of encouraging them to look down upon the Arabs.

In her book on Israel G. S. Nikitina discusses the birth of Zionism, British "colonial policy" in Palestine, and the founding of the state of Israel.[164] One purpose of the book is to show the close ties between American "imperialism" and Zionism. Nikitina gives a detailed description of the Israeli government, of its political parties, and of its relations with the United States, France, Great Britain, and Germany. She discusses in some detail Israel's military organization and the Arab-Israeli War of 1967. After a sketchy survey of Israel's history, economy, and agriculture, and of American subsidies, German reparations, and foreign capital, Nikitina turns to an analysis of Zionism as an ideology and finds it full of contradictions.[265] Like other Soviet writers, she warns that Israel will not solve the Jewish problem but will merely worsen it.

The manner in which Britain used Zionism to strengthen its rule over Palestine is explained by S. A. Andreev,[266] who defines Zionism as the reactionary nationalist ideology of the Jewish upper bourgeoisie, which is closely linked to imperialism. Disagreeing with the Zionists, he insists that there is no single Jewish nation and culture. He accuses Zionists of racism and chauvinism, and does not consider that Jewish settlement in Palestine is the sole solution to the Jewish problem. Thousands who migrated to Israel, writes Andreev, found in their new home the very discrimination from which they had sought to escape. He says that the "black Jews" from Africa and Asia are discriminated against, and that there is a class conflict in Israel between the rulers and the ruled, the exploiters and the exploited.

In Andreev's view the liberation of Palestine was a result of the struggle of both the Jews and the Arabs against the British in 1945. He finds that the war of 1948-49 between the Arabs and the Jews was provoked by Anglo-American imperialism. Israel won the war, but instead of establishing good relations with its neighbors it allowed itself to become a base for aggression against the Arabs. Had it not been for the Soviet Union, Andreev says, Israeli aggression against the Arabs would have developed into a major armed conflict.[267] Israel's attack on Egypt in 1956, in the opinion of Andreev, was the outcome of imperialist intrigues and of the aggressive foreign policy of the Israeli government, which acted as an agent of the Western powers and the United States. He thinks that the majority of Israelis opposed further territorial expansion at the expense of the Arab states. He minces no words in his criticism of the Israeli government, of Israel's political parties, and of the workers' federation. He criticizes also Israel's conduct of foreign affairs: her activities in Africa, her cooperation with Germany, and the aggression against the Arabs. He, too, discredits what he calls the kibbutz myth and Israel's financial dependence on the United States and Western Europe.

Another Soviet book on Israel lauds the struggle of the working masses of Israel against the "reactionary" and "unpopular" policy of the Israeli government. It also comments on the "special role" which the Western powers have assigned to Israel in the Middle East, and describes Israel as "a capitalist state." Zionism is characterized as the most reactionary wing of international Jewry, which has directed the Jewish masses toward nationalism and away from the struggle against capitalism. The book commends the Arabs for their stand against Israel and Western colonialism and imperialism. Like much of the Soviet writing on Israel, it is monotonously repetitious: Zionism is a reactionary ideology; Israel has not kept its promises since 1948; it is dependent on the United States and other imperialist powers; the kibbutz is a far cry from socialism; the Israeli economy is in a shambles; the Israeli government is capitalist; the existence of Israel will not end anti-Semitism; anti-Semitism adversely affects not the rich Jew but the poor Jew, the Jewish workers, and the Jewish intelligentsia; and the only hope for Israel is the Communist Party of Israel, founded in 1948.[268]

Turkey

Some of the best work done in the Soviet Union on the Ottoman Turks concerns medieval and early modern history.[269] Valuable studies have been published on the Seljuk state, on the origin of the Ottoman Turks, on the founding of the Ottoman state, on various Ottoman institutions, on Ottoman feudalism,[270] and on peasant insurrections and other kinds of social unrest. A great deal has been written on the historical significance of the Ottoman conquest of Constantinople.[271]

The Ottoman reform movements in the eighteenth and nineteenth centuries have been treated in several works. There are excellent studies, for example, on Mustafa Bairaktar and on the Young Turks.[272] The Tanzimat, the New Ottomans, Pan-Turkism, Pan-Islamism, and the development of Turkish bourgeois nationalism have all been investigated. Ottoman foreign relations, especially with Russia, have been treated at great length;[273] and the results of various Russian military and naval engagements with the Turks, as well as the activities of Russian generals and admirals, have been assessed. The influence of Russian revolutionary activity, such as the Revolution of 1905[274] and the October Revolution, on the development of the Turkish revolutionary movement and on Turkish nationalist resistance to Western occupation is the subject of several Soviet studies.[275] The influence of Lenin on Turkey has also commanded a great deal of interest.[276]

Turkish activities in the First World War, especially during the closing stages, have received considerable attention from Soviet historians, who have discussed Turco-German relations on the eve of the First World War, the Russo-Turkish military engagement in 1918,[277] Baku Bolshevik resistance to the Turkish-German intervention in Azerbaijan (1918),[278] the Greco-Turkish War,[279] and American imperialism and designs on Turkey.[280] A few short studies have appeared on the Turkish-Dashnak War, which is said to have been provoked by the imperialist powers when the Turks decided to annex certain Armenian and Georgian lands.[281]

The national liberation movement in Turkey (1908-23) was investigated in its various ramifications by Soviet writers both before and after the Second World War,[282] and more recently by A. Miller and A.M. Shamsutdinov. Soviet authors maintain that the Turkish national liberation revolution had a bourgeois character and that the Turks won national independence but failed to introduce basic social and economic changes.[283] In describing the manner in which the Turkish national liberation movement was inspired by the October Revolution,[284] Soviet writers point out that the first Turks to learn of the Revolution were some 63,000 Turkish officers and men who were prisoners of war in Russia.[285] The revolutionary ideas were transmitted also by the fifty or sixty thousand Russian citizens of Turkish origin interned at the beginning of the First World War and later settled in various places deep inside Russia. Some news of the October Revolution may have been provided by Ottoman Turks who had come to Russia as wage earners and lived largely in Turkestan (Tashkent, Ashkhabad, Alma-Ata), the Volga Region (Kazan, Astrakhan, Samar, Saratov), Central and South Russia (Ryazan, Odessa), and in the Urals and Siberia.

Soviet-Turkish relations during and since the Turkish War of Independence is another subject that has greatly interested Soviet historians.[286] Their studies treat Turkish military involvement against the Bolsheviks in 1918,[287] Soviet-Turkish cooperation and the Treaty of Friendship (March 16, 1921), and the Kars Conference. In addition, M. V. Frunze's notes and observations on his travels to Turkey in November 1921 have been published. The many offshoots of the Turkish struggle for independence, such as the founding of the Turkish Communist Party,[288] the "Green Army," and the Kemalist successes against the Entente Powers, have received a good deal of attention. While the Kemalist Turks are praised for their struggle against imperialism, they are criticized for having subjected the Turkish communists to "White terrorism and barbarism,"[289] which allegedly weakened the liberation movement. Soviet historians make much of the fact that the Soviet government was the first to recognize the

Turkish Grand National Assembly and to establish diplomatic relations with it.

The relations between Kemalist Turkey and the Soviet Union continued to expand between the two wars; and on December 17, 1925, the two countries concluded a Treaty of Friendship. The Soviet Union was content with the Turkish anti-imperialist policy but could not forgive the Turks for neglecting the workers at home.[290] When Turkey, under the influence of the Western powers, refused in 1939 to sign a Mutual Security Pact with the Soviet Union, relations between the two became strained.[291] Soviet authors criticize the Turks for joining the Anglo-French "imperialist camp" in 1939 and accuse them of cooperation with the Axis during the Second World War. The fact that Turkey after the war suspended relations with Germany and declared war against that country on February 23, 1945, did not improve relations between Ankara and Moscow.[292] Soviet historians repeatedly take the Turks to task for joining the Western camp and for becoming a tool of the British and American governments.

Several Soviet writers have investigated Kemal's political views[293] and economic, cultural, and political developments in Kemalist Turkey. There are works on the transformation of the Turkish state from a theocracy and monarchy into a republic,[294] on Turkish foreign affairs,[295] on the policies of the Western powers in regard to the Kemalist movement, on the development of the Turkish bourgeoisie, on the workers' movement,[296] on the industrial proletariat in Turkey,[297] on the Turkish government,[298] and on Turkish geography.[299]

Topics relating to the economy have received a great deal of attention as well. P. P. Moiseev, for example, surveys the development of agriculture from the beginning of the First World War to 1960.[300] He examines the Kemalist anti-peasant policy,[301] the plight of the peasantry, agricultural capitalism, the Kemalist land laws (1923-29), postwar agrarian reform (1945-50), and other aspects of Turkish agriculture. He concludes that in view of the Turkish government's involvement in aggressive military blocs, the only hope for the peasants is to unite with the workers in a common struggle for peace, land, and freedom. By other writers high priority is given to the study of the development of capitalism in Turkey.[302] According to Soviet experts, the Turkish experience serves as a fine example of a semi-colonial country that won national independence in the first stage of the crisis of world capitalism and then proceeded to achieve economic independence through etatism and state capitalism. In the opinion of these experts, under certain conditions, etatism can play a positive role in the economic development of the country and can help the country win its economic independence. Turkish etatism, according to Soviet writers, grew stronger from year to year. By the Second World War, the Turkish national bourgeoisie greatly benefited from etatist policies, and thereby considerably strengthened the material base of its rule.

After a brief statement on Turkey's two revolutions (1908 and 1919-23), Iu. N. Rozaliev gives a detailed analysis of Turkish capitalism before 1960.[303] He discusses the different stages of the development of Turkish capitalism under the government of the national bourgeoisie, the higher and lower forms of capitalistic activity, the importance of state capitalism, and the ways in which the imperialist monopolies are making inroads in Turkey. Other writers, such as I.V. Alibekov, and B.M. Dantsig, seek to explain how various Turkish government policies weakened the system of etatism after the Second World War. They point out that the departure from etatism became more obvious after the Democratic Party came to power. Rozaliev explains the growth of private capital in the Turkish economy and concludes that this along with imperialist monopolies has intensified the struggle in Turkey between the proletariat and the peasantry on the one hand and the ruling class on the other. N. G. Kireev examines the role of state capitalism and private capital in Turkey's foreign trade, as well as Turkey's unsuccessful attempts to control the invasion of foreign capital. Turkish progressive circles, according to Kireev, believe that a strong state sector and noncapitalist measures are essential for the development of the country.

Numerous short studies have been published on the impact of the Second World War on Turkey, on Turkish foreign affairs, and on Soviet-Turkish relations after the Second World War. Soviet authors hold that the defeat of Germany, which created a serious crisis in Turkey, stimulated the growth of the "progressive forces." Dissatisfied with the government's foreign and domestic policies, the peasants, the workers, and the "progressive" intelligentsia began to clamor for reforms, for democratization of the government, and for improvement of the economic condition of the masses. As a result, the ruling Republican People's Party was compelled to introduce land reform, to adopt social insurance for workers, and to liberalize the electoral system. In the opinion of Soviet writers, however, these were only stopgap measures that failed to satisfy the popular opposition. Discontent spread to the ranks of the Republican People's Party itself, and a group split off to form a separate Democratic Party. The new party wanted Turkey to limit etatism and to encourage private capital; otherwise it endorsed the country's existing pro-Western foreign policy. In 1946 the Socialist Party, originally founded in 1919, was reborn out of the new political climate.[304]

The changes in Turkish government and political life since the military coup of May 27, 1960, are discussed in many recent Soviet works. There are short studies on the contemporary Turkish parliament, on the rights of citizens under the new constitution, on the electoral system, and on the increase in middle-class political activity. Soviet writers have analyzed the Turkish constitution of 1961 with special reference to the rights it guarantees and the benefits it grants to Turkish citizens.[305] They conclude that the new constitution represents a considerable victory for the workers. According to Karim-zade, the "democratic forces" and the Workers' Party of Turkey are steadfast in their demand for constitutional rights and freedoms because they are convinced that the "struggle for democracy" is an integral part of the struggle for socialism.[306] The electoral system introduced in 1950 and the new electoral system of "national balance," in force since 1964-65, have received a good deal of attention. Soviet publications point out, however, that the new electoral system tends to increase factionalism and the importance of small parties, and to strengthen the opposition parties in parliament.

Contemporary Turkish political parties are discussed in a book by Vdovichenko,[307] who examines the Turkish multiparty system and the struggle within the "ruling bourgeois bloc" that weakened bourgeois parliamentarism and intensified antagonisms within the developing capitalist society. Special attention is given to the Republican People's Party and to the formation of the Democratic Party. Vdovichenko explains the interparty conflicts during the first period of multiparty existence (1946-50), the role of social classes and substrata between 1950 and 1960 in Turkey's political life and in the coup d'etat of May 27, 1960, and the trends in the workers' and socialist movements since then. According to Vdovichenko, all bourgeois parties in Turkey claim allegiance to Kemalism. The Workers' Party participates in legal struggle but demands the independence development of Turkey and a united front of progressive forces against imperialism.[308]

Some Soviet writers have no sympathy for the Democratic Party that came to power in 1950, because it has allegedly been backed up by large landowners, commercial bourgeoisie, and foreign capitalism. These writers argue that the policy of the Democratic Party while in power was neither popular nor national,[309] and they welcome the opposition to the government and the growing anti-American sentiment.

In a short book, V. I. Danilov discusses the role of the middle class in Turkey's contemporary political and social life. He analyzes the strength of the middle class and its economic position and social outlook, and discusses the antagonism between the middle class and the ruling circles. The coup of 1960, Danilov says, did not significantly alter the position of the working class.[310] He notes that the spread of the ideas of petty bourgeois socialism, the increased student activity, and the behavior of the military reflect a deep internal antagonism within Turkish society. After 1960, he says, the upper bourgeoisie preserved its dominant position in the country's economy and politics.

Certain Soviet writers note that an increase in the political activity of the urban middle sector has tended to polarize relations between the different political forces.[311] The anti-capitalist elements have been consolidated on a broad "national democratic" basis. The idea of socialism and a non-capitalist way of development has in more recent years been promoted not only by workers but also by broad strata of the intelligentsia and students. The "patriotic officers" have themselves urged reform, and the left wing of the national bourgeoisie has been driven closer to the democratic forces. All of this has prepared the ground for a "united front" of various political and social organizations.[312]

From the beginning of the Second World War until 1964, Soviet writers were harsh in their criticism of the Turks and their history. Much attention was given to Turkish "anti-Soviet policy." Soviet historians deplored Turkish membership in NATO and in the Baghdad Pact and condemned the foreign policies of the Bayar and Gursel governments. They were unsparing in their criticism of Turkish cooperation with the Western powers and of the presence of American military bases in Turkey. They argued that Turkey's foreign policy did not serve the popular cause and that it was opposed by Turkish workers, peasants, and patriotic groups, all of whom were becoming increasingly class-conscious.

From 1964 on, however, the Soviet attitude has changed and Moscow has begun to woo the Turks. Although Turkish history and contemporary activities are still criticized, there is evidence of some restraint; and once again Soviet writers are full of praise for Kemal[313] and Kemalism and express great satisfaction with the steadily improving relations between their country and Turkey. Since 1963 various agreements between Turkey and the U.S.S.R. have been signed and high government officials have exchanged visits. In June 1967 the Soviet Union and Turkey signed an agreement by which the Soviet Union promised to help Turkey build an oil refinery called for by the Turkish Second Five-Year Plan (1967-72).

Soviet scholars interested in Turkey continue their studies of the social changes and the class struggle there.[314] In a recent book, Iu. N. Rozaliev assesses the strength of the individual social classes in Turkey and notes that there is a conflict between those favoring economic nationalization and etatism and those supporting a strong private sector. He concludes that in Turkey there is not only a class conflict between the bourgeoisie and the proletariat but also among different segments of the bourgeois class. Other Soviet authors have been following with keen interest recent ideological trends in Turkey, including the one toward "Turkish socialism."[315] Since the 1960 coup, Soviet observers have noted that the workers' unions and the workers' movement in general have become more active, that there has been a growth of democracy, and that Turkey's relations with the socialist countries have been strengthened. Alarmed by the strong opposition in the country to the Americans and to the compradors, the Turkish bourgeoisie has been attracted to the Western theory of the "evolutionary transformation of capitalism into socialism," and of the "democratization" and "humanization" of capitalism.

When the Society of Socialist Culture was founded in December 1962, several members of the national assembly joined it. In September 1964 a group of bourgeois reformists, who included the head of the Socialist Party, founded the Social Democratic Party. According to K. A. Belova, however, this social reformism failed to win social support, which was natural, she says, because the kind of socialism the Turks had in mind could not work.[316] Like other Soviet writers, she believes that "social reformism" and "Western socialism" will not solve Turkey's problems and cannot satisfy the needs of the Turkish workers.[317] Soviet writers have been critical of the Turks who advocate Western "pseudo-socialism" for their country. That kind of socialism, it is argued, will not satisfy the masses who want "full liberation of the country from the feudal and imperialist yoke."[318] One Soviet author concludes, however, that even though the "socialist ideas" espoused by the Turkish intelligentsia are of the Western pseudo-socialist kind, they do express the desire of the masses for liberation from feudal and imperialist oppression.[319]

Since the Second World War, Soviet scholars have written on many other aspects of Turkish history and culture, including the ethnogenesis of the Turks, health in Turkey, Turkish art and architecture, and the origins of the Turkomans. There are books and articles on Turkish nomads,[320] on the history of the workers' movement,[321] and on various aspects of the economy, such as mining,[322] transportation,[323] and foreign trade.[324] Many articles have been published on Turkish politics and government and on the founding of the Turkish Communist Party.[325] There are several studies dealing with Turkey in the Second World War and a few on Turkish foreign relations.[326] In addition, there are books and articles on Turkish anti-American sentiment,[327] on Turkey and NATO,[328] and on Soviet-Turkish trade relations.

A first-class synthesis of Ottoman history has yet to be produced in the Soviet Union, although the history of the Ottoman empire and of modern Turkey receives good coverage in the ten-volume Soviet *Vsemirnaia istorii* (University history), in the *Bol'shaia Sovetskaia Entsiklopediia*, and in a number of collective works and general histories.[329] In view of Moscow's wavering political line, however, it is hazardous to write syntheses that must invariably deal with many controversial questions. An author's attitude toward Turkey is dictated by the government's policies at the time when he is writing. Thus A. F. Miller, whose works appeared in 1948, and who was at first accused of "bourgeois objectivism," of excessive sympathy for Mustafa Kemal, and of insufficient appreciation for Russia's progressive role in coming to the assistance of the oppressed peoples of Turkey,[330] would have been spared such criticism a few years later.

The most comprehensive Soviet survey of Ottoman history is A. D.

Novichev, *Istoriia Turtsii* (History of Turkey); the first of three projected volumes under this title appeared in 1963.[331] This volume, which treats the history of the Ottoman Turks from the seventies of the eleventh century to the forties of the seventeenth century, contains an excellent bibliography, including Turkish sources. The author discusses Ottoman expansion into Europe and the causes of the Ottoman decline, the transformation of Ottoman feudalism, the repercussions of the military setbacks, and the significance of the Russo-Turkish wars in the eighteenth century. He shows how the Ottoman government came to depend politically and economically on the Western powers. Novichev believes that the Ottoman decline resulted from the backwardness of the feudal social order, incessant wars, the absence of conditions for the development of a middle class, and the "demoralization" of the ruling aristocracy. He says that the Ottoman Empire, like Poland in the eighteenth century, failed to keep up with the European states in economic and scientific progress and in developing trade, industry, a middle class, and large urban centers.[332]

A briefer work by Novichev provides sketchy coverage of Turkish history from the seventies of the eleventh century up to 1965.[333] Published in 1965, it is written in an attitude of sympathy toward the "southern neighbor." Novichev points out how the Soviet peoples manifested friendly feeling when the Turks, following the Soviet example, rose against the Western interventionists and their "sultanic servants." He deals with Turkish culture, the Turkish national movement, the struggle of the subject peoples against Ottoman rule, the class conflict in Turkey, and the plight of the proletariat. He examines in some detail Russo-Turkish relations and the pro-Axis leanings of the Turkish government during the Second World War,[334] and criticizes Turkey's involvement in Western military schemes despite Soviet efforts to improve relations.[335] He does, however, recognize the improvement that has taken place since the 1960 military coup.

One collective work on modern Turkey contains several informative chapters on Turkish art, culture, communications, economy, and politics.[336] The authors of *Noveishaia istoriia Turtsii* (The more recent history of Turkey)[337] have provided the most up-to-date history of modern Turkey from 1917 to 1967 to appear in the Soviet Union. They discuss the Turkish national liberation movement (1918-23), Turkish-Soviet relations between 1918 and 1921, the founding of the Turkish republic, the Dashnak-Turkish War, the consolidation of Kemalist power (1923-29), Turkey and the world economic crisis (1929-33), Turkey's internal and foreign affairs before, during, and after the Second World War, and developments in Turkey since the 1960 putsch. Like many others before them, the contributors contend that the Turkish national liberation movement emerged under the direct influence of the October Revolution. The Turks, they say, succeeded in building on the ruins of the Ottoman Empire "the first bourgeois republic" in the Middle East and in improving significantly the living conditions of the Turkish people.[338] The work contains a bibliography and a chronology of major events.

Iran (Persia)

Since the Second World War Soviet scholars have produced many important studies on ancient Iran and on its precursors. Much good work has been published on feudalism, on medieval towns and guilds, and on peasant insurrections. The best general study on medieval Islam in Iran, which consists of the lectures the author gave at Leningrad University, is I. P. Petrushevskii, *Islam v Irane v VII-XV vekakh* (Islam in Iran from the seventh to the fifteenth century).[339] The author first analyzes the appearance of Islam in Arabia and traces the founding of the Islamic state to the disintegration of the patriarchal-communal order and the formation of a class society. He then discusses the Islamization of Iran and the emergence of the Sunni, Shiah, and Kharijite sects. The ascendancy of the Abbasids, he says, gave the Caliphate a half-Iranian character. He contends that until the establishment of the Safavid state in about 1500, Sunnite Islam was the class ideology of the feudal Iranians, while Shiite Islam was the religion of the political and social opposition. He takes up Islamic beliefs, ritual, law, and mysticism, and writes that although Muslim dissident sects and heretics were persecuted, such persecution never reached the extremes of the Spanish and Portuguese inquisitions.[340] As we have already seen, Ismailism has fascinated several Soviet scholars. Peasant and artisan participation in this movement has been investigated by A. E. Bertel's[341] and by L. V. Stroeva.[342]

A long list of historians have written on Iranian history from the fifteenth to the eighteenth century. Dzh. Ibragimov, for instance, has investigated the social and economic structure of Azerbaijan in the fifteenth century; Petrushevskii, feudal relations in Azerbaijan and Armenia from the sixteenth to the nineteenth century; O. A. Efendiev, Safavid rule in Azerbaijan; and Ibragimov, Safavid rule in Ardabil. N. D. Miklukho-Maklai has studied the tax policy of Shah 'Abbas I, the relations between Iran and Central Asia, and Afghan rule in Iran in the eighteenth century.[343] Iranian Shiism and land tenure under the Safavids have been studied by N. Fil'roze; Safavid diplomatic relations with Western powers, by F. M. Shakhmaliev; and feudal exploitation in Iran in the eighteenth century, by M. P. Arunova.

Several works have been published on Russo-Persian relations and on Persia's relations with the peoples of what is now Soviet Central Asia. There is an interesting paper on the mission of Fazl Alibeg to Russia in 1711-13,[344] and one on social conditions in Persia in the time of Nadir Shah.[345] Besides Miklukho-Maklai's study on eighteenth-century Afghan rule in Iran, K.

Ashrafian's work on the fall of the Safavids deserves mention. Short accounts have appeared on Iranian relations with Turkestan and the Central Asian khanates; on Ermolov's mission to Iran (1816-17); on Anglo-Russian rivalry over Iran at the beginning of the nineteenth century; on the Treaty of Turkmanchai, which regulated relations between Russia and Iran until 1917; on Griboedov's activity in Iran; and on the Russo-Persian War of 1826-28. According to Soviet authors, the Russians played the role of liberators, not conquerors, in the Transcaucasus. Hence Russia's annexation of Transcaucasia is regarded as a progressive historical development.[346]

Many subjects dealing with the internal history of Iran in the nineteenth century have been thoroughly researched. Among the authors who have investigated the Babi and the Bahai movements and have criticized them for their middle-class ideology are A. M. Arsharuni, I. Darov, M. Tomara, and M. S. Ivanov.[347] There are studies on the Anglo-Persian War of 1856-57,[348] on the agrarian and economic situation in the nineteenth century,[349] and on Iran's international position in the first third of the nineteenth century.[350] Short papers have appeared on nineteenth-century feudalism and agriculture, on the origins of bourgeois ideology, on the British tobacco monopoly (1891-92), and on the influence of M. F. Akhunov on social thought in Persia.

Far more historical work has been published on the twentieth than on the nineteenth century, although much of the material is undistinguished. Tsarist economic policy as it affected Iran (1904-1906) has been reviewed. The revolutionary period of 1905-11 attracted many Soviet historians in the twenties, among them G. V. Shtit, F. Bor-Ramenskii, G. N. Il'inskii, G. S. Artiunian, N. K. Belovaia, A. M. Matveev, S. Aliev, and M. S. Ivanov.[351] Soviet scholars have analyzed the role played in the Revolution of 1911 by different social, economic and other groups and attempted to show the bourgeois character of the revolution. In this connection Soviet writers assessed the activity of the democratic organization of some of the *mujtahids* and the social-democratic groups, and sought to explain the imperialistic machinations of Germany, Britain, and the United States.[352]

Later Soviet critics have pointed out errors in earlier works on the Iranian revolution. Artiunian, for example, is accused of mislabeling groups and individuals and of equating adventurers with revolutionaries, feudatories with democrats, and large merchants and exporters with constitutionalists.[353] Even though the latest Soviet studies on the 1911 Revolution are considered better than the earlier ones—those by pre-Revolution Russian scholars such as I. A. Zinov'ev, A. Medvedev, and N. P. Mamantov, for example—they still do not satisfy Soviet critics, who find in them errors of fact and mistakes in methodology.

Other topics covered are Qajar rule,[354] the national liberation movement,[355] the spread of Marxism and Leninism in Iran,[356] modern political development,[357] the agrarian situation in modern Iran,[358] workers' and professional movements,[359] the oil consortium,[360] and American and British imperialism.[361]

Iranian history between the two world wars has received high priority, with many aspects of Iranian life being investigated. A number of works have appeared on the national liberation movement (1917-20),[362] on the national liberation movement in Persian Azerbaijan in 1918-21, on the ascendancy of Reza Shah Pahlevi,[363] on the democratic and anti-imperialist movement in Iran, on the socioeconomic transformation of Iran,[364] on the formation of the national bourgeoisie, and on the policies of German,[365] British,[366] and other European imperialist powers toward Iran. Since 1966, the *Narody Azii i Afriki* has carried several items on the coup of February 21, 1921.[367]

Relations between the U.S.S.R. and Iran since 1917 are treated in a number of works. One author has written a brief article on the Iranian socialists before the founding of the Comintern and on their relations with the Iranian liberation movement.[368] Another discusses the Comintern's policy toward Iran.[369] There is a substantial literature on the influence of the October Revolution on Iran. Lenin and his impact on Iran and on the Iranian liberation movement are examined by several authors, especially during 1970, the anniversary of Lenin's birth.[370] Several works have appeared on the spread of Marxist-Leninist ideas to Iran before the Second World War and on the development of the social and philosophical thought in Iran.[371]

Soviet historians have published valuable analyses of revolutionary Iranian organizations in Central Asia. In the early twentieth century the number of Iranian immigrants into Russian Central Asia increased steadily until it exceeded the number of Turkish immigrants. By 1920 there were 200,000 Iranians in Central Asia and an additional number in other parts of the U.S.S.R. The Iranian immigrants, a few of them middle class,[372] were for the most part wage earners.

The internal and external affairs of Iran during the Second World War have not yet been dealt with exhaustively by Soviet historians. In 1971 a short book appeared on the Teheran Conference.[373] The Iranian working class movement and American "imperialism" in Iran during the Second World War are popular topics of inquiry in Soviet historical circles.[374]

Soviet writers continue to investigate the political, cultural, and economic relations between Iran and the Soviet Union, the Soviet role in the development of the Iranian fishing industry, the economic influence and the oil policy of the United States in Iran (1951-53), the Iranian government, economy, and economic geography,[375] the working class and the professional movements, agriculture, oil, labor legislation, and Japanese economic penetration of Iran. The books best received in the Soviet Union are those discussing British and American imperialist designs on Iran after the Second World War.[376] According to Rozhdestvenskaia, Western aid to Iran during the country's Second Seven-Year Plan (1955-62)[377] gave Iran momentary relief, but failed to eliminate the semi-colonial structure of Iran's economy, her dependence on foreign monopolies, and the basic socioeconomic antagonisms. I. I. Korobeinikov and a few others have written useful works on the Iranian economy, industry and press.[378]

Soviet Iranists have written also on the formation of the Iranian nation, on Iranian nationalism, and on the development of different nationalities and tribes in the country. For instance, in recent years books have appeared on the origin and distribution of the Baluchis,[379] on the tribes of Fars province,[380] and on the Kurds,[381] the Bakhtiaris,[382] and the Armenians. A considerable amount of work has been devoted to textual criticism and to translations of manuscripts. Many documentary materials have been collected, classified, analyzed, and published. The description of the documents in the various Soviet repositories and the publication of catalogues have been major undertakings.[383] Numerous manuscripts have been translated with comments and annotations.[384]

Only one important survey of Iranian history, a collective work, covers the period up to 1800.[385] Of considerable value, however, is M. S. Ivanov, *Ocherk istorii Irana* (Outline of the history of Iran), which traces the history of Iran from ancient times to the end of the Second World War,[386] though it lacks balance in that it emphasizes recent history and slights the period before 1800. Other works that deserve mention are a bulky guidebook,[387] M. S. Ivanov, *Noveishaia istoriia Irana* (Most recent history of Iran),[388] and B. N. Zakhoder's work on contemporary Iran (Moscow, 1967). The Soviet *Vsemirnaia istoriia* and the *Bol'shaia Sovetskaia Entsiklopediia* contain brief surveys of Iranian history and Soviet interpretations of major problems in that history.

It is impossible in a brief review to list and comment on all the works published on the Middle East by Soviet authors since the end of the Second World War. In fact, it is not even possible to deal with all the Middle Eastern peoples and countries on which Soviet scholars have written. Thus significant work on Kurdish history and culture,[389] as well as important Afghan studies,[390] have not been discussed. Similarly, it is difficult to make generalizations that will do justice to the enormous body of Soviet scholarship on the Middle East. The pressure to make historical writing conform to often changing political objectives has accounted for many hastily compiled volumes and narrowly doctrinaire interpretations. Nevertheless, Soviet research on the Middle East in other areas of the social sciences and humanities has yielded many examples of sound scholarship, providing valuable data and fresh perspectives for further investigations.

Notes

1: HISTORICAL INTRODUCTION

[1]"From the Nile to the Neva, from the Elbe to China—From the Volga to the Euphrates, from the Ganges to the Danube . . . That is the Kingdom of Russia . . ." F.I. Tiutchev, *Polnoe Sobranie Sochinenii,* ed. by P. V. Bykov (St. Petersburg, 1913), 2:190.

[2]See V. T. Pashuto, *Vneshnaia Politika Drevnei Rusi* (Moscow, Nauka, 1968).

[3]See Sergius Yakobson, "Russia and Africa," in Ivo J. Lederer, ed., *Russian Foreign Policy: Essays in Historical Perspective* (New Haven and London, Yale University Press, 1962), p. 454. For a skeptical view on this, see George Vernadsky, *Kievan Russia* (New Haven and London, Yale University Press, 1966), chap. 1 and 5.

[4]See M. N. Tikhomirov, *Srednevekovaia Rossiia Na Mezhdunarodnikh Putiakh* (Moscow, Nauka, 1966), chap. 1 and 5.

[5]See Boris Nolde, *La formation de l'Empire Russe* (Paris, 1953), 2 vols.; A. Lobanov-Rostovsky, *Russia and Asia* (Wahr, Ann Arbor, Mich., 1951); C. de Grunwald, *Trois siècles de diplomatie russe* (Paris, Calmann-Lévy, 1945); Norman E. Saul, *Russia and the Mediterranean, 1797-1807* (Chicago and London, University of Chicago Press, 1970).

[6]See Czesław Jeśman, *The Russians in Ethiopia* (London, 1958).

[7]Ironically, in the 1930s and during World War II Arab nationalists turned to Hitler's Germany for help, having given up much earlier on the U.S.S.R.

[8]*The Times* (London), June 3, 1969.

2: THE CONTINUING CRISIS

[1]Vernon V. Aspaturian, "Soviet Foreign Policy at the Crossroads," in *The United States and International Organization: The Changing Setting,* Lawrence S. Finkelstein, ed. (Cambridge, M.I.T. Press, 1969), pp. 42-43; Philip E. Mosely, "The Kremlin and the Third World," *Foreign Affairs,* Oct. 1967, pp. 65-68; John C. Campbell, "The Soviet Union and the Middle East, Part II," *Russian Review,* July 1970, pp. 247-53.

[2]Adam B. Ulam, *Expansion and Coexistence: The History of Soviet Foreign Policy, 1917-1967* (New York, Praeger, 1968), pp. 679-94; Alexander Dallin et al., *The Soviet Union and Disarmament: An Appraisal of Soviet Attitudes and Intentions* (New York, Praeger, 1964), pp. 265-76.

[3]His alleged memoirs, *Khrushchev Remembers* (Boston, Little, Brown, 1970), offer no answer.

[4]Lin Piao, "Report to the Ninth National Congress of the Communist Party of China," *Peking Review*, Special Issue, April 28, 1969, pp. 27-30.

[5]Lawrence W. Martin, "The Changing Military Balance," in *Soviet-American Rivalry in the Middle East*, J. C. Hurewitz, ed. (New York, Praeger, 1969), pp. 63-65; Ph. Masson and J. Couhat, "La présence navale soviétique en Méditerranée," *Revue de Défense Nationale*, May 1968, pp. 858-73.

[6]See Michel Salomon, *Méditerranée Rouge: un nouvel empire soviétique?* (Paris, Robert Laffont, 1970), pp. 44-45, 88-95.

[7]*Soviet Sea Power*, Special Report Series, no. 10 (Washington, Center for Strategic and International Studies, Georgetown University, June 1969), p. 54.

[8]For comment on this point, see Walter Z. Laqueur, *The Road To Jerusalem* (New York, Macmillan, 1968), pp. 71-108, 160-83; Robert E. Hunter, *The Soviet Dilemma in the Middle East, Part I: Problems of Commitment*, Adelphi Papers, no. 59 (London, Institute for Strategic Studies, Sept. 1969), p. 10.

[9]V. Rumyantsev, in *Pravda, June 6, 1969.*

[10]See A. Y. Yodfat, "Moscow Reconsiders Fatah," *The New Middle East*, Dec. 1969, pp. 15-18.

[11]Hunter, *Soviet Dilemma*, p. 16.

3: THE SOVIET UNION AND TURKEY

[1]U.S. Department of State, *Nazi-Soviet Relations, 1939-1941: Documents from the Archives of the German Foreign Office* (Washington, 1948), pp. 217-59.

[2]George Kirk, *The Middle East in the War* (London, 1954), p. 445.

[3]For the text of the Soviet note of Aug. 7, 1946, see U.S. Department of State, *The Problem of the Turkish Straits* (Washington, 1947), pp. 47-49.

[4]*Ayin Tarihi* (History of the Month), May 1945, pp. 452-53.

[5]U.S. Department of State, *Papers Relating to the Foreign Relations of the United States, 1945*, 8 (Washington, 1968): 1260-62, 1268, 1270-71.

[6]Aras wrote articles reminding his readers that Ataturk's foreign policy was based on friendship with the U.S.S.R. See his "Ataturk'un Dis Siyaseti" (Ataturk's foreign policy), *Tan*, Nov. 10, 1945.

[7]Feridun Cemal Erkin, *Les relations turco-soviétiques et la question des Détroits* (Ankara, 1968), p. 324, reports that as secretary general of the Turkish Foreign Office he warned the Soviet ambassador that the U.S.S.R. had more to lose than gain from basing territorial demands on such historical claims.

[8]On this incident, see Kemal Karpat, *Turkey's Politics* (Princeton, 1959), pp. 150-51.

[9]G. Akopian, "K polozheniiu v Turtsii" (On the situation in Turkey), *Pravda*, Dec. 21, 1946.

[10]George Kirk, *The Middle East, 1945-1950* (London, 1954), p. 33.

[11]Erkin, *Les relations turco-soviétiques*, p. 350.

[12]*Ibid.*, pp. 324-25.

[13]*Ibid.*, pp. 325-26.

[14]*Ibid.*, pp. 343 ff. This cooperation led *Pravda* and other Soviet organs to charge that the Turkish note of Oct. 18, 1946, was merely a copy of an Anglo-American original. (*Pravda*, Oct. 20, 1946.)

[15]For the Soviet accusations, see I. Vasil'ev, "Ankara i Amman" (Ankara and Amman), *Izvestiia*, Jan. 24, 1947.

[16]Erkin, *Les relations turco-soviétiques*, pp. 329 ff.

[17]*Ayin Tarihi*, Oct. 1947, pp. 72-73, 76-78; *Pravda*, Oct. 27, 1947.

[18]Huseyin Cahit Yalcin, "Ruslara karsi Amerika Uyanmistir" (America is aroused against the Russians), *Tanin*, Nov. 3, 1947.

[19]D. Zaslavskii, "Dollarovaia likhoradka v Turtsii" (Dollar fever in Turkey), *Pravda*, Mar. 31, 1947.

[20]For an early expression of this concern, see G. Vershinin, "K Amerikanskim planam 'modernizatsii' Turtsii" (On American plans for "modernization" of Turkey), *Pravda*, June 12, 1947.

[21]For examples of these charges, see G. Vershinin, "Amerikanskaia 'pomoshch' Turtsii" (American "aid" to Turkey), *Krasnaia Zvezda*, July 29, 1947; A. Anatol'ev, "V Turtsii" (In Turkey), *Krasnaia Zvezda*, Jan. 9, 1948; S. Belinkov, "Amerikanskie ekspansionisty v Turtsii" (American expansionists in Turkey), *Izvestiia*, Jan. 28, 1948.

[22]R. Rybakov, "Mezhdunarodnye otkliki: Komediia Turetskikh 'vyborov' " (International comment: comedy of the Turkish elections), *Literaturnaia gazeta*, May 13, 1950. Moscow radio broadcast this text on the same date.

[23]Baku radio broadcast in Turkish, May 29, 1950.

[24]Among the RPP leaders opposed to Turkish participation in the Korean war was Necmeddin Sadak, former foreign minister. See his "Kore Savasi ve Turkiye" (The Korean War and Turkey), *Aksam*, July 16, 1950.

[25]V. M. Alekseev and M. A. Kerimov, *Vneshniaia politika Turtsii* (Foreign policy of Turkey) (Moscow, 1961), p. 70.

[26]*Ayin Tarihi*, July 1950, pp. 8-10; Aug. 1950, pp. 111-12.

[27]It was indicative of Turkey's attitude that Foreign Minister Koprulu, in a 16-page survey of foreign relations in 1951, devoted only a single paragraph to the U.S.S.R. and the "Soviet War of Nerves" (*Turkey's Foreign Relations in 1952*, Turkish Information Office, New York, 1952, *passim*).

[28]Denise Folliot, ed., *Documents on International Affairs, 1951* (London, 1954), pp. 68-70.

[29]*Pravda*, Jan. 29, 1952.

[30]V. Kudriavstev, "Na mezhdunarodnye temy" (On international themes), *Izvestiia*, May 11, and Aug. 24, 1952; Y. Bochkaryov, "The Trojan Horse in the Moslem World," *New Times* (Moscow), May 21, 1952, pp. 14-16.

[31]M. Gushchin, "Na mezhdunarodnye temy: Balkanskii blok podzhigatelei voiny"

(On international themes: the Balkan bloc of warmongers), *Moskovskaia Pravda*, Mar. 24, 1953.

[32]*Pravda*, July 19, 1953. Text also in *The Current Digest of the Soviet Press*, 1953, vol. 5, no. 29, pp. 21-22 (hereafter cited as *Digest*).

[33]*Dunya*, Oct. 31, 1954.

[34]George M. Kahin, *The Asian-African Conference, Bandung, Indonesia, 1955* (Ithaca, 1956), p. 20.

[35]*Pravda*, Aug. 1, 1953 (*Digest*, 1953, vol. 5, no. 31, pp. 16-17).

[36]Erkin, *Les relations turco-soviétiques*, p. 411.

[37]Altemur Kilic, "Konusma mi, Fiiliyat mi?" (Words or deeds?), *Vatan*, Dec. 2, 1954.

[38]In *Dunya*, Feb. 19, 1955, Yakup Kadri Karaosmanoglu opined that, with Beria's purge and Malenkov's removal, military dictatorship had come to the U.S.S.R.: "We hear not the sound of sickles, but the pounding of hammers forging swords for tomorrow's invaders."

[39]May 16, 1955.

[40]"Speech by N. S. Khrushchev," *New Times*, Jan. 5, 1956, supplement, pp. 16-32, especially p. 30.

[41]"Report . . . to the 20th Party Congress," *New Times*, Feb. 16, 1956, no. 8, supplement, p. 19.

[42]Kh. Grigoryev, "Soviet-Turkish Relations," *International Affairs* (Moscow), April 1956, no. 4, pp. 61-62.

[43]Anatoli Miller, "Unfounded Doubts," *New Times*, May 10, 1956, p. 13.

[44]Huseyin Cahit Yalcin in *Ulus*, Aug. 4, 1956.

[45]*Keesing's Contemporary Archives*, vol. 10, 1955-56, p. 15226.

[46]Huseyin Cahit Yalcin, "S. Rusya Medeniyet Disi" (S. Russia outside civilization), *Ulus*, Nov. 18, 1956.

[47]Bulent Ecevit, "Yanlis Hesap Bagdattan Donecek mi?" (Will the false account return from Baghdad?), *Ulus*, Nov. 13, 1956.

[48]Omer Sami Cosar, "Rus Gonulluleri!" (Russian volunteers), *Cumhuriyet*, Nov. 11, 1956.

[49]*Ulus*, Nov. 13, 1956.

[50]Altemur Kilic, *Turkey and the World* (Washington, 1959), p. 196.

[51]*Milliyet*, Sept. 8, 1957.

[52]Ankara radio, Sept. 14, 1957, broadcasting a communiqué from the Public Relations Office of the Turkish Ministry of Defense.

[53]*Zafer, Sept. 25, 1957*.

[54]*New York Times, Oct. 26, 1957*.

[55]*Ibid.*, Sept. 11, 1957.

[56]*Izvestiia*, Sept. 10, 1957.

[57]*New York Times*, Sept. 14, 1957.

[58]In his reply of Jan. 17, 1958, to Bulganin's note of Nov. 22, 1957, Adnan

Menderes alleged that the Soviet exchange of messages was "designed to create an artificial danger to exploit at the UN" (Ankara radio, Jan. 19, 1958).

[59]*Zafer*, Feb. 26, 1958.

[60]Gromyko speech at the United Nations, Sept. 20, 1957.

[61]*New York Times*, Nov. 27, 1957.

[62]For an expression of this attitude, see M. Nermi, "Yunanistan'a Guvenilemez" (Greece can't be trusted), *Yeni Istanbul*, Dec. 19, 1954.

[63]Broadcast of May 20, 1958.

[64]*New York Times*, July 26, 1958. Turkish troop deployments were apparently of small scale, and in view of the terrain difficulties were probably intended merely as a psychological gesture.

[65]*Ulus*, July 16, 17, 23, 1958; and A. Ihsan Barlas, "Nasir ve Komunizm" (Nasser and communism), *Dunya*, Nov. 23, 1958.

[66]*Ulus*, July 28, 1958. The issues of *Ulus* and *Yeni Gun* of July 27, 1958, were confiscated as "inflammatory" for publishing the RPP foreign policy declaration after the first extraordinary session of parliament. For the second extraordinary session, see *Ulus*, Aug. 22, 1958; and *Zafer*, Aug. 22, 1958.

[67]*Pravda*, Jan. 25, 1957. See also Maj. Gen. E. A. Boltin, "Atomic Task Forces," *New Times*, Apr. 25, 1957, pp. 7-10.

[68]D. T. Shepilov, "Report . . . to the Sixth Session of the Supreme Soviet," *New Times*, Feb. 21, 1957, supplement, p. 16.

[69]*Zafer*, Dec. 10, 1957.

[70]*Zafer*, Feb. 26, 1958.

[71]*Soviet News*, Dec. 16, 1957, pp. 194-6.

[72]*New York Times*, Jan. 22, 1958. In July 1959, the Turks formally rejected Soviet proposals for a "zone free of nuclear arms" in the Adriatic-Balkan area. See the *New York Times*, July 15, 1959.

[73]I. Aleksandrov, "Blizkim sosediam neobkhodimo 'druzhit'" (Close neighbors should be friends), *Pravda*, June 4, 1958 (*Digest*, 1958, vol. 10, no. 22, p. 19).

[74]On Jan. 7, 1959, Zorlu assured parliament that "we have not yet concluded an agreement" to deploy missiles and he promised to inform the deputies "when an agreement is to be concluded" (*Zafer*, Jan. 8, 1959).

[75]Y. Plotnikov, "Plain Speaking: A Jarring Note," *International Affairs* (Moscow), Apr. 1961, pp. 94-95; Walter F. Weiker, *The Turkish Revolution 1960-1961* (Washington, 1963), p. 18n.

[76]A. H. Ulman and R. H. Dekmejian, "Changing Patterns in Turkish Foreign Policy, 1959-1967," *Orbis*, Fall 1967, no. 3, p. 773.

[77]Bizim Radyo, Apr. 12, 1960, suggested that economic accords would be concluded during these visits.

[78]*Zafer*, Apr. 12, 1960.

[79]M. Piri, "Menderes'in Rusya Seyahati" (Menderes's Russian trip), *Cumhuriyet*, Apr. 13, 1960.

[80]Bizim Radyo, Apr. 30, 1960. On Apr. 22, 1960, this radio urged action, "not to

bring Inonu to power," but to install "a government depending on the people." This organ characterized the rising protest against the DP as the start of a "national liberation struggle."

[81]*Pravda,* May 14, 1960 (*Digest,* 1960, vol. 12, no. 20, pp. 32-33).

[82]B. Alexeyev, "Turkey Faces Choice," *International Affairs* (Moscow), July 1960, p. 47. Italics in the original.

[83]*The Turkish Yearbook of International Relations, 1962* (Ankara, 1964), p. 158, quoted Gursel's June 1962 announcement that the economic aid offered the junta by the U.S.S.R. had amounted to some $500 million.

[84]For Khrushchev's note of June 28, 1960, and Gursel's reply of July 8, 1960, see *Ulus,* Sept. 1, 1960; also *The Mizan Newsletter,* Sept. 1960, vol. 2, no. 8, pp. 15-17.

[85]For excerpts from the Soviet note of Feb. 3, 1961, and the Turkish reply of Feb. 24, 1961, see *Ulus,* Feb.25, 1961; *Kudret,* Feb. 25, 1961.

[86]M. Yurev, "Turkey at the Cross-Roads," *International Affairs* (Moscow), Oct. 1962, p. 44.

[87]*New York Times,* Oct. 28, 1962; *Soviet News,* Oct. 29, 1962.

[88]Robert F. Kennedy, *Thirteen Days* (New York, 1969), pp. 94-95.

[89]*Milliyet,* Oct. 26, 1962.

[90]Dogan Avcioglu, "Fuze Usleri" (Missile bases), *Yon,* Oct. 31, 1962, p. 3.

[91]Kennedy, *Thirteen Days,* p. 94.

[92]*Moscow News,* June 15, 1963, p. 7.

[93]*Pravda,* Oct. 29, 1963.

[94]Erkin, *Les relations turco-soviétiques,* pp. 436-37.

[95]The text of this letter and the Turkish reply were released in 1966. See *The Middle East Journal,* Summer 1966, vol. 20, no. 3, pp. 386-93.

[96]Moscow radio, Dec. 26 and 28, 1963.

[97]Moscow radio in English, June 9, 1964.

[98]*New Times,* Aug. 26, 1964, p. 3.

[99]*Ibid.*

[100]"International Notes: Turkey: Provocation in Izmir," *New Times,* Sept. 9, 1964, p. 23.

[101]Erkin, *Les relations turco-soviétiques,* p. 443.

[102]*Ibid.* p. 448.

[103]Moscow regularly protested visits of U.S. naval units to the Black Sea; see *Krasnaia zvezda,* Sept. 3, 1966.

[104]Yakup Demir and Halis Okan, "Turkey: Ways of Development," *World Marxist Review,* May 1965, pp. 45-49.

[105]"Turkish-Soviet Relations," commentary on Bizim Radyo, June 25, 1966.

[106]According to *Son Havadis,* Nov. 2, 1968, in response to the Turkish government's official representations, the Kremlin insisted that such radios operated outside its knowledge or control.

[107]Moscow radio in Turkish, Mar. 25, 1967, hailed this agreement as "an impor-

tant step in the development of Soviet Turkish economic cooperation."

[108]*Cumhuriyet*, Nov. 9, 1967.

[109]*Milliyet*, Apr. 14, 1968, quoting TLP Executive Board member Yusuf Ziya Bahadanli.

[110]See the draft RPP policy paper published in *Milliyet*, July 5, 1968.

[111]*Cumhuriyet*, Aug. 29, 1968.

[112]*Ibid.*, Oct. 16, 1968.

[113]*Milliyet*, Aug. 22, 1968; and *Vatan*, Aug. 24, 1968.

[114]*Milliyet*, Oct. 7, 1968. Aybar said: "Turkish socialism has nothing to do with Soviet Bolshevism . . . . Our socialism is for men. We reject [the idea] that man is a tool of socialism."

[115]Moscow radio in Turkish, Oct. 14, 1969. This broadcast attributed the JP victory to its "growing cooperation with the Soviet Union" and to its "realistic attitude" toward a number of important issues.

[116]E. Gasanova, "Novye veianiia obshchestvennoi zhizni Turtsii (o 'Turetskom sotsializme')" (New trends in Turkish social life: on "Turkish socialism"), *Narody Azii i Afriki*, Jan-Feb. 1965, no. 1, pp. 26-34.

4: SOVIET-IRANIAN RELATIONS

[1]Lev Vasil'ev, *Puti sovetskogo imperializma* (New York, 1954).

[2]Hassan Arfa, *Under Five Shahs* (London, 1964), p. 316.

[3]Sepehr Zabih, *The Communist Movement in Iran* (Berkeley, 1966), pp. 90-91.

[4]Arfa, *Under Five Shahs*, p. 329.

[5]The negotiations and their consequences are mentioned in George Lenczowski, *Russia and the West in Iran, 1918-1948* (Ithaca, 1949), pp. 222-23; John Marlow, *The Persian Gulf in the Twentieth Century* (New York, 1962); Peter Avery, *Modern Iran* (New York, 1965).

[6]For Kurdistan see William Eagleton, Jr., *The Kurdish Republic of 1946* (London, 1963). No such well-documented study has appeared on the much more important events in Azerbaijan.

[7]Eagleton, *Kurdish Republic*, pp. 23-24.

[8]*Ibid.*, pp. 43-46.

[9]*Ibid.*, p. 55.

[10]*Ibid.*, p. 59.

[11]Arfa, *Under Five Shahs*, p. 347.

[12]Avery, *Modern Iran*, p. 388. See also Mohammad Reza Shah Pahlvai, *Mission for My Country* (London, 1961), p. 115.

[13]Arfa, *Under Five Shahs*, p. 352.

[14]*Ibid.*, p. 349.

[15]George Kirk, in *Survey of International Affairs: The Middle East, 1945-1950* (Oxford, 1954), p.63.

[16]Ramesh Sanghvi, *Aryamehr: The Shah of Iran* (London, 1968), p. 120.

[17]See Firuz Kazemzadeh, *Russia and Britain in Persia, 1864-1914: A Study in Imperialism* (New Haven, 1968), chap. 8 and 9.

[18]Arfa, *Under Five Shahs*, p. 362.

[19]For some speculations on the mission, see Raymond Lacoste, *La Russie sovietique et la question d'Orient* (Paris, 1946).

[20]Mohammad Reza Shah, *My Country*, p. 116.

[21]Harry S. Truman, *Memoirs by Harry S. Truman* (Garden City, N.Y., 1955-56), 2:94.

[22]*Ibid.*, p. 95.

[23]Mohammad Reza Shah, *My Country*, p. 116.

[24]Truman, *Memoirs*, 2:95.

[25]Arfa, *Under Five Shahs*, p. 378.

[26]Mohammad Reza Shah, *My Country*, p. 117.

[27]Dean Acheson, *Present at the Creation* (New York, 1969), p. 198.

[28]Mohammad Reza Shah, *My Country*, pp. 117-18.

[29]Avery, *Modern Iran*, p. 399.

[30]Arfa, *Under Five Shahs*, p. 385.

[31]Sanghvi, *Aryamehr*, p. 153.

[32]Lenczowski, *Russia and the West in Iran*, pp. 310-11.

[33]Avery, *Modern Iran*, p. 400.

[34]*Ibid.*

[35]Royal Institute of International Affairs, *Documents on International Affairs: 1952* (London, 1955), pp. 334-35.

[36]David J. Dallin, *Soviet Foreign Policy after Stalin* (Philadelphia, 1961), p. 211.

[37]*Ibid.*

[38]Avery, *Modern Iran*, p. 425.

[39]Mohammad Reza Shah, *My Country*, p. 94.

[40]M. S. Ivanov, in *Sovetskaia istoricheskaia entsiklopedia* (Moscow, 1965), 6:243.

[41]*Pravda*, August 19, 1953, as cited in Dallin, *Soviet Foreign Policy*, p. 212.

[42]*Black Book on Tudeh Officers Organization*, pp. 270-71, as cited in Dallin, *Soviet Foreign Policy*, p. 213.

[43]Mohammad Reza Shah, *My Country*, p. 119.

[44]Arfa, *Under Five Shahs*, pp. 412-13.

[45]Sanghvi, *Aryamehr*, pp. 247-48.

[46]Royal Institute of International Affairs, *Documents on International Affairs, 1954* (London, 1957), pp. 189-90.

[47]John C. Campbell, *Defense of the Middle East* (New York, 1958), p. 55.

[48]Royal Institute of International Affairs, *Documents on International Affairs, 1955* (London, 1958), p. 305.

[49]*Ibid.*, pp. 305-06.

[50]*Ibid.*, pp. 309-13.

[51]*Ibid.*

[52]Avery, *Modern Iran*, p. 459.

[53]Mohammed Reza Shah, *My Country*, pp. 118-20.

[54]Royal Institute of International Affairs, *Documents on International Affairs, 1958* (London, 1962), pp. 330-32.

[55]Mohammad Reza Shah, *My Country*, p. 122.

[56]*Ibid.*

[57]"Statement by Mr. Semyonov to the Persian Government regarding Soviet Persian relations, 10 February 1959," in *Documents on International Affairs 1959* (London, 1963), pp. 327-36.

[58]Statements in the Persian Senate, by Mr. Ali Hekmat regarding the breakdown of negotiations with the Soviet Union, Teheran, 14 February 1959, quoted in *Documents on International Affairs 1959,* pp. 336-40.

[59]*Documents on International Affairs 1959,* p. 335, n. 1.

[60]Mohammad Reza Shah, *My Country*, p. 123.

[61]Cited in Donald N. Wilber, *Contemporary Iran* (New York, 1963), p. 133.

[62]*Pravda*, July 4, 1965, *Vneshniaia politika Sovetskogo Soiuza i mezhdunarodnye otnosheniia*, years 1964-65 (*The foreign policy of the Soviet Union and international relations*) (Moscow, 1966), pp. 271-72.

[63]*Pravda*, July 29, 1967, *Vneshniaia politika Sovetskogo Soiuza*, 1967 (Moscow, 1968), p. 204.

5: THE SOVIET UNION AND NORTH AFRICA

[1]Pre-emptive strategy is common in Soviet policy toward most of the LDCs. See R. S. Walters, "American and Soviet Aid to Less Developed Countries: A Comparative Analysis," Ph.D. dissertation, Department of Political Science, University of Michigan, 1967; and H. S. Dinerstein, "Soviet Doctrines on Developing Countries: Some Divergent Views," in Kurt London, ed., *New Nations in a Divided World* (New York, Praeger, 1963), p. 78 (cited by Walters).

[2]Vyshinsky was the Soviet representative. See a report of his talks with de Gaulle in Charles de Gaulle, *Mémoires de guerre: l'Unité* (Paris, Plon, 1956), 2:603-606.

[3]On this episode, see Majid Khadduri, *Modern Libya: A Study in Political Development* (Baltimore, Johns Hopkins Press, 1963), p. 114; and Maurice Pernot, "The Soviet Union and the Mediterranean," *Fortnightly* (Dec. 1945), pp. 363-68.

[4]Pernot, "Soviet Union and Mediterranean," p. 363.

[5]Few informed observers believe that the Russians have taken over Mers-el-Kebir. See, for instance, Curt Gasteyger, "Conflict and Tension in the Mediterranean," *Adelphi Papers*, no. 51 (1968), p. 4.

[6]On all these points, see Gasteyger, "Conflict and Tension," p. 3.

[7]In this scheme the Black Sea straits became superfluous—as well as the Black Sea

fleet itself—since fuel, supplies, and repair facilities can be found in friendly Mediterranean and Asian ports. In the future the use of the straits may be found convenient but not indispensable. The Suez Canal, however, is much more important, since it furnishes the crucial link with the Indian Ocean and the Far East. Although confined at the western end of the Mediterranean by Spain and Morocco, the Straits of Gibraltar are an important but surmountable barrier. Thus the U.S.S.R. has sidestepped the Turkish nemesis only to fall victim to the Israelis.

[8]See Geoffrey Kemp, "Strategy and Arms Levels, 1945-1967," in J. C. Hurewitz, ed., *Soviet-American Rivalry in the Middle East* (New York, Academy of Political Science, 1969), pp. 33-34. There are reports that both Egyptian and Soviet aircraft are based in Algeria, particularly at Batna and Laghouat. How many aircraft are there and for what purpose is not known. See John Cooley, *Christian Science Monitor*, Aug. 7, 1969.

[9]See Alexander Dallin, "The Soviet Union: Political Activity," in Zbigniew Brzezinski, ed., *Africa and the Communist World* (Stanford, Calif., 1963), p. 47.

[10]See King Hassan's speech in *Le Petit Marocain*, July 10, 1967.

[11]See "Soviet Interest in Middle East Oil," *MIZAN*, vol. 10, no. 3 (June 1968), pp. 79-85; "Soviet Oil Trading in 1967: Outlook for Exports Grow Dim," *Research Departments of Radio Free Europe* (Communist Area), Jan. 13, 1969; Gardner Patterson, "Declining American Investment," in Hurewitz, ed., *Soviet-American Rivalry*, pp. 91-104; Walter Laqueur, "Russians vs. Arabs," *Commentary*, vol. 53, no. 4 (April 1972), p. 64.

[12]For a résumé, see "China, the Arab World, and Africa," *MIZAN*, vol. 6, no. 5 (1964).

[13]This analysis is taken from Walters, *American and Soviet Aid.*

[14]See W. T. Shinn, Jr., "The National Democratic State: A Communist Program for Less Developed Areas," *World Politics*, vol. 15, no. 3 (1963), pp. 377-89; A. Bennigsen, "The 'National Front' in Communist Strategy in the Middle East," in W. Z. Laqueur, ed., *The Middle East in Transition* (New York, Praeger, 1958), pp. 360-69; David Morison, *The USSR and Africa 1943-63* (Oxford University Press, 1964), pp. 1-58; and John Kemp, "The Soviet Union and the Third World," *Survey*, no. 72 (1969), pp. 19-38.

[15]See, for instance, G. I. Mirski, "Changes in Class Forces and Ideas on Socialism," in *MIZAN* (Special issue: "The USSR and the Developing Countries"), vol. 6, no. 10 (1964). His categorization of political and administrative elites and class structure in certain Middle Eastern states is insightful and, with some modifications, in consonance with my own views. His notion and his analysis of the "bureaucratic bourgeoisie" are not far removed, it seems to me, from Manfred Halpern's "new middle class." See also D. S. Carlisle, "The Changing Soviet Perception of the Development Process in the Afro-Asian World," *Midwest Journal of Political Science*, vol. 8, no. 4 (1964), pp. 385-407.

[16]See Uri Ra'anan, "Moscow and the Third World," *Problems of Communism*, 14 (Jan.-Feb. 1965): 22-31.

[17]*Ibid.*, p. 26. It is argued that the Mirski-Khrushchev approach, blurring the issue of the vanguard role of communists in the transition to socialism, was an important

element in the Sino-Soviet dispute (Carlisle, "Changing Soviet Perception," p. 397). While this may have been true on the level of the "church" debate between the communist powers, it was not an issue of any great relevance to either of them on the level of policy toward the LDCs.

[18]See R. A. Yellon, "The Winds of Change," *MIZAN*, vol. 9, no. 4 (1967), pp. 155-73.

[19]See "National Liberation Movements: A Lower Soviet Rating?" *MIZAN*, vol. 9, no. 2 (1967), pp. 41-49. See also David Morison, "Africa and Asia: Some Trends in Soviet Thinking," *MIZAN*, vol. 10, no. 5 (1968), pp. 167-84. In the new African pecking order, Ghana and Mali have dropped out, and Tanzania and Congo-Brazzaville have been added. See R. A. Ulianovsky, "On the Modern Stage of the National Liberation Movement," *Narody Azii i Afriki*, no. 5 (1967); and Robin Buss, "Wary Partners: The Soviet Union and Arab Socialism," *Adelphi Papers*, no. 73 (Dec. 1970), entire issue.

[20]Yellon, "Winds of Change," p. 163. However, the Russians are always vulnerable to Chinese attack on precisely this point.

[21]The $110 million arms deal with Iran in 1967 may be indicative of this trend.

[22]Why local communists should gladly pay the price of Soviet cooperation with the national bourgeoisie is set forth by a member of the Tudeh party of Iran, I. Iskandary, in "Iran: Present Situation and Perspective," *World Marxist Review*, vol. 8, no. 5 (1965), pp. 68-76. For a general discussion of the plight of Middle Eastern communist parties, see Manfred Halpern, "The Middle East and North Africa," in C. E. Black, ed., *Communism and Revolution* (Princeton University Press, 1964), pp. 303-29.

[23]See *Le Parti Communiste Marocain lutte pour son existence légale* (Damascus, 1960) and *Un procès d'inquisition* (Paris, 1960).

[24]See Ali Ya'ta, "Unity—The Way to Firm Up Moroccan Independence and Democracy," *World Marxist Review*, vol. 11, no. 3 (1968), pp. 15-19. For reasons that are not entirely clear, Ali Ya'ta and two associates were arrested in Aug. 1969.

[25]"Nationalism and Communism in Tunisia," *MIZAN*, vol. 5, no. 2 (1963); and Ibn Chaldoun, "Tunisia a Year Later," *World Marxist Review* (March 1964).

[26]On the charges, see "Le procès de subversion et l'opposition en Tunisie," *Maghreb*, no. 30 (Nov.-Dec. 1968), pp. 8-12. Also accused were Ba'athists and Trotskyites.

[27]Quoted in Hervé Bourges, *L'Algérie à l'épreuve du pouvoir* (Paris, 1967), p. 84.

[28]The PCA's position is stated in Larbi Bouhali, "The Algerian Revolution Goes On," *World Marxist Review*, vol. 6, no. 1 (1963), pp. 43-46.

[29]See Khadduri, *Modern Libya*, p. 106.

[30]Walters develops this point in *American and Soviet Aid*, p. 114.

[31]Yellon, "Winds of Change," p. 159.

[32]Figure from U.S. Department of State (Intelligence and Research), *Research Memorandum RSB-65* (Aug. 4, 1965), Table 1, p. 6.

[33]Estimate of Yellon, "Winds of Change," p. 156.

[34]*Ibid.*

³⁵Figure from U.S. Department of State (Intelligence and Research), *Research Memorandum RSE-120* (Aug. 14, 1968), p. 1.

³⁶On this point, see R. K. Ramazani, "Soviet Military Assistance to the Uncommitted Countries," *Midwest Journal of Political Science,* vol. 3, no. 4 (1959), pp. 356-73. A general treatment of Soviet military aid is given in *The Soviet Military Aid Program as a Reflection of Soviet Objectives,* Atlantic Research Corp. (submitted to Air Force Office of Scientific Research), Washington, D.C. (June 24, 1965).

³⁷See, for instance, the rankings of Mirski and Avakov, "Klassovoi Strukture v Slaborazitykh Stranakh," *Mirovaia Ekonomika i Mezhdunarodnye Otnosheniia* (April 1962); cited by Carlisle, "Changing Soviet Perception," p. 404.

³⁸The steelworks will enter into production in 1971 and will produce initially, 400,000 tons a year.

³⁹For a detailed breakdown, see Stuart Schaar, "The Arms Race and Defense Strategy in North Africa," *AUFS Report* (North Africa Series), vol. 13, no. 9, (1967), Table IV, p. 25.

⁴⁰In 1967, Czechoslovakia supplied Morocco with ca. fifty reconditioned T-54 tanks in a $16 million arms deal (see Schaar, "Arms Race," pp. 3-4).

⁴¹In general, see Carole A. Sawyer, *Communist Trade with Developing Countries 1955-1965* (New York, Praeger, 1966); Walters, "American and Soviet Aid," *passim;* André Tiano, *Le Maghreb entre les mythes* (Paris, 1967), pp. 445-94; and Elizabeth Valkenia, "New Soviet Views on Economic Aid," *Survey,* no. 76 (Summer 1970), pp. 17-29.

⁴²For the importance of Algerian vineyards to the economy, see H. Isnard, "La viticulture nord-africaine," *Annuaire de l'Afrique du Nord* (1965), pp. 37-48.

⁴³See I.W. Zartman, "North Africa and the EEC Negotiations," *Middle East Journal* (Winter 1968), pp. 1-17; and Tiano, *Le Maghreb,* pp. 478-87.

⁴⁴See *La Vie Economique,* Casablanca, March 1, 1968.

⁴⁵For a résumé, see *CEDIES Informations,* Casablanca, no. 665 (April 5, 1969), pp. 1, 2.

⁴⁶More recent trade statistics confirm these judgments formulated in 1969. For instance, in 1970 only 5.5 percent of Algeria's exports and 3.6 percent of her imports went to or came from the U.S.S.R. See *Middle East International,* Feb. 1972.

⁴⁷See C. A. Gallagher, "The Death of a Group," *AUFS Report* (North Africa Series), vol. 9, no. 4 (May 1963).

⁴⁸Ali Ya'ta of the PCM attacked AATUF in the *World Marxist Review,* on the grounds that it neglected the fundamental necessity of organizing workers according to Marxism-Leninism. See Dallin, "Soviet Union," pp. 28-29. For an account of the formation of AATUF, see Jean Meynaud and Anisse Salah Bey, *Le syndicalisme africain* (Paris, 1963).

⁴⁹At the time of the Algerian-Moroccan border conflict in October 1963, the U.S.S.R. backed Algeria, claiming (in *Pravda,* Oct. 17) that the war had been instigated by the United States so that it would have an excuse to reactivate its military bases in Morocco. For more on the border conflict, see "The Algerian-Moroccan Conflict: 1962-1963," in *The Control of Local Conflict,* ACDA, 3 (1967): 507-34; and Edouard Meric, "Le conflit algéro-marocain," *Revue Francaise de Science Politique,* vol. 15, no. 4 (1965), pp. 743-52.

[50]A. G. Virabov, "Economic Integration of the Maghreb," *Narody Azii i Afriki*, no. 6 (1967). The new warmth in relations between Algeria and Morocco in 1968 and 1969 was underscored and approved by Podgorny during his visit to both countries in the spring of 1969.

[51]See, for instance, R. Landa, *Natsional'no-osvoboditel'noe dvizhenie v Alzhire* (The national liberation movement in Algeria), Institute of Asian Peoples, Academy of Sciences of the U.S.S.R., 1962.

[52]Bachir Hadj Ali, "Some Lessons of the Liberation Struggle in Algeria," *World Marxist Review* (Jan. 1965), pp. 50-58; also R. Landa, "The Surge of the Patriotic Movement in the Cities of Algeria: 1960-61," *Narody Azii i Afriki*, no. 2 (1962), pp. 30-38. This article reads like a rehash of some of Hadj Ali's ideas.

[53]Charles-Henri Favrod, *Le FLN et l'Algérie* (Paris, 1962), p. 103.

[54]Cited in Arslan Humbaraci, *Algeria: A Revolution That Failed* (London, 1966), p. 175.

[55]Cited by M. K. Clark, *Algeria in Turmoil* (New York, 1960), pp. 116-17; see also W. G. Andrews, *French Politics and Algeria* (New York, 1962).

[56]See Yves Courrière, *Le temps des léopards* (Paris, Fayard, 1969), pp. 293-99.

[57]Clark, *Algeria in Turmoil*, p. 320.

[58]Amar Ouzagane, *Le meilleur combat* (Paris, 1962), p. 184.

[59]"Extraits du procès-verbal du congrès du 20 août 1956," *El-Moudjahid* (FLN), numéro spécial, 29 pp.; quote from p. 13. Excerpts from this document are to be found in André Mandouze, *La révolution algérienne par les textes* (Paris, 1961), pp. 85-100.

[60]Favrod, *Le FLN et l'Algérie*, p. 121; see also Jeanne Favret, "Le syndicat, les travailleurs, et le pouvoir en Algérie," *Annuaire de l'Afrique du Nord* (1964), pp. 44-62; and Mohammed Lebjaoui, *Vérités sur la révolution algérienne* (Paris, Gallimard, 1970), p. 36. Lebjaoui claims to have sired the idea of joining ICFTU to promote a split between the United States and France; and it was his assumption that the ICFTU would have to back the UGTA anyway.

[61]A whitewash of the PCF is to be found in Yu. V. Shchirovskii, *Bor'ba Frantsuzskoi Kommunisticheskoi Partii Protiv Voiny v Alzhire* (The struggle of the French Communist Party against the war in Algeria), Academy of the Central Committee of the CPSU (Moscow, 1962).

[62]A good example of Russia's prudent handling of de Gaulle on this issue is to be found in "The USSR and France," *International Affairs,* vol. 6, no. 3 (1960), pp. 3-7. Belkacem Krim, known to be an anti-communist, was the GPRA foreign minister at this time (although a known Marxist, Mohammed Harbi, was a member of his cabinet), and it was Krim's policy to pursue the opening to the east with trips to Moscow and Peking. See Yves Courrière, *Les feux du désespoir* (Paris, Fayard, 1971), pp. 117 and 218.

[63]For this period, see Larbi Bouhali, "A New Stage in Algeria's Struggle for Freedom," *International Affairs*, vol. 8, no. 2 (1962), pp. 29-35; and "New Programme of the Algerian Communist Party," *World Marxist Review*, vol. 5, no. 9 (1962), pp. 57-61.

[64]This point of view is recorded in Bachir Hadj Ali, "The Algerian Revolution and the Algerian Revolutionary in 1964," *World Marxist Review*, vol. 7, no. 8 (1964), pp. 98-103. *Alger Républicain* became an official organ of the FLN in 1964.

[65]The text is in "L'Algérie en marche vers le socialisme," *Economie et Politique*, no. 130 (May 1965), pp. 150-52.

[66]Ben Bella had a penchant for treading on the toes of the mighty. Just as he had capped off his state visit to the United States and to John F. Kennedy with a meeting with Castro in Havana, so too he proceeded to make a state visit to Tito (with lavish praise of the Yugoslavian system of socialism) about a month before his visit to the U.S.S.R.

[67]See, for instance, Yu. Potemkin, "The Algerian Revolution: Achievements and Perspectives," *Mirovaia Ekonomika i Mezhdunarodnye Otnosheniia*, no. 10 (1964), pp. 26-36.

[68]See R. Landa, "Specific Features of Algeria's Non-Capitalist Development," *Narody Azii i Afriki*, no. 5 (1964), pp. 10-21. That self-management in Algeria is still viewed favorably by the U.S.S.R. is evident in "Soviet Publicist Praises Workers' Self-Management—but for Algeria," *Research Departments of Radio Free Europe* (Soviet Union), June 13, 1969.

[69]Bouhali, "The Algerian Revolution Goes On"; and Bourges, *L'Algérie à l'épreuve du pouvoir*, p. 83.

[70]See "Algeria: a Fruitful Dialogue," *MIZAN*, vol. 6, no. 2 (1964); "Algeria's Difficulties," *MIZAN*, vol. 7, no. 6 (1965), pp. 7-11; and Potemkin, "Algerian Revolution."

[71]For a sample of their diverse approaches, see Mohammed Harbi, "L'Algérie et ses réalités," *Economie et Politique*, no. 130 (May 1965), pp. 51-61; and Ouzagane, *Le meilleur combat, passim*. In Jan. 1963, at the Moshi Afro-Asian Conference, the Algerians supported the Chinese position that the Soviet delegation should not be allowed to attend.

[72]Ait Ahmad Hocine, who founded his Front des Forces Socialistes in opposition to Ben Bella in 1963, joined with Lebjaoui to create the Organisation Clandestine de la Révolution Algérienne (OCRA), which later became the Mouvement Algérien pour l'Unité Nationale et la Démocratie. On the repression under Boumedienne, see Bachir Hadj Ali, *L'Arbitraire* (Paris, 1966).

[73]See A. M. Goldobin, "Some Problems of the Non-Capitalist Development of Algeria and the UAR," *Narody Azii i Afriki*, no. 5 (1966), pp. 43-49; and the reply of R. Landa, "Again about the Non-Capitalist Path of Development," *Narody Azii i Afriki*, no. 6 (1966), pp. 30-38.

[74]I do not view the war in Vietnam as an exception to my statements so much as an indication of how poorly the lessons of the fifties were learned and of how easy it is for the United States to relapse into the old rhetoric and thought patterns.

7: THE SOVIET UNION IN LEBANON, SYRIA, AND JORDAN

[1]Louis Fischer, *The Soviets in World Affairs* (London, Cape, 1930), 1:399. See also

Walter Z. Laqueur, *The Soviet Union and the Middle East* (New York, Praeger, 1959); and Ivar Spector, *The Soviet Union and the Muslim World, 1917-1958* (Seattle, University of Washington, 1959).

[2]See Gerhard L. Weinberg, *Germany and the Soviet Union, 1939-1941* (Leiden, Brill, 1954); J. C. Hurewitz, ed., *Soviet-American Rivalry in the Middle East* (New York, Praeger, 1969); Harry N. Howard, "Germany, the Soviet Union and Turkey during World War II," *Department of State Bulletin*, vol. 19, no. 472 (July 18, 1948), pp. 63-78; and Harry N. Howard, "The Entry of Turkey into World War II," *Belleten*, vol. 31, no. 122 (April 1967), pp. 221-75.

[3]See *Foreign Relations of the United States. Diplomatic Papers 1943*, 4:953-1056; 1944, 5:774-813 (hereafter cited as *USFR*). On the long-standing Russian interest in Syria, see Theophanis G. Stavrou, *Russian Interests in Palestine, 1882-1914: A Study of Religious and Educational Enterprise* (Thessalonike, Institute of Balkan Studies, 1963); and Derek Hopwood, *The Russian Presence in Syria and Palestine, 1843-1914: Church and Politics in the Near East* (London, Oxford, 1969).

[4]Among other things, see Harry S. Truman, *Memoirs* (Garden City, N.Y., Doubleday, 1956), vol. 2, *passim*; Dean G. Acheson, *Present at the Creation: My Years at the State Department* (New York, Norton, 1969), *passim*; Feridun Cemal Erkin, *Les relations turco-soviétiques et la question des Détroits* (Ankara, 1968), Chap. 8.

[5]*USFR*, 1945, 8:1049 ff.

[6]United Nations, Security Council, no. 1, *Official Records*, 21st-23rd Meetings (Feb. 15-16, 1946), pp. 206-368.

[7]For detailed accounts of Syrian politics after World War II, see Patrick Seale, *The Struggle for Syria: A Study of Post-War Arab Politics, 1945-1958* (New York, Oxford [RIIA], 1965); Gordon H. Torrey, *Syrian Politics and the Military, 1945-1958* (Columbus, Ohio State University, 1964); Kamel S. Abu Jaber, *The Arab Ba'ath Socialist Party: History, Ideology, and Organization* (Syracuse, N.Y., Syracuse University, 1966); and Leonard Binder, *The Ideological Revolution in the Middle East* (New York, Wiley, 1964), *passim*.

[8]See Michael W. Suleiman, *Political Parties in Lebanon: The Challenge of a Fragmented Political Culture* (Ithaca, Cornell, 1967), especially chap. 2; Michael Hudson, *The Precarious Republic: Political Modernization in Lebanon* (New York, Random House, 1969), passim; and Leonard Binder, ed., *Politics in Lebanon* (New York, Wiley, 1966).

[9]See Aqil Hyder Hasan, *Jordan: A Political Study, 1948-1957* (New York, Asia Publishing House, 1965); and P. J. Vatikiotis, *Politics and the Military in Jordan: A Study of the Arab Legion, 1921-1957* (New York, Praeger, 1967).

[10]Department of State, *American Foreign Policy: Current Documents 1957*, pp. 1015-22.

[11]See Royal Institute of International Affairs, *Documents on International Affairs 1957*, p. 288; King Hussein of Jordan, *Uneasy Lies the Head* (New York, Random House, 1962), chaps. 9-11. In the course of these events, two chiefs of staff, Ali Abu Nuwar and Maj. Gen. Hayari, left the country and went into exile in Damascus.

[12]See esp. United Nations, *The External Financing of Economic Development* (New

York, 1968), pp. 16-17, which puts the total of Soviet bilateral aid commitments to Syria at $448,000,000 (1954-66), as compared with $1,408,000,000 to Egypt. See also Franklyn D. Holzman, "Soviet Trade and Aid Policies," and Charles Issawi, "Regional Economies in the 1970s," in Hurewitz, *Soviet-American Rivalry*, pp. 104-20, and 121-36; and Alec Nove and J. A. Newth, *The Soviet Middle East: A Communist Model for Development* (New York, Praeger, 1967).

[13]Department of State Publication 6632, *The Sino-Soviet Economic Offensive in the Less Developed Countries* (Washington, D.C., USGPO, 1958); Laqueur, *Soviet Union and the Middle East*, Part II, chap. 5-6.

[14]*Documents on International Affairs 1957*, pp. 319-24.

[15]See also the sketch and report of the Syrian economy by the International Bank for Reconstruction and Development, *The Economic Development of Syria* (Baltimore, Johns Hopkins University, 1955). Syria rejected IBRD assistance, as it had American, on the ground that it prejudiced Syrian sovereignty and independence.

[16]See also *The Mizan News Letter: The Middle East*, vol. 1, no. 8 (Aug. 1959), Appendix, pp. 1-5, for Syrian Communist Party Declaration in Nov. 1956.

[17]Department of State, *American Foreign Policy; Basic Documents, 1950-1955*, 2:2180-87; J. C. Hurewitz, *Diplomacy in the Near and Middle East* (Princeton, N. J., D. Van Nostrand, 1956), 2:332-35.

[18]Raymond Dennett and Robert K. Turner, *Documents on American Foreign Relations 1948* (Boston, World Peace Foundation, 1950), 10:660-79.

[19]See Kennett Love, *Suez the Twice Fought War* (New York, McGraw-Hill, 1969).

[20]See basic documents in Department of State Publication 6392, *The Suez Canal Problem, July 26-Sep. 22, 1956* (Washington, D.C., USGPO, 1956); Department of State Publication 6505, *United States Policy in the Middle East, Sept. 1956-June 1957* (Washington, D.C., USGPO, 1957); *American Foreign Policy: Current Documents 1956*, pp. 579-703; and *ibid., 1957*, pp. 872-1015.

[21]*American Foreign Policy; Current Documents 1959*, pp. 783-831.

[22]*Ibid.*, pp. 831-71; République Libanaise, Ministère des Affaires Etrangères, I: *Documents sur la Politique Extérieure du Liban* (Beirut, Jan. 1958).

[23]John C. Campbell, *Defense of the Middle East: Problems of American Policy* (New York, Harper, 1958), chap. 9.

[24]See Muhammad Khalil, *The Arab States and the Arab League* (Beirut, Khayats, 1962), 2:337-42; *Documents on International Affairs 1957*, pp. 66-81; *American Foreign Policy: Current Documents 1957*, pp. 761-71.

[25]*Ibid.*, pp. 1015-28.

[26]Khalil, *Arab States and Arab League*, 2:390-95, 916-20; *New York Times*, April 25, 1957.

[27]*American Foreign Policy: Current Documents 1957*, pp. 1034-38. The Syrian government charged that the United States was prepared to offer some $400,000,000 to have the government overthrown, and a new government was not only to make peace with Israel but to attack Lebanon. For good measure the United States was also to oust the French from Algeria. See *L'Orient* (Beirut), Aug. 13, 1957, for

documentation; also *New York Times, New York Herald-Tribune, Beirut Daily Star*, Aug. 13 and 14, 1957. The charges were duly denied.

[28]*American Foreign Policy: Current Documents 1957*, pp. 1037-39.

[29]*Ibid.*, pp. 1038-39; *Documents on International Affairs 1957*, pp. 324-69.

[30]*American Foreign Policy: Current Documents 1957*, pp. 1041-43.

[31]*Ibid.*, pp. 1046-48.

[32]*Ibid.*, pp. 1048-53. The Soviets supported also the Saudi offer to mediate the controversy, which was accepted by Turkey. See also U.N. Docs. A/PV.714; L. 226, 227.

[33]For basic texts see Khalil, *Arab States and Arab League,* 1:70-92, 601-17.

[34]See Camille Chamoun, *Crise au Moyen-Orient* (Paris, Gallimard, 1963); Fahim Qubain, *Crisis in Lebanon* (Washington, D.C., Middle East Institute, 1961); Leila M. T. Meo, *Lebanon: Improbable Nation* (Bloomington, Indiana University, 1965); and Hudson, *Precarious Republic, passim.*

[35]U.N. Doc. S/4007.

[36]U. N. Docs. S/PV.823, S/4023, 4029, 4038; *American Foreign Policy: Current Documents 1958*, pp. 942-44. For UNOGIL Reports, see U. N. Docs. S/4040, 4052, 4069, 4085, 4100, 4114. See also David W. Wainhouse et al., *International Peace Observation: A History and Forecast* (Baltimore, Johns Hopkins Press, 1966), pp. 373-90. The Lebanese government never did submit direct, probative evidence of "massive" U.A.R. intervention. UNOGIL found no such evidence, partly because of limitations as to observation. See the Lebanese circular note of July 2, 1958, in *L'Orient*, July 3, 1958.

[37]U. N. Doc. S/4047.

[38]*American Foreign Policy: Current Documents 1958*, pp. 959-74.

[39]*Ibid.*, pp. 984-87; U. N. Docs. S/4053; S/PV.831, pp. 5-7.

[40]U. N. Doc. S/4047/Rev. 1.

[41]*American Foreign Policy: Current Documents 1959*, p. 989; U.N. Doc. S/4057. See also Robert Murphy, *Diplomat Among Warriors* (New York, Pyramid, 1965), chap. 27.

[42]*American Foreign Policy: Current Documents 1958*, pp. 993-94.

[43]*Ibid.*, pp. 995-99.

[44]*Ibid.*, pp. 999-1000.

[45]*Ibid.*, pp. 1001-1002.

[46]*Ibid.*, pp. 1003-1005. See also, for interview with Khrushchev, *New York Herald-Tribune* and *New York Times,* Aug. 6, 1958.

[47]*American Foreign Policy: Current Documents 1958*, pp. 1011-17.

[48]*Ibid.*, pp. 1018-25; U.N. Docs. S/4056/ Rev. 1, S/4057/Rev. 1.

[49]U. N. Docs. A/PV.732, pp. 45-50; A/3870. No vote was taken on the Soviet proposal in view of the passage of Resolution 1237 (ES-III), of Aug. 21, 1958.

[50]*American Foreign Policy: Current Documents 1958*, pp. 1032-39.

[51]U. N. Docs. A/3876, 3877.

[52]U.N. Docs. A/3878, 3905, 3934/Rev. 1/Annex 1, 3934/Rev. 1, 3986, 4056, 4113,

4115; *American Foreign Policy: Current Documents 1958*, pp. 1061-62.

[53]*American Foreign Policy: Current Documents, 1961*, pp. 671-72: Richard P. Stebbins, *Documents on American Foreign Relations 1961* (New York, Harper, for the Council on Foreign Relations, 1962), pp. 281-84.

[54]See *Mizan Newsletter*, vol. 1, no. 8 (Aug. 1959), Appendix, pp. 1-5, with the declaration of the Syrian Communist Party on the close ties with the Soviet Union.

[55]For convenience see Hisham B. Sharabi, *Nationalism and Revolution in the Arab World* (Princeton, D. Van Nostrand, 1966), pp. 138-39, 160-61.

[56]Prime Minister Zayen visited the U.S.S.R. in April 1966, and was granted a $120,000,000 credit for hydroelectric, dam, and irrigation projects.

[57]George Mirsky, *The New Times*, 34 (1963):13-14.

[58]*American Foreign Policy: Current Documents 1957*, pp. 1025-28.

[59]*Pravda*, Dec. 2, 1964, reported decisions of the Jordanian Communist Party Central Committee, which noted positive advances in recent Jordanian policy, especially the establishment of relations with the U.S.S.R. and other Socialist countries, and the restoration of normal relations with the U.A.R., and the recognition of the Yemeni Arab Republic. It condemned the "terrorism" of the Jordanian security police and declared that the party should strive for a more positive course (*Mizan Newsletter*, vol. 7, no. 1 [Jan. 1965], pp. 14-15)

[60]*American Foreign Policy: Current Documents 1964*, pp. 712-13.

[61]See the statement of Deputy Undersecretary of State U. Alexis Johnson, Jan. 20, 1964; *ibid.*, pp. 677-79, 679-81.

[62]*Department of Defense Appropriation, 1965: Hearings before the Subcommittee on Department of Defense of the Committee on Appropriations and the Committee on Armed Services*, U. S. Senate, 88th Congress, 2d Session, on H. R. 10939, pt. 1, pp. 18-20.

[63]*American Foreign Policy: Current Documents 1964*, pp. 685-86, 708-11; U. N. Doc. S/6061 and Corr. 1. On the other hand, Syrian extremists during this period complained that the U.S.S.R. did little but talk, while Communist China was really ready to assist, and some suggested converting Syria into a "second Albania."

[64]*See American Foreign Policy: Current Documents 1966*, pp. 525-26, 528-30, 530-37; and U. N. Docs. S/PV.1291, S/7436, 7437, 7584. King Hussein charged on Nov. 21, 1966, that the U.S.S.R. was instigating trouble in the Middle East.

[65]One may consult such disparate accounts as Nadav Safran, *From War to War: The Arab-Israeli Confrontation, 1948-1967* (New York, Pegasus, 1969); Theodore Draper, *Israel and World Politics: Roots of the Third Arab-Israeli War* (New York, Viking, 1968); Walter Z. Laqueur, *The Road to War* (Baltimore, Penguin, 1969); Fred J. Khouri, *The Arab-Israeli Dilemma* (Syracuse, Syracuse University, 1968); Hisham B. Sharabi, *Palestine and Israel: The Lethal Dilemma* (New York, Pegasus, 1969); Charles W. Yost, "The Arab-Israeli War: How It Began," *Foreign Affairs*, vol. 46, no. 2 (Jan. 1968), pp. 304-20; Ibrahim Abu Lughod, ed., "The Arab-Israeli Confrontation of June 1967," *Arab World*, vol. 14, nos. 10-11 (1969).

[66]Arthur Lall, *The UN and the Middle East Crisis, 1967* (New York, Columbia, 1968),

[67]See *Al-Anwar*, Jan 10, 1969; and *New York Times*, Jan. 11, 1969. See also *Com-*

munist States and Developing Countries: Aid and Trade in 1970, Department of State Bureau of Intelligence and Research, RECS-15 (Sept. 22, 1971), one of the best summary studies of Soviet assistance in the Middle East; and Wynfred Joshua, *Soviet Penetration into the Middle East* (New York, National Strategy Information Center, 1971), chaps. 1-3. A bloodless coup in Damascus on Oct. 26, 1968, had removed Prime Minister Yusuf Zayen and replaced him with a provisional government under the head of state, Dr. Nur al-Din al-Atassi. The leader of the coup, Defense Minister Maj. Gen. Hafiz al-Asad, also demanded the removal and exile of Maj. Gen. Salah Jadid and Lt. Col. Abd al-Karim al-Jundi, both of whom were considered pro-Moscow. An unsuccessful coup against the Ba'ath took place on May 22, 1969.

[68]See *Pravda*, Oct. 3, 1967; and *Mizan Supplement, Middle East, 1967*, pp. 3-4.

[69]See Walter Z. Laqueur, "An Independent Radical Movement for the Middle East," *New Middle East* (London), no. 11 (Aug. 1969), pp. 14-22; Sharabi, *Nationalism and Revolution*, chap. 8; Michael Hudson, "The Palestinian Arab Resistance Movement: Its Significance in the Middle East Crisis," *Middle East Journal*, vol. 23, no. 3 (Summer 1969), pp. 291-307.

[70]See *New York Times* and *Washington Post*, Oct. 19, ff, Oct. 30, and Oct. 31, 1969; and *Fateh*, Nov. 20, 1969, for charges that the United States was seeking to instigate another counterrevolutionary move, whether in Lebanon or in support of the Zionist movement.

[71]*New York Times*, Oct. 24 and 25, 1969.

[72]Quoted in *New York Times*, Oct. 26, 1969. See also the interview of an official of the Palestine Liberation Movement in *Fateh*, Nov. 10, 1969, denouncing the United States and declaring that any American intervention would be resisted.

[73]For a concise expression of American views and policy see *U. S. Foreign Policy for the 1970's: A New Strategy for Peace. A Report to the Congress by Richard Nixon, President of the United States, February 18, 1970* (Washington, D. C., USGPO, 1970), pp. 77-83. See also *New York Times*, Oct. 26-28, 1969. For guerrilla views, see Yusif A. Sayigh, *Towards Peace in Palestine* (Beirut, 1970); *The Palestine National Liberation Movement, Al-Fateh* (Beirut, 1970); *The Palestine National Liberation Movement, Fateh, Dialogue with Fateh* (Beirut, 1970); *The Palestine National Liberation Movement, Fateh, Revolution Until Victory* (Beirut, 1970).

[74]For Soviet and American statements see *New York Times* and *Washington Post*, Nov. 1, 1969. See also *New York Times*, Nov. 4 and Dec. 3-5, 1969.

[75]For text see *The Near East Conflict*. Hearings before the Subcommittee on the Near East of the Committee on Foreign Affairs, House of Representatives. 91st Congress, 1st Session, July 21, 22, 23, 28, 29, and 30, 1970 (Washington, D. C., USGPO, 1970), pp. 295-96.

[76]For backgrounds see John K. Cooley, "Moscow Faces a Palestinian Dilemma," *Mid East*, vol. 11, no. 3 (June 1970), pp. 32-35; Robert A. Mertz, "Why George Habash Turned Marxist," *ibid.*, vol. 11, no. 4, (Aug. 1970), pp. 31-36.

[77]*U. S. Foreign Policy for the 1970's. Building for Peace. A Report to the Congress by Richard Nixon, President of the United States, February 25, 1971* (Washington, D. C., 1971), pp. 127-28. See also Benjamin Welles, *New York Times*, Oct. 8, 1970.

[78]Terence Prittie, *Manchester Guardian Weekly*, Dec. 6, 1969.

8: THE SOVIET UNION AND ISRAEL: 1947-1969

[1]See, for example, the resolution on Zionism adopted at the Communist International Second Congress, August 1920.

[2]Walter Z. Laqueur, *The Soviet Union and the Middle East* (New York, Frederic A. Praeger, 1959), p. 147.

[3]The Jewish minority in the Soviet Union is variously put at between 2 and 3 million, while America's Jews number some 5 million.

[4]The article read in part: "Soviet Jews are rebuilding their Socialist motherland together with all the Soviet people. They are not looking toward the Near East; they are looking to the future."

[5]In theory, the New Look policy was adopted because of the limitations of the containment policy demonstrated in Korea. These limitations were mainly that the communists retained the initiative and its advantages, and that one action might, as in Korea, tie down enough of the West's military capacity in one place to impair its defense capability in other potential theatres.

[6]As we now know, Israeli fears about the extra strength to accrue to Arab countries from their participation in the Western-sponsored pact were quite exaggerated; but this is unimportant in this context, for it is what the Israelis believed at the time that matters.

[7]"The State Department said today that it had indications that the Soviet Union might be willing to supply arms to Israel as well as to the Arab states" (*New York Times*, October 13, 1955).

[8]See Nadav Safran, *From War to War: The Arab-Israeli Confrontation, 1948-1967* (New York, Pegasus, 1969), chap. VI and VII.

[9]The reader may wish to consult on this my article, "The Alternatives in the Middle East," *Commentary*, May 1969.

9: SOVIET STUDIES ON THE MIDDLE EAST

[1]For a brief history of VNAV and Soviet Oriental studies, see Wayne S. Vucinich, "The Structure of Soviet Orientology," in Wayne S. Vucinich, ed., *Russia and Asia* (Stanford, Calif., Hoover Institution, 1972), pp. 52-134.

[2]Stephen Page, *U.S.S.R. and Arabia* (London, Central Asian Research Center, 1971), 150pp.

[3]*Pravda*, August 7, 1947.

[4]Page, *U.S.S.R. and Arabia*, pp. 19-20.

[5]*Kommunist*, May 8, 1955, pp. 74-83.

[6]*Sovetskaia istoricheskaia entsiklopediia* (*SIE*) (Moscow, 1965), pp. 589-90.

[7]S. S. Korneev, *Nauchnye sviazi Akademii Nauk S.S.S.R. so stranami Azii i Afriki*

(Moscow, 1963); and I. V. Samylovskii, *Nauchnye i kul'turnye sviazi S.S.S.R. so stranami Azii i Afriki* (Moscow, 1963).

[8]N. A. Kuznetsova and L. M. Kulagina, *Iz istorii sovetskogo vostokovedeniia* (hereafter cited as *Iz istorii*). (Moscow, 1970), p. 144.

[9]Alvin Z. Rubinstein, *The Foreign Policy of the Soviet Union* (New York, 1960), pp. 393-97.

[10]*Ibid.*, p. 296.

[11]*Ibid.*, pp. 299-302.

[12]"XX S'ezd Kommunisticheskoi partii Sovetskogo Soiuza i zadachi izucheniia sovremennogo vostoka," *Sovetskoe vostokovedenie*, no. 1 (1956), pp. 3-12.

[13]Page, *U.S.S.R. and Arabia*, pp. 57-58.

[14]*Ibid.*, pp. 58-61; F. Zhukov, "Znamenatel'nyi faktor nashego vremeni: O nekotorykh voprosakh sovremennogo natsional'no-osvoboditel'nogo dvizheniia," *Pravda*, August 26, pp. 3-4; and *Kommunist*, no. 13 (1960), pp. 10-27.

[15]Page, *U.S.S.R. and Arabia*, p. 32.

[16]*Iz istorii*, p. 160-161.

[17]Rubinstein, *Foreign Policy of Soviet Union*, pp. 400-402.

[18]Page, *U.S.S.R. and Arabia*, p. 48.

[19]*Iz istorii*, pp. 160-61.

[20]There are cabinets for the study of the ancient East, the Near East, the Kurds, Iran, Turco-Mongolia, India, China, Korea, Japan, the Arabs, Burma, and the Caucasus.

[21]The institutes of Ancient History, the History of Material Culture, Ethnography, the Economy of the World Socialist System, etc.

[22]*Sektor zarubezhnogo vostoka Instituta istorii iskusstv, Institut Marksizma-Leninizma pri TsK KPSS, Akademiia obshchestvennykh nauk pri TsK VKP (b)*, etc.

[23]The Armenian, Azerbaijan, Georgian, Kirghiz, Tadzhik Turkmen, Uzbek, and certain other academies and republican instututes and centers of research.

[24]See A. S. Tvertinova, *Vostokovednye fondy krupneishikh bibliotek Sovetskogo Soiuza*. Stat'i i soobshcheniia (Moscow, 1963), 240pp.

[25]V. I. Beliaev, "Arabskie rukopisi v sobranii Instituta vostokovedeniia," *Uchenyi Zapiski Instituta Vostokovedeniia* (hereafter UZIV), no. 6 (1953), pp. 54-103; A. A. Kartsev, "Arkhivnye istochniki po istorii russko-arabskikh sviazi v XIX-nachale XX v.," *Kratkie Soobshcheniia Instituta Narodov Azii* (hereafter KSINA), no. 58 (1962), pp. 16-23; and A. L. Khalidov and A. I. Mikhailova, *Akademiia Nauk*, 3 vols. (Moscow, 1960-65).

[26]N.D. Miklukho-Maklai, *Opisanie tadzhikskikh i persidskikh rukopisei Instituta vostokovedeniia* (Moscow, 1955), 106 pp.; S.I. Baevskii, *Opisanie persidskikh i tadzhikhskikh rukopisei Instituta narodov Azii*, 2 vols. (Moscow, 1961-62); N. D. Miklukho-Maklai and collaborators have also edited a two-volume catalogue (published in 1964) of Persian and Tadzhik documents.

[27]A. Kh. Rafikov, *Istoricheskaia literatura na turetskom iazyke, khraniashchaiasia v bibliotekakh Leningrada* (Leningrad, 1968). See also, by the same author,

"Sobranie russkikh izdanii XVIII v. o Turtsii v Biblioteke Akademii nauk SSSR," *Sbornik statei i materialov Biblioteki AN SSSR* (Leningrad, 1965), pp. 282-320.

[28]M.B. Rudenko, *Opisanie kurdskikh rukopisei leningradskikh sobranii* (Moscow, 1961), 125 pp. There are catalogues that list and describe Arabic, Persian, and Turkish documents in the possession of the Armenian, Georgian, Uzbek, and Tadzhik academies of sciences. See *Persidskie, arabskie i tiurskie ofitsial'nye dokumenti Matenadarana XIV-XIX vekov i ikh znachenie dlia izucheniia sotsial'noekonomicheskoi zhizn' stran Blizhnego Vostoka* (Moscow, 1960); *Ukazy persidskikh shakov* (Erevan, 1956); *Persidskie dokumenty Matenadarana* (Erevan, 1959); V. S. Puturidze, *Persidskie istoricheskie dokumenti v knigo-khranilishchakh Gruzii* (Tbilisi, 1962); V. S. Puturidze, "Persidskie istoricheskie dokumenty v drevne khranilishchakh Gruzinskoi SSR," *Materialy Pervoi vsesoiuznoi nauchnoi konferentsii vostokovedov v Tashkente 4-11 iiunia 1957 g.* (Tashkent, 1958), pp. 900-905; A A. Semenov, ed., *Sobranie vostochnykh rukopisei Akademii nauk Uzbekskoi SSR,* 2 vols. (Tashkent, 1952-54); and a catalogue of manuscript collections in the Uzbek Academy of Sciences. See also *Katalog vostochnykh rukopisei fonda AN Tadzhikskoi SSR,* 2 vols. (Stalinabad, 1960-62).

[29]See D. I. Tikhonov, "Vostochnye rukopisi Instituta vostokovedeniia Akademii nauk SSSR," *UZIV,* no. 6 (1955), pp. 3-35.

[30]Tvertinova, *Vostokovedenye fondy,* pp. 156-57.

[31]T. I. Kukhtin, *Bibliografiia Afganistana, Literatura na russkom iazyke* (Moscow, 1962), 272 pp.

[32]A. K. Sverchevskaia, ed., *Bibliografiia Irana* (Moscow, 1967); and N. A. Kuznetsova, *Bibliografiia Irana, Literatura na russkom iazyke* (Moscow, 1967).

[33]A. K. Sverchevskaia and T. P. Cherman, *Bibliografiia Turtsii (1713-1917)* (Moscow, 1961), 267pp.; and by the same authors, *Bibliografiia Turtsii (1917-1958)* (Moscow, 1959), 190pp.

[34]On Russian and Soviet historiography before and since the October Revolution, see N. N. Tikhomirov et al., eds., *Ocherki po istorii istoricheskoi nauki v SSSR,* 5 vols. (Moscow, 1955-71); and V. I. Avdiev, N. P. Shastina, and V. A. Zhukovskii, *Ocherki po istorii russkogo vostokovedeniia,* 5 vols. (Moscow, 1953-60). There is a vast literature on the history of Russian and Soviet Oriental studies which, according to A. M. Kulikova, was initiated before the time of G. J. Kehr (1733), who is usually regarded as the father of Oriental studies. Kulikova notes that Peter the Great had authorized the German, G. V. Leibnitz (1711-16), to devise a program of higher studies that would include instruction in Arabic and Hebrew. See A. M. Kulikova, "Proekt vostokovednogo obrazovaniia v Rossii," *Narody Azii i Afriki (NAiA),* no. 4 (1970), pp. 133-39.

[35]I. Iu. Krachkovskii, *Ocherki po istorii russkoi arabistiki* (Moscow, 1950), 298pp.

[36]N. A. Smirnov, *Ocherki istorii izucheniia Islama v SSR* (Moscow, 1954), 275pp.

[37]At least three books have appeared in this series. G. L. Bondarevskii et al., *Politika Anglii na Blizhnem i Srednem Vostoke (1945-65)* (Moscow, 1966), 432pp., discuss political developments in the Persian Gulf, Yemen, Southern Arabia, and Iraq, and various British activities in regard to oil. B. G. Gafurov et al., *Politika SShA na Arabskom Vostoke* (Moscow, 1961), 282pp., cover mainly American ac-

tivities, including the economic penetration of the Arab World, during the 1955-58 period. B. G. Gafurov et al., eds., *Politika SShA na Blizhnem i Srednem Vostoke (SShA i strany SENTO)* (Moscow, 1960), 344pp., discuss American military, political and economic penetration into Turkey, Iran, and Pakistan.

[38]See N. M. Postovskaia, *Izuchenie drevnei istorii Blizhnego Vostoka v Sovetskome Soiuze (1917-1959) gg.* (Moscow, 1962), 438pp.; V. I. Avdiev, *Sovetskaia nauka o drevnem Vostoke za 40 let* (Moscow, 1958), 103pp.; and *Ocherki istorii istoricheskoi nauki v S.S.S.R.*, 4:559-89. For a bibliography on the ancient history of the Middle East, see *Iz istorii*, p. 209 (n.179). For Soviet interpretations of the major questions concerning the ancient Middle East one may consult also textbooks by S. S. Struve and V. I. Avdiev, published in 1941 and 1948, respectively.

[39]M. A. Korostsev, *Egyptology* (Moscow, Institute of the Peoples of Asia of the Academy of Sciences of the U.S.S.R., 1967), 11pp.

[40]On Semitic studies in Russia and the Soviet Union, see Konstantin Tsereteli, *Semitics* (Moscow, Institute of the Peoples of Asia of the Academy of Sciences of the U.S.S.R., 1967), 28pp.

[41]See G. A. Melikishvili and G. G. Giorgadze, *Urartology and Hittitology* (Moscow, Institute of the Peoples of Asia of the Academy of Sciences of the U.S.S.R., 1967), 26pp. Among the pioneer Urartologists were K. P. Patkanov, M. V. Nikol'skii, V. S. Golenishchev, V. F. Minorskii, A. A. Florenskii, S. V. Ter-Avetisian, A. N. Kaznakov, Mesrop Smbatiants, and A. Kapantsian.

[42]*Problemy Vostokovedeniia (PV)*, no. 2 (1960), and *NAiA*, no. 2 (1970), are dedicated almost entirely to Lenin, his ideas, and his influence on the Asian peoples. See M. A. Dandamaev's paper on Leninism and the social and economic formations in ancient Oriental societies in *NAiA*, no. 3 (1970), p. 238. See also G. F. Kim, ed., *Obshchee i osobennoe v istoricheskom razvitii stran Vostoka* (Moscow, 1966); and *Materialy diskussii ob obshchestvennykh formatsiiakh na Vostoke (Aziatskii sposob proizvodstva)* (Moscow, 1966), 248pp., which discusses the development of communes and communal relations, slave-owning relations, slavery during the feudal period, the Asiatic mode of production, etc.

[43]See A. T. Grigor'ian, ed., *Iz istorii nauki i tekhniki v stranakh Vostoka*, 3 vols. (Moscow, 1960-63); and A. T. Grigor'ian *Fiziko-matematicheskie nauki v stranakh Vostoka* (Moscow, 1966).

[44]A. V. Bank et al., *Byzantine Studies* (Moscow, Institute of the Peoples of Asia of the Academy of Sciences in the U.S.S.R., 1967), 24 pp., Z.V. Udal'tsova, *Sovetskoe vostokovedenie za 50 let* (Moscow, 1969).

[45]*Voprosy istorii*, no. 11 (1971), pp. 155-60.

[46]They are to be found in such collective works as *Ocherki po sotsial'no-ekonomicheskoi istorii Blizhnego Vostoka* (Tbilisi, 1968), 203pp. The essays, based on documentary materials, describe the socioeconomic relations of the Caucasus and the Near East in medieval times. See also A. I. Falina, ed., *Blizhnii i Srednii Vostok* (Moscow, 1962), 185pp., a collection of articles on topics covering the period from the history of Sumeria to the nineteenth century. The work is dedicated to Boris Nikolaevich Zakhoder.

[47]See, for example, F. M. Atsamba, ed., *Istoriia stran Azii i Afriki v srednie veka*

(Moscow, 1968), 495pp.; B. N. Zakhoder, *Istoriia vostochnogo srednevekovia*. *Kurs lektsii* (Moscow, 1944); *Istoriia stran zarubezhnogo vostoka v srednie veka* (Moscow, 1957), 373pp.; *Istoriia stran Azii i Afriki v srednie veka* (Moscow, 1968), 496pp.; V. I. Beliaev and I. P. Petrushevskii, "Istoriia stran Blizhnego vostoka v novom uchebnike po istorii srednevekovogo vostoka," *Sovetskoe vostokovedenie*, no. 6 (1958), pp. 95-105; and *Istoriia stran zarubezhnoi Azii v srednie veka* (Leningrad, 1970).

⁴⁸N. A. Smirnov, *Ocherki istorii izucheniia Islama v SSSR* (Moscow, 1954), pp. 58-66. See also K. Marks and F. Engel's, *Sochinenii*, 21:484 and 490-95; and K. Marks and F. Engel's, *O religii* (Moscow, 1955), p. 244; also L. Klimovich, "Marks i Engel's ob Islame i problema ego proiskhozhdeniia v sovetskom islamovedenii," *Revoliutsionnyi vostok, no. 3-4 (1933)*, pp. 59-92.

⁴⁹Page, *U.S.S.R. and Arabia*, p. 20.

⁵⁰On the Soviet explanation of the origin of Islam, see Evgenii A. Beliaev, *Sovremennyi Islam* (Moscow, 1959); and by the same author, *Araby, Islam i arabskii khalifat v ranee srednevekovie* (Moscow, 1965); 2nd ed. (Moscow, 1966), 279pp.; also B. N. Zakhoder, *Istoriia vostochnogo sredenevekovi'ia: Khalifat i Blizhnii vostok* (Moscow, 1944); and *Vsemirnaia istoriia* (Moscow, 1957), vol. 3, chap. 7, pp. 102-25.

⁵¹For a detailed discussion of this debate, see Smirnov, *Ocherki istorii izucheniia Islama v SSSR*, pp. 180-271.

⁵²On the founding of the Islamic state, see E. A. Beliaev, *Obrazovanie arabskogo gosudarstva v VII v.* (Moscow, 1954). See also L. I. Nadiradze, "Voprosy obshchestvenno-ekonomicheskogo stroia gosudarstva Arabov i Khalifata VII i VIII vv. v sovetskoi istoriografii," in *Istoriografiia stran Vostoka* (Moscow, 1969), pp. 5-82.

⁵³ *Vsemirnaia istoriia, vol. 3, chap. 7, p. 106* .

⁵⁴*Ibid.*, p. 106.

⁵⁵For a brief statement on the Arab conquest of Central Asia and the Caucasus by the well-known historians A. Iu. Iakubovskii and I. P. Petrushevskii, see *Vsemirnaia istoriia*, vol. 3, chap. 8, pp. 126-39; see also Vucinich, "Structure of Soviet Orientology," pp. 52-134.

⁵⁶L. I. Klimovich, *Islam* (Moscow, 1962). See reviews of the book in *Nauka i religiia*, no. 5 (1962), pp. 93-94; and *Voprosy istorii*, no. 3 (1962), pp. 108-109. Volume 6 of the collected works of V. V. Bartol'd contains his essays on the history of Islam and the Arab caliphate. See A. B. Khalidov, *Raboty po istorii islama i arabskogo khalifata*, vol. 6 (Moscow, 1966), 784 pp., in the collection of V. V. Bartol'd, *Sochineniia*, 6 vols. (Moscow, 1963-66).

⁵⁷I. P. Petrushevskii, "K istorii rabstva v khalifate VII-X vekov," *NAiA*, no. 3 (1971), pp. 60-71; L. I. Nadiradze, "K voprosu o rabstve v Aravii v VII v.," *Voprosy istorii i literatury stran zarubezhnogo vostoka* (Moscow, 1960), pp. 136-56; and L. I. Nadiradze, "Vopros o rabstve v khalifate VII-VIII v.," *NAiA*, no. 5 (1968), pp. 75-85.

⁵⁸Much has been written on Shamil and Miuridism, a question that has produced heated polemics over several years. See, for example, S. Bushuev, *O dvizhenii Shamilia* (Makhach-Kale, 1949). See also an earlier book by the same author, *Bor'ba gortsev za nezavisimost' pod rukovodstvom Shamilia* (Moscow, 1939). For an excellent

discussion of the Shamil question, see Lowell Tillett, *The Great Friendship* (Chapel Hill, N.C., 1969), pp. 130-170.

[59]T. Izimbetov, *Kritika ideologii sovremennogo Islama* (Moscow, 1962); and S. M. Gadzhiev *Osnovnye cherty sovremennogo Islama* (Makhach-Kale, 1962). Many widely scattered and largely fragmentary materials on Soviet policy toward Islam and the Muslims in general have been published in Soviet journals and newspapers.

[60]N. A. Smirnov, *Sovremennyi Islam* (Moscow, 1959); and T. Izimbetov, *Islam i sovremennost'* (Nukus, 1963), 161pp.

[61]E. A. Beliaev, *Musul'manskoe sektantstvo* (Moscow, 1957).

[62]E. A. Beliaev, *Klassovuiu sushchnost' Islama* (Moscow, 1934); and D. A. Petrushev, *Islam i ego reaktsionnaia sushchnost'* (Moscow, 1960).

[63]I. P. Tsamerian et al., eds., *Stroitel'stvo kommunizma i preodolenie religioznykh perezhitkov* (Moscow, 1966); O. A. Sukharev, *Islam v Uzbekistane* (Tashkent, 1960); and G.S. Snesarev, "O nekotorykh prichinakh sokhraneniia religiozno-bytovykh perezhitkov u Uzbekov Khorezma," *Sovetskaia etnografiia*, no. 2 (1957), p. 68.

[64]I. Iu. Krachkovskii, *Koran* (Moscow, 1962), 714pp.

[65]M. N. O. Osmanov, *Sufizm i sufiiskaia literatura*, vol. 3 (Moscow, 1965), 524pp., in collected works of E. E. Bertel's, *Izbrannye trudy*, 4 vols. (Moscow, 1960-65). The volume contains works on Sufism and Sufi ideas selected from classical Arabic, Persian, and Uzbek literature.

[66]For a short discussion of the Mazdikites, see I. P. Petrushevskii, "K istorii mazdakitov v epokhu gospodstva Islama," *NAiA*, no. 5 (1970), pp. 71-80.

[67]For Soviet studies of the Ismailites, see L. V. Stroeva, "Ismaility Irana i Sirii v zarubezhnoi i sovetskoi istoriografii," in G. V. Eftimov, *Istoriografiia i istochnikovedenie*, 1:138-48. In the fifties Stroeva wrote half a dozen short articles on various aspects of Ismailism.

[68]E. A. Beliaev, *Puritane Islama?* (Moscow, 1967), 262pp.

[69]V. V. Bartol'd, "K istorii krestianskikh dvizhenii v Perzii," in *Iz dalekogo i blizhnogo proshlogo* (Leningrad-Moscow, 1923), pp. 57, 60, 61. A collection of essays in honor of N. I. Kareev. Works of Bartol'd have been published in six volumes under the main editorship of B. G. Gafurov, each volume being edited by a prominent Orientalist. See V. V. Bartol'd, *Sochineniia*, 6 vols. (Moscow, 1963-66).

[70]I. P. Petrushevskii, "Gorodskaia znat' v gosudarstve Hulagidov," *Sovetskoe vostokovedenie*, no. 5 (Moscow, 1948), pp. 85-110.

[71]*Vsemirnaia istoriia*, vol. 3, chap. 34, pp. 494-510.

[72]A. E. Bertel's, *Nasir-i Khosrov i ismailizm* (Moscow, 1959). In the twenties V. A. Ivanov investigated Ismailis. He described the manuscripts on Ismailis in the Asiatic Museum and wrote a book on the dogma of the Pamir Ismailis. See *K dogmatike pamirskikh Ismailitov* (Tashkent, 1926).

[73]T. Izimbetov, *Islam i sovremennost'* (Nukus, 1963), 160pp.

[74]E. A. Beliaev, *Araby, Islam i arabskii khalifat v ranee srednevekovie*, 2nd ed. (Moscow, 1966), 279pp.

[75]L. I. Klimovich, *Islam, ego proiskhozhdenie i sotsial'naia sushchnost'* (Moscow, 1956); and by the same author, *Koran i ego dogmaty* (Alma-Ata, 1958).

[76]I. A. Genin and B. M. Dantsig, *Strany Iugo-zapadnoi Azii i Severnoi Afriki* (Alma-Ata, 1958).

[77]*K kritike teoreticheskikh osnov zapadno-evropeiskogo burzhuaznogo islamovedeniia* (Tashkent, 1962), 36pp.

[78]L. R. Gordon-Polonskoi, *Musul'manskie techeniia v obshchestvennoi mysli Indii i Pakistana* (Moscow, 1963); T. Izimbetov, *Kritika ideologii sovremennogo Islama* (Moscow, 1962), 22pp.; and Izimbetov, *Islam i sovremennost'*.

[79]In recent years the Muslim religious administration in Central Asia and Kazakhstan (SADUM) has issued a number of *fetwas* attempting to adjust Islam to modern conditions. See Tsamerian et al., *Stroitel'stvo kommunizma i preodolenie religioznykh perezhitkov*, p. 56. See also S. M. Gadzhiev, *Osnovnye cherty sovremennogo Islama* (Makhach-Kale, 1962); and Izimbetov, *Islam i sovremennost'*, pp. 7-9.

[80]Izimbetov, *Kritika ideologii sovremennogo Islama*, pp. 6-7; and *Islam i sovremennost'*, p. 7.

[81]D. A. Petrushev, *Islam i ego reaktsionnaia sushchnost'* (Moscow, 1960), a rather superficial treatment of the subject. See also O. A. Sukharev, *Islam v Uzbekistane* (Tashkent, 1960).

[82]Izimbetov, *Kritika ideologii sovremennogo Islama*, pp. 9-13.

[83]Izimbetov, *Islam i sovremennost'*.

[84]N. A. Simoniia, "O kharaktere natsional'no-osvoboditel'nykh revoliutsii," *NAiA*, no. 6 (1966), pp. 3-21; G. F. Kim and A. S. Kaufman, "Nekotorve problemy natsional'no-osvoboditel'nykh revoliutsii v svete leninskikh idei," *NAiA*, no. 5 (1969), pp. 3-17; and N. A. Simoniia, *O osobennostiakh natsional'no-osvoboditel-nykh revoliutsii* (Moscow, 1968), 90pp. Simoniia describes various tendencies in national liberation movements. Besides proletarian socialism, there are also independent socialisms, which he describes as Arab, African, and Indonesian socialisms, wrapped in national garb. See also R. A. Il'ianovskii, "K. Marks i problemy natsional'no-osvoboditel'nogo dvizheniia," *NAiA*, no. 6 (1968), pp. 3-19; and V. V. Asheva and G. G. Zhitovskii, *Tezisy iubileinoi nauchnoi sessii po problemam natsional'no-osvoboditel'nogo dvizheniia i ekonomicheskogo razvitiia osvoboditel'shikhsia stran na sovremennoi etape* (Moscow, 1970), 131pp. On the specifics of the national liberation movement, nationalism and bourgeois ideology, and the reliance of national liberation movements on the socialist countries, see S. N. Gregorian, ed., *Ideologiia sovremennogo natsional'nogo osvoboditel'nogo dvizheniia* (Moscow, 1966), 232pp.; A. A. Iskenderov, *Natsional'no-osvoboditel'noe dvizhenie i problemy zakonomernosti i perspektivy* (Moscow, 1970), 391 pp.; and the editorial, "Dal'neishee razvitie marksistskoleninskogo ucheniia o natsional'no-kolonial'nom voprose," *PV*, no. 1 (1961), pp. 3-12. See also G. S. Akopian, *Bor'ba narodov Blizhnego i Srednego Vostoka za natsional'nuiu nezavisimost'* (Moscow, 1953).

[85]A. N. Kheifets, "Leninskaia vneshnaia politika i natsional'no-osvoboditel'nye dvizheniia," *NAiA*, no. 12 (1970), pp. 211-16; *Lenin i natsional'no-osvoboditel'noe dvizhenie v stranakh vostoka* (Moscow, 1970), 504pp.; "XXIV S"ezd KPSS i problemy natsional'no-osvoboditel'nogo dvizheniia," *NAiA*, no. 3 (1971), pp. 3-14; and I. Iu. Semenov, "Iz istorii teoreticheskoi razrobotki V. I. Leninym natsional'nogo voprosa," *NAiA*, no. 4 (1966), pp. 106-09, 207-16.

[86]*Protiv fal'sifikatsii istorii kolonializma. Sbornik statei* (Moscow, 1962), 228pp.; M. L. Bondarevskii et al., *Protiv fal'sifikatsii istorii Vostoka. Sbornik statei* (Moscow, 1961); E. D. Modrzhinskaia, *Ideologiia sovremennogo kolonializma* (Moscow, 1961); N. P. Shmelev, *Ideologiia imperializma i problemy slaborazvytykh stran* Moscow, 1962); B. A. Shabas, *Ideologicheskie osnovy sovremennogo kolonializma* (Moscow, 1961); K. M. Popov et al., *Kolonializm vchera i segodnia* Moscow, 1964), 316 pp.; K. M. Popov, *Kolonializm zleishei vrag narodov Vostoka* (Moscow, 1964), 190pp.; K. M. Popov, *Protiv kolonializma. Sbornik statei* (Moscow, 1960), 172 pp.; I. S. Shern-Borisov, *Khristianskaia religiia i sovremennyi kolonializm* (Moscow, 1965), 115 pp. For views of Marx and Engels on the national and colonial question, see K. L. Seleznev, "K. Marks i F. Engel's o natsional' nokolonial'nom voprose," *NAiA*, no. 5 (1970), pp. 161-71.

[87]B. G. Gafurov, ed., *Politika SShA na Arabskom Vostoke* (Moscow, 1961), 282pp.; V. L. Bodionskii et al., *Politika SShA na Arabskom Vostoke* (Moscow, 1961); B. G. Gafurov, ed., *Politika SShA na Blizhnem i Srednem Vostoke (SShA i strany SENTO)* (Moscow, 1960), 344 pp.; I. V. Samylovskii, *Ekspansiia amerikanskogo imperializma na Blizhnem i Srednem Vostoke* (Moscow, 1955); O. E. Tuganova, *Politika SShA i Anglii na Blizhnem Vostoke* (Moscow, 1960); V. M. Kollontai, *Inostrannye investitsii v ekonomicheski slaborazvitykh stranakh* (Moscow, 1960); L. A. Fituni, *Problemy pomoshchi ekonomicheski slaborazvitym stranam* (Moscow, 1961); G. Andreev, *Ekspansiia dollara* (Moscow, 1961); G. A. Kochukova, "K voprosu o strukture ekonomicheskoi pomoshchi SShA stranam Blizhnego Vostoka," in L. M. Kulagina et al., *Strany Blizhnego i Srednego Vostoka* (Moscow, 1969), pp. 105-14; O. E. Tuganova, *Mezhdunarodnye otnosheniia na Blizhnem i Srednem vostoke* (Moscow, 1967).

[88]E. L. Shteinberg, *Istoriia britanskoi agressii na Srednem Vostoke* (Moscow, 1951); and G. L. Bondarevskii, ed., *Politika Anglii na Blizhnem i Srednem Vostoke (1945-1965)* (Moscow, 1965), 432pp., which discusses a whole list of problems—British imperialism in Egypt, the Sudanese question, the Palestinian war, the Anglo-Egyptian dispute before the United Nations, the Suez conflict (1951-52), the Baghdad Pact, the Iranian oil crisis, the Cyprus question, relations among the Middle Eastern peoples, national liberation movements, and several other topics. See also V. Prokof'ev, *Aggressivnyi blok SENTO* (Moscow, 1963), 105pp. Soviet writers blame English imperialism for backward conditions on Cyprus and insist that the people of Cyprus themselves determine their fate in line with the purpose of the United Nations and the Declaration of the Rights of Man. See E. Dzelepi, *Pravda o Kipre* (Moscow, 1958); and S. Beregov, "Kiprskii vopros i mezhdunarodnoe pravo," *Sovetskii ezhegodnik mezhdunarodnogo prava* (Moscow, 1958), p. 427.

[89]B. M. Dantsig, ed., *Politika Frantsii v Azii i Afrike (1945-1964 gg.)* (Moscow, 1965), 408pp.

[90]I. I. Etinger, *Ekspansiia FRG v arabskikh stranakh i Afrike* (Moscow, 1961). See also A. S. Silin, *Ekspansiia Germaniia na Blizhnem vostoke v kontse XIX veke* (Moscow, 1971).

[91]N. Khalfin, *Soviet Orientology and Studies in the History of Colonialism* (Moscow, Institute of the Peoples of Asia of the Academy of Sciences of the U.S.S.R., 1967).

[92]See Rubinstein, *Foreign Policy of the Soviet Union*, pp. 357-58; and Page, *U.S.S.R. and Arabia*, p. 15.

[93]Soviet authors consider oil exploitation the backbone of Western imperialism in the Middle East and see it as a plundering of the national resources of the Middle Eastern peoples. See V. S. Baskin, *Neftianie monopolii na Blizhnem i Srednem Vostoke* (Moscow, 1971); and R. N. Andreasian and A. Ia. El'ianov, *Blizhnii Vostok. Neft' i nezavisimost'* (Moscow, 1961), 319pp. These authors discuss the oil intrigues of imperialist states, the anti-imperialist movement among oil workers and the national bourgeoisie.

[94]*Vestnik AN SSSR*, no. 3 (1966), pp. 182-86.

[95]A. A. Guber, ed., *Velikii Oktiabr' i narody Vostoka. Sbornik 1917-1957* (Moscow, 1957), 420pp. For a brief statement on how Soviet writers interpret the influence of the October Revolution on Eastern peoples, see *NAiA*, no. 1 (1967), pp. 5-18; A. N. Kheifets, *Sovetskaia Rossiia i sopredel'nye strany Vostoka v gody grazhdanskoi voiny (1918-1920)* (Moscow, 1964), 471pp.; and I. V. Grankovskii et al., *Velikaia Octiabr'skaia sotsialisticheskaia revoliutsiia i natsional'no-osvoboditel'noe dvizhenie narodov Azii, Afriki, i Latinskoi Ameriki. Mezhdunarodnaia nauchnaia konferentsiia* (Baku, 1967), 397pp. The purpose of the last-named work is to show that the Soviet Union protects the peoples of Asia, Africa, and South America, and that the United States threatens their existence. The authors describe the U.S.S.R. as an anti-imperialist power and discuss the impact of the October Revolution on peoples of Soviet Asia. Despite its essentially propagandistic format, this symposium contains much useful information. See also *Velikii Oktiabr' i osvoboditel'naia bor'ba narodov Blizhnego i srednego Vostoka* (Baku, 1967).

[96]A. N. Kheifets, *Sovetskaia diplomatiia i narody Vostoka, 1921-1927* (Moscow, 1968), 326pp., discusses diplomatic relations with Asian countries and the conclusion of agreements with them (the Soviet-Iranian agreement of 1921, the Soviet-Afghan agreement of 1921, the Soviet-Turkish agreement of 1921, the Soviet-Chinese agreement of 1924). Up to 1927 the U.S.S.R. had agreements with only ten Asian countries; in 1967 it had diplomatic relations with sixty-four. The book shows how the Soviet Union supported the national liberation movements and encouraged the struggle against imperialism and colonialism. It concentrates on the diplomatic activities of Lenin and some Soviet diplomats (V. Chicherin, L. M. Karakhan, A. A. Ioffe, F. A. Ratshtein, and S. A. Arabov). It contains a detailed statement on M. V. Frunze's mission to Turkey. Other subjects discussed at length are the influence of the Bolshevik Revolution and Leninist ideas on the Orient, the impact of the Soviet victory on Germany and Japan, and the transformation of socialism into a world system. See also A. N. Kheifets, "Piatidesiateletie pervykh dogovorov sovetskoi strany s Iranom Afghanistanom i Turtsiei (1921 g.)," *NAiA*, no. 1 (1971), pp. 50-62.

[97]L. P. Deliusin et al., *Komintern i vostok* (Moscow, 1969), 512pp. The authors discuss the origin and purpose of the Comintern and Lenin's part in it. They criticize Mao Tse-tung and other Chinese leaders for alleged attempts to discredit and distort the aims and activities of the Comintern. They treat in addition the Comintern position on nationality, colonialism, and national liberation, as well as the establishment of the communist movement in China (1920-27) and other developments in China.

[98]On various kinds of Soviet economic and cultural help to Asian countries and on Soviet backing of the national liberation movement against colonialism, see D. G.

Chertkov et al., *SSSR i razvivaiushchiesia strany* (Moscow, 1966), 105pp.; *Ekonomicheskoe sotrudnichestvo Sovetskogo Soiuza s ekonomicheski slaborazvitym stranami (Moscow, 1962); SSSR i strany Vostoka* (Moscow, 1961); and V. Rimanov, *SSSR i ekonomicheski slaborazvitie strany* (Moscow, 1963).

[99]A. G. Bel'skii, "Kontseptsiia 'istinnogo natsionalizma' i ee reaktsionnaia sushchnost'," *NAiA*, no. 4 (1966), pp. 16-26. On nationalism of the oppressed and developing nations, see G. S. Akopian, "O dvukh tendentsiiakh natsionalizma ugnetennykh i razvivaiushchikhsia natsii," *NAiA*, no. 5 (1970), pp. 3-16, which includes a discussion of nationalism in the U.A.R. and Syria. On Lenin and the nationality question, see Iu. I. Semenov, "Iz istorii teoreticheskoi razrabotki V. I. Leninym natsional'nogo voprosa," *NAiA*, no. 4 (1966), pp. 106-109, 207-16.

[100]See, for example, S. D. Skazin et al., *Genezis kapitalizma v promyshlennosti i sel'skom khoziaistve* (Moscow, 1965), 495pp. The proceedings of this symposium are dedicated to the eightieth birthday of Nikola M. Druzhinin. See also by Skazin, *O genezise kapitalizma v stranakh vostoka (XV-XIX vv.). Materialy obsuzhdeniia* (Moscow, 1962).

[101]See, for example, R. G. Lana, "Esche raz o nekapitalisticheskom puti razvitiia," *NAiA*, no. 6 (1966), pp. 30-38. On revolutionary-democratic dictatorship and the noncapitalist way of development, see N. A. Simoniia, "Leninskaia ideia revoliutsionno-demokraticheskoi diktatury i nekapitalisticheskii put' razvitii," *NAiA*, no. 2 (1968), pp. 3-14. See also A. N. Kheifets, "Bor'ba V. I. Lenina protiv mel'ko-burzhuazno-narodnicheskikh vzgliadov na nekapitalisticheskoe razvitie," *NAiA*, no. 1 (1969), pp. 3-15, and *Iz istorii*, p. 208, n. 170.

[102]A. I. Levkovskii et al., eds., *Gosudarstvennyi kapitalizm v stranakh Vostoka* (Moscow, 1962), 292pp.

[103]See the proceedings of the symposium on classes and class struggle in developing countries published as *Klassy i klassovaia bor'ba v razvivaiushchikh stranakh* (Moscow, 1967), and Kheifets, "Bor'ba V. I. Lenina," pp. 3-15.

[104]I. V. Milovanov et al., *Rabochii klass i rabochee dvizhenie v stranakh Azii i Afriki* (Moscow, 1965), 316pp.; *Imperializm i bor'ba rabochego klassa* (Moscow, 1960); A. A. Iskenderov, ed., *Polozhenie rabochego klassa i rabochee dvizhenie v stranakh Azii i Afriki 1959-1961* (Moscow, 1961); A. A. Iskenderov, "Issledovanie sovetskikh uchenykh o rabochem klasse Azii i Afriki," *NAiA*, no. 3 (1963), pp. 110-23; by the same author, *Rabochii klass stran Azii i Afriki* (Moscow, 1966); and *Istoriia profsoiuznogo dvizheniia za rubezhem* (Moscow, 1958).

[105]*Iz istorii*, p. 208, n. 171. See also M. I. Luk'ianov, ed., *Agrarnye reformy v stranakh Vostoka* (Moscow, 1961), 234pp.; *Agrarnye reformy v razvivaiushchikhsia stranakh vysherazvitogo kapitalizma* (Moscow, 1965); and *Agrarnye otnosheniia v stranakh Vostoka* (Moscow, 1968).

[106]*Vestnik*, no. 2 (1966), pp. 173-75. The peasant movements in Asia and Africa were the main topics of discussion at a conference held October 28-November 2, 1965.

[107]*Iz istorii*, p. 208, n. 172.

[108]N. A. Kuznetsova, ed., *Problemy ekonomiki i istorii stran Blizhnego i Srednego Vostoka* (Moscow, 1966), 238pp.

[109]O. E. Tuganova, *Mezhdunarodnye otnosheniia na Blizhnem i Srednem Vostoke* (Moscow, 1967).

[110]B. G. Gafurov et al., *Lenin i Vostok* (Moscow, 1960), 306pp.; and A. N. Kheifets, ed., *Lenin—velikii drug narodov Vostoka* (Moscow, 1960), 248pp. See also report on the proceedings of the conference on Leninism and the development of democratic social thought among Eastern peoples, in *NAiA*, no. 2 (1970), pp. 161-71; *V.I. Lenin-drug narodov Vostoka. Sbornik dokumentov i materialov 1917-1924*, 2 vols. (Baku, 1967).

[111]See Grigor'ian, *Iz istorii* and *Fizikomatematicheskie nauki v stranakh Vostoka.*

[112]See, for example, *Istoriko-sotsiologicheskii traktat ibn Khalduna 'Mukaddima'* (Moscow, 1964), 223pp.

[113]See *NAiA*, no. 4 (1966), pp. 3-15, 264-69.

[114]al-Kavakibi abd ar-Rakhman, *Priroda despotizma i gibel'nost poraboshcheniia* (Moscow, 1963), 204pp.

[115]Z. I. Levin, *Filosof iz Fureiki. Amin ibn Fares ar-Reikhani* (Moscow, 1965), 71 pp.

[116]Kh. T. Kil'berg has translated Abd ar-Rahman al-Jabarti's monumental study of Egypt under Muhammad 'Ali, first published in 1879. The translator comments on the book and on al-Jabarti's interpretation of Muhammad 'Ali's relations with Napoleon. He displays no interest in evaluating al-Jabarti as an historian, but rather in rendering the work into Russian because of the valuable information it contains. See Abd ar-Rahman al-Dzhabarti, *Egipet pod vlast'iu Mukhammada Ali (1806-1821)*,, vol. 4 (Moscow, 1963), 787 pp.

[117]M. S. Ivanov, ed., *Etnicheskie protsessy i sostav naseleniia v stranakh Perednei Azii* (Moscow, 1963), 172pp. See also *Narod Perednei Azii* (Moscow, 1957) and *Perednoaziatskii etnograficheskii sbornik*, vol. 1 (Moscow, 1958).

[118]Many classics and modern works have been translated, among them the works of Firdausi, Rudaki, Vasifi, Nakhichevani, Qasimi, and others. For Arabic, Persian, Turkish, and other Middle Eastern sources on the history of the peoples of Eastern Europe and the Soviet Union, see A. S. Tvertinova, ed., *Vostochnye istochniki po istorii narodov Iugo-vostochnoi i Tsentral'noi Evropy. Sbornik statei i materialov* (Moscow, 1964), 304 pp. For Arabia and Persian sources on the history of Eastern Europe and the Volga region, see B. N. Zakhoder, *Kaspiiskii svod svedenii o Vostochnoi Evrope. Gorgan i Povolozh'e* (Moscow, 1962), 279pp. Also see I. Iu. Krachkovskii, "Arabskie istochniki po istorii Turkmen i Turkmenii IX-XIII v.," *Materialy po istorii Turkmen i Turkmenii*, vol. 1 (Moscow-Leningrad, 1939). A. P. Kovalevskii published the translation of Ahmad ibn Fadlan's book on travels in the Volga region in 921-22 A.D. Various other Arabic sources, including those on Africa, have been published as well.

[119]V. Nikitina et al., *Literatury drevnego Vostoka* (Moscow, 1962). This work discusses the literatures of Mesopotamia, Egypt, Palestine, Phoenicia, Iran, India, and China.

[120]B. B. Parnikel', "Ob osnovakh literaturnoi periodizatsii," *NAiA*, no. 6 (1965), pp. 136-40.

[121]See, for example, K. O. Iunusov, "Novye formy dramaticheskikh proizvedenii v

egipetskoi literatury," *NAiA*, no. 4 (1970), pp. 139-43. Much of the discussion in this article was occasioned by the seventieth anniversary of the Egyptian writer Tewfik al-Hakim.

[122]See, for example, a collection of essays entitled *M. Gor'kii i literatury zarubezhnogo Vostoka* (Moscow, 1968); Z. G. Osmanova, *M. Gor'kii i literatura Irana* (Moscow, 1961), 128pp.; A. I. Shifman, *Lev Tolstoi i Vostok* (Moscow, 1960), 480pp.; and P. I. Tartakovskii, "Poeziia Bunina i arabskii Vostok," *NAiA*, no. 1 (1971), pp. 106-21.

[123]B. Guseinov, *Poety Irana o Sovetskom Soiuze* (Moscow, 1965), 310 pp.

[124]See, for example, N. I. Konrad, *Zapud i Vostok* (Moscow, 1965), 310pp.; and I. S. Braginskii, ed., *Vzaimosviaz literatur Vostoka i Zapada* (Moscow, 1961), 251pp.

[125]See, for example, I. S. Braginskii et al., *Problemy stanovleniia realizma v literaturakh Vostoka. Materialy diskussii* (Moscow, 1964), 357pp.; and *Problemy realizma v literaturakh zarubezhnogo Vostoka* (Moscow, 1966).

[126]I. S. Braginskii et al., *Problemy teorii literatury i estetiki v stranakh Vostoka* (Moscow, 1964), 340pp.

[127]See, for example, V. Solov'ev et al., *Arabskaia literatura* (Moscow, 1964).

[128]Several series are being published: *Literatura Vostoka* (Oriental literature), *Pamiatniki literatur narodov Vostoka* (Monuments of the literatures of the peoples of Asia), *Perevody* (Translations), *Pamiatniki pis'menosti vostoka* (Monuments of Oriental writing), *Sovremennaia vostochnaia novella* (The contemporary Eastern novel), *Literatura i fol'klor narodov Azii, Afriki, Avstralii i Okeanii* (Literature and folklore of the peoples of Asia, Africa, Australia, and Oceania), and *Skazki i mify narodov Vostoka* (Stories and myths of the peoples of the Orient). Many special volumes are published, including translations of ancient and medieval writings.

[129]I. I. Fil'shtinskii, *Arabskaia klassicheskaia literatura* (Moscow, 1965). See also I. Ia. Gamidov, "O trudakh ibn Kutaiby 'Poeziia i poety' i "Istochniki soobshchenii," *NAiA,* no. 5 (1970), pp. 147-53.

[130]V. Solov'ev, I. Fil'shtinskii, D. Kusupov, *Arabskaia literatura. Kratkii ocherk* (Moscow, 1964).

[131]See G. Sh. Sharbatov, *Arabic Studies (Philology)* p. 6, for listing of published, works.

[132]Ibragim Tatarly, "Sabakhattin Ali i A. S. Pushkin," *NAiA*, no. 3 (1971), pp. 86-92, an article that discusses Pushkin's influence on Sabakhattin Ali (1907-48).

[133]N. A. Aizenshtein, *Iz istorii turetskogo realizma. Zametki o turetskoi proze (70-e gody XIX v.-30-e gody XX v.)* (Moscow, 1968), 283pp., contains an index of names and titles of works.

[134]Kh. Kiamilev, *U istokov sovremennoi turetskoi literatury* (Moscow, 1969), pp. 125-26.

[135]N. A. Baskakov, *Tiurskie iazyki* (Moscow, 1960), 247 pp., supplies a short account of the development and formation of all Turkic languages and their relationships. It includes useful charts and indexes. See also E. N. Nadzhip, "Bol'shoe dostizhenie sovetskoi tiurkologii (k vykhody v svet 'Drevnetiurskogo slovaria')," *NAiA*, no. 2 (1970), pp. 169-79. In 1969 there appeared the best edition thus far of *Drevnetiurskii slovar'* (An ancient Turkic dictionary) (Leningrad, 1969),

676pp. See also A. N. Kononov, *Turkic Philology* (Moscow, 1967), 52pp.

[136]See, for example, M. N. D. Osmanov, "Tip, metod i stil' persidskoi poezii X veka," *NAiA*, no. 1 (1970), pp. 151-56.

[137]On the literature of Persia and the study of this subject in the Soviet Union, see I. S. Braginskii, *Persidskaia literatura* (Moscow, 1963), 213pp. See also Iu. F. Borshchevskii and Iu. E. Bregel', "O sozdanii bibliograficheskogo svoda istorii persidsko-tadzhikskoi literatury," *NAiA*, no. 3 (1970), pp. 104-19.

[138]N. A. Kuznetsova, "Problema 'Oktiabr" i Iran v sovetskoi literature" in L. R. Polonskaia, *Sovremennaia istoriografiia zarubezhnogo Vostoka. Oktiabr' i natsional'no-osvoboditel'naia bor'ba* (Moscow, 1969), pp. 46-57.

[139]M. N. Ivanov, *Oktiabr'skaia revoliutsiia i Iran* (Moscow, 1958).

[140]Osmanova, *M. Gor'kii i literatura Irana*; and Z. G. Fil'shtinskaia, "Maksim Gor'kii v sovremennoi progressivnoi persidskoi literature," *KSIV*, no. 4 (1952), pp. 45-51.

[141]I. M. Oransky, *Old Iranian Philology and Iranian Linguistics* (Moscow, Institute of the Peoples of Asia of the Academy of Sciences of the U.S.S.R., 1967).

[142]I. M. Oranskii, "Iz zametok o novykh sovetskikh rabotakh po iranskoi dialektologii," *NAiA*, no. 1 (1971), pp. 174-76, a review of Soviet work on Iranian dialectology which includes an extensive bibliography. On October 20-22, 1970, a Conference on Iranistics was held in the U.S.S.R. under the auspices of the Institute of Linguistics of the Academy of Sciences of the U.S.S.R. See *NAiA*, no. 3 (1971), pp. 229-31.

[143]M. N. Bogoliubov, "Iranskoe iazykoznanie v Leningrade (1917-1957)," *Uchenye zapiski IVAN*, 25 (1960):303-318.

[144]For the list of Iranists associated with this school, see Oransky, *Old Iranian Philology*, pp. 8-9.

[145]Oransky, *Old Iranian Philology*, 10-11.

[146]*Nauchnaia konferentsiia po iranskoi filologii. Tezisy dokladov* (Leningrad, 1962). See *Voprosy istorii*, no. 5 (1962), pp. 252-54; and *Ocherki po istorii izucheniia iranskikh iazykov* (Moscow,1962),148pp. The Institute of Language and Thought of N. Ia. Marr published a two-volume proceedings of a symposium on the Iranian language entitled *Iranskie iazyki* (Moscow-Leningrad, 1950), in which several Iranian languages, including Kurdish, were discussed.

[147]Oransky, *Old Iranian Philology*, pp. 36-38.

[148]On Semitics in Russia and the Soviet Union, see Konstantin Tsereteli, *Semitics* (Moscow, Institute of the Peoples of Asia of the Academy of Sciences of the U.S.S.R., 1967), 28pp.; G. Sh. Sharbatov, ed., *Semitskie iazyki. Sbornik statei* (Moscow, 1963), 250pp.; and A. M. Gazov-Ginzberg, *Byl li iazyk izobrazitelen v svoikh istokakh? (Svidetel'stvo prasemitskogo zapasa kornei)* (Moscow, 1965).

[149]See "Vahhabity," in *Bol'shaia Sovetskaia Entsiklopediia (BSE)*, 7 (1951):64-65; "Iemen," *BSE*, 19 (1953):179-83.

[150]Page, *U.S.S.R. and Arabia*, pp. 25-26.

[151]*Ibid.*, pp. 27-30.

[152]The first Conference of Arabists was held in May 1959 and the second in January 1963.

[153]See N. A. Arsharuni, "Aktuel'nye zadachi arabisticheskikh issledovanii," *Vestnik AN SSSR*, November 1969, pp. 134-35.

[154]*NAiA*, no. 2 (1970), pp. 221-22.

[155]See, for example, *Ocherki po sotsial'no-ekonomicheskoi istorii Blizhnego vostoka* (Tbilisi, 1968), 203pp. The essays in this work, based on documentary materials, describe socioeconomic relations in the Caucasus and the Near East in medieval times. See also A. I. Falina, ed., *Blizhnii i Srednii Vostok* (Moscow, 1962), dedicated to Boris Nikolaevich Zakhoder, 185pp., a collection of articles on topics covering the period from the history of Sumeria to the nineteenth century.

[130]B. G. Gafurov, ed., *Politika SShA na Arabskom Vostoke* (Moscow, 1961); and I. I. Etinger, *Ekspansiia FRG v arabskikh stranakh i Afrike* (Moscow, 1961).

[157]M. S. Lazarev, *Krushenie turetskogo gospodstva na Arabskom Vostoke (1914-1918 gg.)* (Moscow, 1960).

[158]For general works on the Arabic world and the Middle East, see E. A. Lebedev, ed., *Arabskie strany. Istoriia* (Moscow, 1963); E. A. Beliaev, ed. *Arabskie strany. Istoriia. Ekonomika* (Moscow, 1966), 283pp.; and *Afrikanskii sbornik. Istoriia*, vol. 1 (Moscow, 1963), a collection containing essays on economic relations between the African countries and the U.S.S.R., on contemporary politics, on workers' movements, on the problem of education, on relations between the Arab states, and on foreign monopolies in Egypt before the Second World War. There are, of course, general works on particular subjects, on the Arab world, and on the Middle East as a whole. See, for example, a work on Arab government by I. Levin and V. Mamaev, *Gosudarstvennyi stroi stran arabskogo vostoka* (Moscow, 1963, 1966). See also *Ocherki po istorii arabskikh stran* (Moscow, 1959); I. S. Isaikin, *SSSR: Arabskie strany 1917-1960 gg. Dokumenty i materialy* (Moscow, 1961); Basistov and I. Ianovskii, *Strany Blizhnego i Srednego Vostoka* (Tashkent, 1958); N. I. Proshin, *Strany Araviiskogo Poluostrova* (Moscow, 1958); I. M. Reisner and B. K. Rubtsov, eds., *Novaia istoriia zarubezhnogo Vostoka,* 2 vols. (Moscow, 1952); 2nd ed. (Moscow, 1971); *Noveishaia istoriia stran zarubezhnogo Vostoka,* 4 vols. (Moscow, 1954-60); *Novaia istoriia zarubezhnoi Azii i Afriki* (Leningrad, 1969); I. A. Genin, *Strany Iugozapadnoi Azii i Severnoi Afriki* (Moscow, 1960); *Noveishaia istoriia stran zarubezhnoi Azii i Afriki* (Leningrad, 1963); and *Strany Blizhnego i Srednego Vostoka* (Moscow, 1964).

On Egypt exclusively, see N. A. Dlin, *Ob'edinennaia arabskaia respublika* (Moscow, 1963), 141pp. V. I. Kiselev, L. L. Lenov, and many others have written on Egypt and the U.A.R. See also Sh. Isavi, *Egipet v seredine XX veka* (Moscow, 1958).

[159]See, for example, L. A. Semenova, *Salkakh as-Din i mamluki v Egipte* (Moscow, 1966).

[160]See the statement by T. V. Eremeeva in *Izvestiia AN SSSR*, vol. 5, no. 2 (1948).

[161]L. A. Fridman, *Kapitalsticheskoe razvitie Egipta, 1882-1935* (Moscow, 1963). N. A. Ivanov and L. A. Semenova have also written on the genesis of capitalism in Egypt. See N. A. Ivanov, "Agrarnye otnosheniia v Egipte v poslednoi chetvrti XVIII-nachale XIX veka," in *O genezise kapitalisma v stranakh Vostoka.* See also *Eksport kapital i kolonial'naia eksploatatsiia Egipta v 1882-1913 godakh.*

[162]*Voblikov, Noveishaia istoriia*, p. 19.

[163]I. S. Isaikin, *SSSR i arabskie strany 1917-1960 gg. Dokumenty i materialy* (Moscow, 1961). See also A. E. Ioffe, "Nachal'nyi etap vzaimootnosheniia Sovetskogo Soiuza s arabskimi i afrikanskimi stranami (1923-1932)," *NAiA*, no. 6 (1965), pp. 57-66.

[164]Voblikov, *Noveishaia istoriia*, p. 19.

[165]F. M. Atsamba, *Formirovanie rabochego klassa v Egipte i ego ekonomicheskoe polozhenie 1914-1952* (Moscow, 1960).

[166]A. F. Sultanov, *Polozhenie egipetskogo krest'ianstva pered zemel'noi reformi 1952 g.* (Moscow, 1958).

[167]See Sh. N. Kurdgilashvili, *Revoliutsiia 1952 g. i krakh britanskogo gospodstva v Egipte* (Moscow, 1966), 166 pp.; B. G. Seiranian, *Egipet v bor'be za nezavisimost' 1945-1952* (Moscow, 1970), 299pp., examines the history of Egypt between 1945 and 1952 in some detail, and analyzes the class struggle, the general political situation, the essence of English imperialism, and the English attempts to control Egypt. See also R. M. Avakov and G. I. Mirskii, "Desiat let anti-imperialisticheskoi bor'by egipetskogo naroda (1952-62)," *NAiA*, no. 4 (1962), pp. 39-42.

[168]Voblikov, *Noveishaia istoriia*, pp. 20-21 and 24.

[169]*Ibid.*, pp. 24-25.

[170]*Ibid.*, pp. 29-30.

[171]*Ibid.*, pp. 32-37.

[172]*Ibid.*, p. 33.

[173]*Ibid.*, p. 34.

[174]*Ibid.*, pp. 34-36.

[175]B. G. Seiranian, *Egipet v bor'be za nezavisimost'*, pp. 285-88. See also L. N. Vatolina, "Rost natsional'nogo samoznaniia narodov arabskikh stran (1945-1955 gg.)," *Sovetskoe vostokovedenie*, no. 5 (1955), pp. 56-58.

[176]Seiranian, *Egipet v bor'be za nezavisimost'*, p. 287.

[177]*Ibid.*, pp. 286-87.

[178]Voblikov, *Noveishaia istoriia*, pp. 31-32.

[179]A. M. Goldobin, "Razgrom assotsiatsii brat'ev-musul'man v Egipte v 1954 g.," *Uchenye zapiski leningradskogo universiteta. Seriia vostokovedcheskikh nauk*, vol. 302, no. 14 (Leningrad, 1962).

[180]Seiranian, *Egipet v bor'be za nezavisimost'*, p. 68.

[181]*Ibid.*, pp. 286-87.

[182]On the Revolution of 1952, see Kurdgilashvili, *Revoliutsiia 1952*.

[183]*Seiranian, Egipet v bor'be za nezavisimost'*, p. 287.

[184]*Ibid.*, pp. 287-88.

[185]See H. I. Kil'berg, *Egypt's Struggle for Independence, 1918-1924* (Leningrad, 1950).

[186]Voblikov, *Noveishaia istoriia*, pp. 31-32.

[187]Kurdgilashvili, *Revoliutsiia 1952*, and A. S. Protopopov, *Sovetskii Soiuz i Suetskii krizis 1956 goda* (Moscow), 252pp. On the Suez, see also an earlier work by I. A. Dement'ev, *Suetskii kanal* (Moscow, 1954); and N. N. Lebedev,

"Imperialisticheskaia aggressiia protiv Egipta v 1956 g.," *Voprosy istorii*, no. 9 (1953), pp. 66-81. See also G. V. Fokeev, "Bor'ba za likvidatsiiu posledstviia agresii protiv Egipta v 1956-1957 godakh," *Voprosy istorii*, No. 8 (1972), pp. 64-78.

[188]Protopopov, *Sovetskii Soiuz i Suetskii krizis*, p. 213.

[189]*Ibid.*

[190]*Ibid.*, pp. 216-17.

[191]*Krasnaia zvezda*, April 29, 1950.

[192]See, for example, L. N. Vatolina, "Rost natsional'nogo samoznaniia narodov arabskikh stran (1945-1955 gg.)," *Sovetskoe vostokovedenie*, no. 5 (1955), pp. 56-58.

[193]Protopopov, *Sovetskii Soiuz i Suetskii krizis*, p. 236.

[194]*Ibid.*, p. 241.

[195]Page, *U.S.S.R. and Arabia*, p. 47.

[196]*Ibid.*, p. 217.

[197]*Ibid.*, p. 219.

[198]Voblikov, *Noveishaia istoriia*, pp. 36-37.

[199]D. A. Ol'derogge, *Zapadni Sudan v XV-XIX vv. Ocherki po istorii i istorii kultury* (Moscow-Leningrad, 1960).

[200]S. R. Smirnov, *Istoriia Sudana* (Moscow, 1968), 294pp., contains a brief sketch of Sudanese history before the nineteenth century and a discussion of Turkish-Egyptian rule, of the Mahdi uprising, of the Sudan under British rule, of socioeconomic development, and of the struggle for independence.

[201]I. I. Potekhin, *Afrika smotrit v budushchee* (Moscow, 1960), 86pp.

[202]On the most recent Soviet view regarding the problem of "unity" in the Sudan, see N. A. Pozdniakov, "Problema natsional'nogo edinstva Sudana," *NAiA*, no. 4 (1970), pp. 27-36.

[203]S. R. Smirnov, *Vosstanie Makhdistov v Sudane* (Moscow-Leningrad, 1950).

[204]On Anglo-Egyptian administration of the Sudan, see Iu. D. Dmitrievskii, *Anglo-Egipetskii Sudan* (Moscow, 1951).

[205]P. A. Petrov, *Sudan. Ekonomika i vneshnaia torgovlia* (Moscow, 1961).

[206]T. F. Fiodorov, *Finansy i kredit Sudana* (Moscow, 1962).

[207]On the struggle for the independence of the Sudan, see V. I. Kiselev, *Put' Sudana k nezavisimosti* (Moscow, 1958).

[208]The All-Union Conference of Africanists held in Moscow on October 20-24, 1969, considered many theoretical questions concerning sub-Saharan countries as well as North Africa. See *NAiA*, no. 3 (1970), pp. 211-17.

[209]See, for example, N. Arsharuni, *Liviia* (Moscow, 1965).

[210]V. Smirnov, *Tunis. Ekonomicheskii ocherk* (Moscow, 1962).

[211]N. I. Ivanov, *Gosudarstvennyi stroi Tunisa* (Moscow, 1962).

[212]I. V. Potemkin, *Ekonomicheskaia politika Frantsii v stranakh Magriba* (Moscow, 1960).

[213]N. A. Ivanov, *Sovremennyi Tunis* (Moscow, 1959).

[214]R. G. Landa, *Natsional'no-osvoboditel'noe dvizhenie v Alzhire* (Moscow, 1962);

and also by the same author, *Alzhir sbrasivaet okovy* (Moscow, 1961), and "Novaia ekonomicheskaia politika Alzhira (1365-1969 gg.)," *NAiA*, no. 1 (1970), pp. 15-28. 28.

[215]N. S. Lutskaia, *Respublika Rif* (Moscow, 1959), 211pp.

[216]G. Kanaev, *Profsoiuznoe dvizhenie v Marokko* (Moscow, 1962).

[217]Iu. M. Golovin, *Marokko* (Moscow, 1964).

[218]I. M. Smilianskaia, *Siriia i Palestina pod turetskim pravitel'stvom v istoricheskim i politicheskim otnosheniiam* (Moscow, 1962), 326pp.; and by the same author, *Krestianskoe dvizhenie v Livane v pervoi polovine XIX v.* (Moscow, 1965), 226pp., which discusses the anti-feudal movements, the Druze-Maronite conflicts (1841-55 and 1860), the peasant movement in the 1850s, general socioeconomic development, and cultural rebirth. In addition it compares the uprisings of 1782, 1784, 1840, 1845, and 1860.

[219]M. T. Panchenkova, *Politika Frantsii na Blizhnem Vostoke i Siriiskaia ekspeditsiia 1860-1861 gg.* (Moscow, 1966), 270pp.

[220]K. M. Bazili, *Siriia i Palestina pod turetskim pravitel'stvom* (Moscow, 1962).

[221]For a short work on the founding of the independent Syrian republic, see N. O. Oganesian, *Obrazovanie nezavisimoi Siriiskoi Respubliki (1939-1946)* (Moscow, 1968), 115pp.

[222]E. N. Mel'nikov, "Osobennosti razvitiia sovremennogo Livana," *NAiA*, no. 3 (1971), pp. 51-59.

[223]See, for example, V. B. Lutskii, *Natsional'no-osvoboditel'naia voina v Sirii (1925-1927 gg.)* (Moscow, 1964), 336pp.

[224]See, for example, V. K. Katin, *Livan. Ekonomika i vneshnaia torgovlia* (Moscow, 1961).

[225]Smilianskaia, *Krestianskoe dvizhenie v Livane.*

[226]See, for example, *Sovremennyi Livan* (Moscow, 1963).

[227]See, for example, A. A. Dolinina, "Livanskii poet o Lenine," *NAiA*, no. 2 (1970), pp. 116-21; and G. Sh. Sharbatov, "Arabskie poety o Lenine," *NAiA*, no. 2 (1970), pp. 93-99.

[228]L. N. Kotlov, *Iordaniia v noveishee vremia* (Moscow, 1962). See also *Sovremennaia Iordaniia* (Moscow, 1964).

[229]See, for example, A. Iu. Iakubovskii, "Ob ispol'nykh arendakh v Irake v VIII v.," *Sovetskoe vostokovedenie*, no. 4 (Moscow-Leningrad, 1947). pp. 171-84.

[230]See, for example, L. N. Kotlov, *Natsional'no-osvoboditel'noe vosstanie 1920 goda v Irake* (Moscow, 1958), 214pp.

[231]G. I. Mirskii, *Iraq v smutnoe vremia, 1930-1941* (Moscow, 1961).

[232]I. M. Reisner and B. K. Rubtsov, *Novaia istoriia stran zarubezhnogo Vostoka*, 2 vols. (Moscow, 1952).

[233]See *Problemy vostokovedeniia*, no. 1 (1961), pp. 94-105. See also O. Gerasimov, *Irakskaia neft'* (Moscow, 1969), 180pp.

[234]See, for example, A. Al'badari, "Front natsional'nogo edinstva v Irake (1946-1958)," *NAiA*, no. 6 (1965), pp. 62-73. See also D. Ruindezh, *Bor'ba irakskogo*

naroda protiv Bagdadskogo pakta (1954-1955 gg.) (Baku, 1966).

[235]G. S. Chiparshvili, *Razvitie sel'skokhoziaistvennogo kooperativnogo dvizheniia v Irane* (Tbilisi, 1968), 152pp.

[236]See, for example, B. M. Dantsig, *Irak v proshlom i nastoiashchem* (Moscow, 1960), 255pp.; S. S. Pegov and S. N. Alitovskii, *Iraq* (Moscow, 1966); and *Sovremennyi Iraq* (Moscow, 1966). In 1970 it was announced that a major study of Iraq by A. Ch. Seiranian and A. F. Fedchenko was in press.

[237]K. P. Matveev and I. I. Mariukhania, *Assiriiskii vopros vo vremia i posle pervoi mirovoi voiny (1914-1933 gg.)* (Moscow, 1963), 143pp., discusses Iraqi oppression of the Assyrians and Muslim religious antagonism toward them. See also M. A. Kamal', *Natsional'no-osvobodit'noe dvizhenie v Irakskom Kurdistane* (Baku, 1967).

[238]Page, *U.S.S.R. and Arabia*, p. 20, and V. B. Lutskii, *Angliiskii i amerikanskii imperializm na Blizhnem Vostok* (Moscow, 1948).

[239]See, for example, "Ideologiia rannego vakhabizma," *NAiA,* no. 6 (1965), pp. 113-21.

[240]A. M. Vasil'ev, *Puritane Islama?* (Moscow, 1967), 262pp.

[241]*Araby v bor'be za nezavisimost'* (Moscow, 1957), p. 16.

[242]"XX S"ezd Kommunisticheskoi Partii," *Sovetskoe vostokovedenie,* no. 1 (1956), p. 6; and Page, *U.S.S.R. and Arabia,* p. 32.

[243]See, for example, A. I. Levin, "Saudovskaia Araviia," in *Araby v bor'be za nezavisimost'* (Moscow, 1957); and I. P. Beliaev, *Amerikanskii imperializm v Saudovskoi Aravii* (Moscow, 1957).

[244]N. I. Proshin, *Saudovskaia Araviia. Istoriko-ekonomicheskii ocherk* (Moscow, 1964), 302pp.

[245]See references on Saudi Arabia in I. Levin and V. Mamaev, *Gosudarstvennyi stroi stran Arabskogo vostoka* (Moscow, 1957).

[246]Page, *U.S.S.R. and Arabia,* p. 50.

[247]A. I. Pershits, "Rodoplemennaia organizatsiia i plemennyi sostav kochevnikov severnoi Aravii v XIX-XX vv.," *Kratkie Soobshchenia Instituta Etnografii* (hereafter *KSIE*), no. 7 (1949), pp. 70-74; A. I. Pershits, "Khoziaistvennyi byt' kochevnikov Saudovskoi Aravii," *Sovetskaia etnografiia,* no. 1 (1952), pp. 104-12; A. I. Pershits, "Proizvodstvennye otnosheniia u kochevnikov severnoi Aravii v XIX-nachale XX vv.," *KSIE,* no. 21 (1954), pp. 51-58; and A. I. Pershits, "Araby Saudovskoi Aravii," *Sovetskaia etnografiia,* no. 3 (1955), pp, 127-41.

[248]A. I. Pershits, *Khoziaistvo i obshchestvenno-politicheskii stroi Severnoi Aravii v XIX-pervoi treti XX vv.* (Moscow, 1961), 221pp.

[249]*Ibid.,* p. 221.

[250]Page, *U.S.S.R. and Arabia,* pp. 16-17.

[251]G. L. Bondarevskii, "Osvoboditel'naia bor'ba narodov Iemena v kontse XIX v. i pozitsiia Velikobritanii," *Voprosy istorii,* no. 6 (1971), pp. 100-115; also Page, *U.S.S.R. and Arabia,* pp. 16-17.

[252]On the anti-imperialist policies of Saudi Arabia and Yemen, and the soft and optimistic Soviet line regarding these countries, see E. Primakov, *Strany Aravii i*

kolonializm (Moscow, 1956). See also Page, *U.S.S.R. and Arabia, p. 33.*

[253]Page, *U.S.S.R. and Arabia,* p. 48.

[254]*Ibid.,* p. 49.

[255]*Ibid.,* pp. 37-39.

[256]E. K. Golubovskaia, *Iemen* (Moscow, 1965).

[257]See, for example, G. Akopian, "O natsional'no-osvoboditel'nom dvizhenii narodov Blizhnego i Srednego Vostoka," *Voprosy ekonomiki,* no. 1 (1953), p. 67.

[258]See A. I. Levin, "Angliiskie vladeniia v Aravii," in G. L. Bondarevskii, ed., *Poslednie kolonii v Azii* (Moscow, 1958); and Page, *U.S.S.R. and Arabia,* pp. 49-50.

[259]Page, *U.S.S.R. and Arabia,* p. 51.

[260]See, for example, L.V. Val'kova, *Angliiskaia kolonial'naia politika v Adene i adenskikh Protektoratakh* (Moscow, 1968), 157 pp. For an excellent survey of Soviet policy toward the governments of the Arabian Peninsula, see George S. Rentz, "The Soviet Union and the Arabian Peninsula" (Hoover Institution, unpublished manuscript).

[261]L. S. Zvereva, *Kuveit* (Moscow, 1964).

[262]*BSE,* 15 (1952):377-79; 17 (1952):515-17; and 39 (1956):138.

[263]G. S. Nikitina, *Gosudarstvo Izrail'* (Moscow, 1968), 413pp.

[264]*Ibid.,* pp. 366-68.

[265]*Ibid.* The most recent Soviet publications on Zionism are a collection of essays entitled *Ochag sionizma i agressii. Sbornik statei* (Moscow, 1971), 111pp.; and books by Iu. Ivanov, *Ostorozhno: Sionizm! Ocherki po ideologii, organizatsii i praktike sionizma,* 2nd ed. (Moscow, 1971), 206pp.; and M. Gol'denberg, *Mify sionizma* (Kishinev, 1971), 160pp. See also a collective work, *Reaktsionnaia, sushchnost sionizma. Sbornik materialov* (Moscow, 1972), 206 pp. On Zionism as an instrument of American foreign policy, see A. K. Kislov, "Belyi dom i sionistskoe lobbi," *Voprosy istorii,* No. 1 (1973), p. 48-61.

[266]S. A. Andreev, *Izrail'* (Moscow, 1962), 118pp.

[267]*Ibid.,* pp. 4-9.

[268]K. Ivanov and Z. Sheinas, *Gosudarstvo Izrail'. Ego polozhenie i politika* (Moscow, 1959), 188pp. See pp. 2, 13, 97-98, 121-31, 147, 171.

[269]On Turkish studies in the Soviet Union, see B. Dantzig, *The History, Economy and Geography of Turkey* (Moscow, Institute of the Peoples of Asia of the Academy of Sciences, 1967), 31pp. The late Vladimir Aleksandrovich Gordlevskii, foremost Soviet Orientalist, published many works on the Turkish language, on the history of Turkish literature and folklore, and on the medieval history of Asia Minor. His selected works have been published in three volumes under the editorship of N. A. Baskakov et al. The first volume contains Gordlevskii's historical works, the second his studies on the Turkish language and literature, and the third the writings on Turkish culture and society. See V. A. Gordlevskii, *Izbrannye sochineniia,* 3 vols. (Moscow, 1960-62). The fourth volume is yet to appear. See also A. N. Kononov, ed., *Tiurkologicheskii sbornik, 1971* (Moscow, 1972), 290pp.

[270]See A. S. Tvertinova, "Vtoroi traktat Kochibeia," *UZIV,* no. 6 (1953), pp. 212-68, a document written by a seventeenth-century Ottoman author. On the basis of

this document, Tvertinova analyzes the character of Ottoman feudalism. See also *BSE*, 43 (1956):494; A. S. Tvertinova, "Nekotorye nereshenye problemy v kharakteristike turetskogo feodalizma," in *Blizhnii i Srednei Vostok* (Moscow, 1968), and by the same author, "K voprosu o demenial'nom zemlevladenii feodalov-lennikov v Osmanskoi imperii v XV-XVIII vv.," *KSIV*, no. 38 (Moscow, 1960).

[271]*Literaturnaia gazeta*, May 27, 1952, p. 2; and *Voprosy istorii*, no. 1 (1956), pp. 216-19. *Vizantiiskii vremennik*, no. 7 (1953), is dedicated to the conquest of Constantinople and the significance of this event. See especially M. N. Levchenko, "Zavoevanie turkami Konstantinopolia v 1453 g. i istoricheskie posledovaniia etogo sobytiia, *Vizantiiskii vremmenik*, no 7 (1953), pp. 3-8. On the controversial question regarding the final stages of the Byzantine Empire, see also Z. V. Udal'tsova, "K voprosu ob otsenke trudov akad. F. I. Uspenskogo," *Voprosy istorii*, no. 6 (1949), p. 126.

[272]A. Miller, *Mustafa pasha Bairaktar* (Moscow, 1947), 507pp.; and G. Z. Aliev, *Turtsiia v period pravleniia maladoturok (1908-1914)* (Moscow, 1972), 388 pp. On Young Turks, also see Iu. A. Petrosian, *Mladoturetskoe dvizhenie* (vtoraia polovina XIX-nachalo XX v. (Moscow, 1972). On the Tanzimat, see F. Sh. Shabanov, *Gosudarstvennyi stroi i pravovaia sistema Turtsii v periode Tanzimata* (Baku, 1967). On the "New Ottomans," see Iu. A. Petrosian, *"Novye osmany" i bor'ba za konsti-tutsiiu 1876 g. v Turtsii* (Moscow, 1958).

[273]See, for example, O. P. Markova, *Rossiia, Zakavkaz'e i mezhdunarodnye ot-nosheniia v XVIII veke* (Moscow, 1966), 321pp.; Ministerstvo Inostrannykh del SSSR, *Vneshnaia politika Rossii XIX i nachala XX veka. Seriia pervaia* (Moscow, 1960—); and N. A. Smirnov, *Rossiia i Turtsiia v XVI-XVII vv.*, 2 vols. (Moscow, 1946). On German imperialism and Turkey, see M. G. Orudzhev, *Iz istorii proniknoveniia germanskogo imperializma v Turtsii s kontsa XIX v po 1914 g.* (Baku, 1971).

[274]Kh. M. Tsovikian, "Vliianie russkoi revoliucsii 1905 goda na revoliutsionnoe dvizhenie v Turtsii," *Sovetskoe vostokovedenie*, no. 3 (1945), pp. 15-35.

[275]Sh. Tagieva and Iu. Bagirov, *Vliianie Oktiabr'skoi revoliutsii na natsional'noe dvizhenie v Irane i v Turtsii* (Baku, 1957), 63pp.; E. K. Sarkisian, *Velikaia Oktiabr'skaia sotsialisticheskaia revoliutsiia i natsionalno-osvoboditel'naia bor'ba v Turtsii* (Erevan, 1958); and by the same author, "Vliianie Oktiabr'skoi revoliutsii na natsional'no-osvoboditel'noe dvizhenie v Turtsii (1918-1922)," in *Izvestiia Akademii nauk Armianskoi SSR*, no. 1 (1957), pp. 7-12. See also A. D. Novichev, "Vliianie velikoi Oktiabr'skoi sotsialisticheskoi revoliutsiia na sud'bu Turtsii," in *Vestnik Le-ningradskogo universiteta*, vol. 20, no. 4 (1957), pp. 95-107; A. M. Shamsutdinov, "Oktiabr'skaia revoliutsiia i natsional'no-osvoboditel'noe dvizhenie v Turtsii (1919-1922)," in A. A. Guber, ed., *Velikii Oktiabr' i narody Vostoka* (Moscow, 1957), pp. 384-407; and F. F. Ludshuveit, "Posleoktiabr'skii revoliutsionnyi pod'em v Turtsii," in *Vestnik Moskovskogo universiteta*, Seriia obshchestvennykh nauk, vol. 7, no. 3 (1949), pp. 39-54. On Turkish resistance to French occupation, see N. Z. Efen-dieva, *Bor'ba turetskogo naroda protiv frantsuzskikh okkupantov na iuge Anatolii* (Baku, 1966).

[276]A. K. Sverchevskaia, "Izdanie proizvedenii V. I. Lenina v Turtsii," *NAiA*, no. 2 (1971), pp. 133-38.

[277]A. M. Shamsutdinov, "Uchastie sultanskoi Turtsii v interventsii protiv Sovetskoi Rossii v 1918 g.," *UZIF*, no. 14 (1956), pp. 163-96. On Turkey in the First World War, see G. Z. Aliev, *Turtsiia v period pervoi mirovoi voiny* (Baku, 1965).

[278]E. A. Tokarzhevskii, "Bakinskie bol'sheviki-organizatory bor'by protiv germano-turetskikh interventov v Azerbaidzhane v 1918 gody," *Trudy*, Azerbaidzhanskii filial IMEL pri TsK VKP(b), VI (1947), 1-212; XIII (1949), 203-43.

[279]N. G. Korsun, *Greko-Turetskaia voina 1919-1922 gg.* (Moscow, 1940), 55pp.

[280]V. I. Spil'kova, *Imperialisticheskaia politika SShA v otnoshenii Turtsii (1914-1920)* (Moscow, 1960); and A. F. Miller, "Amerikanskii plan zakhvata Konstantinopolia i prolivov v 1919 g.," *Voprosy istorii*, no. 3 (1951), pp. 61-79. There are also one or two items on the Turkish question before the U. S. Senate and on the American commission in Turkey in 1919.

[281]See, for example, S. Kuznetsova, "Krakh turetskoi interventsii v Zakavkaz'e v 1920-1921 godakh," *Voprosy istorii*, no. 9 (1951), pp. 143-56.

[282]See A. K. Sverchevskaia, "Obzor nekotorykh robot po istorii Turtsii, opublikovannykh v 1965-1966 gg.," in L. M. Kulagina et al., eds., *Strany Blizhnego i Srednego Vostoka* (Moscow, 1969), pp. 73-77.

[283]M. A. Gasratian et al., *Noveishaia istoriia Turtsii* (Moscow, 1968), p. 67. Experts from the Institute of the Peoples of Asia of the Soviet Academy of Sciences, the Azerbaijan Institute of the Near East and the Middle East, and the Armenian Sector of the Institute of Oriental Studies participated in writing this book.

[284]A. M. Shamsutdinov, *Natsional'no-osvoboditel'naia bor'ba v Turtsii, 1918-1923 gg.* (Moscow, 1966), 358pp.; and by the same author, *Turetskaia respublika. Kratkii ocherk istorii 1923-1926* (Moscow, 1962). See also A. Miller, "Burzhuazno-natsional'naia revoliutsiia v Turtsii," in *Sovetskaia Rossiia i kapitalisticheskii mir v 1917-1923 g.* (Moscow, 1957).

[285]M. A. Pershits, "Vostochnye internatsionalisty v Rossii. . .," in L. P. Deliusin et al., *Komintern i Vostok* (Moscow, 1970), pp. 53-119, 54-55. See also *Zhizn' natsional'nostei*, January 4, 1920, p. 1. In the proceedings of the symposium on *Velikii Oktiabr' i narody Vostoka 1917-1957* (Moscow, 1957), there is a chapter on the influence of the October Revolution on Turkey.

[286]I. Iu. Bagirov, *Sovetsko-turetskie otnosheniia v 1920-1922 gg.* (Moscow, 1965), 144pp.; and P. P. Moiseev and Iu. Rozaliev, *K istorii sovetsko-turetskikh otnoshenii* (Moscow, 1958). See also S. I. Aralov, *Vospominaniia sovetskogo diplomata 1922-1923 gg.* (Moscow, 1960), p. 287; and A. M. Shamsutdinov, "Uchastie sultanskoi Turtsii v interventsii protiv Sovetskoi Rossii v. 1918 g.," *UZIV*, no. 14 (1956), pp. 163-96; A. Abdurakhmanov, *Azerbaidzhan v Russko-iranskikh i Russko-turetskikh otnosheniiakh v pervoi polovine XVIII v* (Baku, 1963).

[287]A. M. Shamsutdinov, "Uchastie sultanskoi Turtsii v interventsii protiv Sovetskoi Rossi v 1918 g.," *UZIV*, no. 14 (1956), pp. 163-96.

[288]A. D. Novichev, "Zarozhdenie rabochego i sotsialisticheskogo dvizheniia v Turtsii," *Uchenye zapiski Leningradskogo universiteta*, no. 304 (1962), pp. 3-29; R. P. Kornienko, *Rabochee dvizhenie v Turtsii 1918-1963 gg.* (Moscow, 1965); B. Potskhveriia and Iuri Rozaliev, "Trebovaniia rabochei gruppy na Izmirskom

ekonomicheskom kongresse 1923 g.," *Kratkie soobshcheniia vostokovedeniia, AN SSSR,* 22 (1956):82-87; A. M. Shamsutdinov, "Pervyi s"ezd kommunisticheskoi Partii Turtsii," *Kratkie soobshcheniia Instituta narodov Azii,* 30 (1961):227-37; E. F. Ludshuveit, "Konferentsiia levykh turetskikh sotsialistov v Moskve letom 1918 goda," *Vostokovedcheskii sbornik,* 2 (Erevan, 1964):174-92. For an excellent study of Turkish communism, see George S. Harris, *The Origins of Communism in Turkey* (Stanford, Hoover Institution, 1967), 215pp.

[289]Gasratian, *Noveishaia istorii Turtsii,* p. 61.

[290]*Ibid.,* pp. 101, 138.

[291]*Ibid.,* p. 171.

[292]*Ibid.,* pp. 192-93.

[293]A.F. Miller, "Formirovanie politicheskikh vzgliadov Kemalia Atatiurka," *NAiA,* no. 5 (1963), pp. 65-85. See also by the same author,"Kemal' Atatiurk. Rannye gody," *NAiA,* No. 6 (1970), pp. 81.

[294]R. I. Karim-zade, "K voprosu ob obrazovanii parlamenta respublikanskoi Turtsii," in Kulagina, *Strany Blizhnego i Srednego Vostoka,* pp. 1-28. See also an earlier work by G. Astakhov, *Ot sultanata k demokraticheskoi Turtsii. Ocherki iz istorii Kemalizma* (Moscow-Leningrad, 1926).

[295]V. M. Alekseev, *Vneshnaia politika Turtsii* (Moscow, 1961).

[296]D. I. Vdovichenko, *Natsional'naia burzhuaziia Turtsii* (Moscow, 1962), 267 pp; E. Iu. Gasanav, *Ideologiia burzuaznogo natsionalizma v Turtsii* (Baku, 1966).

[297]Iu. N. Rozsaliev, *Ocherki polozheniia promyshlennogo proletariata Turtsii posle vtoroi mirovoi voiny* (Moscow, 1956).

[298]Karim-zade, "K voprosu ob obrazovnii parlamenta respublikanskoi Turtsii," p. 21.

[299]D. S. Zavriev, *K noveishei istorii severo-vostochnykh vilaetov Turtsii* (Tbilisi, 1947), 367pp.

[300]P. P. Moiseev, *Agrarnye otnosheniia v sovremennoi Turtsii* (Moscow, 1960), 224pp.; and P. P. Moiseev, *Agrarnyi stroi sovremennoi Turtsii* (Moscow, 1970), 312pp. See also A. D. Novichev, *Krest'ianstvo Turtsii v noveishee vremia* (Moscow, 1959); E. K. Sarkosov, "Agrarnye otnosheniia v kemalistskoi Turtsii," *Trudy sektora ekonomiki AN Armianskoi SSR,* vol. 1 (1949); A. S. Tvertinova, "Ob agrarnoi politike i sostoianiiu krest'ianskogo khoziaistva v Turtsii v 1923-1929 gg.," *Kratkie soobshcheniia IVAN SSSR,* no. 19 (1956); and an earlier book by P. M. Zhukovskii, *Zemel'cheskaia Turtsiia* (Moscow-Leningrad, 1933), 908pp.

[301]A. D. Novichev, "Antikrest'ianskaia politika kemalistov v 1919-1922 godakh," *Voprosy istorii,* no. 9 (1951), pp. 56-75; and by the same author, *Krest'ianstvo Turtsii v noveishee vremia* (Moscow, 1959).

[302]Iu. N. Rozaliev, *Osobennosti razvitia kapitalizma v Turtsii, 1923-1960 gg.* (Moscow, 1963), 354pp., a well documented book with an extensive bibliography, including Soviet studies of many different phases of Turkish economy. See also A. I. Levkovskii et al., *Gosudarstvenny kapitalizm v stranakh Vostoka* (Moscow, 1960), which contains a chapter on state capitalism in Turkey; I. V. Alibekov, *Gosudarstvennyi kapitalizm v Turtsii* (Moscow, 1966), 243pp.; and B. M. Dantsig,

"Etatism, ego sushchnost i znachenie v ekonomike Turtsii," *Uchenye zapiski IVAN SSSR*, no. 17 (1959).

[303]Rozaliev, *Osobennosti razvitiia kapitalizma v Turtsii*, discusses the economic policy of the Turkish government in the period from 1923 to 1933, the evolution of "lower forms of capitalism," and the development of large private capital.

[304]Gasratian, *Noveishaia istorii Turtsii*, pp. 200-201.

[305]R. I. Karim-zade, "Sotsial'no-ekonomicheskie prava Turetskikh grazhdan po konstitutsii 1961 goda," in Kulagina, *Strany Blizhnego i Srednogo Vostoka*, pp. 29-33.

[306]Karim-zade, "Sotsial'no-ekonomicheskie prava," p. 33.

[307]D. I. Vdovichenko, *Bor'ba politicheskikh partii v Turtsii 1944-1965 gg.* (Moscow, 1964), 308pp.

[308]*Ibid.*, p. 297.

[309]Gasratian, *Noveishaia istoriia Turtsii*, pp. 356-57.

[310]V. I. Danilov, *Srednie sloi v politicheskoi zhizni sovremennoi Turtsii* (Moscow, 1968), pp. 132-34. See review of this book in *NAiA*, no. 5 (1970), pp. 202-203.

[311]A. I. Prokopovich, "O vozrastanii politicheskoi aktivnosti gorodskikh srednikh sloev Turtsii," in Kulagina, *Strany Blizhnego i Srednego Vostoka*, pp. 55-63. On the middle sector in Turkey, see also Danilov, *Srednie sloi v politicheskoi zhizni sovremennoi Turtsii*. See also Iu. Rustamov, *Sovremennaia turetskaia burzhuaznaia sotsiologiia* (Baku, 1967).

[312]Prokopovich, "O vozrastanii politicheskoi aktivnosti," pp. 60-62.

[313]A selection of speeches and statements translated into Russian has been published. See Kemal Ataturk, *Izbrannye rechi i vystupleniia* (Moscow, 1966), 439pp. Mustafa Kemal's well-known speech of October 15-20, 1927, was published earlier in four volumes; see Mustafa Kemal, *Put novoi Turtsii*, 4 vols, (Moscow. 1929-34).

[314]Iu. N. Rozaliev, *Klassy i klassovaia bor'ba v Turtsii (burzhuaziia i proletariat)* (Moscow, 1966), 166pp. For a short article on the labor force in Turkey, see G. I. Starchenkov, "Problemy rabochei sily v Turtsii," *NAiA*, no. 1 (1971), pp. 29-71.

[315]E. Iu. Gasanova, "Novye veianiia v obshchestvennoi mysli Turtsii (o 'turetskom sotsializme')," *NAiA*, no. 1 (1965), pp. 26-34.

[316]K. A. Belova, "K voprosu o sotsial-reformizme v Turtsii," in Kulagina, *Strany Blizhnego i Srednego Vostoka*, pp. 3-12.

[317]See also Gasanova, "Novye veianiia."

[318]Gasratian, *Noveishaia istoriia Turtsii*, pp. 356-57.

[319]*Ibid.*

[320]A. D. Novichev, "Turetskie kochevniki i polukochevniki v sovremennoi Turtsii," *Sovetskaia etnografiia*, no. 3 (1951), pp. 100-20. Also see D. E. Eremeev, *Iuryki (Turetskie kochevniki i polukochevniki).* (Moscow, 1969).

[321]R. P. Kornienko, *Rabochee dvizhenie v Turtsii 1918-1963 gg.* (Moscow, 1965). See also a study of the industrial proletariat in Turkey, Iu. N. Rozaliev, *Ocherki polozheniia promyshlennogo proletariata Turtsii posle vtoroi mirovoi voiny* (Moscow, 1956).

[322]V. A. Gordlevskii, "Eksploitatsiia nedr zeml' v Turtsii," *Sovetskoe vostokovedenie*, no. 3 (1945), pp. 109-44.

[323]V. T. Veselov, *Transport sovremennoi Turtsii* (Moscow, 1969), 143pp.

[324]V. P. Smirnov, *Turtsiia, Ekonomika i vneshnaia torgovlia* (Moscow, 1956). On Soviet-Turkish economic relations, see A. Bizhe, *Sovetsko-turetskie ekonomicheskie otnosheniia* (Baku, 1965).

[325]*Voprosy istorii*, no. 9 (1955), pp. 175-96.

[326]One of the better studies is V. M. Alekseev and M. A. Kerimov, *Vneshnaia politika Turtsii* (Moscow, 1961).

[327]For a statement on anti-American trends in Turkey, see *Protiv fal'sifikatsii istorii kolonializma* (Moscow, 1962).

[328]Iu. Iu. Dvoiurov et al., *Turtsiia—aktivnyi uchastnik agressivnykh blokov* (Moscow, 1958).

[329]I. M. Reisner, et al., *Noveishaia istoriia stran zarubezhnogo Vostoka*, vol. 1 (1918-29) (Moscow, 1954), 370pp.; vol. 2 (1929-39) (Moscow, 1955), 278pp.

[330]See *Voprosy istorii*, no. 3 (1950), pp. 99-119. See also A. F. Miller, *Kratkaia istorii Turtsii* (Moscow, 1948); and *Ocherki noveishei istorii Turtsii* (Moscow-Leningrad, 1948).

[331]For the latest Soviet interpretation of Ottoman history, see sections on the Ottoman Empire and Turkey in *Vsemirnaia istoriia*, 10 vols. (Moscow, 1955-65); A. D. Novichev, *Istoriia Turtsii*, vol. 1: *Epokha feodalizma (XI-XVIII veka)* (Leningrad, 1963), 314pp.; and Gasratian et al., *Noveishaia istoriia Turtsii*. See *Voprosy turetskoi istorii* (Baku, 1972) and Institut Narodov Blizhnego i Srednego Vostoka, A.N. Az. S.S.R., *Voprosy istorii Irana i Turtsii* (Baku, 1966). A collection of essays.

[332]Novichev, *Istoriia Turtsii*, p. 256.

[333]A. D. Novichev, *Turtsiia. Kratkaia istoriia* (Moscow, 1965), 270pp. See also M. A. Gasratian, ed., *Sovremennaia Turtsiia (spravochnik)* (Moscow, 1965).

[334]Novichev, *Istoriia Turtsii*, p. 194. See also I. Vasil'ev, *O turetskom "neutralitete" v vtoroi mirovoi voine* (Moscow, 1951).

[335]On Turkish foreign relations, see V. M. Alekseev and M. A. Kerimov, *Vneshnaia politika Turtsii* (Moscow, 1961). See also Iu. V. Marunov and Iu. V. Potemkin, *Arabo-turetskie otnosheniia na sovremennom etape, 1946-1960* (Moscow, 1961).

[336]A. M. Shamsutdinov et al., *Sovremennaia Turtsiia* (Moscow, 1958), 290pp. See also A. M. Shamsutdinov, *Turetskaia respublika. Kratkii ocherk istorii 1923-1961 gg.* (Moscow, 1962). For history of education in modern Turkey see T.P. Dadashev, *Prosveshchenie v Turtsii v noveishee Vremia (1923-1960 gg.)* (Moscow, 1972).

[337]Gasratian, *Noveishaia istoriia Turtsii*.

[338]*Ibid.*, p. 5.

[339]I. P. Petrushevskii, *Islam v Irane v VII-XV vekakh* (Leningrad, 1966), uses Western and Iranian sources and includes a good bibliography and a glossary of Oriental terms.

[340]*Ibid.*, p. 98.

[341]A. E. Bertel's, *Nasir-i Khosrov i ismailizm* (Moscow, 1959).

[342]Stroeva published at least half a dozen articles on specific aspects of Ismailism. For a listing of her articles, see B. G. Gafurov, ed., *History of Iranian Studies*, p. 24.

[343]N. D. Miklukho-Maklai, "Iz istorii afganskogo vladychestva v Irane (20-ie gg. XVIII g)," *Uchenye zapiski LGU*, no. 4 (Leningrad, 1954). On Iran in the second half of the eighteenth century, see Z. Sharashenidze, *Iran vo vtoroi polovine XVIII v.* (Tbilisi, 1970).

[344]See *Iranskii sbornik* (Moscow, 1963).

[345]M. R. Arunova and K. Z. Ashrafian, *Gosudarstvo Nadir-shakha Afshara. Ocherko obshchestvennykh otnoshenii v Irane 30-40-kh godov XVIII veka* (Moscow, 1958).

[346]*Voprosy istorii*, no. 7 (1971), p. 194. See also B. P. Balaian, *Mezhdunarodnye otnosheniia v 1813-1828 godakh* (Erevan, 1967); and A. R. Ioannisian, *Prisoedinenie Zakavkaz'ia k Rossii i mezhdunarodnoe otnoshenie v nachale XIX stoletiia* (Erevan, 1958).

[347]See particularly M. S. Ivanov, *Babidskie vosstanie v Irane* (Moscow-Leningrad, 1939); and N. Kuznetsova in *Ocherki po istorii russkogo vostokovedeniia*, vol. 6 (Moscow, 1963).

[348]P. P. Bushev, *Gerat i anglo-iranskaia voina 1856-1857 gg.* (Moscow, 1959).

[349]G. M. Eganian, *Agrarnye otnosheniia v Irane v pervoi polovine XIX v.* (Erevan, 1963) (in Armenian). Sh.A. Tagieva, *Formy zemlevladeniia i zemlepol'zovaniia v Irane v kontse XIX—nachale XXV.* (Baku, 1964). By the same author, *Bolozhenie krest'ian Irana v Kontse XIX—nachale XX v* (Baku, 1969).

[350]M. A. Igamberdiev, *Iran i mezhdunarodnye otnosheniia pervoi treti XIX v.* (Samarkand, 1961).

[351]*Mezhvuzovskaia nauchnaia konferentsiia po voprosam istorii stran Azii i Afriki v sovetskoi istoriografii (20-22 dekabria, 1966 g. Tezisy dokladov)* (Moscow, 1966), pp. 52-54. M. S. Ivanov, *Iranskaia revoliutsiia 1905-1911 godov* (Moscow, 1957); and G. S. Artiunian, *Iranskaia revoliutsiia 1905-1911 gg. i bol'sheviki Zakavkaz'ia* (Erevan, 1957). On political societies and organizations in Irane in 1858-1906, see T. A. Ibragimov (Shakhin), *Sozdanie politicheskikh obshchestv i organizatsii v Irane i ikh deiatel'nost' (1858-1906 gg.)* (Baku, 1967).

[352]*Mezhvuzovskaia nauchnaia konferentsiia . . . 20-22 dekabria, 1966*, pp. 52-54.

[353]*Ibid.*

[354]G. V. Shitov, *Persiia pod vlast'iu poslednikh Kadzharov* (Leningrad, 1933).

[355]M. N. Ivanova, *Natsional'no-osvoboditel'noe dvizhenie v Irane 1918-1922 gg.* (Moscow, 1961).

[356]A. Agakhi, *Rasprostranenie idei marksizma-leninizma v Irane (do Vtoroi mirovoi voiny)* (Baku, 1961). A. Shamide, *Lenin i Iran* (Baku, 1970)

[357]M. P. Pavlovich, *Ocherki politicheskoi bor'by v Persii* (Moscow, 1925).

[358]Sh. M. Badi, *Agrarnye otnosheniia v sovremennom Irane* (Moscow, 1959); and A. I. Demin, *Sel'skoe khoziaistvo sovremennogo Irana* (Moscow, 1967).

[359]A. V. Bashkirov, *Rabochee i profsoiuznoe dvizhenie v Irane* (Moscow, 1959); and Sh. M. Badi, *Rabochii klass Irana* (Moscow, 1965). A.I. Shamide, *Rabochee i profsoiuznoe dvizhcnie v Irane v 1941-1946 gg.)* (Baku, 1961). Z.Z. Abdullaev, *Promyshlen-*

nost' i zarozhdenie rabochego klassa v Irane v kontse XIX—nachale XX v. (Baku, 1963). By the same, *Formirovanie rabochego klassa Irana* (Baku, 1968).

[360]M. S. Ivanov, *Neftianoi konsortium i nezavisimost' Irana* (Moscow, 1959).

[361]L. I. Miroshnikov, *Angliiskaia ekspansiia v Irane 1914-1920* (Moscow, 1961); and Z. Z. Abdullaev, *Nachalo ekspansii SShA v Irane* (Moscow, 1963). See also M. S. Ivanov, "Angliiskii imperializm i perevorot 21 fevralia 1921 g. v Irane," *NAiA*, no. 3 (1970), pp. 61-70; A. K.Lavrent'ev,*Imperialisticheskaia politika SShA i Anglii v Irane* (Moscow, 1960); and M. V. Popov, *Amerikanskii imperializm v Irane v gody 2-oi mirovoi voiny* (Moscow, 1956).

[362]Sh. Tagieva, *Natsional'no-osvoboditel'noe dvizhenie v Iranskom Azerbaidzhane v 1917-1920 gg.* (Baku, 1956). G. M. Eganian has written several short studies on this subject; see *Izvestiia AN Armianskoi SSR. Obshchestvennye nauki*, no. 11-12 (1959), pp. 47-50; *KSINA*, no. 73 (1963), pp. 89-95; *Sessiia po voprosam istorii i ekonomiki Afganistana, Irana i Turtsii. Tezisy dokladov* (Moscow, 1962); M. N. Ivanova, *Natsional'no-osvoboditel'noe dvizhenie v Irane v 1918-1922 gg.* (Moscow, 1966); M. N. Ivanova, "Natsional'no-osvoboditel'noe dvizhenie v Iranskom Azerbaidzhane v 1918-1920 gg.," *KSIV*, no. 14 (1955), pp. 3-13; Kh. Ataev, *Natsional'no-osvoboditel'noe dvizhnie v Khorasane* (Ashkhabad, 1962); and A. F. Miller, "Natsional'no-osvoboditel'noe dvizhenie v Irane," in *Sovetskaia Rossiia i kapitalitisticheskii mir* (Moscow, 1957), pp. 586-93.

[363]D. S. Melikov, *Ustanovlenie diktaturi Reza-Shakh v Irane* (Moscow, 1961).

[364]V. S. Glukhoded, *Problemy ekonomicheskogo razvitiia Irana (20-30-e godv)*, (Moscow, 1968). See R. A. Seidov, *Agrarnyi vopros i krest'ianskoi dvizhenie v Irane* (1950-1953 gg.) (Baku, 1963).

[365]S. L. Agaev, *Germanskii imperializm v Irane (Veimarskaia respublika. Tretii reikh)* (Moscow, 1969), 156pp. Agaev published a book on a similar subject in 1966.

[366]Miroshnikov, *Angliiskaia ekspansiia v Irane.*

[367]See, for example, S. L. Agaev, "K voprosu o kharaktere perevorota 3 khuta," *NAiA*, no. 5 (1966); and Z. Z. Abdullaev, "Metodologicheskie i istochnikovedcheskie problemy issledovaniia 'perevorota' 3 khuta 1921 goda v Irane," *NAiA*, no. 5 (1971), pp. 76-84.

[368]See F. B. Beleiutskii and N. K. Belov, "Pervye sviazi sotsialistov s natsional'no-osvoboditel'nym dvizhcniem (do obrazovaniia Kominterna)," *NAiA*, no. 4 (1970), pp. 45-55, for a discussion of the Iranian scene.

[369]See L. P. Deliusin, *Komintern i Vostok*, p. 55.

[370]A conference on this and related subjects was held on February 27, 1970, under the sponsorship of the Georgian Academy of Sciences.

[371]See, for example, A. M. Agakhi, *Rasprostranenie idei marksizma-leninizma v Irane (do Vtoroi mirovoi voiny)*. Agakhi has written several other studies on this subject. A. Aminzade, *Vliianie Velikoi Oktiabr'skoi sotsiialisticheskoi revoliutsii na Razvitie demokraticheskoi mysli v Irane (1917-1925 gg.)* (Baku, 1964). G. M. Agakhi, *Iz istorii obshchestvennoi i filosotskoi mysli v Irane* (Baku, 1971).

[372]See A. M. Matveev, "Iz istorii iranskikh revoliutsionnykh organizatsii v Srednei Azii v nachale XX v.," *Vzaimootnosheniia narodov Srednei Azii i sopredel'nykh stran*

Vostoka (Tashkent, 1963), pp. 134-38; and *Kommunisticheskii internatsional*, no. 4 (1920).

[373]V. Berezhklov, *Tegeran, 1943* (Moscow, 1971), 128pp.

[374]Popov, *Amerikanskii imperializm.*

[375]S. G. Gorelikov, *Iran. Ekonomo-geograficheskaia kharakteristika* (Moscow, 1961).

[376]B. Abdurazakov, *Proiski angliiskogo i amerikanskogo imperializma v Irane 1941-1947 gody* (Tashkent, 1959); A. Kh. Babakhodzhaev, *Proval angliiskoi politiki v Srednei Azii i v Srednem Vostoke (1918-1924)* (Moscow, 1962); and A. K. Lavrent'ev, *Imperialisticheskaia politika SShA i Anglii v Irane* (Moscow, 1960). Many essays have been published on imperialism and colonialism in the Middle East in general. See also A. V. Bashkirov, *Ekspansiia angliiskikh i amerikanskikh imperialistov v Irane* (Moscow, 1954).

[377]D. S. Rozhdestvenskaia, "Ekonomicheskaia dolgosrochnaia pomoshch' zapada Irana v period vtorogo semiletnogo plana (1955-1962 gg.)," in Kulagina, *Strany Blizhnego i Srednego Vostoka,* pp. 122-31.

[378]See, for example, Glukhoded, *Problemy ekonomicheskogo razvitiia Irana.* M. Rabizade, *Razvitie Kapitalisticheskogo predprinimatel'stva v promyshlennosti Irana v 30-kh gg. XX v.* (Baku, 1970). I. Khatemi, *Zarubezhnaia iranistika pressa v bor'be protiv kolonializma i imperializma* (Baku, 1964).

[379]M. G. Pikulin, *Baludzhi* (Moscow, 1959).

[380]M. S. Ivanov, *Plemena Farsa. Kashkaiskie, Khamse, Kukhailuie, Mamasani* (Moscow, 1961).

[381]O. L. Vil'chevskii, *Kurdy. Vvdenie v etnicheskuiu istoriiu kurdskogo naroda* (Moscow, 1961).

[382]V. V. Trubetskoi, *Bakhtiary* (Moscow, 1966).

[383]On the catalogues and descriptions of Persian and Tadzhik documents, see A. D. Papazian, *Persidskie dokumenty Matenadarana,* vol. 1 (VXVI vv.) (Erevan, 1956), vol. 2 (1601-1650) (Erevan, 1959); A. A. Semenov, ed., *Sobranie vostochnykh rukopisei Akademii Nauk Uzbekskoi S.S.R.,* 6 vols. (Tashkent, 1952-64); N. D. Miklukho-Maklai, *Opisanie tadzhikskikh i persidskikh rukopisei Instituta vostokovedeniia,* 2 vols. (Moscow, 1955, 1961); O. F. Akimushkin et al., *Persidskie i tadzhikskie rukopisi Instituta Narodov Azii AN SSSR* (Moscow, 1964); A. T. Tagirdzhanov, *Opisanie tadzhikskikh i persidskikh rukopisei Vostochnogo otdela Biblioteki LGU* (Leningrad, 1952); A. M. Mirzoev and A. N. Boldyrev, eds., *Katalog vostochnykh rukopisei Akademii Nauk Tadzhikskoi SSR,* vol. 1 (Stalinabad, 1960).

[384]For listing, see *History of Iranian Studies,* pp. 26-28.

[385]Pigulevskaia, *Istoriia Irana s drevneishikh vremen do kontsa XVIII veka.*

[386]M. S. Ivanov, *Ocherk istorii Irana* (Moscow, 1952), 467 pp. See also B. G. Gafurov (ed.), *Istoriia iranskogo gosudarstva i kul'tury. K 2500-etiin Iranskogo gosudarstva.* Sbornikstatei (Moscow, 1971), 350pp. For a collection of essays on Iranian history see Institut narodov Blizhnego i Srednego Vostoka A.N. Az. S.S.R., *Voprosy istorii Irana i Turtsii* (Baku, 1966).

[387]*Sovremennyi Iran. Spravochnik* (Moscow, 1957), 718pp.

[388] M. S. Ivanov, *Noveishaia istoriia Irana* (Moscow, 1965).

[389] On Kurdish studies in the Soviet Union, see *Ocherki istorii istoricheskoi nauki v S.S.S.R.*, 3 (Moscow, 1963): 542. See also A. S. Musaelian, *Bibliografiia po kurdovedeniiu* (Moscow, 1963).

[390] On Afghan studies, see V. A. Romodin, *Afghan Studies* (Moscow, Institute of the Peoples of Asia of the Academy of Sciences of the U.S.S.R., 1967), 32pp. See also, by the same author, "Iz istorii izucheniia Afgantsev i Afganistana v Rossii," *Ocherki po istorii russkogo votokovedeniia*, 1 (Moscow, 1953): 148-84. On studies of Afghanistan in Russia before the Revolution, see D. N. Anuchin, ed., *Afganistan*, vol. 1 (Moscow, 1923), a collection of essays. See also V. A. Livshits and I. M. Oranskii, "Izuchenie afganskogo iazyka (pashto) v otechestvennoi nauki," *Uchenye zapiski Tadzhikskogo zhenskogo pedagogicheskogo instituta*, 1 (Stalinabad, 1957): 207-20; and R. T. Akhramovich, "Afganistan," *Ocherki istorii istoricheskoi nauki v SSSR*, 4 (Moscow, 1966): 763-68, which discusses Soviet historiography on Afghanistan. The most prominent Soviet Afghan scholars are R.T. Akhramovich, G. Aslanov, A. Babakhodzhaev, Iu. V. Ganovskii, L. R. Gordon, L. R. Gordon-Polonskaia, N. D. Miklukho-Maklai, and V. A. Romodin. Two important works on Soviet-Afghan relations since 1919 have recently been published. One is a collection of documents issued under the auspices of the Soviet and Afghan foreign ministries (L. B. Teplinskii et al., eds., *Sovetsko-afganskie otnosheniia 1919-1969 gg.* [Moscow, 1971], 439 pp.). The other is a study by L. B. Teplinskii, *50 let sovetsko-afganskikh otnoshenii 1919-1969* (Moscow, 1971), 237pp.

Index

279